Developments in West European Politics

Edited by

Martin Rhodes
Paul Heywood
Vincent Wright

St. Martin's Press
New York

DEVELOPMENTS IN WEST EUROPEAN POLITICS

St. Martin's Press, Scholarly and Reference Division,
175 Fifth Avenue, New York, N.Y. 10010

First published in the United States of America in 1997

This book is printed on paper suitable for recycling and
made from fully managed and sustained forest sources.

Printed in Great Britain

ISBN 0–312–17339–3
ISBN 0–312–17340–7

Library of Congress Cataloging-in-Publication Data
Developments in West European politics/edited by Martin Rhodes,
Paul Heywood, Vincent Wright
p.   cm.
Includes bibliographical references (p.   ) and index.
ISBN 0–312–17339–3 (cloth). – ISBN 0–312–17340–7 (paper)
1. European federation.   2. Europe—Economic integration.
3. Europe—Politics and government—1989–   I. Rhodes, Martin.
II. Heywood, Paul.   III. Wright, Vincent..
JN15.D47   1997
940.55′9—dc21   96–52116
                                                      CIP

ngola   can Politics

Contents

PART TWO: GOVERNANCE

PART THREE: PUBLIC POLICY

PART FOUR: POLITICS, IDEOLOGY AND FUTURE CHALLENGES

List of Contributors

Thomas Christiansen is a Research Fellow in the Department of Government, University of Essex, England.

Ute Collier is a Jean Monnet Fellow in the Robert Schuman Centre, European University Institute, San Domenico di Fiesole, Florence, Italy.

Phil Cooke is Professor of Regional Development and Director of the Centre for Advanced Studies in Social Sciences, University of Wales College of Cardiff, Wales.

Colin Crouch is Professor of Sociology in the Department of Social and Political Science, European University Institute, San Domenico di Fiesole, Florence, Italy.

Renaud Dehousse is Professor of Law in the Department of Law, European University Institute, San Domenico di Fiesole, Florence, Italy.

Michael Gallagher is a Lecturer in Politics, Department of Political Science, Trinity College, University of Dublin, Ireland.

Jonathan Golub is a Research Fellow in the Robert Schuman Centre, European University Institute, San Domenico di Fiesole, Florence, Italy.

Philip Gummett is Professor of Politics and Science and Technology, Department of Government, University of Manchester, England.

Paul Heywood is Professor of Politics, Department of Politics, University of Nottingham, England.

Piero Ignazi is Professor of Political Science, Dipartimento di Politica, Istituzione, Storia, Università degli Studi di Bologna, Italy.

Herbert Kitschelt is Professor of Political Science, Department of Political Science, Duke University, Durham, North Carolina, USA.

Raymond Kuhn is Senior Lecturer in the Department of Political Studies, Queen Mary and Westfield College, University of London, England.

Joni Lovenduski is Professor of Politics, Department of Politics, University of Southampton, England.

Anand Menon is Lecturer in the Politics of European Integration, University of Oxford, England.

Yves Mény is Director of the Robert Schuman Centre, European University Institute, San Domenico di Fiesole, Florence, Italy.

Nick Rengger is Reader in Political Theory and International Relations in the School of History and International Relations, University of St Andrews, Scotland.

Martin Rhodes is Senior Research Fellow in the Robert Schuman Centre, European University Institute, San Domenico di Fiesole, Florence, Italy.

Gerd Schienstock is Director of the Work Research Centre, University of Tampere, Finland.

Loukas Tsoukalis is Professor of European Integration at the University of Athens and Director of European Studies at the College of Europe in Bruges.

Bastiaan van Apeldoorn is a PhD student at the European University Institute, San Domenico di Fiesole, Florence, Italy.

Vincent Wright is an Official in Politics, Nuffield College, Oxford, England, and a Fellow of the British Academy.

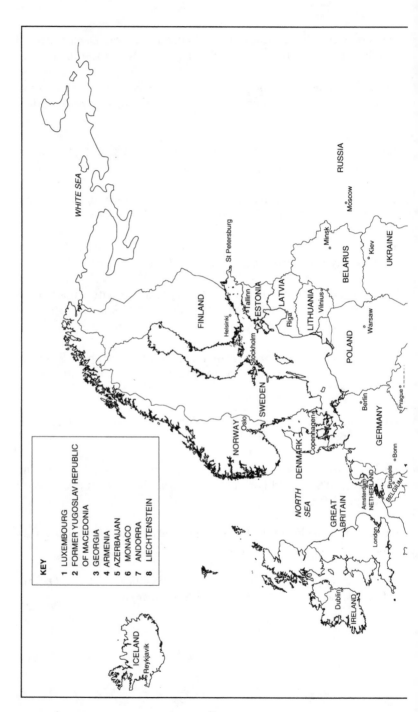

KEY

1 LUXEMBOURG
2 FORMER YUGOSLAV REPUBLIC
  OF MACEDONIA
3 GEORGIA
4 ARMENIA
5 AZERBAIJAN
6 MONACO
7 ANDORRA
8 LIECHTENSTEIN

WHITE SEA

RUSSIA

Moscow

St Petersburg

Minsk

BELARUS

Kiev

UKRAINE

FINLAND

Helsinki

Tallinn

ESTONIA

LATVIA

Riga

LITHUANIA

Vilnius

POLAND

Warsaw

SWEDEN

Stockholm

Oslo

NORWAY

DENMARK

Copenhagen

Berlin

GERMANY

Prague

Bonn

NORTH
SEA

GREAT
BRITAIN

Amsterdam

NETHERLAND

Brussels

BELGIUM

London

Dublin

IRELAND

ICELAND

Reykjavik

xii

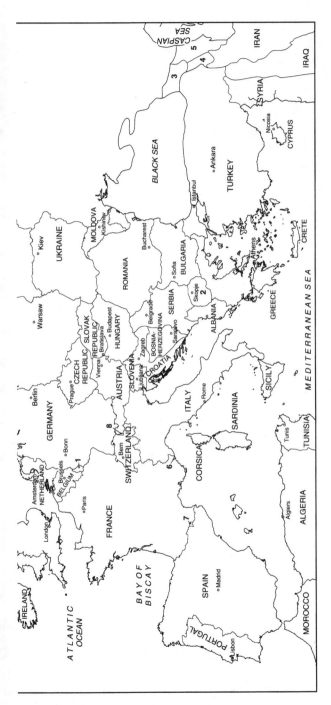

1

Towards a New Europe?

MARTIN RHODES, PAUL HEYWOOD AND VINCENT WRIGHT

Western Europe is undergoing a process of accelerating change. This process is simultaneously supranational, national and subnational in its origins and manifestations. It is of such complexity that there is not as yet – and perhaps will never be – a single formula or theory for comprehending it. The nature of the changes themselves are easily identified: they include the emergence of a transnational economy and polity in the European Union, the redefinition of the nation-state and national identities, and the erosion of traditional political values, beliefs and certainties. But explaining them and accounting for their multifaceted character is far more difficult. This volume neither aspires nor pretends to present an overarching explanation for the tumultuous changes currently being experienced by West European political, social and economic systems. Its more modest aim is to provide a survey of developments in West European politics, taking into account the multiple levels of the new (and still evolving) European political order. In doing so, the authors are highly conscious of the interrelationship of these political levels with the international and global arenas where many of the origins of these developments lie. Thus, while all the chapters stand alone as analyses of the particular phenomena with which they are concerned, important themes link them.

An Era of Political Change

Had this book been written fifteen or twenty years ago, no doubt its central preoccupations would have still been with the *choix de société* – the fundamental social alternatives – that lay at the heart of West European political organisation and activity. Although the great communist monolith in the East was showing signs of beginning to

1

crumble, the Cold War still provided the central paradigm through which the prevailing political order was articulated and analysed. Western European variants of the socialist – and, to a lesser, more marginal extent, communist – tradition were still vibrant: the choices they counterposed to liberal, conservative and Christian democratic parties were still clear and the focus they provided for political loyalty – and even social identity – were only just beginning to be questioned. Collectivist and state interventionist, their continuing impact on the economic organisation of Western Europe was also evident in the expansion of the public sector in many countries in the 1970s, and especially in France under the Mitterrand Government in the early 1980s – perhaps the last gasp of the old-style socialist project before its demise.

Political parties were essentially still divided by ideological positions that had characterised European societies since the nineteenth century, and despite the rumblings of the student protests of 1968, these had yet to translate into new types of radical political expression – even if embryonic manifestations of feminism, post-materialism and 'life-style' politics were starting to become evident. Furthermore, while economic restructuring in response to new forms of international competition was beginning to undermine traditional forms of industrial relations, collective organisation in the labour movement was still strong. The Keynesian welfare state was well entrenched – and underpinned by a cross-party consensus in most countries – although in some cases the fiscal strains were beginning to show. As for 'Europe', the Common Market had yet to impinge significantly on national politics or domestic economic regulation. Far from eroding the nation-state, the early decades of European integration – limited largely to trade liberalisation – were accompanied by a significant strengthening of the state in European countries: not only did they become more interventionist from the 1950s to the 1970s, but they were still in a position to control the boundary between their domestic economies and the outside world.

Since then much has changed. The old ideological and geo-political certainties of the postwar world have disappeared with the collapse of the Soviet bloc. While this has allowed the spread of Western capitalism – and in some cases liberal democracy – into new parts of Europe, it has also contributed to the erosion and loss of meaning of the old ideological oppositions (left versus right, capital versus labour) and produced new 'threats' to the West European status quo. As Philip Gummett shows in Chapter 12, significant uncertainties have been created for European security by the end of the Cold War and the the emergence of diverse new risks, such as ethnic or nationalist conflict (for instance, in the former Yugoslavia and Soviet Union), and pressure from immigrants and refugees at western borders. These make it difficult for countries to plan their defence policies and have triggered a revision of traditional assumptions about European security.

At the same time, the international or global context of Western Europe's political economy has been transformed in a very short time. For example, since the 1970s, the end of the Bretton Woods system of managed exchange rates has given way to an era of floating exchange rates, followed by the emergence of the European Monetary System. The liberalisation of capital controls has produced a rapid globalisation of financial markets, accompanied by the surrender by governments of many of their traditional tools of economic policy. The expansion of international trade and the transnationalisation of company activities link ever greater parts of national economies into an increasingly global market place and subject them to influences beyond their control. As part of this process, radical changes have been occurring in the organisation of production systems, with a shift – albeit uneven – away from Fordist mass production to post-Fordist flexible specialisation, a process driven by international competition and the global spread of 'best-practice' work relations and technology.

Although its relationship with these other manifestations of internationalisation or globalisation are complex, the emergence since the 1980s of the European Community/Union as a new type of polity – one that simultaneously is transnational and still rooted in the European nation states – has had a profound impact on the way in which politics is conducted in Western Europe. The old boundaries between the domestic and the international are becoming increasingly blurred. Indeed, the very nature of national political and economic systems has altered, in both organisational and ideological terms. All the institutions of West European democracies have been affected, including public administrations, parliaments, political parties and interest groups. Moreover, traditional channels of citizen participation and representation – interest groups and conventional political parties – are facing a series of new challenges, the most obvious of which is widespread disillusionment with traditional politics and the rise of 'lifestyle' or anti-party politics on both the left and far right.

Many of these changes are linked to the changing nature of the nation-state and threats to traditional forms of governance. A whole series of pressures has led to the retreat of the state in many domains – including a shift in the dominant macroeconomic paradigm from Keynesianism and government interventionism to monetarism and the primacy of the market, as well as the processes of internationalisation and European integration referred to above. Deregulation and privatisation as generalised phenomena across Western capitalist societies are difficult to disentangle from the more general process of globalisation: as Colin Crouch and Anand Menon argue in Chapter 9, they are clearly both a cause and effect of this process, as is the reorganisation of production consequent upon them. But at the same time, the nation-state retains a key presence. What we may in fact be witnessing, as Renaud Dehousse points out in Chapter 3, is less the demise of the nation-state than its redeployment. That seems certainly to be the case at the European level – where nation-states continue to be the principal actors – but it is also true at the domestic level where, although in many instances the substance of state authority has been eroded or intentionally reduced, in other areas, as Müller and Wright (1994) have argued, the focus or form of that authority has merely been displaced.

This is true especially of traditional areas of intervention in the economy, or through the welfare state, where national patterns of state–society relations remain highly distinctive. Although, as Held (1991) has argued, the nation state is to an extent being 'hollowed out' by a transfer of powers upwards to international organisations (such as the European Union) and sometimes downwards to regional levels – as demonstrated by Phil Cooke, Thomas Christiansen and Gerd Schienstock in Chapter 11 – this is a highly variable process, in terms both of country and policy sectors. It is also a process in which the nation state retains a central role as a mediator and as a source of the rule of law and political legitimacy (Hirst and Thompson, 1995). Yet, at the same time, traditional sources of legitimacy – especially territoriality – are being undermined by internationalisation and globalisation.

Globalisation

Globalisation is a contested term: many prefer the more limited term 'internationalisation' to describe an as yet incomplete process whereby national and regional political economies are becoming assimilated within global transactions, markets and political dynamics. As Hirst and Thompson (1995) have pointed out, economic 'globalisation' has really occurred only in the triad of industrialised nations in Western Europe, North America and Asia. Yet, if carefully conceptualised (precisely in terms of its differential speed and impact), globalisation does provide a useful analytical framework – although not necessarily a complete explanation – for understanding many of the changes identified in this volume.

First of all, globalisation needs to be distinguished from integration. Whereas the latter refers to a higher level of trade and greater technological uniformity, globalisation refers to greater transnational uniformity in culture, communications, information, financial regulation and national economic policies. Globalisation is therefore a more complete and penetrating stage of the internationalisation process. One way of understanding the phenomenon is to construe it in terms of the position of nation-states in the international political economy. Cerny (1995) has argued that the more the scale of goods and assets produced, exchanged and/or used in a particular economic sector or activity diverges from the structural scale of the national state, the more the authority, legitimacy, policy-making capacity and policy-implementing effectiveness of states will be challenged. In these circumstances, states will find it difficult to provide and control particular 'public' goods – arguably the most important consequence of globalisation for the nation state. These include *regulatory public goods* (the establishment and protection of property rights, a stable currency, legal regulations for production and trade, trade protection, control of communications); *productive/distributive-productive goods* (full or partial public ownership of certain industries, direct or indirect provision of infrastructure and public services, direct or indirect involvement in finance capital); and *redistributive public goods* (health and welfare services, employment policies, corporatist bargaining processes and environmental protection). But the loss of state capacity and control in these three areas is highly variable.

The chapters in this volume provide evidence of the differential impact of globalisation in all these areas: while states are manifestly having difficulties in providing such public goods, globalisation is affecting public goods to quite different degrees. Thus, whereas a globalisation of provision is clearly occurring in the area of regulatory public goods (currency, trade and communications regulation has become progressively elevated to supranational levels), public goods provision in other areas remains generally based at the national level, even if this provision is made problematic by the constraining impact of globalisation. Thus, globalisation is least advanced in labour markets and most advanced in the areas of financial markets, mass media and entertainment, and organisational ideologies. Trade and investment come somewhere in between. Globalisation also has contradictory effects, as in the case of the apparently paradoxical connection between globalisation and localisation – discussed by Cooke *et al.*, and by Crouch and Menon – whereby small and medium-sized firms rely on a high level of *local* linkages and networks for competitiveness in *international* markets. Waters (1995) explains the differential extent of globalisation in terms of the 'mediation' of financial markets, organisational ideologies and the media by 'symbolism' – that is, their transfer from the material to the non-material has gone further than elsewhere, allowing their markets to escape territorial controls and to become increasingly 'virtual' in their operation, although still very real in their consequences. There is a connection here, too, with the process of European integration which, as a process of regional economic integration, is closely related to the globalisation process. Once again, financial integration has probably gone furthest in the European Union – although antipathy to proposals for a single currency reveal both symbolic and political limits to this process. The globalisation of mass media and entertainment, on the other hand, has outpaced its European integration: as Raymond Kuhn remarks in Chapter 15, European television audiences watch their national programmes first, programmes from the United States second, and those from other European nations a distant third. Media policy and regulation is shaped by the increasingly global nature of transmission, facilitated by new technologies and by the transnationalisation of media companies and their ownership. Meanwhile, labour markets and welfare, although increasingly affected by European integration, are among the least Europeanised policy sectors.

It is not surprising that while the 'weight' of supranational or 'global' influences on national social, political and economic systems has increased, the response of these systems has been highly varied, preventing any simple process of pan-European convergence either in politics or policy-making. With regard to welfare states, the pressures facing all European countries are similar: the problems of cost-containment in the areas of health, pensions and more general welfare provision (created by demographic pressures, life-cycle changes, and fiscal strains), and the constraints created by economic interdependence (regional economic integration, competitive trade pressures and the liberalisation of international financial flows). But these are being dealt with in quite different ways that are consonant with the institutional and political differences of individual nations. Similar distinctions persist in the organisation of national economies, despite the spread of privatisation, deregulation and the impact on financial systems and corporate governance of the same global pressures. For what are ostensibly common phenomena frequently take different forms. Privatisation, for example, while everywhere involving a retreat of the state from the economy, frequently has a nationally specific character and may even maintain a state presence, albeit in slightly different form. In France, for example, traces of the traditional *dirigiste* state role are still strong within the privatised sector.

In some respects, globalisation – and European integration – are producing pressures for change which generate convergence, that is a growing institutional uniformity across political systems. It is certainly the case that the globalisation of financial markets and the European integration of banking regulation has had an important impact on continental financial institutions. However, this does not mean that their distinctive character is being destroyed. For example, German banks may have 'gone global' and operate much like any other bank when based in London, but they have not abandoned their traditional characteristics when operating in Germany. At the same time, while many aspect of the Anglo-Saxon financial model are emerging in continental systems, aspects of the German system are also becoming more common, as in the case of Italy, where there is evidence of a shift towards the German system of universal banking. Similarly, as Crouch and Menon point out, the impact of globalisation is leading firms to shrug off state regulation and sometimes their own collective organisa- tion – business associations – as well; meanwhile, large firms have the added incentive of going global themselves and transcending national governmental and associational frameworks. Here again, though, there are contradictory tendencies at work. On the one hand, such moves are very damaging to neo-corporatist and consociational arrangements – the linkages that have traditionally bound organised interests together and to national policy structures. On the other hand, corporatism in some countries has been strengthened as governments try to make organised interests an additional instrument of governance in times of economic uncertainty. Germany in its post-unification phase is a case in point. At the same time, there is some evidence that small and medium-sized firms are becoming more rather than less embedded in associational networks, although this is generally at the local rather than the national level.

This issue is explored by Cooke, Christiansen and Schienstock and raises important questions not just about the effects of globalisation on domestic economies, but also about the nature of the nation-state. They argue that the demise of Fordism as a regulatory model has led to new approaches to competitive advantage. One of these – the emer- gence of regional innovation systems – has become a feature of high- profile regions such as those in north–central Italy, Baden–Württem- berg and Rhône–Alpes. The co-operative relationships between eco- nomic actors and local political authorities that characterise these regions are now being encouraged in less developed regions by the

EU as a means of promoting economic development. Again, there is a link to globalisation here: in a continuing climate of 'global monetarism', the pursuit of low inflation and balanced budgets by governments implies a new period of institutional and policy innovation. Complex processes of learning and innovation have become critical for success in the global economy and 'region-states' may be the more appropriate level for this to occur than the nation-state. This does not mean that the nation-state is necessarily being supplanted by the subnational state as the primary tier of economic regulation: national policy clearly remains important in areas such as education, training and finance. But it may mean that in many parts of Europe a regional capacity for institutional innovation will become a critical component of innovation in the industrial and service economies and therefore of competitiveness in the global economy. Those countries with highly centralised political systems may find it more difficult to adapt their production systems to this new era of global markets and locally embedded production. Centralised states – such as Britain, Portugal and Greece – are also finding it more difficult to adapt to the new system of relations being established between the European Commission and Europe's regions for the promotion of regional development through the Structural Funds.

European Integration

A second major development influencing the political order in Western Europe is European integration. The emergence of the European Community (EC) – now the European Union (EU) – as a transnational form of governance has many implications for the ways in which politics are conducted in Western Europe's national polities. In many ways European integration is difficult to distinguish from globalisation, and the real loss of national autonomy seems to have been less to new levels of supranational government than to markets. Thus, as Loukas Tsoukalis and Martin Rhodes discuss in their analysis of European monetary union in Chapter 2, European economic integration has involved only a slow movement towards a supranational system of economic management, with the nation-state only gradually ceding authority in recent years to European authorities. Perhaps the most important surrender of national economic autonomy has been to the market – a phenomenon linked to the wider process of globalisation as much as to the creation of an integrated *European* market – rather than supranational institutions. Again, this is most evident in financial services, where governments have had to bow to international pressures and surrender traditional control over banking and financial markets, introducing regulatory frameworks that pose few impediments to international capital flows. But attempts to preserve a system of stable intra-EU exchange rates and plans for economic and monetary union (EMU) imply both a strengthened role for markets *and* a loss of autonomy to new, politically independent institutions at the EU level – representing a significant qualitative step in regional integration and a distribution of power away from the nation-state.

For the time being, however, nation-states retain their strength in many respects. As Dehousse makes clear, the nation-state is not being subsumed into a supranational political system: it remains a key agent in determining the pace of European integration and the extent to which sovereignty is being pooled within that polity. But at the same time, a state-centred approach no longer allows us to understand some essential features of the integration process, indicated, for example, by the fact that many member states have begun to question the extent and direction of European integration. Finding a way between the two competing arguments about what drives European integration – a realist, state-centred approach, which sees the European Union as essentially a bargain between states pursuing their own preferences, and a neo-functionalist approach, which sees integration as a quasi-automatic process whereby nation-state sovereignty is gradually eroded and undermined by the accretion of ever more powers above and beyond its influence – Dehousse's analysis says as much about the changing nature of the nation-state as it does about the emerging European polity.

He argues that a unitary view of the state which sees relations between the EC and member-states as a zero-sum game is too reductionist to account for European integration. In some ways the nation-state *has* seen an erosion of its autonomy: this is not simply a result of European integration, but the result of a more general process of internationalisation. Thus, the interaction between domestic and international affairs has been blurred to the point where often there is no clear distinction between the two: independent national policies can no longer deal with many cross-boundary issues. European integration has simply added a further dimension to this process by creating a complex form of interdependence – not just in terms of the trade relations, but in terms of a functional interdependence in policy and a growing institutional interdependence manifested in sectoral co-operation and networks linking executives, judiciaries and, more recently, legislatures. Dehousse notes in particular the fundamental role of the

European Court of Justice (ECJ) in 'constitutionalising' the EU's legal order: judicial co-operation between the ECJ and national courts has ensured the EU's decisions an effectiveness that most rules of international law do not have. At the same time, as Paul Heywood and Vincent Wright indicate in Chapter 5, national executives can sometimes increase their power by exploiting interdependence to their advantage: this is what occurs when governments use the EU's decision-making machinery to further policies that at the national level might confront too many obstacles, either from national parliaments or organised interests.

The complexity of the relationship between member-states and the EU is well illustrated in several chapters in this book. For example, as Crouch and Menon show, the emergence of the EU as a focus for interest group activity has affected, though to differing extents, national patterns of interest mediation. While more pluralist political systems have not been altered fundamentally by the impact of the EU, more *étatiste* systems such as the French are increasingly experiencing the need for wider consultation than was previously the case. Again, it is evident that there is no zero-sum game between the nation-state and the EU as targets of interest group activity: while the EU has increased the number of lobbying contact points, there has been no simple shift away from the national level of interest intermediation. This is partly because, as already mentioned, European integration – like globalisation – has occurred to different degrees in different areas. Interest group activity has tended to 'supranationalise' in those policy areas where the EU plays an important role, such as macroeconomic policy, industrial policy and competition policy. It has been much less marked in other policy areas, such as education and social welfare, reflecting the fact that in large part these policy arenas remain rooted in national political systems.

In those areas where the EU does play an important role, the nature of decision-making has become highly complex. In the area of regional policy, new linkages have been established between regions, and between these regions and the European Commission. Globalisation and European integration have triggered not just new competitive, but also new co-operative, relations among regions as they compete for both European funds and private international capital. The nation-state – which generally intervenes as a filter or 'gatekeeper' between its regions and the supranational authorities – may in certain circumstances be bypassed by new direct relationships between the Commission and the regions. This adds a complex, multilevel character to the EU, although this should not be confused with a form of regionalisation which 'hollows out' the nation-state: regardless of the fact that it is regions that implement many EU initiatives, 'hollowing out' on a significant scale has yet to occur. Environmental policy provides another example of complex, multilevel policy-making in which the nation-state retains a key role, but politics and policy bear an increasingly European imprint. As Ute Collier and Jonathan Golub note in Chapter 13, since the early 1980s, the EC has become perhaps the most important source of environmental policy in Western Europe, so much so that the primary decision making centre for all states has shifted to Brussels. Illustrating the more general points made by Dehousse, they show that a state-centred analysis is incapable of explaining the nature of policy outcomes. While an intergovernmentalist perspective would suggest that the EU is unlikely to produce outcomes that are anything other than lowest-common-denominator standards, or levels of regulation that conform with the standards of one high regulation state, the domestic politics of the member states in the environmental area have been transformed by EU policies that have ratcheted up standards for *all* member states. At the same time, however, European policies are implemented via state institutions, and in this respect the nation-state retains a central role. New arguments regarding subsidiarity may delimit the extent to which supranational policies can override national preferences. In media policy too, as discussed by Kuhn, there are strict limits to the development of a coherent EU audio-visual policy, precisely because national interests prevail so strongly in an area in which national governments, regulatory bodies and media organisations still dominate what is still largely a national policy-making process. Even when the policy forum is transferred to the supranational level, the policy debate often continues to reflect national concerns. As in other areas of policy, governments use the EU to 'cut slack' – that is, as a means for promoting their own domestic policies.

The Future of Democracy and the Nation-State

How, then, can we make sense of the various developments outlined above? How precisely are they all related? It would be wrong to claim that there is a consensus among social scientists on the significance of these changes, or on how to interpret them. While for the more conventional among them it is either a question of 'business as usual' in European politics or else a slow, incremental adjustment to a context that is changing only gradually, others perceive a dramatic process of restructuring and even a rupture between eras – between Fordism and post-Fordism (affecting forms of political organisation as much as the economy), or between modernity and 'postmodernity' (eroding traditional forms of identity and human interaction as much as conventional forms of politics). This volume does not aim to arbitrate between these positions. But it is clear from all the analyses presented here that fundamental transformations are occurring. Why, then, should there be any dispute on the matter?

Part of the reason for this conflict of views is, as Herbert Kitschelt points out in Chapter 8, that change is occurring to various different degrees at different levels of political systems. In some cases this change is quite profound, in others it is restricted. It is this differential speed and extent of change that makes it so difficult to grasp exactly what is happening to contemporary West European democracies. On the one hand, there seems to be a general transformation of political identity across Western societies: as Piero Ignazi argues in Chapter 17, behind the inability of traditional parties to retain their 'grip' on civil society lies a socioeconomic transformation and the emergence of new social alignments, which has resulted in conflicts over economic resources becoming much less salient. For even if employment, inflation and welfare provision are still important for the bulk of the population, the economy is less central than it once was in defining political allegiances. In the absence of the older 'integrative orders' (of Marxism and organised religion) that have also collapsed or been eroded, there has been the emergence of what Ignazi refers to as a bric-à-brac style of value formation. Evidence of new identity-related politics has been apparent for some time. After all, while often neglected by conventional politics text books, the emergence of gender politics alongside traditional concerns with class inequalities has long been a feature of the national and, increasingly, supranational politics of Western Europe and elsewhere, as demonstrated by Joni Lovenduski's analysis of feminism and politics in Chapter 16. Nick Rengger, meanwhile, in Chapter 14 interprets this fragmentation of identity – and hence forms of political expression – in terms of a 'crisis of modernity'.

Elsewhere, Kitschelt illustrates how structural – or system – changes affecting all countries produce such different effects. Some common changes can be perceived in all political systems: for example, since the 1960s, international competition and welfare state expansion have reinvigorated economic left–right divisions, leading to a new division between an educated libertarian class and a more authoritarian lower-class culture. At the same time, large parties – such as industrial companies – have had to engage in 'flexible specialisation' and appeal to much narrower segments of the electoral market, much like firms searching for market niches. Whether this works or fails will depend on the success of other strategies to counter a growing discontent with the functioning of democracy in Western societies. However, other effects are specific to *particular* party systems: thus, where in the 1960s party systems were differentiated by a high number of effective parties, existing parties could more readily absorb new issues by altering their appeals; but, as Chapter 6 by Yves Mény and Martin Rhodes indicates, where party systems in the 'golden age' of the Keynesian welfare state were based on clientelism and highly segmented subsocieties, conventional parties have experienced a steep decline caused by a rebellion of the electorate against clientelism and the spread of a new ethos of 'efficiency' among sections of the middle classes – the political upheavals of the early 1990s in Italy providing the most striking case. We must be careful, then, to distinguish between general forces for change and their particular effects in different political systems.

All the foregoing has implications for the future of the nation-state and traditional forms of democracy. Many of the contributors to this book identify problems of democratic legitimacy in contemporary Europe. If we restrict ourselves just to domestic politics, both Piero Ignazi (in Chapter 17) and Michael Gallagher (in Chapter 7) suggest a number of explanations for the growth of either 'anti-party' and 'anti-system' political movements or political disillusionment and abstention. Ignazi concludes that the reason for the growth of new anti-party or anti-system parties lies not so much in a crisis of democracy as such, but in the incapacity of traditional parties to represent new issues. Gallagher points to a parallel phenomenon – a widespread withdrawal of individuals from participation, party membership and activism – which he attributes to a disinclination to become involved in politics rather than a disillusionment with democracy as such. He also explains this is in part by the rise of new movements and forms of activity (such as the emergence of the feminist movement as a rival to parties – especially where gender issues are concerned, as discussed by Lovenduski), and an increasing recourse to the legal system rather than to parties for the expression and resolution of grievances.

But a closer examination of this issue quickly takes us beyond the boundaries of national politics and into the realm of European and international politics and their impact, once again, on the domestic politics of nation-states. In terms of a traditional approach to understanding these developments, we are faced with two complementary views of the impact of the EU and the emergence of a supranational political system on national politics. Kitschelt argues there is as yet little evidence that 'Europe' has become a major new source of political division and cleavage in the party systems of Western Europe (although it may do so as political integration proceeds). Yet, as Gallagher points out, the information overload (generated by the media) that may be responsible for a withdrawal of parts of the populations from the public sphere is exacerbated by the increasing interpenetration of regional, national and European politics and policy. Both he and Dehousse point to the depoliticisation that European developments portend: while at the national level, the growth in the size and the activities of bureaucratic structures has been accompanied by a weakening of the bodies supposed to control them – especially parliaments – this process has been compounded by the influence of national administrations in the European decision-making process and the failure to provide any effective supranational substitute for weakened national forums of representation. The European Parliament has not been able to replace national parliaments as a focus of political representation and identity, even though the importance of the latter has declined. While it is true that the powers of the European Parliament have increased, this has been achieved via byzantine methods that are generally not understood by the European public.

Whether it is possible to create a focus for European representation and identity in the contemporary era is a moot point, and leads into wider issues such as the nature of 'European identity' and the implications for the latter of the current transformation of international politics. As Rengger argues, 'deterritorialisation' is one aspect of the changes currently eroding traditional concepts of the nation-state. The nation-state is not disappearing, but it is increasingly a mediator in the process of transferring powers down to regions and up to supranational authorities. Of course, this process has gone further in some countries and in some sectors than in others. But, in hand with the more general process of internationalisation in political and economic life, the glue that binds territorial units together does seem to be dissolving, although not without resistance (witness the growing enthusiasm across Europe for the notion of 'subsidiarity' that would reserve certain powers for nation states against the encroachment of supranational powers). In the process, the division between internal domestic politics and external international politics is being blurred. This in itself is playing a part in the alienation of national publics from their domestic institutions. At the same time, however, the external dimension has become steadily more uncertain – and, one could argue, risk-laden – as the bipolarisation since the end of the Second World War between capitalism and communism has fragmented. As Gummett discusses, one aspect of this change is the need for a complete revision of the assumptions and institutions on which European security has been based – security in this case being the defence strategy of a still-evolving EU, the centre of gravity of which is itself gradually moving eastwards.

However, as Rengger points out, 'security' has a wider significance, related closely to the politics of 'desire, fear and risk'. The international and domestic dimensions of this general 'security' problem in the post-Cold War world are encapsulated in the clash between the forces of radical particularism (Jihad) and those of increasingly global capital-ism (McWorld): while the latter dissolves the boundaries between national and global political and economic spheres, populations either seek identities in new and narrow types of social and political move-ments, or retreat into the private sphere altogether. The implications of these developments for liberal democracies are important. A plurality of identities is difficult for either national governments or the EU authorities to accommodate; and a retreat from the public sphere undermines the participatory essence of civil society. The postmodern thesis that the EU rests on a number of logics that the politics of 'desire, risk and fear' undercut is a perceptive one: indeed, the emergence of the EU as an incomplete and novel form of polity has arguably contributed to a situation in which identity and a sense of political belonging have become problematic. In these circumstances, neither clinging to state sovereignty nor shifting power to a suprana-tional state can cope with the rise of a postmodern politics of identity. Although they would not all accept the premise of this argument, most of the contributors to this volume would agree that what is required in Western Europe is a re-emphasis on civil society. In an era of radical transformation, ambitious institution building and challenges to tradi-tional political structures and identities, the recreation of civil society – a public sphere – congruent with these changes is perhaps the greatest challenge facing Europe today.

PART ONE

Integration, Globalisation and the Nation-State

2

Economic Integration and the Nation-State

LOUKAS TSOUKALIS AND MARTIN RHODES

The development of European economic integration is often seen as a process whereby nation-states have steadily surrendered economic policy-making to the European institutions. But while there has been evidence of this in the most recent phase of integration, especially with plans for a shift towards full monetary union at the end of the 1990s, the external constraints imposed on their freedom of action have been at least as much the result of international economic interdependence as of European integration. The main constraint in terms of national economic autonomy was for long the result of increased international capital mobility, and for many years regional integration had very little effect on it. This situation has changed with the internal market programme, although beyond the deregulatory thrust of the Single European Act (SEA), the liberalisation of capital movements decided at the European level has been at least partly an attempt to make virtue out of necessity, given the increasing ineffectiveness of existing controls in the international economy.

The following analysis focuses on the changing relationship between the nation-state, the European institutions and the market in the process of European economic integration. The central argument is that this process has involved only a very slow evolution towards a supranational system of economic management, with the nation-state only gradually ceding authority in recent years to European authorities. This process of integration has been strongly influenced by ideological trends: both the internal market programme and the section of the Maastricht Treaty on Economic and Monetary Union (EMU) bear clearly the signs of the new economic orthodoxy. Thus the most important surrender of national economic autonomy has been to the market rather than to supranational institutions. But attempts to preserve a system of stable intra-EU exchange rates and plans for monetary union imply both a strengthened role for markets *and* a loss of autonomy to new, politically independent institutions at the European level – a significant qualitative step in regional integration and the distribution of power away from the nation-state in Western Europe.

State and Market in European Integration

Neither of the traditional routes to understanding European economic integration – via federalist and/or (neo)functionalist theories (see Chapter 3) – reveals the true nature of the dynamics that have driven this process forward. Both sets of theories have treated the relationship between the nation-state and regional integration as a zero-sum game, with a strong element of automaticity – through the process of spill-over – added by the neo-functionalists. As the integration of the European market proceeded, so the role of the state, in this view, should have been steadily reduced. But there is little evidence to support this set of assumptions, at least for the early stages of the integration process. The process of integration before the 1980s is much more accurately conceived of as a combination of external liberalisation and the strengthening of the economic role of the state at the domestic level.

With their recent access to archival material, revisionist historians are beginning to demonstrate how the evolution of the EC was 'an integral part of the re-assertion of the nation-state as an organisational concept' (Milward, 1992, p. 3). The best proof of this argument is that, beyond the Common Agricultural Policy (CAP), for many years nation-states resisted a transfer of economic policy-making authority to the European institutions, and European economic integration was essentially limited to trade in goods: the progressive elimination of economic border controls – most notably tariffs and quantitative restrictions – was the major factor behind the rapid growth in trade in goods between the members of the European Community. At the same time, this process was accompanied by a much more complex one in which the state extended its influence over domestic economies.

The increasing openness of national economies was an integral part of the economic miracle of the 1950s and 1960s, during which decades of high growth, full employment and low inflation were all fortuitously combined. This, in turn, was based on a remarkable strengthening of the mixed economy and the Western European welfare state as governments became increasingly interventionist at both the micro- and the macroeconomic levels. At the macroeconomic level, state expenditure rose spectacularly as a proportion of GDP, and states used fiscal and monetary policies (in different ways) to maximise growth and employment. At the microeconomic level, governments also resorted to regional, industrial and incomes policies, albeit with varying degrees of enthusiasm and with different instruments, to influence the domestic allocation of resources and the distribution of income. Each member state devised a distinct institutional structure and style of economic management. Meanwhile, the growing strength of trade unions combined with welfare state provisions and job security legislation to create highly regulated labour markets as each West European country realised its own domestic political compromise for governing the capitalist economy (Boltho, 1982) (see Chapters 4 and 10).

To some extent, then, these years witnessed the emergence of a paradox in the West European political economy, as the increasing openness of European economies, closely related to both international and European liberalisation processes, was accompanied by the conscious attempt by the state to regulate the market. Numerous contradictions were apparent in this process, including the fact that domestic intervention sometimes led to the replacement of the border controls that had been negotiated away in the context of either the EEC or GATT – the General Agreement on Tariffs and Trade – with non-tariff barriers. But, arguably, without intervention through the mixed economy and the welfare state, the process of internationalisation and European integration could not have proceeded so smoothly. For governments played a critical role in facilitating and sometimes delaying the necessary adjustments (the impact on employment, for example) arising from the greater openness of their economies, while also legitimising this process by alleviating its costs for the losers.

This delicate balance between opening markets and strengthening states underpinned economic integration in Western Europe until the mid-1970s. But economic miracles do not last for ever, and the decades of high growth, low inflation and low unemployment (the so-called 'golden age') were followed by years of stagflation and recession. External liberalisation and domestic economic interventionism could not happily coexist in an era of low growth and unemployment. European integration suffered as a result. During the 1970s and early 1980s, government attempts to regulate the market became increasingly interventionist, and national industrial regimes increasingly fragmented. European regulation was largely limited to the Common Agricultural Policy (CAP), the iron and steel sector (where the Treaty of Paris that founded the European Coal and Steel Community in 1951 gave it special interventionist powers), and some European-level protectionism, most notably in the Multi-Fibre Agreement (MFA), which restricted imports of textile and clothing products. Otherwise, new steps in integration were largely limited to experimentation with monetary co-ordination.

From Common Market to Regional Currency Bloc: The Origins of Monetary Integration

As pointed out above, an important part of the early symbiosis between state and market in the postwar period has been a capacity for controlling the relationship between the domestic and international economies. This applies as much to capital and investment flows as it does to goods. The creation of a regional currency bloc in Europe – which would require the surrender of much of this national autonomy – was not an issue during much of this period. The Treaty of Rome in fact contained little of relevance in this area: apart from some wishful thinking on the co-ordination of policies it was very cautious with respect to the elimination of exchange controls. National governments were committed to an international monetary system based on the dollar standard. Their equally strong commitment to interventionist domestic policies meant they were zealous in retaining monetary and fiscal policy independence, and a heavy armoury of exchange controls, for domestic stabilisation objectives (Tsoukalis, 1977).

Why, then, has Europe moved progressively towards European economic and monetary union (EMU)? The reasons range from the mundane and practical to the ideological and symbolic. To some extent, regional monetary integration has to be understood as a reaction to developments in the international economy – an attempt by national governments to reconcile different and often increasingly incompatible economic objectives. In a world of increasingly mobile capital, governments have to choose between fixed exchange rates and an autonomous monetary policy. European governments have generally opted for the former in an attempt to safeguard their external trade and also as a means of avoiding competitive devaluations. Thus the subject of EMU really only appeared prominently on the European agenda from the end of the 1960s, when the dollar-based international monetary system known as Bretton Woods collapsed. This exchange rate system had promoted successfully exchange rate stability, currency convertibility – mainly for current account transactions – and a progressive liberalisation of trade. But it could only last as long as the United States was prepared to guarantee the value of the dollar. However, the United States was forced to abandon the system when the dollar itself came under increasing pressure of devaluation. The subsequent system of floating exchange rates created a degree of international instability which the Europeans sought to contain at the European level. The central problem (and a key factor in the asymmetry that has always bedevilled attempts at EC monetary co-ordination) was that the expansion of intra-EC trade made European economic relations highly susceptible to the fluctuations in the value of the Deutschemark (DM). Reflecting the confidence of international investors in the strength of the German economy, the DM tended to rise in value as the dollar declined. The search for exchange rate stability to cover trade between the Community countries – which has risen to approximately 60 per cent of their total – has been a very important motivation behind the various plans for European monetary union.

But money has also been treated as part of high politics – especially by the French. While the EMS was at one level a regional response to instability in international markets, it was also central to a reassertion of Europe's role in world affairs. European monetary union also became associated symbolically and politically with the internal construction of Europe and the achievement of political union – the desire to integrate Germany more closely into the EC via stronger economic linkages, and the general objective – especially on the part of France and Italy – of joint monetary policy-making. Consequently, monetary union has often been treated as an economic means for the achievement of political ends. Thus, geopolitical considerations, European ideology and symbolism have all characterised the debate on economic and monetary union conducted at the highest political levels. Practical and pragmatic measures concentrating on the short-term goal of stable intra-EC exchange rates (as in the early stages of the European Monetary System) have always been linked to long-term, politically-driven plans for more complete monetary union.

The first real steps in the direction of monetary union were taken in the early 1970s with the Report of the Werner Committee which advocated a central monetary authority, unified capital markets, some co-ordination of fiscal policy, EC regional and structural policies, and closer consultations among the social partners (trade unions and employers) (Taylor, 1995). Inspired by this report, the first step towards

EMU was taken with the introduction of the so-called European currency snake in 1972 and the European Monetary Co-operation Fund in 1973. Member currencies of 'the snake' – which included the original EEC-6 (France, Germany, Italy, Belgium, the Netherlands and Luxembourg) plus Britain, the Republic of Ireland, Denmark and Norway – were linked within a plus or minus 2.25 per cent fluctuation band. But the experiment failed, largely because of divergent macro-economic policies and inflation rates in the wake of the rise in oil prices.

The 'snake' was replaced in 1979 by the European Monetary System (EMS). Politically, the motive was to revive the flagging project of European integration, as proclaimed in a key speech by Commission president Roy Jenkins in 1977. This spurred negotiations among a small group of member-state representatives on the creation of a new system – outside the normal channels of consultation and despite the lack of support from technical advisers and central banks (Padoa Schioppa, 1994, p. 76). These gave 'Community' backing to the Franco-German collaboration (between Helmut Schmidt and Giscard d'Estaing) that was critical in launching the project. For both, the EMS was an economic construct linked to their mutual political ambitions: apart from cementing the Germans more closely into the Community, France wanted a larger platform for its role in the international economy and some influence over German monetary policy; while for the Germans, monetary union was the essential condition for political union – a goal to which the federalist Schmidt was deeply committed. The UK, meanwhile, declined to join.

Nevertheless, in practical terms, the EMS was a rather pragmatic response to the instability generated by the collapse of Bretton Woods and the subsequent weakness of the dollar: indeed, when the EMS was negotiated in 1978, there was a careful avoidance of the issues of free capital flows, common monetary policy and the single currency, because of the fears of the German Bundesbank that the EMS might be a more politicised version of the snake, to the detriment of its own independence. Although Germany retained its monetary centrality in the new system, the burden of adjustments was formally more symmetrical and the Bundesbank found that its adjustment obligations were quite onerous. Until the crises of 1992–3 (see below), most currencies within the system were supposed to diverge by no more than plus or minus 2.25 per cent relative to each other, or by 6 per cent for 'weaker' currencies such as the Italian lira, the British pound or the Spanish peseta.

While the daily running of the EMS has been left to central bankers, politicians have played an important role in adjustments in the system when the realignment of central rates has been negotiated. Until the 1992 crisis of the system, tensions were resolved by compensating for inflation differentials with periodic realignments of intra-EC exchange rates. Nevertheless, the EMS has, in fact, exhibited the same characteristic as the snake: a fundamental asymmetry relating to the central role of the Deutschemark – the so-called 'anchor' of the system. Despite the collective nature of the system, Germany's low propensity to inflate, combined with its economic weight and the priority attached by its EMS partners to exchange rate stability and low inflation, has enabled Germany to set the monetary standard. Thus, no realignment of ERM central parities has ever involved a depreciation of the DM. At the same time, an often restrictive monetary policy has been accepted by the participating countries. In some cases, most notably Italy, this has been welcomed by central bankers who thereby increased their independence *vis-à-vis* national politicians in the pursuit of anti-inflation policies. This has not been caused especially by the preferences of the Bundesbank, but rather by a political and ideological shift in terms of macroeconomic management and the almost universal adoption of the new orthodoxy among central bankers – and, increasingly, by politicians as well.

In practice, only Germany set its monetary policy independently. The other countries had either to adjust to German policy, devalue or leave the system. The problem was that exchange rate realignments did not always fully compensate for inflation differentials. There was a deliberate attempt by governments and central banks to use the exchange rate as an additional anti-inflationary instrument; hence the resistance to devaluation. This meant the progressive overvaluation of these currencies and the loss of external competitiveness, which was in turn translated into growing trade deficits. In the end this acted as a boomerang. The crisis of September 1992 was fundamentally a crisis of confidence for the currencies of countries with higher inflation rates and large trade deficits. At this point, the disadvantages of asymmetry were magnified: at a time of economic recession and growing unemployment, internal resistance to the continuation of the link with the DM and high German interest rates grew in several countries, while markets began to doubt the sustainability of existing policies, thus creating a vicious circle which ended in a speculative crisis. The result was the withdrawal of sterling and the lira from the ERM and the repeated devaluations of the peseta and the escudo (De Grauwe, 1994; Johnson and Collignon, 1994). They were followed by a more systemic crisis which led to the abandonment of the old narrow margins of fluctuation in August 1993.

Integrationist aspirations had once again run aground on market realities. But the real winners were not the national governments; they were the markets. In the exchange crises of 1992–3, markets won a decisive victory over governments in a game in which the latter had already deprived themselves of most of their weapons. Markets won because they had become more powerful and also because governments had shown themselves unable to make use of the flexibility offered by a system they had themselves designed. Intergovernmental co-ordination at the European level had revealed its limits.

Deregulation, Internationalisation and the Single Market Programme

While monetary co-ordination between the European Community's member states became increasingly sophisticated, economic integration remained largely stagnant until the middle-to-late 1980s. The new and most recent phase of integration – the internal market programme – was launched in the mid-1980s by the European Commission President, Jacques Delors. In the background, pressures for a resurgence of European integration were coming from multiple sources: economic stagnation in Europe; concern about the competitiveness of European firms in international markets; and the costs to Europe, already discussed above, of international economic uncertainty. All these combined to create a new European agenda – one increasingly influenced by European business: labour, never central to European policy making, was not part of the new set of bargains that underpinned the launch of the new '1992' programme (Sandholtz and Zysman, 1989).

Emphasis shifted from external liberalisation to the mixed economy. The elimination of tariffs and quotas had produced a very incomplete common market, which was inevitable given the growth and complexity of national mixed economies. The new phase of integration set out to tackle the market implications of national regulation in the key areas of competition policy, technical standards and regulations, the supervision of financial institutions and, to a lesser extent, taxation policy. This involved an important new development: the liberalisation of capital and services. For, despite the movement towards a regional currency area after 1979, many European capital markets remained nationally regulated. In the early 1980s, the overall degree of capital market liberalisation was still quite low.

During the 1980s, a free-market conception of the European Community steadily prevailed over the alternative 'neo-mercantilist' vision, most notably promoted by the French after the failure of their own *national*-level industrial policies early in the decade. The legacy of 'neo-mercantilism' – the view that the European economy could be promoted via the consolidation of a large, united market as the base for new 'Euro-champion' companies – is to be found in technology promotion and collaboration programmes such as ESPRIT (information technology), BRITE (materials), RACE (telecommunications) and EUREKA – promoting high technology Euro-projects such as HDTV (high definition television) – and JESSI (semiconductors). Large-scale, state-funded collaborative programmes include, notably, the European Space Agency and the heavily subsidised Airbus consortium. However, this approach to integration has not been dominant. In the first place, the idea of a 'European' approach to competition and technological advance has been undermined by globalisation: large companies operating in world markets also market their products, secure technology transfer and raise finance internationally – as signalled by the proliferation of alliances between European and US or Japanese firms and the large number of US multinational subsidiaries that now participate in the Community's technology promotion programmes.

In the second place, the Single European Act (SEA) of 1987 has not created any basis for a 'fortress Europe' conception of integration. Rather, this predominantly deregulatory programme is accelerating tendencies towards internationalisation (Grahl and Teague, 1990). The 300 or so measures in the SEA aim to release the forces of competition, thereby overcoming the obstacles that were seen as impeding European economic growth. These are being implemented faster in some countries and sectors than others, but they are none the less changing the European economy radically. In some respects, this regulatory shift reduces the influence that national governments have over their economies; and some of this power is being surrendered to centralised European institutions. But in many sectors, national regulatory latitude is possible, even though this may be reduced steadily as the implementation of the internal market proceeds. The real change, as already suggested, lies in the abandonment of policy influence by national authorities to increasingly globalised markets, both in industrial products and financial services.

There are numerous cases where European regulatory powers are being asserted; but they remain contingent on the acquiescence of national governments. In most cases a 'two-tier' regulatory structure is being created. Take state aids, for example. Here, as in other areas, the EC has attempted to create an overall framework for industry. This framework allows the provision of national aid only in some cases – in lagging regions, where an industry is in crisis or if it promotes projects of 'European interest'. But there remains ample scope for national discretion. Not only do these vague categories permit scope for non-compliance, but the Commission has often been forced to bow to national political imperatives. In sectors where it has well-established powers – notably iron and steel – it has been able to create a regime with detailed and enforceable rules. But even here it has been unable to prevent politics from prevailing over economic logic – explaining in large part the collapse of its steel restructuring plan in 1994. Heavy subsidies for national champions (Iberia, Air France) or 'Euro-champions' (such as Airbus) have also been permitted.

Similarly, in competition regulation, while the Merger Control Regulation of 1989 ostensibly centralises competence in the hands of the Commission, only a small number of mergers – those that have 'a Community dimension' (where aggregate world-wide turnover exceeds Ecu 5 bn) – are dealt with at the European level. Furthermore, there are certain instances – such as public security, the plurality of the media, or when the member state makes a special case – where national jurisdiction prevails. In competition policy, there is some evidence of convergence on European norms, as set out in Articles 85 and 86 of the EC Treaty, especially among the smaller countries. But each member state retains its own national system, and those of the larger countries, such as Britain and Germany, have been slow to change. But here, too, regulatory change is being driven as much by the internationalisation of industrial sectors as by the development of a Community dimension (Davison, Fitzpatrick and Johnson, 1995).

Market-driven regulatory change has been most evident in financial services. Since the 1970s an ongoing process of re-regulation in financial services has occurred in response to the internationalisation of finance. In the 1950s and 1960s, demands from American capital for more open financial markets and the expansion of international trade placed increasing pressure on traditional regulatory systems. Even before the collapse of Bretton Woods and the arrival of a floating exchange rate regime – which saw a massive expansion in private capital flows to hedge against changes in currency values – this pressure found an outlet in London's 'Euro-markets', which were free from UK or US exchange and domestic interest rate controls (Cerny, 1993, pp. 57–9). The rapid expansion of the Euro-markets in the 1970s and 1980s placed pressure, in turn, on other financial markets to adapt. Multinational companies engaged in a process of 'regulatory arbitrage' as they sought out lower-cost environments. The international and domestic financial environment has been transformed by the emergence of global markets in short-term securities and cross-border equity trade; by rapid innovation in new financial instruments such as derivatives (swaps, futures and options); and by the appearance of actors with transnational investments, including insurance companies, mutual investment funds and pension funds. Confronted by this challenge, national authorities have had to surrender traditional control over banking and financial markets, and monetary instruments such as credit control, and replace them with regulatory frameworks that permit international capital flows. Once-cosy relations between central banks and domestic financial communities have been undermined (Grahl and Teague, 1990, pp. 111–18; Dyson *et al.*, 1995).

The first step towards the creation of a free European financial area began in 1988 with the Capital Movements Directive. As in other sectors, rather than a shift in governance to the European level, a two-tier structure has been created. While the Commission is responsible for removing national barriers and controls, the main policy instruments – and responsibility for domestic market regulation – remain with the member states. The governing principle here is mutual recognition rather than harmonisation. Under the Second Banking Directive of 1989, for example, banks of one country can offer a full range of services in another. But while a financial institution must comply with the market rules of the country in which it operates, responsibility for regulating that institution lies with its home country. Moreover, a full surrender of national influence is unlikely in the near future. Some countries enjoy derogations, preventing access to various parts of their financial sectors, while tax differences affecting many financial products remain extensive, and most directives allow governments to apply local conduct-of-business rules to foreign firms (Vipond, 1993).

Since the mid-1980s, then, deregulatory measures, the wide application of the principle of mutual recognition, and the adoption of common rules at the European level, have steadily brought integration to the previously sealed domains of the national mixed economy. But in contrast to the views of economic 'nationalists', the most important transfer of power has not been from the nation-state to the European institutions, but from the state to the market. The weakening of state power has been perhaps as much by design as by default. There has been an ever widening gap between economic and political integration (sometimes described as a conflict between 'negative' and 'positive' integration) as political realities only slowly adjust to the growing Europeanisation (and internationalisation) of economic forces. It is the weakness of the European political system – where agreement on the abolition of barriers has been much easier than the creation of new political or social structures – that partly accounts for the shift in the balance of power from the state to the market (Tsoukalis, 1997).

Restoring that balance – by providing a social dimension for the single market, for example – has been (and will be) extremely difficult (see Chapter 4). This is because the creation of that market has been one of the factors eroding specific national social compromises and creating the potential for 'regulatory arbitrage' among different welfare regimes, as companies search for the most 'competitive' locations in terms of social costs. At the same time, the creation of a social regime at the European level is impeded by the relative weakness of European employer and union organisations, and their marginalisation from negotiations on the economic dimensions of the integration process (Rhodes, 1995b). While national regulations are being harmonised by the Community in product-related areas – such as health, safety, environmental and consumer protection – creating high European standards in *process*-related environmental and welfare regulation is proving much more difficult, largely because of the problems of reconciling the diverse interests of the most advanced and the least developed economies. It has been argued that an erosion of standards in these areas may occur unless double standards are allowed (for example, a two-speed Europe, allowing higher levels of regulation in certain countries, while others are given time to catch up) and the perfectionism of market integration is balanced against the legitimacy of national priorities in areas such as social welfare, health care and industrial relations (Scharpf, 1996); but this argument exaggerates, perhaps, the possibilities of arbitrage between different national systems, while also underestimating the enormous differences that still exist between labour productivity levels.

Maastricht and the Political Economy of Monetary Union

As is suggested by the above, the process of integration has been strongly influenced by ideological trends. Beyond the internal market programme, the part of the Maastricht Treaty on EMU also clearly bears the signs of the new economic orthodoxy – of independent central banks, beyond the influence of politicians, and 'sound money'. As Sandholtz (1993) argues, the conversion of a core group of EC states to anti-inflation discipline as their overriding macroeconomic objective was the critical precondition for their acceptance of the Maastricht terms for EMU. As in the past, the most recent plans for EMU are inextricably linked with high politics. But these plans now imply a conscious decision to cede an important and also highly symbolic part of national economic sovereignty.

Until recently, discussions on EMU had been characterised by a large amount of relatively costless rhetoric. But now, although it is based on a typical Community compromise (the French got a clear commitment to, and specific date, for EMU, the Germans made sure the new European model conformed closely to their own, the British and Danes secured 'opt-outs', and the poorer Southern Europeans obtained a greater redistribution of resources), monetary union constitutes the most important and concrete part of the Maastricht Treaty. As a result, we now have a precise timetable for EMU – planned to start in 1999 – and detailed plans for its institutional architecture.

EMU will involve the irrevocable fixity of intra-EU exchange rates, to be followed by the adoption of a common currency, and the centralisation of monetary policy. A European Central Bank (ECB) will be responsible for the conduct of monetary policy for the Union as a whole, and for most foreign exchange operations. National central banks will be part of the new federal structure (the European System of Central Banks – ESCB) and they will operate in accordance with the guidelines and instructions of the ECB. The treaty and the attached protocol refer explicitly to the political independence of the ECB and national central banks, thus following the German model, which has also been adopted progressively by individual member countries. The monetisation of deficits will not be permitted within the monetary union, nor will there be any 'bailing out' of national, regional or local authorities by the EU. In the intermediate stages leading to EMU, there will be no substantial shift in the balance of power between national and central institutions. The European Monetary Institute (EMI) acts as a precursor to the ECB, but with no real powers in terms of monetary policy. But during the run-up to EMU, the definition of 'economically correct' behaviour has included the setting of criteria that are effectively the ticket for entry to the final stage of EMU. The convergence criteria refer to public deficits (which should be less than 3 per cent of GDP); public debt (less than 60 per cent of GDP); and exchange rate stability; while inflation must be no more than 1.5 per cent higher and long-term interest rates no more than 2 per cent higher than the average of the three states with the lowest inflation and interest rates. These criteria are now acting as a very important reference point for the macroeconomic policy of most member countries. They can be criticised on many grounds: they are mechanistic, some of them arbitrary and, perhaps, also superfluous (De Grauwe, 1994); moreover, in 1995, only one country, namely Luxembourg, fulfilled all four criteria. They do, however, reflect the strong influence of Germany as well as prevalent economic orthodoxy; and the two are closely related.

Convergence on the new economic orthodoxy of sound money and independent central banks raises important questions about the forces involved in shaping EMU's final stage. Recent research suggests that the triumph of the new economic orthodoxy within these arrangements has much to do with the power exerted by central bankers in the EMU negotiation process; but in the background, the internationalisation of economies is the major structuring variable. Given the challenge to central banks created by increased capital mobility (reducing the effectiveness of traditional monetary and exchange rate policies) and the relaunch of EMU in the late 1980s, Dyson *et al.* (1995) argue that central bankers have been the primary force in shaping a system of monetary integration that limits their loss of power. Pointing out that the final stage of EMU was negotiated almost exclusively by central bankers, they suggest that 'central bank independence provides the key connection between changes in global financial markets and EMU': a professional ideology based on political and economic independence for central banks and on the importance of price stability has become institutionalised within the arrangements for EMU and secures the control of central bankers within the new monetary system (ibid.).

The role of the Bundesbank as the guardian of the 'anchor' currency has been critical in the process of defining EMU, and underlines the asymmetry that persists within the present system of monetary co-ordination and emerging system of monetary integration. For the solutions adopted after the crisis of 1992–3 (see above) did not remove asymmetry as the fundamental problem of the system. Instability became more systemic: German unification produced a policy mix which relied exclusively on monetary policy as an anti-inflationary instrument. Consequently, interest rates were kept high by the Bundesbank at a time when Europe had entered the depths of economic recession, though, since 1993, the situation has calmed down in line with a steady fall of German interest rates. Faced with the size of private funds shifting across national borders and currencies, and the relatively recent dismantlement of the old and increasingly ineffective system of capital controls, European governments finally gave in to the pressures in the system in August 1993, announcing that the margins of fluctuation were to be widened to 15 per cent.

The deflationary consequences for the rest of Europe of the EMS were manifestly clear: fixed exchange rates, combined with the continuing central role of the DM, meant that other EMS countries could not lower their own interest rates, and unemployment kept on rising. There was still the option of devaluing their currencies against the DM. However, there was a general resistance to a new realignment of central rates – tantamount to a devaluation against the DM. This was not just because of a political commitment to anti-inflationary policies. Much more was at stake, namely the prestige and credibility of governments – and this was apparently felt most strongly in France, which continued to adhere to its *franc fort* policy of close alignment with the DM, in order to ensure that a strengthened Franco-German axis underpinned moves towards the final stages of EMU. The political consequences were reaped by the Juppé Government in the strikes of November–December 1995.

The strict application of the convergence criteria will unavoidably imply a further step in the institutionalisation of different tiers inside the Union; and this time, it will be even more important than before. The inevitability of asymmetry in this context leads us to ask a number of more fundamental questions about EMU. These concern both the feasibility of the arrangements being adopted and the changing relationship between nation-states, the supranational authorities and the market in the European Union.

Among the advantages expected to result from EMU are the removal of transaction costs and the costs and uncertainty (the currency risk premium) of long-term, cross-border investment. At the same time, it is expected that a central European bank will be able to ensure price stability. The link between EMU and the achievement of a fully-functioning – and durable – open internal market and political union should also be mentioned. While it is argued that a single currency will remove the temptation for countries to improve their competitiveness via devaluation (which, EMU enthusiasts would maintain, provides only short-term gains that are quickly eroded by subsequent inflation), the threat to political union created by the calculation of its costs and benefits in national terms by politicians should also be diminished (Goodhart, 1995).

However, such gains may be overwhelmed by the costs and strains of an artificially constructed monetary area. The asymmetry between Germany (and the bloc of neighbours dominated by its economy, including the Benelux countries and Austria) and the periphery of Britain and the southern member states would create the most tension, especially in the need for different policies to deal with external shocks. Given the lack of geographical flexibility in European labour and housing markets, the safety valve of migration cannot operate in Europe as it does in the United States. And the consequent problems of unemployment and uneven development under EMU could not be alleviated on a European-wide basis in conventional nation-state fashion, with fiscal and other redistributive policies (social transfers), since these functions will not be centralised under EMU. 'Euro-pessimists' fear a political – and even extreme nationalist backlash – in these circumstances (see Goodhart, 1995), although the balance between gains and losses remains an open and fiercely debated question among economists.

This leads directly to a second set of questions regarding the relationship between national governments, the supranational authorities and markets. The emphasis on price stability, together with the political independence of the new institution to be created in the final stage of EMU, are consistent with the new economic orthodoxy (Tsoukalis, 1997): and, as such, responsibility for monetary policy will not simply be transferred to the new institution, but it will also be taken away from politicians, be they national or European. While the objective of intra-EU exchange rate stability has involved substantial limitations to date in terms of national monetary autonomy (with the possible exception of Germany), this loss of autonomy will be completed – and made irreversible – by the final stage of EMU. On the other hand, given the asymmetry in past European arrangements, and the leading role of the Bundesbank in it, the creation of the ECB will at least allow other Europeans to share with the Germans the responsibility for conducting European monetary policy – one of the principal reasons for the strong commitment of the French and Italians to the project.

While the treaty does not create any new institutions for the co-ordination of fiscal policies, it does make provisions aiming at the strengthening of the existing mechanisms, while also defining what constitutes 'economically correct' behaviour. On the basis of reports by the Commission, which is therefore given the role of watchdog, the ECOFIN Council (Economics and Finance Ministers) will examine the policies of individual countries. A whole series of measures will be available to the Council in order to exert pressure on profligate members, ranging from public recommendations to the imposition of fines. In between, the Council may resort to other measures, always adopted on the basis of qualified majority votes (excluding the member states concerned), such as requiring the European Investment Bank to reconsider its lending policy to the particular member country and asking the latter to make non-interest-bearing deposits with the Union. Thus the treaty provisions rely mainly on the combination of peer and market pressure, the two being sometimes mutually reinforcing. The poorer countries which also happen to be major beneficiaries of the Structural Funds (there is in fact an explicit link in the treaty between transfers from the new Cohesion Fund and macroeconomic policy) will undoubtedly prove more vulnerable than others to collective pressure for a change in their macroeconomic policy. On the other hand, there is absolutely nothing in the treaty to prevent a deflationary bias resulting from excessively contractionary policies – which returns us, once again, to the political implications of EMU.

For at the heart of the movement towards monetary union lies a major question of political authority and legitimacy. Can there be a central bank without corresponding centralised political authority? (Cohen, 1994). This has no historical precedent. Unless political union acquires real meaning after the next intergovernmental conference, the independence of the ECB will be even greater in real terms than that enjoyed by the more privileged of its old national counterparts. In these circumstances it is difficult to see how decisions that have a direct impact on unemployment in places as diverse as Lille, Liverpool, Andalusia and Attica can be legitimised.

Conclusion

There has already been a substantial reduction in national economic autonomy in the process of European integration. But, as this chapter has emphasised, until recently this has not been to the advantage of the European institutions, but rather to the less controllable forces of the market. This has been in part the result of pressures beyond the influence of national governments – the globalisation of production and pressures for the liberalisation of national controls on the flow of capital from powerful actors in the new global market. But governments have also willingly surrendered their capacities to control the economic borders of the nation-state, and the deregulatory thrust of the single market programme has contributed to this shift in the balance between the market and the state.

As far as monetary union is concerned, we shall be witnessing a loss of national economic control to both the markets *and* to new European institutions – in particular the European Central Bank. There has already been a substantial reduction in national economic autonomy in the various attempts to preserve a system of stable intra-EU exchange rates. Yet the entry into the final stage of EMU, if and when it occurs, will mark a significant step in regional integration and the distribution of power between EU and national institutions. As with the other aspects of regional economic integration discussed above, EMU will also involve further changes in the economic order – that is, in the interaction between state and market. A weak European political system in an increasingly integrated regional economy will impose serious constraints on the allocation, distribution and stabilisation functions performed by the state in the context of the modern mixed economy. Thus it will also have important consequences for the balance between different economic and social groups.

The key question for the future is whether the EU and its institutions enjoy the political legitimacy for important decisions that will be seen to affect directly large sections of the population. Are national electorates ready to accept the consequences of an increasing Europeanisation and internationalisation of economic forces, especially in times of high unemployment and growing income inequality? Losers may rally behind nationalist flags, and the number of losers has been on the rise in recent years. Will politics necessarily adjust to economic changes?

3

European Integration and the Nation-State

RENAUD DEHOUSSE

The state remains the starting point for many analyses of European integration. The Community, and after it the European Union (EU), were created by national states. If they did so, it is generally stressed that it is because they felt the development of international co-operation was likely to bring a number of collective benefits. In order to make sure it would serve their interests, structures and procedures were designed to preserve their control over decision-making; hence the weight of the member states in the European political system (Hoffmann, 1966; Garrett, 1992).

The most refined variants of this intergovernmentalist model do accept that state structures are not operating in a political vacuum: they are subject to pressures from quite varied interests – sectoral, occupational or regional. However, the state remains the primary *political arena*. This is the level where the various interests at stake confront each other, and where the adjustments necessary to accommodate the position of each state come about. Integration is therefore viewed as a two-level political process: determination of national preferences, then intergovernmental negotiations at European level. This process is well summarised by Andrew Moravcsik's formula: 'national interests → state preferences → international negotiations → outcome' (Moravcsik, 1993).

However dominant it may be, this approach has recently been criticised from a number of directions. Some of the criticisms have questioned the centrality of the state as an actor, and assert that the development of European integration has owed much to supranational agencies – the Commission and Court of Justice of the European Communities – whose actions cannot be seen as an expression of the will of states (Dehousse and Majone, 1994). Others have noted the development of direct action by representatives of various interest groups at the European level, which suggests that the state is not necessarily the only political arena in which European policies are being discussed and shaped, and that national governments might not be the only actors influencing European policies (Mazey and Richardson, 1993; Marks *et al.*, 1995).

The fact is that the state-centred approach does not allow us to explain some essential features of the integration process. Thus, in recent years, subsidiarity has emerged as a major issue in the political debate over integration. Many voices have been raised against Community intervention, which is said to be both too frequent and too meddlesome. Several governments have not been slow in joining this chorus of criticism. This debate may have been more conjunctural than structural in nature, reflecting mainly a reaction to the renewed dynamism of the integration process after the mid-1980s. But the fact remains that the problem is rather hard to explain if one adheres to the canons of the intergovernmental approach: if the member states are so solidly and firmly in command of the Community institutional machine, how can the latter produce results so removed from their preferences?

Similarly, in legal terms, the EC had initially been conceived of as a classical international system, even if endowed with specific supranational features. Yet a system has evolved in which Community decisions take precedence over the rules of national law, even constitutional law. Thus, Community law has acquired an effectiveness which is closer to that of national law in federal systems than to that of international law (Weiler, 1981). Symptomatically, the Court of Justice readily refers to the Community's 'constitutional charter' in talking of the Treaty of Rome (Case 294/83, *Les Verts*). In the eyes of intergovernmentalists, this development involves a twofold anomaly: not only does it owe little to a combination of national wills; but states have adjusted to it, even if it restricts their freedom of manoeuvre considerably. The aim of this study is to show that 'anomalies' of this type are easily explainable by taking into consideration the effects of the integration process on state structures.

The classical intergovernmentalist approach tends to reify, not to say personalise, the state: it is treated as an individual, endowed with a capacity for understanding, a will of its own and a concern to act consistently. But this approach ignores the fact that behind the notion of 'the state' there lies a range of institutions whose objectives and interests vary. France is not just the Elysée, but also the Quai d'Orsay,

Place Beauvau, sometimes the Palais Bourbon or even the region of Aquitaine or Pas-de-Calais. Britain is not just Downing Street, but also Whitehall or Westminster. And each of these institutions may itself be a theatre of confrontation between differing interests. Yet, it is rarely acknowledged that European policies mobilise a large number of institutions within the state, and give rise to enormous co-ordination problems (Metcalfe, 1994). With few exceptions (see, for example, Moravcsik, 1994), states are considered to be independent variables and are treated implicitly as unitary structures that are hierarchically (and therefore efficiently) organised.

The object of this chapter is threefold. First, it suggests that while much integration theory has focused on the role of nation-states in the integration process, our understanding of that process requires a study of its impact, in turn, on the structures and behaviour of the states themselves. Second, it demonstrates that the conventional (unitary) vision of the state ignores the centrifugal effects of integration, which have led to a fragmentation of state structures and the emergence of functional networks among the institutions of governance in the various member states. Third, it argues that an approach centred on these networks allows a better understanding of the dynamics of the integration process. But before doing so we need to consider the context in which these developments have taken place.

Interdependence and the Nation-State

It has become a commonplace that the twentieth century has seen an enormous growth in interdependence among nation-states. The technological revolutions, the development of communications and of international trade, and the accumulation of means of mass destruction are among the factors that have contributed to this evolution. Such a thorough transformation was bound to have effects on the conduct of international relations. It has called into question the two classical postulates of international life: the separation between foreign and domestic policy, and the unitary character of the state.

International co-operation now covers such varied areas as culture, technological growth, improvement in living conditions, the fight against drugs, and environmental protection. It is hard to imagine an area that by its nature would be incapable of having an international dimension. Instances of interaction between domestic affairs and international questions are so numerous that it is no longer possible to make a clear distinction between the two levels. Quite naturally, this

evolution has affected the state apparatus. For states, the interpenetration of contemporary societies is reflected in a 'loss of control'
(Keohane and Nye, 1971, p. 742). Independent national policies are
often inadequate for dealing with a widening range of economic,
environmental or security issues (to mention but a few), which cut
across national boundaries. To meet this challenge, states have developed diverse forms of international co-operation and concerted action.
While the centripetal (or centralising) implications of interdependence
are generally acknowledged, the centrifugal (or fragmentary) forces
accompanying them have received less attention. Yet, it seems clear
that within the machinery of state, the diversification of interstate
contacts has gone hand in hand with their development. To be sure, at
the formal level, constitutional procedures generally grant to the
executive a leading – though not exclusive – role in foreign policy
formation. However, the importance of this apparent centralisation
should not be overestimated, as it is undermined by the development of
informal contacts, which are much more difficult to regulate. Most
state institutions (including even subnational actors) now struggle to
conduct an external policy of their own. More importantly, within the
executive, the time when 'foreign policy' concerned only the chancel-
leries is over for good. If only for reasons of time, it has become
impossible for foreign ministries to monopolise contacts abroad:
instead, one has seen line departments setting up *ad hoc* structures
for handling the external aspect of their policies. As a result, 'bureaucratic fragmentation', once seen as the special feature of domestic
affairs (Rosenau, 1967), is nowadays equally characteristic of the
foreign relations of states.

  While this phenomenon affects the whole of international relations,
it is *a fortiori* even more characteristic of the EU, since interdependence
is much more pronounced there. For even if the Treaties observe a
prudent silence on the possibility of a state withdrawing from the
Community, the links among EU member states are so highly developed in the mid-1990s that it is hard to envisage any one of them
pulling out unilaterally (Weiler, 1985). The French 'U-turn' in 1983
forcefully underlined this fact. Constrained to choose between an
(inflation-prone) policy of 'independent economic growth', which was
undermining the stability of the franc, and adopting a more orthodox
macro-economic policy in order to remain in the European Monetary
System, the socialist government of President Mitterrand opted for the
latter, showing that even if governments remain jealous of their
independence, they are not always willing to pay the high price
demanded for it.

The are several types of linkage between the national and supranational levels of the EU. Functional interdependence has grown enormously: in a common market, areas as diverse as environment, consumer protection, and social or cultural policy, though largely in the hands of member states, cannot be conducted entirely autonomously. Organisational elements also aggravate the centrifugal trend. The fact that the EU covers a wide range of policies, the division of the Council into over twenty specialised meetings, and the mushrooming of expert groups of various kinds offer multiple lines of communication, thereby making policy co-ordination a daunting task (Metcalfe, 1994, p. 277). Political interdependence is also increasing: we have seen examples of political crises unleashed at domestic level in connection with the European debate (Prime Ministers Margaret Thatcher and John Major have had experience of this, with different outcomes). In contrast, skilful politicians have learnt that they can 'cut slack', that is, use international commitments to loosen constraints imposed on them by legislatures, interests groups, or other domestic actors (Moravcsik, 1994). With the inclusion of the 'economic convergence criteria' in the Maastricht Treaty, for example, the need to stick with the European 'pack' has been invoked repeatedly to justify budgetary cuts that circumstances made necessary in any case.

All this, of course, is bound to have effects on the way European affairs are conducted at the national level, especially since the Treaties multiply the points of contact among institutions.

Integration and the Fragmentation of State Structures

Called on to handle an increasingly broad and complex set of tasks, state structures are evolving towards ever more advanced forms of specialisation. This trend is accentuated by the integration process. The phenomenon is twofold: integration has not only led to the development of manifold forms of *sectoral* co-operation (among specialists in a given area); it has also given rise to a phenomenon of *functional* differentiation, encouraging the creation of networks linking the executive agencies, judicial bodies and, more recently, legislatures of member states and of the EU. Though distinct, these two tendencies nourish each other.

Given the development of these forms of co-operation, the unitary conception of the state is often a fiction. Let us take the example of the EU Council. Legally, this is a body in which the will of the various member states is expressed. In practice, however, the Council consists of a myriad of specialised formations, bringing together the ministers of finance and the treasury, of youth and of sport, of home affairs and so on. The 'General Affairs' Council (bringing together the foreign ministers), to which a co-ordinating role has been assigned, has too much to do with its own sectoral business, the embryonic European foreign policy, to be able to handle this role effectively. Each formation of the Council thus tends to act autonomously, without always showing much consideration for what is decided at the other meetings. The European Council (which brings together the heads of state or government of the member states), has neither the material time nor the administrative resources needed to make up for this shortfall.

One of the original features of the Community system is that the political figures responsible – the ministers – act much more systematically than they do in most international organisations (Wessels, 1990, p. 235). This is easy to explain considering the binding power of decisions in the EU, which contrasts with the vagueness of resolutions adopted in other contexts. The political level is, however, only the tip of the iceberg. The available figures suggest a growing number of national bureaucrats becoming involved in developing and applying Community policies (ibid. p. 234). The possibilities of interaction among national administrations and the Community administration are manifold and include expert groups set up by the Commission to test the reactions of national administrations and interested circles, EU Council working groups and intergovernmental committees mandated to monitor the implementation of Community decisions by the Commission.

At this level too, a sectoral logic dominates. Community policies affect in one way or another all departments of the member states' cabinets. This has often led to the creation of European desks or offices in a large number of departments (Lequesne, 1993). Some traditionally highly centralised states have sought to mitigate this centrifugal development by setting up *ad hoc* bodies responsible for co-ordinating their Community policy: the 'Secrétariat général du comité interministériel pour les questions de coopération économique européenne' (SGCI) in France, or the European Secretariat of the Cabinet Office in Britain are the best-known examples. However, the influence of these bodies seems to be declining relative to the role of the 'technical' ministries (Siedentopf and Ziller, 1988, pp. 59–60). In his study of French European policy, for instance, Christian Lequesne has shown that even in a state where the administration is impregnated with a deeply-rooted hierarchical tradition, each ministry tries to defend as a priority the logic of its sector, reflecting its own interests and these of its clientele. Given the multiplicity of communication lines, the SGCI is not in a position to control all contacts with specialised departments in other member states, or with European institutions. This may occasionally give rise to contradictions up to the highest levels, culminating in contrasting positions being defended within different specialised sessions of the Council of Ministers (Lequesne, 1993, pp. 28, 265).

The tendency towards fragmentation is even stronger in other countries. Germany, with its combination of federalism and constitutionally guaranteed autonomy for ministries, has notorious difficulties in co-ordinating its European policies. The Ministry of Foreign Affairs has retained its leading role only with regards to political aspects of the integration process (Fromont and Siedentopf, 1987, p. 17). Similarly, in Italy, ministries generally have a strong sense of their own identity and tend to act in an uncoordinated fashion. It is therefore natural for each department to manage its European policy in a relatively autonomous way (d'Auria, 1987). A comparative survey of policy coordination has shown that in six member states of the EU twelve (namely Germany, Spain, Portugal, Italy, Greece and Luxembourg) no arbitration mechanism existed that could settle conflict between specialised departments (Metcalfe, 1994, pp. 285–6). The emergence of a sectoral logic is facilitated by the fact that a large number of European decisions are, in fact, taken at a fairly low level: not only does the Council of Ministers rely heavily on the preparatory work of COREPER, which brings together the Permanent Representatives of the member states in Brussels, but COREPER is often inclined to ratify choices made in specialised Council Working Groups (González Sánchez, 1992). Thus, unless an issue acquires a high political salience, the chances that a sectoral consensus will prevail are fairly high. Even Permanent Representatives, who are supposed to be the eyes and voices of their countries in the EU machinery, often see the search for compromise as one of their primary functions, which may lead them occasionally to interpret their instructions 'constructively' (Rutten, 1992). All these findings are, of course, in contrast with the basic postulate of intergovernmentalist approaches, which assume the capacity of the state to define and defend the national interest.

The attention that has been given to the development of the 'Europe of the administrations' (Siedentopf and Ziller, 1988, p. 367) has to some extent eclipsed the fact that a parallel development was taking place at other levels. The fundamental role of the Court of Justice in 'constitutionalising' the Community legal order, thanks particularly to the principles of direct effect and primacy of Community law, cannot be understood in isolation from the close relations it has established with national jurisdictions.

The vehicle of this privileged relationship was the preliminary ruling procedure introduced by Article 177 of the Treaty of Rome. This mechanism allows national courts, when dealing with a case involving questions of Community law, to ask the Court of Justice what interpretation should be given to Community provisions, or what is the validity of the acts adopted by its institutions. This has created a division of labour among judicial institutions, with the Court of Justice ensuring the uniform interpretation of Community law, and national courts applying it to specific cases.

Of all the procedures laid down by the Treaty of Rome, this is the most widely used. Preliminary rulings have accounted for over a third of the decisions handed down by the Court of Justice since its creation (Dehousse, 1994, p. 34). Some of the most important rulings in Community case law find their origin in questions raised by national courts. Through this channel, private individuals, whose direct access to the Court of Justice is relatively restricted, have succeeded in bringing before it a sizeable number of cases. Over two-thirds of the rulings in question saw the Court deciding – very specifically, though indirectly – on the compatibility of national provisions with Community law. Judicial co-operation has thus ensured Community decisions of an effectiveness incommensurable with that of most rules of international law. This success owes much to the enthusiasm many national courts have displayed for this form of judicial dialogue: though only higher courts are bound to remit a case to the Court of Justice where doubt arises as to the interpretation of Community law, almost three-quarters of the preliminary rulings have to do with referrals from lower courts. (The frequency of recourse to Article 177, however, varies heavily from one country to another, which conceal significant local resistance (Dehousse, 1994).)

Parliamentary bodies have been slower to develop such horizontal co-operation relationships. This certainly has to do with a multiplicity of different factors: the European Parliament had to wait until the mid-1980s for the Single European Act to give it the means to bear regularly on Community decision-making. For their part, national parliaments were slow to become aware of the fact that intergovernmental co-operation, by facing them with a *fait accompli*, was depriving them of a considerable part of their prerogative.

Be that as it may, since the early 1990s considerable efforts have been made to make up for this delay. The 'assizes' held in December 1990 between representatives of the European Parliament and national parliaments to discuss possible institutional reforms were a turning point. Since then, forms of co-operation have developed steadily. The specialist committees for Community affairs in the various national parliaments meet twice yearly (at what Community circles have imaginatively dubbed the 'COSAC meetings'), and many parliamentary committees have decided to associate MEPs as a matter of course with their discussions. For some time, too, there has been a multiplication of *ad hoc* initiatives, bilateral or multinational, bringing together members of parliamentary committees dealing with the same subjects at national and at European level (Westlake, 1995), which are similar to the functional co-operation networks that play such an essential role at the administrative level. The influence of these various initiatives remains, of course, to be demonstrated. However, the desire of parliamentary bodies to develop forms of functional co-operation seems undeniable.

Fragmentation and the Depoliticisation of European Public Policies

At the national level, the growth in the size and the activities of bureaucratic structures has gone hand in hand with a weakening of the structures supposed to control them, foremost among them parliamentary bodies. These two convergent tendencies have helped to lessen the legitimacy of public decisions, as shown by the complaints heard from many quarters against the growth of the bureaucratic state. European integration has only worsened things by aggravating these two tendencies: it has increased the power of (national) administrations considerably, while making it more difficult for parliaments to exert their powers of control. The very organisation of decision-making greatly favours national administrations (Moravcsik, 1994). One simple fact suffices to illustrate this. Matters that have been agreed at COREPER appear on the EU Council agenda as so-called 'items A', which are generally approved without discussion. These matters account for 70–75 per cent of decisions taken at Community level (Quermonne, 1994, p. 56). In other words, a large majority of European decisions are, in fact, taken at the bureaucratic level, even though they are adopted formally by a political body such as the Council of Ministers. Parliamentary structures, which traditionally act as a counter-weight to the power of the Executive, are in no position to make up for the influence of national administrations in the European decision-making process. Though strengthened by the Maastricht Treaty, the European Parliament's control powers concentrate on the Commission; this Parliament has no influence at all over national administrations. Moreover, the negotiating logic that prevails at European level, as in any form of intergovernmental co-operation, makes the control exercised by national parliaments haphazard: any parliament can at best keep an eye on the activity of 'its' ministers and the officials acting under their authority. By contrast, the Council as an institution, like the committees that prepare its decisions, are beyond any censure – hence the frequent complaints against what is often depicted as a 'democratic deficit'.

The legislative co-decision procedure set up by the Maastricht Treaty to grant proper legislative powers to the European Parliament illustrates well the peculiarity of the European situation. Though a meeting of a joint conciliation committee is provided where necessary to smooth differences between the Council and Parliament, in many cases the Council delegation consists of the permanent representatives or their deputies. Thus, although co-decision has been conceived to put Parliament and the Council of Ministers on an equal footing, it often takes the somewhat unusual form of a dialogue between diplomats and parliamentarians.

However, the 'democratic deficit' often mentioned in this connection is only one aspect of a broader problem of depoliticisation of European public policy (Dehousse, 1995). The great organised structures, the parties or trade unions, whose actions are the backdrop to the political debate in the eyes of citizens, are only weakly organised at the European level. As for the 'field specialists' who fill the networks of administrations, they tend to operate closely together with their direct interlocutors (sectional interests, pressure groups) without concerning themselves too much with public opinion.

These untypical aspects, combined with the complexity and multiplicity of decision-making procedures – of which there are more than twenty – all make it hard for the average person to comprehend the European debate. They count for much of the feeling of alienation that many sections of the population feel towards the European institutions. In such a heterogeneous whole as the European Union, seeking the common good is an intrinsically difficult task. The absence of a forum where the great issues of the day are debated is felt strongly. The European Parliament has not succeeded fully in taking on this role as a sounding box; as for the media, they barely give European issues a cursory glance. By transferring a large number of decisions to the European level, integration has led to a weakening of the state's role as a political arena; at the same time, however, it has failed to provide any real substitute. This has contributed much to the depoliticisation of public policy.

Fragmentation and Growth of the European Union's Powers

Though the integration process has had its ups and downs, the long-term trend seems to be towards a growth in the powers of the European institutions at several levels. The scope of Community policies has expanded progressively beyond that of economic integration *stricto sensu*, to include areas such as environment or consumer protection, health or education. In parallel, there has been a strengthening of the supranationality of decision-making, thanks to the extension of majority voting and the strengthening of the European Parliament's powers. For its part, the Court of Justice, through bold case law centred on the concepts of direct effect and the primacy of Community law, has brought Community law an effectiveness incommensurable with that of most norms of international law.

All these factors would seem to limit state prerogatives in one way or another. As such, they are difficult to reconcile with state-centred approaches to understanding the integration process, because the 'unitary' view of the state, which is central to these approaches, tends to see relations between the Community and member states as a zero-sum game: powers conferred on the former are necessarily taken away from the latter. To explain the development of integration, intergovernmentalists either refer to the need of independent bodies to ensure the effective implementation of interstate bargains (Garrett, 1992), or they try to identify areas in which national preferences seem to have converged at a given time (Moravcsik, 1991). Yet, useful as they may be, none of these reasons seems sufficient to explain a phenomenon of such considerable extent.

European integration is certainly too complex to be accounted for by some monocausal relationship. The motive forces have varied with time and area concerned (Dehousse and Majone, 1994). None the less, the 'fragmented' approach to the role of state bodies put forward here has the advantage of offering a scheme of analysis that allows an answer to one essential question: why have states adjusted without too much fuss (at least until the Maastricht Treaty) to an evolution that seemingly deprives them of many powers? The answer can be summed up in a few words: because the most directly interested agencies were getting something out of it.

The weight of the specialist departments in Community decision-making was mentioned earlier. Operating, into the bargain, in an only slightly politicised system, the 'field specialists' enjoy considerable freedom of manoeuvre. Many studies of intergovernmental co-operation in federal systems have highlighted the fact that collaboration among experts has often ignored the power-sharing lines between centre and periphery. Trained in the same schools, speaking a common language, moved by similar sectoral concerns, the experts in a given area tend to favour solutions that reflect their common values. In this context, competence problems take second place, which allows a degree of uniformity to develop via these institutional links (Weidner, 1955).

Several recent studies have highlighted the phenomenon of '*copinage technocratique*' ('technocratic collusion') at Community level, identifying, for example, a correlation between the level of influence of technical committees over a given policy and the degree of their members' expertise, their capacity to identify common values through negotiation, the existence of a consensus within the scientific community and so on. (Eichener, 1992; Buitendijk and van Schendelen, 1995). In this context, it is scarcely surprising that Commission initiatives are welcomed as long as they meet its interlocutor's sectoral concerns. The data available on the expert committees with the remit of monitoring Commission activities stress the consensual nature of decision-making: in almost all cases, when they have to take a decision of a technical nature, these committees tend to follow the Commission's proposals (Eichener, 1992). Political considerations are rarely of primary importance (González Sánchez, 1992).

In certain cases, the fragmentation of the decision-making process may even be a source of integrationist pressure. Those in charge of environment policy or consumer protection, for example, often face heavy resistance at national level from their colleagues in the treasury or the board of trade, or even the ministry of labour, who unfailingly stress the economic or social costs of some of their regulatory initiatives. There is nothing of the sort at Community level, where they are dealing with people who often share their concerns and difficulties. This may explain why an appreciable number of European decisions originate in a request from one or several member states, whereas the Commission in principle has an exclusive initiative right in most areas of Community activity (European Commission, 1992). The more consensual atmosphere prevailing at the European level appears to be favourable to innovations. There may therefore be considerable temptation to push through measures in Brussels that have failed at the national level. Eichener thus reports the example of a directive on safety in the workplace, adopted by the Community in 1983 on the initiative of an official who had initially sought to push his views through at the national level without success (Eichener, 1992).

In this institutional context, far from the zero-sum game described by supporters of the state-centred model, sectoral co-operation leads to a positive-sum game, as all agents in a given sector have an interest in achieving a solution that reflects their common values. Given the essential role of national administrations in decision-making at the European level, it would be wrong to see integration as disempowering state structures. On the contrary, it offers national decision-makers the possibility of communicating in a fairly congenial atmosphere, sheltered from indiscreet glances and beyond the control of parliamentary bodies (Weiler, 1991; Moravcsik, 1994). And if their initiatives are criticised, they will always have the possibility of throwing responsibility for them on to the nasty 'Brussels bureaucracy'!

Similar reasoning applies *mutatis mutandis* to the judicial level. If national courts, the direct interlocutors of the European Court of Justice, have as a whole accepted the latter's case law without much resistance, despite the innovations it has often brought with it, this is perhaps because these innovations ended up strengthening their prerogatives (Burley and Mattli, 1992; Weiler, 1994). Judicial bodies may indeed be endowed with extraordinary powers where called on to act to ensure the application of Community law. Even in countries where there is no judicial review of the constitutionality of laws, for example, the Court of Justice has ruled that the judiciary must verify the conformity of laws with Community standards. Similarly, in Italy or France, where the review of constitutionality is the exclusive province of the constitutional court, the judge in ordinary may 'disapply' any law incompatible with Community law. In Britain, where suspensive relief from the application of laws is unknown, it can be imposed, if this is needed, to ensure the efficacy of a Community norm. All these changes in the office of judge, aimed at ensuring the effectiveness of Community law, have the great advantage of increasing the powers of national jurisdictions, which can only create a favourable atmosphere for the reception of innovations in case law.

At this level, as with that of intergovernmental co-operation, a sectoral approach highlights the common interests and values of the main agents in a given network. It thus offers a better understanding of the favourable reception there has been for Community innovations – until concerns of a political and institutional nature returned to prominence with the Maastricht Treaty.

Reorganising the State

Much thinking on European integration is based more or less explicitly on the notion that it is reflected in a loss of power by states. The

transfer of decision-making power to supranational institutions, and the importance at the European level of the so-called 'negative integration' rules, which prohibit restrictions on free movement, are perceived as factors limiting the autonomy of national authorities. It has also been suggested frequently that Community rules, with their emphasis on the free market, enhance the tendency to deregulation that has marked public policy since the early 1980s (McGee and Weatherhill, 1990; Scharpf, 1996). The case law of the Court of Justice, which has exploited systematically the prohibitions contained in the Treaty of Rome, has contributed to the credibility of this thesis at a time when political decision-making was paralysed by the need to reach a unanimous decision on nearly every issue.

The foregoing analysis suggests a more qualified approach. On the one hand, counterposing the states to the European Union is somewhat artificial, given the role the former play at the European level. As shown above, the osmosis in any given policy area between national and Community agencies has contributed to the steady expansion of Community activities. On the other hand, the move to majority voting laid down in the Single European Act for setting up the single market has given a new vitality to the EC institutional system, enabling *inter alia* the Council to decide much more speedily. This meant that a better balance between positive and negative integration could be assured (Dehousse, 1992).

The combination of co-operation among experts and majority voting explains why, since the mid-1980s, Community policies do not merely reflect a common denominator among national preferences, as is widely assumed, but have at times been marked by substantive innovations (Eichener, 1992). At the time of the adoption of the product safety directive, for example, it was more safety-minded than the most progressive national legislation (Fallon and Maniet, 1990). Two direct consequences of the fragmentation of decision-making – the existence of a more favourable climate for innovation and the weakness of political debate – have certainly contributed to this development. Thus, in this case, it can be argued that deregulation at the national level has been followed by reregulation at the European level (Majone, 1990). In other areas, European policies have led to the development of national regulation at least in some member states. Prior to the development of European environmental policy, for example, Mediterranean countries had not been very active in that field. Similarly, the absence of any anti-trust policy in Italy eventually appeared as an anomaly, given the dynamism in this area displayed by the European Commission. If it were not for that contrast, one wonders whether an antitrust authority would have been created in that country at all.

More than once, European policies have been accompanied by the creation of new administrative structures aimed at ensuring the effectiveness of decisions taken at European level. The general directive on product safety adopted in 1992, for example, requires the setting up at national level of administrative structures to ensure that marketed products do not involve risks for consumers. It also happens that Community norms require member states to set up specific structures to check on the implementation of certain rules. Regulation No. 2262/84, adopted in July 1984, provided for the setting up of autonomous agencies to monitor aids to olive oil production introduced as part of the Common Agricultural Policy (OJ No. L208/11 of 3 August 1984). In certain cases, the Community even goes so far as to take on some of the costs linked to the establishment of new administrative structures (see, for example, Regulation No. 405/89 of 21 December 1989, on scrutiny by the member states of transactions forming part of the system of financing by the Guarantee section of the EAGGF (European Agricultural Guidance and Guarantee Fund) (OJ No. L388/18, 30 December 1989).

For some years there has also been a development of specialist administrative networks at the European level. The most outstanding example is undoubtedly that of the European central bank system set up by the Maastricht Treaty. According to the Treaty scheme, monetary policy is to be conducted by a network of central banks in which the national monetary institutions – free of all political supervision – are to handle monetary policy in concert with the European central bank (see Chapter 2). This remarkable scheme was proposed by the Delors Committee, composed principally of the governors of national central banks. This is no doubt an extreme case, owing much to the fact that the need to give the experts considerable institutional freedom is more accepted in the monetary area than in others, since it is perceived as a guarantee of price stability. But it would be wrong to see this as an isolated phenomenon. The many European agencies created in the early 1990s must first and foremost be analysed as networks bringing together the national and Community officials with responsibility for a given area (Dehousse *et al.*, 1992). Here again, the creation of these agencies has acted as an incentive for the establishment of similar structures at the national level. The creation of the European Monitoring Centre of Drugs and Drug Addiction, for example, was followed rapidly by the establishment of a similar structure in France, although this was not made obligatory by the relevant Council regulation. Thus the circle is closed: the fragmentation of decision-making promotes the development of European regulation, which legitimises and cements the existence of autonomously functioning, specialised networks.

Since it is based on a principle of decentralised administration, where applying the norms is a matter primarily for the national bureaucracies, the Community system cannot do without the latters' assistance. One of the primary objectives of integration has therefore been to guide the activity of the national administrations. In doing so, it has accentuated the fragmentation of the nation-state. It is true that these national administrations lose some of their autonomy in the process, as they can no longer take decisions unilaterally. However, national administrations gain to the extent that fragmentation enhances their possibilities of intervention, while largely shielding the organisations responsible for a given policy from political controls. Rather than a retreat of the state, we are witnessing its redeployment.

Conclusion: Transnational Governance – Policies without Politics

The relationship between the states and the process of European integration is a complex one. While there has been much to debate over the role of states in that process, little attention has been paid to the other side of the coin, that is, the impact of integration on state structures themselves. Clearly, the development of transnational co-operation during recent decades could not but have influenced the way state administrations perform their functions. I have tried to show that the main consequence of this evolution has been a growing fragmentation of the state: not only have bureaucracies been given the possibility of evading parliamentary control mechanisms at the national level, even within the executive, each department has engaged in the development of its own European policy. In most member states of the Union, current co-ordination mechanisms seem unable to counteract this centrifugal evolution.

This chapter has also noted the parallel development of functional networks across national borders. All three branches of Montesquieu's *trias politicas* have engaged in a co-operative relationship with their counterparts in other member states. True, this tendency has not affected each of them to the same extent, nor at the same time. Whereas administrative and judicial co-operation dates back to the early years of the Community, parliaments have been slow to follow suit. But the point is precisely that a focus on these forms of transnational functional governance helps us understand both the dynamics of integration and the problem it has created: transnational administrative co-operation has fed the growth of Community competences, judicial co-operation has ensured the acceptance of the European Court's bold jurisprudence, and the slowness with which parliaments have reacted, has contributed to the depoliticisation of European public policies.

While this 'fragmentation' approach contrasts fundamentally with a basic postulate of intergovernmentalist theories, namely that the capacity of states to formulate a centralised and coherent European policy, it does not follow that this evolution has weakened the state. The crux of the matter is that talking about the state 'as a whole' is unhelpful. In fact, some branches of the state – the administration and the judiciary – have clearly benefited from the integration process, while other institutions, such as parliaments, have lost ground. It would therefore be wrong to assume that integration undermines the authority of the state. Within the structures of the state there have been winners and losers, but on the whole, bureaucracy – which plays a growing role at the national level – has not seen its position eroded significantly by the integration process, since administrative co-operation plays such a central role in Community policies. True, bureaucracies have now lost the capacity to decide unilaterally on a number of matters; but in the process, their autonomy *vis-à-vis* national parliaments has increased. The development of a transnational functional network could even be seen as evidence of the state's remarkable capacity to adjust to new forms of governance.

Turning to the state as a political arena, and no longer as a decision-making structure, the evaluation is more complex. It seems clear that most political debate still takes place at the national level. Although many lobbies and interest groups have discovered the European scene in the wake of the Single European Act, the extent of their influence remains unclear, and the institutions that traditionally shape political debates – such as political parties or the media – are still poorly organised at the European level. As a result, few decisions attract the attention of public opinion at large, which may explain the rather low turnout at European elections. In other words, while integration is undermining the relevance of the state as a political arena, it has so far failed to provide any substitute.

This discrepancy between politics and policies is, of course, problematic, as many of the control mechanisms set up at national level to ensure the democratic character of policy choices (parliamentary control) or to protect fundamental values (judicial review) are being eluded as a result of the integration process. There is a clear need for mechanisms to ensure the legitimacy of policy choices made in Brussels and Strasbourg. Yet it seems equally clear that state-based control techniques will not suffice, for the simple reason that the European Community is not a state, but a complex form of transnational governance. The way we think about its legitimacy must somehow reflects its peculiarities. The consolidation of the European Parliament's prerogatives, which is often regarded as the critical remedy to this democratic deficit, is unlikely to suffice in meeting this legitimacy challenge.

PART TWO
Governance

4

The Welfare State: Internal Challenges, External Constraints*

MARTIN RHODES

No account of recent development in west European politics would be complete without an in-depth consideration of the present and future of the welfare state – for three main reasons. First, welfare institutions and programmes are central to the functioning of European economies and labour markets and are underpinned by long-standing political and financial commitments, popular support and vested interests. Second, in recent years the welfare state has risen to the top of the political agenda, not just because of attacks made on it by the neo-liberal right in certain countries but because it now faces a number of unprecedented challenges, both from within domestic political econo-mies and from the external economic environment. And third, con-troversy around attempts to put in place a European 'social dimension' has exposed the different conceptions of social policy among member states and revealed the limits to European intervention.

The following analysis provides a comparative overview of develop-ments in European welfare states. The central argument is that although European welfare states are not in crisis, and are certainly not being dismantled on any significant scale, they are certainly heavily constrained by cost problems and, while still institutionally diverse, are nevertheless converging in terms of their *response* to the present impasse and also, to some extent, in terms of social policy *outcomes*. The discussion begins with a brief account of the central issues before examining the variety of west European welfare states. The current challenges to the welfare status quo – both internal and external – are

---

* This chapter contains material and arguments developed at greater length in Rhodes (1996a).

57

then presented, prior to a discussion of the ways in which welfare states are changing.

Is the Welfare State in Crisis?

The notion of a 'welfare crisis' has been in vogue for some time. It first gained popularity in the mid-1970s at a time when it seemed that the economic slump following the oil price shock signalled a deeper crisis of the capitalist economies. Two celebrated books from the period – James O'Connor's *Fiscal Crisis of the State* (1973) and Ian Gough's *The Political Economy of the Welfare State* (1979) – traced the origins of the welfare state's problems to its contradictory role within capitalism (which it simultaneously legitimised and constrained). From a more conservative standpoint, others began to talk about 'policy overload', a concept which was subsequently hijacked by neo-liberal opponents of the welfare state. At the end of that decade, the OECD produced a volume on *The Welfare State in Crisis* (1981) that produced a range of viewpoints, many of which focused on two further challenges to the welfare state – the emergence both of a post-industrial society (see Chapter 8), with different demands and needs from those addressed by conventional social programmes, and a trade off between equity and efficiency in western economies.

One of the contributors to that book – Harold Wilensky – argued that the new challenges could be accommodated by welfare states without too much disruption and certainly without their demise, especially in those countries with strong 'corporatist' patterns of bargaining between labour, management and government. Indeed, as it turned out, the fiscal strains and 'overload' were absorbed by a return to higher levels of growth and the 'crisis' subsequently corrected by marginal shifts in the emphasis of policy towards income maintenance and protection against risk. Welfare states no longer grew as they had in the past – in the 1980s the ratio of social spending to GDP grew by less than 2 per cent per annum in the EC 12 compared with 5 per cent in the previous decade – but the major social programmes (pensions, health, unemployment compensation, etc.) were sustained in the north and expanded in the south (see Table 4.1).

By the early 1990s, a new set of concerns had emerged. First, while welfare spending reached its limits in those countries Wilensky considered best able to cope with new challenges (by 1993 the costs of welfare in Scandinavia and the Netherlands were equal to or greater than a third of GDP) it also expanded across the European Commu-

TABLE 4.1 *Social expenditure in the EU 12, 1970–93 (% of GDP)*

	B	DK	D	GR	SP	FR	IRL	I	L	NL	P	UK	EU12
1970	18.7	19.6	21.5	–	–	19.2	13.2	17.4	15.9	20.8	–	15.9	19.0
1980	28.0	28.7	28.8	9.7	18.2	25.4	20.6	19.4	26.5	30.1	12.9	20.6	24.1
1985	29.3	28.4	28.4	15.4	20.0	28.8	23.6	22.6	23.4	31.7	14.2	23.8	25.9
1990	27.0	29.8	26.9	16.1	20.6	27.7	19.5	24.1	22.1	32.2	15.0	22.1	25.2
1993	27.6	33.2	27.6	16.3	24.0	30.9	21.4	25.8	24.9	33.6	18.3	27.3	27.7

Source: Adapted from European Commission (1995), Table 1.

nity in line with higher unemployment: if the ratio of social spending to GDP grew by an average 4.4 per cent per year between 1990 and 1993, unemployment benefits rose by 14.0 per cent. Second, those challenges already identified in the 1980s appeared to become more pressing, in particular demographic changes (the ageing of the European popula- tion) and the emergence of new family and labour market patterns. These changes transformed the nature of 'needs' and altered the gender/family/work nexus in which welfare states had traditionally been based. And third, the nature of the international political econ- omy has been fundamentally altered, by the liberalisation of the flow of capital and goods and the abandonment of exchange controls (Rhodes, 1995a). Although these fundamentals of the 'age of embedded liberal- ism' had already begun to give way from the mid-1970s (see Ruggie, 1984 and Chapter 2 in this volume), the internationalisation of trade and the globalisation of finance accelerated in the 1980s, altering the balance of power between organised interests (capital and labour) and imposing new exogenous constraints on government autonomy.

Whether this amounts to a 'crisis' is debatable. First, globalisation seems to have fuelled welfare state expansion rather than retrenchment: for while growing competitive pressures are making businesses – and governments – more attentive to non-wage labour costs (employer contributions to social insurance systems), social programmes of both the passive (social assistance) and active (retraining) type have borne the cost of higher unemployment and industrial adjustment. Second, a wide variety of welfare reforms across Europe have made changes only at the margins, even if they are beginning to cut close to the bone of some programmes in certain countries. For, as Pierson (1996) argues, the politics of welfare retrenchment are very different from the politics of expansion. In most EU countries, the support of electorates for a 'fat' rather than 'lean' welfare state, buttressed by the defence of the status quo by vested interests, makes anything other than tinkering very difficult.

Yet neither of these points detracts from the fact that, for a variety of reasons, welfare states are at an impasse. For while the expansion of spending in response to globalisation has created its own problems (unemployment is one of the major contemporary challenges), policy inertia has compounded the problems and contradictions of the welfare state. Moreover, welfare systems are failing in many areas. Even if in most countries welfare programmes have been sustained, social change is accelerating at such a pace that new risks are emerging and previously minor risks are being aggravated: higher unemployment, for example, means more 'risk-prone' environments, with reduced access to welfare for those who do not qualify for benefits linked to labour market participation (Sigg *et al.*, 1996). At the same time, although public opinion polls continue to indicate widespread support for the welfare state, among politicians of all parties there is a profound loss of confidence in 'collective', public-sector solutions in favour of either privatised or 'marketised' social services. How far this loss of confidence will feed through into policies that question the fundamentals of European welfare systems depends on a host of factors, notably the institutional make-up of those systems and factors largely beyond the control of policy makers, primarily levels of economic growth and the impact of changes in the global economy.

Varieties of Welfare: Categorising West European Social Systems

Social systems generate their own particular problems and contradictions. Esping-Andersen's *Three Worlds of Welfare Capitalism* (1990) has made a seminal contribution to our understanding of how welfare systems work, how they differ and why they get in trouble. His is a complex but elegant thesis. Beginning with T. H. Marshall's proposition that 'social citizenship constitutes the core idea of a welfare state' (Esping-Andersen, 1990: 21), he explores the institutional conditions in which social rights are granted, setting out three main principles for a theoretical specification of the welfare state: the effects of social citizenship on the position of the individual *vis-à-vis* the market (the less dependent the individual on the market for his/her status, the more that status is 'de-commodified'); the system of social stratification thereby created (status as a citizen will compete with, and in some cases replace, one's class position); and the relationship between the state, the market and the family's role in social provision. The welfare-state variations that result from applying these principles cluster into three regime-types (noting, however, that none of the countries within them are 'pure' types):

- *The social-democratic type* (the Scandinavian countries) where the social democrats who dominated these political systems in the period before and after the Second World War created a highly universal and de-commodifying set of programmes. Services and benefits were upgraded to levels expected by the middle classes and equality ensured by giving workers full access to those rights. All are entitled to the same amounts when risk occurs, though those employed receive additional benefits through mandatory occupational schemes. This model 'crowds out the market' and creates a cross-class solidarity in favour of an extensive system of welfare support. Its strength lies in its commitment to a full-employment guarantee, in which the right to work is as important as the right to income protection. But this is also a source of weakness, for sustaining such a system is highly costly and requires that revenue be maximised and social problems minimised. An inability to prevent rising levels of unemployment will create serious problems, not just of funding but of maintaining the system's core, legitimising, ideal of solidarity.
- *The liberal, Anglo-Saxon type* (into which both Britain and Ireland fall, albeit imperfectly) which, by contrast, minimises solidarity and de-commodification and delivers modest benefits via means-tested assistance and universal transfers, catering largely to a clientele of low-income, largely working-class dependants. Unlike the Scandinavian model – where the middle classes and their support have been central – this is a more residual welfare state and increasingly dependent on the support of a restricted class coalition. This in itself is a weakness because it creates political space for anti-welfare pressures as a growing number resort to private-sector health and pensions' provision. A further weakness is created by the growing gaps in the safety net and the creation of poverty traps by means-testing and the proliferation of low-paid, temporary or part-time jobs. The net result has been a significant increase in inequality and poverty rates.
- *The conservative, corporatist type* (Austria, France, Germany, the Benelux countries and Italy) includes strong elements of de-commodification but is most distinctive for its 'status differentiating' welfare programmes, for income maintenance and health care are strongly related to employment and family status. Only the Netherlands has shifted strongly towards universal schemes. The 'Bismarckian' insurance principle still determines the distribution of benefits (which,

apart from family allowances, are earnings-related) and their funding (via employer and employees' contributions with distinct provisions and regulations applying to different occupational groups). Employers' organisations and unions play an important role in the management of the social insurance funds. While social assistance programmes fill the gaps left by social insurance, the traditional family is strongly defended by the system which, bearing the influence of the Church, excludes non-working wives from social insurance. The current weaknesses in this model lie in the high incidence of social charges (a non-wage labour cost) on employers, a policy and spending bias towards pensions and an apparent inability to respond to growing levels of unemployment.

This interpretation of European welfare states has not gone unchallenged. There have been two principal critiques: that it caters insufficiently for the 'gender' character of welfare state regimes, and that the model is too general. A growing, but inconclusive literature has argued that the regime approach needs to be complemented or revised by greater emphasis on the role of gender in shaping (and being shaped by) welfare systems (e.g. Lewis, 1992; Bussemaker and van Kersbergen, 1994). Attention should be paid in particular to the role of unpaid work and the status of women beyond the labour market, as wives, mothers and citizens (Sainsbury, 1994). This issue is addressed briefly below when considering the implications of increasing female work force participation. As for the critique of excessive generality, in itself this argument is invalid for no theory seeks to explain diversity: rather it tries to identify underlying patterns and mechanisms. More justifiable, however, is criticism of the absence of the southern European countries, with the exception of Italy which is included under the conservative–corporatist type. Leibfried (1992) sought to specify a distinctive southern or 'Latin Rim' form of welfare in which the church, family and private charity combined with residual public welfare institutions to create a 'rudimentary welfare state'. Ferrera (1996) has gone further, identifying and exploring in detail four main traits of a 'southern model':

- A highly fragmented and 'corporatist' income maintenance system characterised by dualism and polarisation in terms of income maintenance and pensions – between the 'hyper-protected' (public employees, white-collar workers and private wage-earners of medium-sized and large enterprises working on full contracts) and the 'under-protected' (the unemployed – who have little income support – and workers in weak sectors without job security or in the extensive informal economy).

- A departure from corporatist traditions (typical of Esping-Andersen's conservative, continental model) in the field of health care and the establishment of national health services, as in Britain, Ireland and Scandinavia.
- A weak role for the state (reflected in still low levels of welfare spending in these countries, apart from Italy – see Table 4.1); and the persistence of a peculiar welfare mix between public and non-public actors and institutions (family/church/charity).
- Extensive clientelism and 'patronage machines' which distribute cash subsidies to political client groups (e.g. invalidity pensions in southern Italy and in certain parts of Spain and the need for contacts within the party–union network to exploit the complicated regulations of the Greek pension system).

Whether the identification of these features requires the addition of a new 'variety' of welfare regime to Esping-Andersen's 'three worlds' is debatable. Katrougalos (1996) argues convincingly that the case of Greece – and by implication the other three southern European countries – fits rather well the 'organisational matrix' of the conservative, continental model, given an occupationally highly segmented social insurance system, a disproportionate bias towards pensions, entitlements related to the employment and contribution record and an emphasis on the role of the family as the core unit of social care. Where they differ is in their level of development and the uneven institutionalisation of these principles. For the purposes of the following discussion we can accept his conclusion that in terms of their underlying mechanisms, the southern welfare systems form a 'sub-category' or 'discount edition' of the continental model, while also acknowledging their peculiar features and weaknesses.

Challenges to Welfare – I: Domestic Developments

Each of these regime types is responding in its own way to the internal and external challenges to welfare. The domestic challenges to welfare stem from the interaction of the following developments.

Demographic Change

The ageing of the EU population, resulting from declining birth rates and increased life expectancy, poses a major challenge due to the shift in the ratio of active (tax paying, social contribution making) citizens to passive welfare recipients. Spending will have to rise, not only on retirement pensions but also on health and other forms of care. The European Commission (1995) notes that in 1995 around 15 per cent of the population in the European Union were aged 65 or over, equal to 23 per cent of the working-age population (15 to 64). By 2005 the over-65s will rise to 26 per cent of the working-age population and to 30 per cent by 2015. The problem varies greatly across Europe, ranging from Ireland, which has the lowest dependency ratio, to Italy where the over-65s are projected to increase to almost 40 per cent of those of working age over the next thirty years.

The Rising Cost of Health Care

Health-care spending in the OECD area more than doubled its share of GDP between 1960 and 1992, from under 4 per cent to just over 8 per cent, although spending in the European Union varies from a low of 5.4 per cent in Greece to 9.8 per cent in Finland. According to recent research, less a half of this increase can be explained by 'demand-side' factors, i.e. ageing, higher incomes and increased insurance coverage. The rest can be accounted for by 'supply' effects, including technological change (techniques, drugs, equipment and procedures), a growth in medical personnel and facilities and increases in real health care prices (Oxley and MacFarlan, 1995). Thus the health-care sector, broadly defined, contains its own 'inflationary dynamic', quite apart from new demands placed on the system. The escalating costs this generates places significant strains on health care funding.

Low Economic Growth and High Unemployment

The strain imposed by ageing and rising health care costs will be much more difficult to bear if economic growth stays depressed and unemployment high. In themselves, low growth and high unemployment imply higher spending on income support for those unable to find work and on active labour market measures to improve their employability. None of the European regime types are responding particularly well to the unemployment challenge (Esping-Andersen, 1996b). For while the Scandinavian solution of expanding public-sector employment (especially for women) has hit its limits, the conservative, continental solution of subsidising exit from the labour force via early retirement has become costly and imposes higher non-wage costs on firms, making them reluctant to hire new recruits. The unemployment problem is accentuated in southern Europe, where the labour market has become divided rigidly (due to a distorted system of employment regulation) between the 'hyper-protected' (employed in the public sector or large private-sector companies) and the young – especially female – unemployed. Meanwhile the neo-liberal, Anglo–Saxon, approach has been to deregulate the labour market and create a mass of low productivity 'junk jobs' which entails a welfare 'double-jeopardy' (Esping-Andersen, 1996a): it requires higher levels of social assistance while also producing poverty traps (low wages create disincentives to work unless social assistance is drastically curtailed). This approach also creates new risks, with growing levels of poverty, especially among the unskilled and single-parent households.

The Changing Nature of the Labour Market

Two developments in the labour market have critical implications for the future of west European welfare: the growing proportion of non-standard forms of employment and the increasing participation of women. Although a proliferation of 'precarious' jobs has been a particular feature of the Anglo–Saxon labour market, an increasing number of those in work in all countries now work on part-time and/or fixed-term contracts. Just as the traditional welfare state – especially the 'Bismarckian', continental model – assumed a life-time of full-time, stable employment, it also assumed that women were 'inactive', i.e. primarily involved in unpaid family work. Now female participation rates are above 50 per cent in virtually all countries and are over 60 per cent in many.

None of the systems described above is well-equipped for the growing number of people who now alternate between employment and unemployment, between 'typical' and 'atypical' jobs. Nor will they easily deal with the large number of young people in long-term unemployment or whose work experience is infrequent or in the black economy. For in many countries there are minimum legibility thresholds preventing workers from either contributing to or receiving benefits from social security schemes. An 'atypical' worker may never qualify for benefits (Sigg et al., 1996). Germany is a case *par excellence* of this problem, for the allocation of benefits for sickness, unemployment and old age depends on whether the person (or the claimant's spouse) has been in full-time employment. High unemployment and increasing divorce rates (the rise of the 'atypical' family) mean that fewer will have 'sufficient' claims on the system to protect them from poverty (Plaug, 1995). This is an example of how the changing labour market produces 'implicit disentitlement' (Standing, 1995). 'Explicit disentitlement' is occurring as well, as countries respond to cost and so-called 'disincentive' or 'moral hazard' problems – the idea that welfare prevents people working and 'creates' welfare dependency – by limiting access to unemployment benefits or social assistance.

Increased female activity rates also raise serious issues, not just because family work still tends to fall on women's shoulders, especially in the southern countries, but also because social protection is geared to *male* breadwinners and tends to penalise female careers: interrupting employment, even temporarily, for family reasons can cause a considerable loss of pension in some countries (Ferrera, 1994). Only in the Scandinavian countries has the welfare regime been 'women-friendly' in this respect, by providing extensive child-care services and adequate social security cover. Women, it should be noted, are more likely to suffer various forms of disentitlement than men because they are more concentrated in part-time and temporary employment (Standing, 1995).

Challenges to Welfare – II: External Constraints

As discussed above, the issue of globalisation is a controversial one and its effects on the welfare state apparently contradictory. Nevertheless, the interaction of globalisation with internal challenges suggests there is a new dynamic at work in the international economy that compounds the problems of the advanced welfare states while also making them more difficult to resolve. 'Europeanisation' also has numerous implications for all of the region's welfare regimes, as both a 'sub-set' of globalisation (in creating an unfettered internal market) and the source of new pan-European social policies and programmes.

Globalisation

The process of globalisation has a number of implications for welfare states. The first of these derive from its impact on inequality and unemployment:

- Relocation to low labour cost countries outside Europe has been occurring at an increasingly rapid pace in manufacturing, especially in sectors where production can easily be separated from production and design and where the market is global. This, and the parallel increase in the growth of manufactured exports from the newly industrialised countries (NICs), has been driven by their growing manufacturing cost advantage and rising productivity. To date, the major casualties have been unskilled or low-skilled workers in labour intensive manufacturing. In the future, semi-skilled and certain skilled workers will also be threatened by the globalisation of information technology to those NICs (mainly in the Asia-Pacific region) that have made massive investments in education and training (Freeman and Soete, 1995).

- Despite the institutional barriers to market forces created by different welfare systems, there is growing evidence that intensified international competition and the changes induced in industry are increasing earnings inequality, in part because the relative wages of more skilled workers are being bid up in western countries and those of lower skilled workers are falling (Gottschalk and Joyce, 1995).

The second set of implications derives from the impact of globalisation on national government autonomy:

- The 'golden age' of the welfare state between the 1950s and 1970s was dependent on internal and external supports (Singh, 1995). The key domestic arrangements included, with varying degrees of success, a compromise on wages and profits between capital and labour and a commitment by the state to a certain level of welfare, living standards and domestic demand. Externally, a stable international monetary and trading regime depended on the support of a hegemonic power – the United States. As explained in Chapter 2, the relative decline of that power and of the dollar as the monetary bedrock of the system meant that those arrangements could no longer be sustained. The end of the international regime of 'embedded liberalism' – based on fixed exchange rates and capital controls – has witnessed a loss of control by governments over financial transactions as credit and exchange controls have been abandoned.
- In consequence, domestic economies have become hostage to international markets and their demands for 'credibility'. Governments – and especially social democratic ones – have had to shift their priorities away from traditional goals of redistribution, welfarism and full employment towards restraining the expansion of credit and money stock effected by international markets, defending the

balance of trade and payments and controlling inflation (Moses, 1995). Meanwhile – and partly in consequence – domestic welfare arrangements have become harder to sustain as corporatist welfare coalitions (between employers and unions – the 'social partners') have been undermined: for increased capital mobility immeasurably strengthens the owners of capital over other groups (Frieden, 1991). The most dramatic example of this shift has been in the Scandinavian model where employers have broken with the long-standing-corporatist consensus (Stephens, 1996). Nevertheless, even if it is under stress, corporatist decision-making may prove to be essential in managing welfare retrenchment and change: pension reform, for example, may prove impossible without it in many countries (as revealed recently in France, Germany and Italy).

- Finally, the 'competitive imperative' generated by greater economic interdependence has encouraged the pursuit of policies designed to preserve or create competitive advantage. The main concern is to avoid burdening firms with higher non-wage labour costs or corporate taxes and to alleviate those they currently bear.

Europeanisation

Increased integration of the European economy poses a new and parallel set of problems. The critical question is how far the various welfare regimes can retain their diversity in an open trading, finance and, eventually, currency region. The first set of implications relates, again to the impact on employment and welfare arrangements. For in a more open European trade area – the single market – a contest may be emerging among the regimes due to their different social costs. There are two dimensions to this phenomenon:

- First, the greater scope created for 'regulatory arbitrage' on the part of firms (i.e., their capacity to choose between locations on the basis of the relative costs of regulation) could lead to 'regime shopping'. Arguably, this is already happening as firms from high-cost jurisdictions such as Germany transfer to lower-cost countries like Britain, where other assets – such as an educated work force and access to finance – are also in good supply.
- The second, related, prospect is that, if 'regulatory arbitrage' becomes extensive, member state governments could engage in 'social devaluation, a problem likely to be compounded by progress towards European monetary union (EMU). The austerity policies

demanded from countries in preparation for EMU (reductions in deficits and debts, a prioritisation of anti-inflation policies) have already had an impact on welfare programmes. Under fully-fledged monetary union, reducing wage (and non-wage) labour costs will become the only tool left in the hands of governments seeking to improve the competitiveness of their economies. Those countries able to compete on productivity may be able to sustain existing welfare arrangements; those having to compete on price will be forced to reduce the costs of welfare for firms as well as bidding down real wages. The threat of a further increase in polarisation and inequality begins to loom large under these circumstances.

Of course, these aspects of 'negative integration' are the downside of European Union. 'Positive integration' is also occurring as new regulations are put in place to protect the European 'social model'. However, the balance between the positive and negative effects seems strongly biased towards the latter (Scharpf, 1997). Part of the problem lies in the diversity within Europe's 'social model', despite the existence of common principles across the various welfare regimes. Other difficulties derive from the complex, multi-tiered structure of the EU.

Over the last twenty years or so, a great deal of political capital has been invested in the so-called European 'social dimension', precisely to prevent 'negative integration' from occurring. However, despite major advances in recent years, it has failed to live up to the hopes of its promoters (Rhodes, 1995b). There are four areas of European policy that can broadly be conceived as 'social': the social security and distributive aspects of the Common Agricultural Policy (CAP); the funds for pan-European transfers – the regional fund, the social funds and the new 'cohesion fund' created at Maastricht; regulations on the environment, product safety and consumer protection; and regulatory policies for the labour market. But none of these, alone or in combination, herald a European welfare state, for the following reasons:

• The Common Agricultural Policy operates in a highly distorted fashion. Because its social policy-like measures are subordinated to its institutional price system they do not discriminate among farmers or rural areas on the basis of *need*. Indeed, its net effect has been to redistribute resources to the more prosperous farmers of the north under its various subsidy and income-maintenance programmes.
• The regional funds are redistributive and inspired by principles of pan-European solidarity. Conceivably, they could provide the basis

for a system of inter-regional social transfers and risk insurance, but to do so they would have to be expanded and reoriented towards social inequality and deprivation rather than broad regional disparities

• While the harmonisation of health and safety standards and consumer and environmental protection has made considerable advances – preserving conditions in the work place and protecting consumers from the market – they do not affect social entitlements or the central, distributive, functions of welfare.

• The same can be said of innovations in European labour market policy. For while the European Commission's action programmes, inspired by the 1989 Social Charter, have begun to have an impact on *workers'* rights and entitlements across the Community – with significant innovations in equal opportunities, working hours' legislation, the rights of women in the work place and representation in transnational companies – European policy does not address the issue of *social* citizenship. At the same time, attempts to build a European system of industrial relations are being undermined by the opposition of capital, the weaknesses of employers and union organisation at the European level, and the fragility of the European legal basis for institution-building in this area (for further detail, see Rhodes, 1992, 1995b)

Beyond these limitations, the strong links between social policy development and political legitimacy mean that multi-tiered institutional systems such as the European Union are vulnerable to *competitive state building* – as revealed by the new centrality of the concept of 'subsidiarity' in European policy discourse and the opposition of the numerous European member states to European social programmes on the grounds of sovereignty. This is not say that sovereignty is not being conceded in this area: indeed, the broad interpretation given by the European Court of Justice to various European social regulations (in pensions and dismissals, for example) have exceeded the limits originally accepted by many member states. But those states are also resisting a significant transfer of fiscal capacity to the European Union and remain protective of their social policy authority (Leibfried and Pierson, 1995). In sum, the role of Europe in defending the European 'social model' will be restricted to general objectives and 'framework' agreements influencing, and being influenced by, existing national diversity. The burden of adjustment of welfare states to the new challenges and constraints will necessarily be shouldered by the national policy makers.

How are Welfare States Changing?

As already discussed, the combination of internal challenges and external constraints is producing less of a crisis and more of an impasse for west European welfare. Nevertheless, important changes are occurring and although regime diversity is being maintained, there are some signs of convergence.

Even during the phase of welfare state expansion there was a degree of convergence in terms of funding and the spread of benefits between the two broad welfare types: those which emerged from the 'Bismarckian' insurance tradition (relating welfare rights to wage-earners' and employers' contributions) and those based on the Beveridgean concept of social assistance funded from taxation. In the 'insurance group' (Germany, France, Italy and Spain), the contributory system was supplemented by measures to allow the payment of benefits to non-wage earners and the population as a whole (e.g. family allowances and medical care), pension schemes were set up for non-wage earners and a right to a guaranteed minimum incomes was recognised – apart from the southern countries where a national minimum income safety net has been conspicuous by its absence (Gough 1996). In the assistance group (the Scandinavian countries, Britain and Ireland), an inverse evolution led to a guarantee in the case of average or above average salaries of a higher rate of replacement income in the event of unemployment and the progressive adoption of an insurance approach for old age pensions (Chassard and Quintin, 1992).

This process of 'golden age' convergence was driven by interest group lobbying and electoral pressures. In the contemporary era of welfare austerity, the pressures identified above are producing a rather different form of policy convergence (European Commission, 1995):

• *Modifying funding arrangements.* A common concern has been to reduce dependency (and therefore costs) and shift funding away from employers in the cause of competitiveness and job creation. In Scandinavia there has been a move to increase the role of contributions relative to taxation – partly to link benefit payments more closely to employment and discourage working in the informal economy. In insurance countries (e.g. France and Germany) attempts have been made to widen the sources of funding and reduce the burden of costs on employers by identifying those elements of the social protection system which are not employment-related – such as health care and family allowances – and financing these from taxes (Sigg *et al.*, 1996). This has also been a central component of

European Commission thinking on tackling unemployment, for if costs can be shifted from pay-roll taxes to general taxation, then the propensity of firms to create new jobs may be increased. Most countries have tied the reduction of social charges explicitly to employment creation among problem categories such as the young, older and long-term unemployed, the lower paid and disabled. As yet, however, there is little evidence that such policies are working.

- *Tightening regulations and qualifying conditions.* Germany, Greece, Italy, the UK and Finland (for public sector workers), have all increased the official age of retirement, while the amount of pension received has also been reduced, either by lowering the maximum proportion of earnings receivable (Finland), by taking more account of other income in the calculation of tax (Denmark and the Netherlands) or altering the number of earning years on pension assessment is based (France and Portugal). Women will be adversely affected by such reforms because they typically spend fewer years in employment (Sigg *et al.*, 1996). There has also been more restricted access to unemployment benefits. In Britain, a fifth of those registered as unemployment benefit claimants receive no income because for one reason or another they do not qualify. Across the rest of Europe, between 30 and 40 per cent of the jobless do not receive benefits (Standing, 1995). Explicit or implicit disentitlement is therefore widespread.
- *Increasing targeting.* Greater targeting also produces disentitlement. While targeting has been increasingly popular across Europe, as Ferrera (1997) points out, only in the Anglo–Saxon countries has it been extensive, partly because it conforms with a tradition of means-testing but also because there are fewer obstacles: the social partners are not involved in the management of social programmes as in the conservative regime, and the principle of universalism is less well entrenched than in Scandinavia. Nevertheless, income limits have been set for the receipt of certain benefits in Germany, the Netherlands, Italy and Spain (where family allowances have been linked to income), and eligibility criteria have been strengthened. In Scandinavia, however, resistance to targeting has meant that child allowances have been reduced for all income groups.
- *Increased emphasis on active rather than passive measures.* For a number of years there has been a common trend to integrate social protection into employment promotion programmes, i.e. transforming entitlements into incentives (Gilbert, 1992). The most notable example has been the shift from conventional unemployment benefits in the UK to a so-called 'job-seekers'' allowance, linking compensation closely to job search. When similar measures have

been adopted elsewhere, usually, as in Scandinavia, by tying the receipt of benefits to retraining, the employment prospects of the individual will be improved. But by adding to the rules that dissuade claimants – including qualifying periods, a requirement to be 'actively' seeking work, and penalties (disqualification periods for refusing a job or becoming 'voluntarily unemployed') – more draconian approaches represent a strong shift away from income security towards a crude form of 'workfare'.

- *Privatisation and 'marketisation'.* Although it is on the policy agenda of a number of member states, as yet, privatisation has not been widespread beyond the development of complementary pension schemes. In Britain, however, there has been an explicit policy of encouraging personal, private pension schemes by limiting the role of public provision (Sigg *et al.*, 1996). A form of 'creeping' privatisation has been much more common in health care, where private treatment has expanded and the state has unloaded costs on to the individual through 'co-payments' for prescriptions and visits to doctors. There has also been a common search for greater efficiency in the delivery of health care, and although Britain has gone furthest in introducing 'market principles' into the health care sector, competition is being encouraged in many countries between public schemes and private insurers and even between hospitals and general practitioners by giving them direct responsibility for budgets.

The net result has been progress towards a leaner, more efficient, welfare state alongside an erosion of universalism and greater dualism due to 'explicit' or 'implicit' disentitlement. While the Anglo–Saxon countries have gone furthest along this path, the Scandinavian and continental countries have also begun to move in this direction as they seek to contain costs in the face of competitive pressures and cope with a breakdown in their former social consensus. In the southern countries, reducing large budget deficits implies welfare state cutbacks, despite the fact they are still low social spenders. Since they have little in the way of basic income support, and employ the family and local charity as a substitute, the role of these 'traditional' forms of welfare might offer a buffer – if the traditional family were not also in decline.

Conclusion

In their attempts to come to terms with the numerous challenges to the welfare status quo, Europe's various welfare regimes are adopting similar measures to analogous problems, although the Britain's 'Anglo–Saxon' model has moved much further towards a 'lean' welfare state than the others. Yet, for the time being they are also retaining their distinctiveness, both in terms of their underlying principles and institutions and the particular problems that they generate. The Scandinavian countries are having to adjust their high-spending, 'hyper-egalitarian' welfare states to a decline in support for equality and to a world in which their economies are much more exposed than before to external forces. The continental countries face an on-going problem of high unemployment, high labour costs and the constant threat of relocation by firms to lower labour cost jurisdictions. The southern countries, which have slowly been building up their welfare states over the last twenty years are now being forced by unmanageable deficits to scale back public provision. For the time being, although weakened by pressures for institutional conformity, the core principles which govern these regimes will be sustained and condition the process of adjustment.

Yet despite this diversity, all of these regimes face a period of uncertainty, as exposure to international competition increases and the creation of a single European market and currency area introduces new – and as yet unpredictable – constraints. All must respond to the emergence of a 'post-Fordist' or 'post-industrial' labour market and cope with sustained levels of long-term unemployment. The central problem facing all European countries is the same – maintaining the legitimacy of the welfare state by adjusting political expectations and reshaping domestic coalitions in response to these challenges. In their attempts to do so, they face a dilemma, for they must maintain a difficult balance between the three goals of welfare – insurance against risk, the welfare safety net and income redistribution. As Sigg *et al,.* (1996) note, if they prioritise the insurance function (by tying benefits more closely to employment status), the poor and inactive members of society will be penalised and the idea of 'social citizenship' irreparably damaged. But if they prioritise the assistance objective or income redistribution, they may to lose the support of the middle class for expensive welfare programmes and, ultimately, this too will destroy the ideal of social solidarity. If the essence of the European 'social model' is to be defended, a middle course must be charted between these two futures.

5

Executives, Bureaucracies and Decision-Making

PAUL HEYWOOD AND VINCENT WRIGHT

The Structure of European Executives: Formal Roles and Real Power

It has been argued that a country's size can be a crucial determinant of executive power: Allum (1995, p. xviii) quotes Thucydides' dictum that 'great states do what they may; tiny states do what they must'. A distinction should therefore be drawn, argues Allum, between Europe's principal states – Britain, France, Germany and Italy – and the remainder. None the less, in all states, no matter what their size, national political executives are charged with three basic functions: the elaboration, co-ordination and implementation of public policies (Blondel, 1992, p. 268). How they carry out these functions varies widely, of course, and is affected by numerous factors. One such factor, which is of particular significance in terms of the real power enjoyed by national executives, is the constitutional provisions established in any given state.

Real executive power in most West European democracies lies not with the head of state, but with the executive branch of government. By 'executive' is meant those institutions with responsibility over policy decisions; the 'core executive', meanwhile, refers to what Rhodes (1995, p. 12) has called 'the heart of the machine' – the gamut of departments and committees connected with central government which co-ordinate its overall policy position. Although 'monarchy' remains the formal designation of several European states, most are parliamentary democracies in which the executive department is elected indirectly from the legislature. The main exception is France, which is a semi-presidential republic, although Austria and Portugal may also be seen in some ways as being semi-presidential. Thus, except in the French case, the head of state is not usually the chief executive. Instead, there is generally a clear distinction between the political executive and the formal head of state – whether monarchs (as in Belgium, Britain, Denmark, Luxembourg, the Netherlands, Norway, Spain and Sweden), directly-elected presidents (as in Austria, Greece, Iceland, the Republic of Ireland and Portugal) or indirectly-elected presidents (as in Germany, Italy and Switzerland).

In France, constitutional limits on presidential power mean that the chief executive does not enjoy quite the same extent of political authority as does the president of the United States of America. Indeed, France may usefully be seen as having a 'dual executive', in which the president's power is to some extent counterbalanced by that of the prime minister. By contrast, some parliamentary systems – such as Spain – vest such power in the prime minister that they have been described as 'quasi-presidential'. Most European monarchs and heads of state play primarily a symbolic role, serving to legitimise the political system as a whole, but a number have more far-reaching powers: in Austria, Finland, Greece, Iceland, the Republic of Ireland and Portugal the head of state is able in specified circumstances to exercise significant political power over the executive. None the less, in general terms, European parliamentary democracies are characterised by the fact that real power lies with an indirectly elected chief executive officer, known usually as the prime minister. As chief executive, the prime minister is the leading political figure in European democracies, generally responsible for appointing government ministers and setting policy agendas.

In practice, of course, the constitutional framework tells only part of the story: the real power enjoyed by core executives is conditioned by relationships with a series of other actors, each with his or her own resources (Jones, 1991, p. 163). Most West European executives are organised around a cabinet, in which the prime minister acts as chief executive within a collegial system, although the nature of cabinet government varies widely (Blondel and Müller-Rommel, 1993). While cabinet ministers generally have a dual role, being accountable individually as heads of their departments as well as bound by the rules of collective responsibility, both the manner in which cabinets are formed and the way they operate in practice varies widely. In some European countries, notably the Netherlands and Finland, the head of state plays a formal role in government formation, designating a '*formateur*' to nominate cabinet members. In other countries, the prime minister is given virtually free rein. Normally, cabinet ministers are also members of parliament, although in some countries (France, Norway and the

Netherlands), ministers are obliged to resign from the legislature on being appointed to the cabinet (Gallagher *et al.*, 1995, p. 34). In the United Kingdom and the Republic of Ireland, on the other hand, cabinet members are nearly always members of parliament, a situation which also prevailed in Italy until the effective collapse of its political structure in the early 1990s. The appointment as prime minister in early 1993 of the head of the Bank of Italy, Carlo Azeglio Ciampi, represented a deliberate break with past parliamentary practices. Thereafter, Italy has been governed by a series of 'technocratic' administrations, most of whose members had no connection with parliament.

The most collegial cabinet systems are to be found in the Low Countries and Scandinavia, where there is usually a high degree of interaction between the prime minister and other cabinet members. In such systems, the prime minister acts largely as a chairman rather than a chief. In other countries, notably Britain, France and Germany, the relationship between the prime minister and the cabinet is often much more hierarchical. In practice, of course, the relationship between prime ministers and their cabinets tends to be fluid, influenced by contingent factors such as the size and nature of the government's majority, the party system, the personality of office-holders, the proximity of elections and so on. Thus prime ministers who enjoy secure absolute majorities – such as Margaret Thatcher in Britain and Felipe González in Spain during the 1980s – are often able to exercise enormous political power. However, as both Thatcher and González discovered, political fortunes are fickle: once they were identified as electoral liabilities rather than assets, party support for them weakened rapidly. In contrast, Helmut Kohl was able to maintain a secure hold on power in Germany in spite of being forced to rely on coalition governments since the early 1980s.

There is no necessary causal link between two-party systems and governmental stability, nor indeed between proportional electoral systems, coalitions and governmental instability. More significant in regard to executive power is whether a government is able to command a secure and reliable majority in parliament. Where minority governments are in power, they may rely either on formal coalitions or else on circumstantial pacts constructed according to the issue in question. Naturally, coalitions involving a small number of partners tend to be more stable than those which require several competing interests to be conciliated, as has often been the case in Italy and the Netherlands (Hine and Finocchi, 1991; Andeweg, 1991). However, even a prime minister in charge of a majority government can be severely constrained if the party is split internally and contains rival aspirants for the top job: for example, after the 1992 general election in Britain, John Major found that he had to take increasing account of the views of so-called 'Euro-sceptics'. His space for political manoeuvre was so cur-tailed that he took the unprecedented step in the summer of 1995 of resigning as party leader in order to force an election and reassert his political authority. Although the tactic proved to be successful, party managers nevertheless felt it necessary to protect Major from further contests by changing the rules under which he could be challenged as party leader in the future.

Parliaments (or assemblies) naturally play an important role in the policy process, and can act as an effective constraint on executives. However, most West European paliaments serve primarily to legitimise policies brought before them by the executive and have only limited capacities to initiate policies. Their function is mainly reactive, gen-erally being restricted to modifying or revising legislation. One excep-tion is the Swedish Riksdag, where private members' proposals are as numerous as government bills. To a lesser extent, the States-General in the Netherlands and the Italian parliament have also been able to influence policy-making in a significant manner. In general terms, though, the most important role played by West European parliaments is one of scrutiny. A number of formal mechanisms exist whereby executives are called to account, including the ritualised twice-weekly 'question time' in the British House of Commons, during which 15 minutes are set aside for the prime minister to face questions. A version of 'question time' was adopted in Spain in 1994 following concern over alleged government involvement in corruption scandals, although the prime minister reserved the right to set the general conditions under which they could be asked (Heywood, 1995, p. 288). In Germany and Finland, the system of 'interpellation' involves oral questioning of ministers, often followed by snap votes. Most parliaments also have committee structures designed to oversee the actions of the executive; in practice, though, few committees – with the important exception of audit and public accounts committees – are able to exercise significant influence. The ultimate sanction, of course, is a vote of 'no confidence', which, if successful, obliges the executive to resign. Even here, though, executives can enjoy a degree of protection through such measures as the 'constructive vote of no confidence' (as in Germany and Spain), where an alternative candidate for prime minister must be nominated, or stipulated majorities (as in France), where a certain proportion of the entire parliament must support the motion.

Equally significant in terms of executive control is the territorial distribution of power: in federal or devolved systems, there are certain policy areas which are the responsibility of states or regions. Yet even in unitary systems, decentralisation over specific areas of policy-making can act as a constraint on the core executive. Thus the extent to which governments are able to implement public policies is often dependent on whether political power is concentrated or diffused (Hall, 1994). In states where power is highly concentrated – such as Britain and France – the elected government enjoys considerable autonomy over policy formulation and implementation: relatively few social interests have been able to establish effective countervailing power. This has perhaps been most visible in the field of economic policy, where deregulation of financial markets and privatisation measures have been carried through faster than in other European states. In Germany and Austria, by contrast, power is diffused and powerful interest groups are well-established in neo-corporatist institutional structures: as a result, in these two states, governments found it more difficult to implement deregulation and privatisation measures. An alternative political structure exists in Sweden, for example, where governmental power is concentrated, yet constrained by institutionally represented social interests. Here, deregulation and privatisation in recent years have gone further than in Germany and Austria, but at a slower pace than in Britain and France. The structure and distribution of power resources thus exercises an important impact on the behaviour and political possibilities not of governments, but of all social actors in the policy process.

Executive-Administrative Relations

The relationship between the executive and its central administration is a crucial one, since the latter is a major instrument of the former's policy-making authority (Claisse and Meininger, 1994; Page, 1985; Rowat, 1988; Ziller, 1993). The central administration is also an arena for policy bargaining and co-ordination, an influential and often semi-autonomous motor of public policy which penetrates the principal sectoral policy networks, and a major pressure group intent on protecting the rights and privileges of its members. In some countries it has also become an important source of patronage, an integral player in the game of clientelism.

In its relationship with its central administration, the executive is constantly called to address three essential issues: the efficacy of the administration as an agent of the executive's policy, its control over that agent, and its capacity to restructure and modify the behaviour of

TABLE 5.1 Executive structure of West European Democracies

	Head of state	Role	System of government	Title of chief executive	Method of election	Executive powers[a]	Bi-cameral or unicameral legislature	Electoral term
Austria	President	Procedural	Federal republic	Chancellor	Indirect	Medium	Bicameral	4 years
Belgium	Monarch	Procedural	Parliamentary monarchy	Prime minister	Indirect	Medium	Bicameral	4 years
Denmark	Monarch	Symbolic	Parliamentary monarchy	Prime minister	Direct	Medium	Unicameral	4 years
Finland	President	Executive	Unitary republic	Prime minister	Indirect	Medium	Unicameral	4 years
France	President	Executive	Unitary republic	Prime minister	Direct	Med/Low	Bicameral	5 years
Germany	President	Procedural	Federal republic	Chancellor	Direct	High	Bicameral	4 years
Greece	President	Procedural	Unitary republic	Prime minister	Direct	High	Unicameral	4 years
Ireland	President	Procedural	Unitary republic	Prime minister	Indirect	High	Bicameral	5 years
Italy	President	Procedural	Unitary republic	President of council of ministers	Direct	Low	Bicameral	5 years
Luxembourg	Grand duke	Procedural	Parliamentary monarchy	Prime minister	Indirect	Medium	Unicameral	5 years
Netherlands	Monarch	Symbolic	Parliamentary monarchy	Prime minister	Indirect	Low	Bicameral	4 years
Norway	Monarch	Symbolic	Parliamentary monarchy	Prime minister	Indirect	Low	Unicameral[b]	4 years
Portugal	President	Procedural	Unitary republic	Prime minister	Direct	High	Unicameral	4 years
Spain	Monarch	Diplomatic	Parliamentary monarchy	President of council of ministers	Direct	High	Bicameral	4 years
Sweden	Monarch	Symbolic	Parliamentary monarchy	Prime minister	Indirect	Medium	Unicameral	3 years
Switzerland	President	Procedural	Federal republic	President	Indirect	Medium	Bicameral	5 years
United Kingdom	Monarch	Diplomatic	Parliamentary monarchy	Prime minister	Direct	High	Bicameral	5 years

the agent should it be found wanting. Over the last few years all West European executives – though with different degrees of enthusiasm and success – have striven to introduce reforms designed to address one or more of these issues. However, the results have been far from convincing, as the reforms have generated many unintended and unwelcome consequences. Before turning to the reform programmes it is essential to describe briefly the central administrations that have been the object of the reformers' attention.

The most striking feature of central administrations across Western Europe is the scale of the differences they encompass. Each has been marked by its own distinctive historical trajectory, state and legal traditions, socioeconomic cleavage structure and set of political requirements (Armstrong, 1973; Torstendahl, 1991; Silberman, 1993). Thus France continues to be marked by its Napoleonic past, and countries such as Italy, Belgium and Spain continue to bear the imprint of the French military occupation. However, each of these countries, in its distinctive way, has diverged from the initial Napoleonic model, producing a legacy of institutions with similar sounding names but dissimilar activities. Naturally, there are the common organisational features of all central administrations which Weber (1968, pp. 956–1008) identified in his ideal model, but no administration ever fully conformed to the model – not even in Prussia, the system best known to Weber.

Some of the key differences between the central administrations may be delineated in the following ways.

Size and Composition

The central state apparatus is relatively small in federal Germany and unitary Britain, and relatively large in the Napoleonic states of France, Italy and Spain. Size is heavily dependent upon three factors. First, the definition of a civil servant differs widely across Europe. Hence, civil service status (and the rights that attach to it) is conferred in some countries but not others on schoolteachers, university lecturers and even some categories of workers in the telecommunications and railway industries. Indeed, for most of the nineteenth century, French bishops

---

[a] Based on King (1991)
[b] The *Storting* divides into two chambers after elections, a quarter becoming the upper house (*Lagting*) and the remainder the lower house (*Odelsting*)

enjoyed this status. A second difference concerns the existence or not of ministerial *cabinets* – private offices that are recruited by each minister to act as his or her eyes, ears and source of ideas, and as agents for imposing the minister's agenda on recalcitrant officials. France best illustrates the case of the powerful *cabinet* system. Most other countries have modified or diluted versions of the French model, although the British have so far resisted the temptation to create one. The existence or otherwise of an administrative or technical corps represents the third major difference in the composition of the European central administrations. Again, France and Britain provide the most striking contrast, since the latter completely lacks the powerful French system of corps – both generalist and technical – the most important of which are the *grands corps*, trained in the prestigious *grandes écoles* such as the Ecole Nationale d'Administration, the Ecole Polytechnique and the Ecole des Mines. The Spanish have an equally elaborate and prestigious system of *cuerpos* which, like their French counterparts, attempt to colonise the key posts in the administration.

Functional Penetration

The extent to which a central administration establishes a place within specific policy sectors clearly depends on the scope and nature of central state activity. The size, structure, management and delivery of welfare provision differs widely in Western Europe, and this leads to different configurations of actors and to different levels of potential influence for state officials in the policy networks. Every state depends heavily on a wide range of agents for the implementation of public policy – its own officials, subnational government, self-regulated bodies, professional associations (doctors, engineers, teachers, architects, lawyers), semi-autonomous regulatory bodies (in areas such as broadcasting), quangos and 'third sector' bodies such as charitable and voluntary organisations. But the extent and nature of the dependence varies according to country. Again, there is a sharp distinction to be drawn between, on the one hand, Britain and Germany, which are heavily dependent, and, on the other, France, Italy, Spain, Greece and Portugal, where a relatively high proportion of implementation is left to central state agents.

Availability of Technical Expertise and the Position of Technical Experts

Some central administrations – notably the French – have adequate technical resources made available through the technical corps who are recruited and trained by the state. Moreover, members of the technical corps enjoy great prestige and occupy strategic positions in the central administration. Other systems – notably the British and German – are weak in technical expertise, and technical experts, when they exist in a ministry, are invariably kept under the firm control of generalists.

Political Operating Code

A crucial factor, since it relates to the political assumptions of the administration that structure its dealings with the executive. These assumptions are clearly embedded in the distinctive historical experience of each nation. The British central administration, for example, has been nurtured on a diet of parliamentary sovereignty, ministerial responsibility, and the anonymity and strict partisan neutrality of officials. If the responsibility of ministers has often proved to be fictional, and the principle of anonymity increasingly breached, the concepts of parliamentary sovereignty and of political neutrality remain intact: a government, of whatever political complexion, backed by a majority in Parliament attracts the automatic and unanimous (if not always enthusiastic) loyalty of civil servants. For this reason, changes of government do not trigger purges of administrative personnel, and governments have never pressed for the creation of *cabinets ministériels* – ministerial private officials composed of politically sympathetic officials – following the French model. France has had a turbulent political history marked by several changes of regime, and, until the advent of the Fifth Republic, ephemeral and divided coalition governments. Each new regime suspected the administrative elite of its predecessor: hence, the requirement for purges and, because purges were never complete, the need for ministerial private offices serviced by political supporters who were initially political or family friends, but increasingly came to be politically sympathetic civil servants. The long experience of short-lived and tension-ridden coalition government, often with little electoral legitimacy, was hardly conducive to building the kind of traditions of trust, respect and loyalty among civil servants towards the executive that characterised the British administration.

Political Penetration

Otherwise, the extent to which civil servants have moved into partisan politics. Once again, the contrast between the British experience and most of the rest of Western Europe is striking. A strict separation between administration and political party activity is enforced in the

United Kingdom: only the very occasional civil servant ventures into politics and the move automatically involves resignation with no possibility of return. In continental Europe, numerous civil servants (even if we discount university and school teachers who play a prominent role in many left-wing or ecologist parties) have moved into local and national politics. Most parliaments and several governments contain a cohort of state officials who retain their rights to return to the administration.

Ideological Ethos

Otherwise, the collective *Weltanschauung* of the administration. This is forged by different interlocking perceptions of the proper balance between state, market and society, and between equality and freedom, of the role of the state and its relationship with its citizens, of the concept of citizenship and the rights that flow from its bestowal, of the nature of public goods (whether they are desirable and whether they are superior to private goods), and of the public interest and how it is defined. The ideological ethos of the central administration is given practical expression in a number of ways: in its dealings with pressure groups, its reactions to spending proposals, and its propensity to insulate itself against the private sector. Perceptions of the ideological biases of the central administration have not been without consequence. For example, the allegation that civil servants were part of the great 'distributional coalitions' which had expanded the state budget was taken seriously in neo-liberal circles and was to be one of the reasons for their attempts since the late 1970s to reduce the role of the administration.

Internal Organisational Structures and Culture

In this, differences may be seen at several levels. In the first place, there are differences in the degree of vertical control within each ministry. The British system is extremely hierarchically structured around the powerful figures of permanent secretaries, who have normally witnessed the passage of several successive ministers in their department. They are normally able to deal with the internecine rivalries that afflict the life of ministries elsewhere in Europe. Also, some central administrations, in spite of traditional rivalries based on distinct departmental loyalties and cultures, are heavily integrated by informal networks and elaborate official systems of co-ordinating committees. The British administration provides a text-book illustration of a system in which tight co-ordination (through the Treasury and Cabinet Office) is reinforced by a culture of integration, while the Irish system is poorly co-ordinated at the official level but quite well integrated through unofficial and personalised channels.

Most administrative systems are characterised by weak internal hierarchies, inadequate interdepartmental co-ordination, and ill-developed cultures of integration. A typical case is Italy, where government is 'government by department' and where coalition politics and personal enmities hamper co-ordination. In Germany, federal government is also very segmented and poorly co-ordinated in spite of sporadic attempts by the Chancellor's Office to harmonise policies. No less badly co-ordinated is the Dutch administration, with its entrenched and jealously guarded doctrine of ministerial autonomy. However, some degree of co-ordination is introduced by the initial coalition programme which is negotiated as a binding commitment before the formation of the government. Moreover, in the Netherlands, as in Germany, the internal culture is usually dominated by a pragmatic search for compromise.

The French system combines official hierarchies with extreme fragmentation. While some degree of unofficial co-ordination is afforded by the networks formed by each of the *corps*, the general problem of fragmentation is aggravated by inter-corps rivalries and by the tradition of confrontational bargaining within the co-ordinating committees. Conflicts are such that many have to be arbitrated at higher levels – at the Matignon or even the Elysée. Internal organisational culture refers not only to the propensity for integration on the bargaining style. It also involves the perception of roles and of what constitutes 'good administration'. For example, the German central administration is noted for its stifling legalism, its obsession with due process, and its attachment to rules: it is input-orientated, and good administration is seen as the impartial application of the universal rule. The Italian administration manages to combine an obstructive rule-bound culture with a tradition of negotiating specific cases, while the French administration's attachment to legalism and formalism is constantly undermined by its penchant for *dérogations* – exceptions conceded to political friends.

Constitutional and Juridical Protection

Most systems have elaborate constitutional and legal rules to define and protect the public domain and the rights of civil servants. The equivalent of the French *statut général des fonctionnaires* may be found in most European countries. The notable exception is Britain. Most countries also have elaborate systems of administrative law, much of which is directed towards the protection of individual civil servants.

The capacity of the executive to deploy the central administration as an effective instrument of public policy depends on factors such as its willingness (which is determined by its internal structures, policy style and ideological ethos), the extent of its functional and territorial penetration, and its technical expertise. It is also clearly policy-stage specific. The British central administration may be a powerful and purposive agent at the agenda-setting and formalisation stages of public policy-making, but it is weak at the initiation, implementation and evaluation stages at which the French administration, by contrast, is relatively strong. The role of French state engineers in several areas of technological innovation has no equivalent in Britain. The German federal administration is, in comparative terms, weak in most sectors and at almost all policy stages. In short, in analysing the central issues confronting an executive in its relationship with the central administration, it is necessary to construct a complicated typology embracing all the factors analysed above.

Decision-making: Policy Styles and Networks

A number of studies in recent years have sought to analyse executive performance, particularly in the field of economic policy, by reference to national policy styles (Richardson and Jordan, 1979; Richardson, 1982). Such approaches laid considerable emphasis on cultural factors – the attitudes and orientations of the principal actors involved, their procedures and prejudices, conventions, attitudes and understandings, and their 'referential frameworks' – which are largely shaped by a nation's historical development. In its relations with other actors is the central administration pluralist or elitist in its instincts? *Dirigiste* or hands-off in its behaviour? Confrontational or consensual in its approach? Whatever qualms may be harboured about generalising on these questions, there does appear to be a significant difference between, for example, the bargained and consensus-seeking style of German policy makers and the elitist, *dirigiste* and confrontational approach of French officialdom.

However, national policy styles are just as much shaped by the institutional structure of a given state, as suggested by the examples given above on deregulation and privatisation measures. The number, nature and purpose of the institutions which make up a state are in turn governed by constitutional provisions. Federal constitutions impose effective constraints on national core executives, since they invest significant power in separate, subnational administrations. Second chambers, where they exist, can also act as a constraint, although – with the notable exception of the German *Bundesrat* – most such chambers are of limited significance in European polities. A further institutional factor of significance in shaping national policy styles is the role of the courts, particularly supreme courts and constitutional tribunals. In most West European democracies there are courts expressly charged with ensuring that the executive complies with constitutional provisions.

The interaction between core executives, bureaucracies and particular interests has become an increasingly important focus of research. Much recent work has centred on the so-called 'policy networks' approach, which was developed as an alternative to the widely influential conceptions of pluralism and corporatism. Policy networks approaches posit a 'power-dependence' relationship, in which resources are exchanged between organisations: usually, a public actor (that is, a government department) and an interest group. The relationship is seen as being symbiotic and continuous, but asymmetrical: the public actor exercises a disproportionate influence over access to resources and the policy agenda. In the British case, Rhodes distinguished between different types of policy network, according to the degree of integration between members (Rhodes and Marsh, 1992). Thus policy networks range from policy communities, characterised by a high degree of integration and cohesion, to issue networks, which are loosely integrated and often conflictual. In between, professional, intergovernmental and producer networks are dominated respectively by particular interests. Other analysts have introduced various modifications to the policy networks framework; for example, by highlighting the importance of interpersonal relations, and drawing a distinction between a 'policy universe' – encompassing all those actors with a potential interest in a particular policy – and more narrowly-defined policy communities (those with a common policy focus) and networks (linking two or more communities) (Wilks and Wright, 1987).

The policy networks approach has been used widely to analyse the policy-making process in a number of European countries. Its particular advantage over the national policy styles approach is that its flexibility allows for a more detailed examination of the relationship between government departments and interest groups; equally, it offers a solid basis for comparative analysis. Moreover, the approach provides an important corrective to the institutional emphasis that has characterised much political science literature on the policy process. Instead of focusing on the power of the prime minister, for example, or the role of parliament, the policy networks approach seeks to identify the complex relationships between individual government departments, interest groups and other relevant agencies involved in policy-making. The most telling criticisms of the approach are that it rests on imprecise definitions (hence the competing versions) and that its analytical insight is purchased only at the cost of ever-greater descriptive detail. Ultimately, it might be argued that the policy networks approach presents a sophisticated map of policy formulation and co-ordination, rather than an explanatory model with predictive capacity (Dowding, 1995, pp. 136–58). Nevertheless, studies based on the policy networks approach have continued to proliferate, with a growing emphasis on the impact of Europe-related legislation, and policy-making in the European Union itself (Peterson, 1992; Grant *et al.*, 1988; Lehmbruch, 1991).

The applicability of the policy network approach to EU policy-making has generated lively debate. Kassim (1994) has argued that, within the context of the EU, the approach suffers from three major drawbacks: it fails to capture adequately the fluid and improvisational character of much decision-making within the EU, it lacks an appropriate macro theory of the state within which to locate the highly complex institutional architecture of the EU; and it cannot specify the relevant boundaries that are needed to delineate networks. In response, Peterson (1995) has argued that it is precisely the fluidity and complexity of decision-making within the EU that has occasioned the emergence of policy networks so as to provide some degree of order amid the seeming chaos. While Peterson acknowledges the need to provide more definitional rigour when applying the policy networks approach to the EU, and in particular to focus more attention on the EU's institutional structure, he argues that it nevertheless helps to 'make sense of complex policy-making situations which feature a large number of effective actors' (Peterson, 1995, pp. 392–3). The policy networks approach, for all its definitional uncertainty, remains useful as a heuristic device for analysing the complexities of EU governance.

The Challenges Facing Executives and the Changing Face of Public Administration

The relationship between executives and public administrations throughout Western Europe is slowly being reshaped by a combination of exogenous and endogenous pressures. All West European countries have long been confronted not just with an expansion, but also with what might be termed a 'balkanisation', of public policy-making. Since the early 1980s, governments have been faced with policy challenges in a wide variety of sectors which reflect a series of interlinked pressures: ideological, technological, financial, fiscal, economic and political. In combination with these pressures, the growing protagonism of the EU has led to what is widely perceived to be a loss of policy autonomy within European states; it is now commonplace to refer to a 'Europeanisation' of the policy process in national states, involving a convergence of policy aspirations, programmes and instruments across the EU. Indeed, trends towards 'transnationalisation', particularly regarding economic policy, have promoted speculation about the decline of the nation-state. Many of the tasks traditionally seen as being central to the activities of national governments are now seen as having moved beyond their reach. Economic integration – a central element of the move towards economic and monetary union envisaged in the Maastricht Treaty – will inevitably emasculate nation-states: the ability of national governments to decide upon their exchange rates, interest rates, trade flows, investment and output has been severely undermined.

Public administrations have been faced with a set of similar pressures: budgetary squeeze; anti-statist ideology; public choice onslaughts on bureaucracies; internationalisation which has triggered the need for the new transnational or cross-border administrative agencies or co-operation; membership of the EU which has impacted both indirectly (the budgetary rigour imposed by Maastricht) and directly on the scope of purely national sectoral activity, on domestic administrative structures and on policy networks; the changing policy agenda which now embraces some issues (environment, drug-trafficking, law and order) that require international co-operation and some, such as feminism and consumerism, that demand an adjustment to the internal culture of the administration; technological change, which is transforming organisational structures, working practices and skills, personnel management and service delivery; democratic pressures, which are expressed in many and potentially conflicting and disruptive ways, since they encompass demands for more and better (yet cheaper) services, for greater effectiveness yet increasing transparency, participation and consultation, for greater representativeness (in favour of women, ethnic minorities, underprivileged social classes and handicapped people) yet entry into and promotion within the administration by merit; a diffused discontent about the functioning and output of the administration, which is often depicted as more wedded to its own interests than to the public good.

Public administration has also been affected by the so-called postmodernist managerial revolution, which has called into question traditional procedures, and organisational structures and styles, and which advocates smaller, more flexible, more specialised and more autonomous units run by enterprising managers (and not administrators) aided by flattened hierarchies and a more participative workforce. The new public administration should be less obsessed with due process – ensuring respect for the rules for all citizens – and become more sensitive to questions of efficiency, to output, and to the specific demands of the consumers of public services. It should pay attention to specified goals, and be evaluated constantly in the light of those goals.

The central administration of almost every West European country has been the object of reform, although the scope, intensity and objectives of the reform programme have differed widely (Caiden, 1991; Peters and Savoie, 1993; Pierre, 1995). The British have been the most radical, having dismantled several of the key features of the traditional Whitehall machine. At the other end of the spectrum are the Greeks, who have made sporadic and half-hearted attempts to tamper with a politicised and grossly inefficient state administration; and the Germans, who have felt little need to reform an apparatus which appears to function well. Administrative reform has, however, taken place at *Länder* and local level. Italy and Spain have attempted to modernise their sleepy and inefficient administrations, although the attempts have met with only limited success, while France and the Netherlands have been middle-range reformers, although the pattern of reforms in the two countries differs sharply.

The administrative reform programmes have included a wide variety of policies, ranging from the restructuring of ministries and the creation of new administrative bodies to those designed to democratise the administration and render it more user-friendly. Several major strands may be discerned in the reform programmes. First, attempts have been made to reduce the size, resources and scope of the central administration. The number of civil servants has either been reduced (although generally by very little, and figures can be misleading), or, as is more usually the case, stabilised. In many cases, the result of 'cut back' policies has been a dramatic slowdown in the rate of increase in numbers. Accompanying this policy has been the effort to cope with the wage bill by reducing salaries in real terms. As part of the campaign to reduce the scope and influence of the public administration, many

governments have attempted to enact 'de-bureaucratisation' programmes designed to scrap rules and regulations which are either
obsolete or which hinder efficiency. The second major strand of the
administrative reform programmes is represented by the attempt to
improve monitoring and evaluation capacity by modifying budgetary,
planning and evaluation procedures. Auditing and evaluation according to the criteria of the 'three Es' – economy, efficiency and effectiveness – have penetrated all levels of public activity. Performance
indicators, financial controls and accountability, and contractual
agreements are increasingly common in central state administrations.

Linked with this element in the reform programme is a third set of
policies, conveniently (if not always accurately) described as new public
management (NPM), which has had a major impact on the functioning
of the core executive in several liberal democracies – notably in the
English-speaking world, but also in several European states. NPM
relates principally to the operation of public administrations and is
linked to the notion of 'hollowing out the state' (Rhodes, 1994,
pp. 138–9), whereby many of the activities and responsibilities of the
state have been reassigned. It involves fragmenting decision-making,
with the separation of policy decision from policy execution: a small
group of central-state officials define the main policy guidelines, and
they are served by a constellation of devolved and autonomous
managerial agencies. Most governments have transferred competences
to subnational governments, to semi-autonomous regulatory bodies, to
quangos and to 'third sector' organisations – voluntary, non-profit or
charitable organisations which have become 'the private agents of
public policy'. This process of 'agencification' found its most radical
expression in the United Kingdom with the 'Next Steps Initiative'
launched in 1988, which has involved the transfer to agencies of over
four fifths of the country's civil servants. Another expression of the
push to fragment the civil service may be seen in the purchaser–
provider divide, which renders the state more sensitive to the market-
place and to its clients, more dedicated to tapping the individual
creativity and initiative of civil servants, and less respectful of formal
rules and the legal bureaucratic order.

The extent, mix, timing and pace of the reform programmes differ
widely across Western Europe. Thus, most governments have avoided
the British, Danish and Norwegian Conservative Parties' attempts to
define a radical and overarching reform programme, rooted in and
rationalised by anti-state and anti-bureaucracy ideology. Some, such as
those of Olof Palme in Sweden, Michel Rocard in France and Felipe
González in Spain were keen reformers, but in an attempt to modernise

and strengthen, not to denigrate the administration. The differences in the objectives of the reformers may best be illustrated by comparing the British and Greek programmes, since the latter was inspired by the desire to create the kind of administration the Conservatives were dismantling in the UK. Most governments have eschewed radical programmes and have indulged in pragmatic *ad hoc* adjustments to their central administrations.

The pattern of policies also varies considerably across Europe. Most countries have decentralised – some, such as Belgium and Spain, radically so – although Germany has not done so (in spite of some pressures from the *Länder*), and Britain has experienced unprecedented and unparalleled centralisation. 'Agencification' is a feature of the British, French and Italian reform ambitions, but this does not feature among those of the Germans, the Greeks and the Portuguese. Country-specific reforms include the strengthening of the Court of Accounts in Italy to combat corruption, the creation of French-style *cabinets* in Greece under the Pasok government, the merging of several *cuerpos* in Spain, the assault upon the trade unions in the United Kingdom. Differences in the timing, type and intensity of the pressures for reform are obvious. Thus the United Kingdom felt the budgetary pressure earlier and more intensely than most of its European neighbours, while the pressures emanating from membership of the European Union involve greater adjustments for the newly arrived. Finally, domestic political opportunity structures clearly determine the capacity of reformist governments to pursue their ambitions. As the British and Greek cases underline in totally opposite ways, political will and durability are essential ingredients for success. So, too, are the backing of a united government and a cohesive majority party or coalitions, the absence of constitutional and legal constraints, the capacity to restructure hostile policy networks, and to mobilise pro-reformist elements within the administration.

Conclusion

Have the various reform programmes reshaped the relationship between the executive and the central administrations? Any answer must lie in the intentions of the reformers, in the extent and nature of the programmes, and in the outcomes of those programmes (some of which have been unanticipated and unwelcome). In analysing the intentions of the reformers, a distinction must be drawn between, on the one hand, those policies designed to strengthen the machinery of state and the executive's leverage over that machinery, and, on the other, those aiming to reduce the burden on the state and thereby, paradoxically, allegedly strengthening the executive. Naturally, the impact on the executives has been negligible in those countries – notably Germany – with very limited ambitions and with programmes to match, and in those countries (such as Spain, Greece and Italy) where even moderate programmes have run into severe implementation problems. In other countries, it may be too early to pass judgement, since many of the advantages of the policies were front-loaded, the unpalatable consequences often taking time to emerge. Judgement is also inevitably clouded by the values of the assessor: has the kind of territorial centralisation witnessed in the United Kingdom since the 1970s, or the radical decentralisation experienced in Belgium, weakened or strengthened the state and its political executive? Does transparency, consultation and open government weaken or strengthen the executive? Similar questions could be posed about agencification, customerisation, marketisation, down-sizing, and all the various forms of privatisation and deregulation. What is clear is that in many West European countries the central administrations have suffered a diminution in their role and prestige. They are more divided (because of the politics of cut-back management and the internal scramble for limited resources), more fragmented (as a consequence of agencification), more defensive (because of the constant attacks upon them), and increasingly demoralised. They are also more disorientated, since some of the props and premises of the traditional systems have been undermined or are seriously contested. Creating divided, demoralised and disorientated central administrations may not be part of the reformist strategy. It may be an unintended consequence of the reform programmes, and it may even be the price that some reformers are prepared to pay. However, it is questionable whether either the executive or the state are well served by such administrations.

It has been argued that, as a result of these various trends, core executives are now facing a 'double squeeze': on the one hand, the EU is assuming increasing responsibility from above for policy formulation (especially in sectors such as agriculture, or commercial regulation); and on the other, agencies are assuming increasing responsibility from below for policy implementation. The role of core executives can be seen as being steadily narrowed, or fragmented, as states become more 'hollowed out'. The core executive can no longer be seen as the principal source of policy making; instead, trends towards transnationalisation have undermined some traditional assumptions about the nature and role of states in advanced industrial societies. The picture is rendered even more complex by the fact that in spite of this perceived loss of policy autonomy, European core executives find themselves confronted by ever more challenges. In paticular, new issues which cut across traditional boundaries have emerged (such as environmentalism, feminism, or the regulation of the Internet) to impose intractable demands upon states. Such issues have generated new alliances which have helped to blur the traditional left–right prism through which policy orientations were often focused. Core executives thus find themselves faced with a growing role at the same time as budgetary constraints force them to seek ways of cutting back the size of the state. Within this confusing panorama of changing roles, structures, resources and demands, it is not surprising that many received assumptions about European core executives have been undermined.

6

Illicit Governance: Corruption, Scandal and Fraud*

YVES MÉNY AND MARTIN RHODES

The 1980s and 1990s have seen a proliferation of corruption scandals across Western Europe. In the most spectacular case, Italy, an entire political class has been put on trial and the political system transformed, largely as a result of public outrage at, and the legal prosecution of, corrupt bureaucrats, businessmen, party officials and members of parliament. The investigations of the so-called *Mani Pulite* ('clean hands') enquiries revealed a massive and complex web of corruption spanning all traditional political parties, including the Italian Communist Party which had been excluded from national – though not local – government for most of the postwar period. The Italian case is perhaps an extreme one, because of the unusual domination of government by one party – the Christian Democrats – and its allies between the late 1940s and the early 1980s, and the challenge mounted against that hegemony by Bettino Craxi's Socialist Party. This ferocious struggle for political, economic and cultural power meant colonising and exploiting the public sector and indulging in any practice thought expedient, including widespread illegality.

But it can hardly be over-emphasised that corruption is a phenomenon characteristic of all times and of all governments, be they dictatorships, authoritarian regimes, or democracies. Even totalitarian regimes, which by definition should have been impervious to corruption, have been affected and weakened at the same time. This universal

---

* The sections of this chapter written by Yves Mény were translated by Véronique Tormey.

phenomenon does not, however, carry the same consequences in all places. Nobody will shed any tears over the collapse of a corrupt dictatorship if the regime that follows it is democratic or at least less despotic. On the other hand, corruption strikes at the very heart of democracies. Their legitimacy is called into question and the risk of instability or even collapse may raise the fear of a crisis caused by the rise of authoritarian or populist movements. It is therefore no longer possible to consider corruption as a peripheral phenomenon in the analysis of politics, or as a culturally specific 'syndrome', found only in particular places at certain times. To a greater or lesser extent it infiltrates the political processes and relationships of all countries and poses special problems for political reform and regulation, especially in the area of party finance. The vigilant pursuit of the corrupt and the elimination of illicit political practice is essential for the preservation of political legitimacy.

In the following analysis we explore the causes and manifestations of corruption in Western Europe, examining the social practices, rules and political opportunity structures that differentiate countries from one another, the solutions and anti-corruption measures these countries are adopting, and the challenges that face them – and the European Union – in the future.

Defining Corruption, Scandal and Fraud

First we need to distinguish between corruption, scandal and fraud, since while in reality they are often closely connected, conceptually they need to be differentiated. We can define corruption as the violation of a norm through means of an illegal transaction such that both corrupter and corrupted benefit thanks to the specific position they enjoy within the state or the market. The relationship between the corrupter and the corrupted may be co-operative (for example, when a politician is paid for helping a businessman to secure a public contract), in which case we can refer to 'transactive' corruption. However, there may also be a degree of compulsion or coercion involved (as when a public official or politician forces a businessman to pay a kickback to secure a contract), in which case the corruption is 'extortive' (Alatas, 1990; Heywood, 1996). Scandal is rather different – a sign that society has reached a phase of development such that the separation of the public and private is seen as a basic principle of a sound democracy and public office no longer considered to be a means or private remuneration (Neckel, 1989). Fraud is a criminal activity that may take place exclusively in the private sector. But it is frequently found at the dividing line between the public and the private (involving the fraudulent use and abuse of government funds or evasion of tax) and therefore may well involve corrupt practice. This is a particularly sensitive area. It is especially so in the case of the institutions and spending programmes of the EU where, although fraud is widespread and frequently involves the laxity or complicity of member state officials, the word 'corruption' is rarely used.

The complexity of both corruption and scandal, and of the relationship between them, needs further elucidation. Is corruption primarily a phenomenon to be found at the interface between the state and the market? When does a social practice become 'corrupt' rather than simply the 'way of the world'? When corruption is revealed as 'scandal', what does that tell us about the nature of that society?

Corruption expresses primarily the ambiguity of the relationship between the state and the market, private and public power (Cartier-Bresson 1995). It follows, then, that the characteristics of the state or of the market will shape corruption in a particular way and will give it more or less opportunity to develop: below we shall discuss the differences between societies precisely in terms of the opportunities provided by their rules and institutions. The idea, though, that corruption takes on specific contextual forms should not be taken to suggest that it is simply the product of a *particular type* of relationship between state and market. It would be naïve to think, for example, that corruption is an indirect product of state intervention and that its eradication depends on the supremacy of a market unconstrained by a public sphere. It has never been proved empirically that the level of corruption is linked to the amount of public intervention. Rather, the contrary is the case. To give just one example, mid-nineteenth-century Britain was considered to be one of the most corrupt European countries at a time when public intervention was minimal. On the other hand, during the period when the welfare state and public control had reached their apogee (in the 1960s), Britain knew only one type of scandal – sex based – and corruption was considered to be more or less non-existent. More recently, instances of corruption have multiplied in Britain at a time when the frontiers of the state have receded and 'marketisation' and private-sector management practice have penetrated to all reaches of the civil service (Doig, 1996).

But, of course, what is seen as 'corruption' in a society that has attained a certain phase of development in its social, legal and political norms may simply be everyday practice in another. What would be considered as nepotism, unwarranted intervention or shameless patronage in Britain might be defined as fair practice, or even a moral duty in other countries. The practice of giving gifts, regulated or forbidden in Europe in dealings between civil servants and private individuals, can be perfectly acceptable and integrated within African or Asian customs. Not offering a gift, or not ensuring that one's family, circle of friends or clan benefit from the advantages given by one's power and connections, can be just as shocking in some societies as accepting favours or bribes in others. In many parts of southern Europe such norms of behaviour still persist. It is the *perception* of the practice that makes it corrupt and scandalous. Heidenheimer's (1989) distinction between types of perception is helpful here: 'white corruption' is accepted and tolerated, 'black corruption' is widely rejected and criticised, while 'grey corruption' is accepted and/or rejected in a sort of moral limbo or by different groups. Societies that modernise and democratise tend to move, albeit unevenly, from one phase to another. For example, the recent corruption scandals in Italy and Spain do not reveal that these societies have suddenly become corrupt (although corrupt practice certainly proliferated there in the 1980s), but rather that the previously accepted and routine had become unacceptable and illicit. As Lamo de Espinosa (1997) suggests, when social practices become legally defined as 'corruption', this reveals the moral progress of a community from 'black' to 'grey', then to 'white'. Corruption and scandal in this case is a secondary and unintended consequence of a process of ethical transition, expressed rather dramatically in the case of Italy as a form of 'collective catharsis'.

But as we shall argue below, it is difficult to divide societies into corrupt and non-corrupt, 'black and white', for several reasons. First, certain types of corruption are more or less tolerated within societies where more generally such norms of behaviour are considered unacceptable. For example, even in northern European countries where the public/private divide is rather rigidly drawn and where everyday petty corruption involving officialdom is rare, routine corruption involving various parts of the state apparatus – public works officials (and even ministers), the police, the social services – has been documented. These are precisely those parts of the state most heavily involved in corruption in those European societies (Italy, Spain, Greece) where corrupt practices are more widespread. It seems that certain relationships along the state–market divide lend themselves more readily to corruption than others.

Second, there are a number of areas – typically involving foreign trade with Third World countries – in which many multinational firms and most Western political systems have allowed – when they have not actively encouraged – the use of bribery for contracts. Thus differences in perception and behaviour can exercise a reciprocal influence: Westerners sometimes try to adjust their legal and commercial practices in other places, but thereby let themselves become contaminated by customs of which they disapprove in theory. Furthermore, corruption has not only been able to use official state mechanisms, it has also been justified – for want of being *publicly* legitimised – by fiscal authorities, for example, which have tolerated such practices as a means of improving national export performance: the markets for public works, arms sales and large-scale industrial equipment are at the heart of what Péan (1988, p. 96) has called *'l'affairisme d'Etat'* (state wheeler-dealing). Accepted as unavoidable in the relationships with the Third World, corruption has frequently introduced illicit practice via a feedback effect into Western business.

Third, the presence of scandal is not necessarily an indication that a society is experiencing a period of 'purification'. It may also be a sign of struggle in a political system between traditional and modernising elites, or simply between groups using revelations of corruption for political capital. To cite Marengo (1988, p. 66), 'corruption is corrupt behaviour involving political actors and political scandal is the use made in politics of allegations of corrupt behaviour'.

The Causes of Corruption

Exploring the causes of corruption is a complex task since, as already indicated, the phenomenon varies considerably from one society to the next. There are various ways of approaching the subject, including the notion of 'political culture', or variants thereof, including attempts to define societies in terms of levels of 'trust' ('high trust' societies are much less corrupt than 'low trust' ones) (Fukayama, 1995) or 'civicness' (Putnam, 1993). Such approaches suffer, however, from the fact that apparently 'high trust' societies can contain significant pockets of 'low trust' behaviour. Meanwhile, attempts to define the institutional basis of 'civicness' in the Italian case, for example, have foundered on the fact that those regions defined as 'civic' (the centre and north) have been hit as hard by the corruption revelations of the 1990s as those traditionally considered 'amoral' in their norms of social interaction (the south). 'Political culture', moreover, is a concept that always creates the danger of tautologous explanation, that is, 'things are the way they are because they are the way they are'.

An alternative method is to explore the *political opportunity structures* of different societies and their historical origins. Kitschelt (1986) coined this concept for the analysis of situations far removed from corruption. But it can be of use in explaining variations in the intensity and methods of corruption by indicating the ease or difficulty of access to and exploitation of procedures and institutions in a given political system. Depending on the way political and administrative power is structured, this will be more or less obscure or transparent, open or closed, sensitive or indifferent to pressure, since, whatever the regime or organisation, it is in the nature of things that the agents involved may seek to manipulate rules or exploit resources for private gain. The main differences between systems will lie in their capacity for protection against such behaviour. It is this, in essence, that defines the local 'culture' of corruption.

Before analysing different 'opportunity structures' across Western Europe, it is worth considering why corrupt and illicit practices have proliferated in the contemporary period.

The Financing of Political Parties

One of the first and immediate causes stems from the increased financial needs of political parties. Modern elite parties typically have lacked the developed militant base to meet the needs and costs of mobilising an electorate which, driven by the development of modern communications and increasingly sophisticated campaign techniques, has become increasingly expensive. Consequently, they have turned to alternative or complementary resources. This has often been through state financing, but also through secret financing obtained in whatever manner possible from private economic actors. In many countries, party racketeering has had a formidable impact, because it has undermined conventional norms of behaviour even when it has been relatively small-scale; sometimes it has even been justified by the need for strong parties in a vibrant democracy. Once this gap has been opened in the ethical system, the most diverse and the least acceptable forms of corruption can sweep in. The gravity of this problem has compelled all countries to seek new methods of regulating party finance and, in Europe, the public funding of political parties has often been the preferred option for minimising the political influence of private contributors. This is, after all, one of the key elements of a fair and legitimate electoral system.

The stimulus for corruption thus created would not have been so disastrous had it not been combined with other developments. These practices were neither new nor unknown; but they had previously usually stayed within 'acceptable' limits or were identified with isolated individuals rather than systemic practice. What has changed is the context (and opportunity structure) of political practice – in economic, ideological and institutional terms.

Economic Revolution

The years since the mid-1970s have seen a significant restructuring of economies, including changes in the nature and location of production, the appearance of new services, the internationalisation of trade, and the globalisation of financial markets. In this increasingly global economy, information, and the possession of key posts between public and private sectors (and national and international markets) play a crucial role and give a new dimension to certain deviant behaviour (for example, insider trading, or the manipulation of public markets). The internationalisation of the black market in corruption makes it difficult for judges to untangle the sophisticated bank transactions involved in 'laundering' money through dozens of accounts placed in the world's tax havens (Jersey, Luxembourg, Hong Kong, the Cayman Islands and so on). The creation of the European single market has provided new opportunities for such practices, as traditional barriers to the free flow of capital and people have been removed.

Ideological Change

At an ideological level, the neo-liberal devaluation of the state, public services and public administration has had important side-effects, such as the discrediting of the traditional ideals or values which underpinned these very institutions. If the administration becomes the enemy, if 'the government is a problem' (Ronald Reagan), it is not surprising that certain rules of conduct come to be considered old-fashioned. If efficiency and exhortations to 'get rich' are worshipped blindly, it comes as no surprise when corrupt businessmen become idols of their time. Corruption would not have reached this extent without an exceptional combination of circumstances: in short, the norms of behaviour and old economic structures have been rejected in favour of rules whose foundation, legitimacy and content are still being determined.

Institutional Change

Economic and ideological changes have shaken up traditional institutions. The degree of change since the mid-1970s/early 1980s has been unprecedented: the transformation of regulatory authorities (increasingly international or European, increasingly independent of governments); the weakening of representative bodies, such as parties and unions, with elites or leaders cut off from an ever-diminishing base; the blurring of the dividing lines between public and private sectors by privatisation and the transfer of elite personnel from one sector to the other; the decentralisation of government and public administration (extending opportunities for corruption in Italy and Spain, for example); and the creation of a new, parallel, opportunity structure for corrupt and illicit practice in Europe's transnational polity.

A development emblematic of ideological change and institutional transformation in the recent period has been the wave of privatisations and the extension of private-sector management techniques to bureaucracies across Western Europe. But neither has separated the private from the public sphere, nor politics from markets. Rather, they have blurred the dividing line between the two and increased the scope for discretionary powers. Thus a public bank can now take all the risks of an adventurous banker and is faced with no controlling shareholders; a private business, because of the nature of its markets and contracts, will be dependent on public orders and therefore on the goodwill, complicity or the preferential treatment of elected officials or civil servants. Examples of such incestuous relationships can be found across Western Europe and are made easier by the increasing interplay between political, administrative, economic and financial elites.

The different elements mentioned above are common to different political systems. We now need to consider the variations: why has corruption been more extensive in one country than another, and more or less serious in its consequences? This is where national public institutions and market structures come into play.

Manifestations of Corruption: 'Local' Cultures and Opportunity Structures

Certain settings are more conducive to corruption than others. Although the data and evidence on relative levels of corruption are fragmented and unreliable, extensive surveys of businessmen operating in different countries produce stark differences in the *perception* of these levels. For all its weaknesses, this at least provides us with a starting point for analysis. Table 6.1 is drawn from the results of one such survey.

There is a clear distinction between the Northern Protestant countries and the Latin Catholic countries, with the others ranged somewhere in between. Indeed, it is precisely this division that is usually accounted for in terms of political culture or national character: the presence in Spain of *amiguismo* (Heywood, 1996), *'l'arrangement à la française'* or *'l'arrangiarsi'* of the Italians, are familiar illustrations of a certain way of acting and of facing difficulties in the relationship between public and private spheres. But what these social practices alert us to is not a different or specific southern mentality or culture, but rather differences in the way that societies/political systems are organised. Institutional settings breed certain types of relationship and social practice. The fact that the notion of 'conflict of interest' as an antidote to corruption is much stronger in Northern Protestant cultures than in Latin and Catholic civilisations can be attributed to different 'political cultures' and levels of 'trust', but only if 'culture' and 'trust' are defined in historical and institutional terms. Why is it that in Southern European countries multiple office-holding, patron–client relations across the public–private divide, and informal channels for exercising influence on politicians are more accepted than in the North?

The clearest contrast is between Britain – whose civil service has long had a reputation for integrity, and where patron–client relations in the political sphere have been rare – and a country such as Italy, where patronage and favouritism have been a central feature of relations between parties, bureaucracy and business. As Heidenheimer (1996) points out, already by late nineteenth century Britain had highly guarded borders between the processes of social and political exchange

TABLE 6.1 *Perceptions of the degree of corruption in West European countries*

	Least corrupt	Somewhat corrupt	Quite corrupt
Low ↑	Denmark	Germany	Spain
	Finland	Austria	Turkey
	Sweden	France	Greece
	Switzerland	Belgium	Italy
	The Netherlands	Portugal	
	Norway		
	Republic of Ireland		
High ↓	Britain		

Source: Adapted from Heidenheimer (1996).

on the one hand, and between political and economic exchange on the other. Unlike the case in most continental countries, Britain institutionalised its parties and party system long before it institutionalised bureaucracies, which meant that the penetration of politicians into bureaucratic structures was declining in Britain as it was increasing in countries such as Italy and France. Indeed, one can add that in those continental countries that have experienced dictatorship during the twentieth century, the penetration of bureaucracies, and even judiciaries, by parties was seen as an essential check against threats to democracy. Whereas Britain transformed itself from a country in which corruption was rife into one noted for the propriety and integrity of its public servants, countries such as Italy, Spain and Greece built their democracies around interlocking spheres of influence. Moreover, while corrupt practice in Britain was gradually 'recoded' from 'white' to 'grey' and then to 'black', in the Southern countries, the patron–client relations that had always substituted for rational, administrative interaction in their pre-modern polities were transposed into new institutional structures. As Sapelli (1995, pp. 17–18) has argued, it is precisely the collusion between clientelism, a lack of 'sense of state', and the ubiquity of clannish parties which creates the weakness of Southern politics.

In the process, these countries have built quite different 'political opportunity structures', three key aspects of which can be explored:

- The regulation of public appointments and the role of bureaucracy. As corruption is based on social exchange, the struggle against it emerging and spreading depends on precautionary measures. Most are characterised by prohibitions against civil servants and politicians: for example, the policy of enhancing the autonomy of the civil service has led to rules on 'incompatibility', that is, a prohibition on civil servants simultaneously having other jobs (private or political). Another crucial institutional variable is the role and place taken by the bureaucracy in the political system and in society. Wherever a relatively powerful, efficient and autonomous bureaucracy has been created, the risk of corruption is diminished.
- Regulating the activities of politicians. Many countries have sought to establish a degree of separation between politicians and private interests by instituting incompatibility rules and/or giving elected representatives the financial means to enable them to live not only for politics but also *from* politics. Yet here too these rules are very varied and applied in very different ways from one country to another.

- The system of party finance. Nassmacher (1993) identifies a number of ways in which legitimate party financing may border (or move over into) the corrupt: targeting professional politicians seeking re-election (a party tax), public employees wanting to keep their jobs ('macing'), international or national firms as well as local business-men needing public permits or licences (toll-gating) and government contracts (kickbacks). The borderline with corruption often has to be crossed in order to ensure the flow of party revenue from the spoils of office (graft). In some cases regulation has been unnecessary to secure a legitimate system of public funding (Sweden, the Nether-lands, Britain), while in others (for instance, Italy in the 1970s) quite extensive rules have been overwhelmed by pre-existing practices. In still others the introduction of new and relatively effective rules has accompanied an anti-corruption catharsis in public opinion and prosecution of wrongdoers (France in the late 1980s and Italy post-1992).

The 'Least Corrupt': Britain, Scandinavia and the Netherlands

The British civil service, which has some of the strictest and most rigidly applied rules on incompatibility, stands out as one of the least corrupt European administrations. The other members of this group also have quite rigidly drawn boundaries between the public and private spheres. However, changes in recent years have begun to erode those boundaries.

In the British case, this has been the result of the 'marketisation' of the public sector and the introduction of new management techniques, producing new types of opportunity for illicit practice and conflicts of interest in both central and local government. As Doig (1996, pp. 181–2) discusses, cases investigated by the British Public Accounts Committee reveal major failings in key areas of financial control, compliance with rules and the management of public money and assets. 'Dysfunctional change' has created the preconditions for a proliferation of corruption and fraud, producing potential conflicts of interest over privatisation and public position and a misinterpreta-tion of performance rewards amid a failure to enforce or police regulations and procedures. While the Dutch system has also had a strong reputation for public-sector integrity, as in Britain, this is changing. The opportunity structure for corruption expanded in the 1960s and 1970s with the expansion of government services and intervention, creating a complex network of co-operation, consultation and mutual involvement between private and public bodies, making supervision much more difficult. Those areas most susceptible to corruption have been the state customs department, the police, local administration and the sector of semi-public and subsidised bodies. At the same time, economic morality has changed, producing a much less 'Protestant' view of corrupt practice and the evasion of taxes and social security contributions (Hoetjes, 1986).

As for parliamentary responsibility and party finance, like Britain, both Sweden and the Netherlands have a high level of self-regulation and a very loose set of legal constraints. In the latter two countries, this system seems to have been highly successful, with parties in both countries voluntarily rejecting funding from private companies and instead relying largely on a combination of public funds and membership subscriptions. There have been very few examples of financial scandal in either country (Klee, 1993; Koole, 1994). In Britain, however, there have long been signs that self-regulation does not work. Most of the regulations that do exist date from the late nineteenth or early twentieth centuries (Johnston and Pattie, 1993). Failure to reform in recent years, together with a poor implementation of rules, raises many questions about the nature and purpose of financial interests and the scope for corruption. As Doig (1996) argues, the British Parliament has no clear and uniform standards of conduct for its own members: bribery of MPs does not fall under criminal law, and levels of spending are fixed for local but not national election campaigns; trade union donations to the Labour Party are regulated (they must be approved by membership ballot), but there are no controls on company donations to the Conservative Party. Patronage is dispensed quite blatantly (under Mrs Thatcher, seventeen private-sector industrialists – whose companies contributed more than £5 million to her party – were made peers, although Harold Wilson was also accused of rewarding with peerages industrialists who supported the Labour Party), and relatively low salaries encourage MPs to take positions with private companies. This can be a slippery slope, as illustrated by a few cases in the 1990s which showed that some politicians were not indifferent to the pleasures of trips or sumptuous receptions, or to being paid by generous – but not disinterested – businessmen.

The 'Somewhat Corrupt': Germany, Austria, France and Belgium

These countries have very different political systems, yet extensive corruption has been a feature of two of them (France and Belgium), while, in addition to a number of sporadic and spectacular scandals, Germany has failed to create a system of political party finance that prevents more routine forms of corruption. Two institutional features stand out, in contrast to the 'least corrupt countries': all have politicised public services and have, or have had, versions of proportional representation. While the first creates opportunities for conflicts of interest, the latter ensures that parties will secure for themselves systems of public finance – although this does not necessarily prevent corruption.

In France, there is a tension between a high esteem for formal legal values and hierarchies, and a vulnerability to favouritism through cliques and networks. At the national level there are too few checks and balances on executive power, and Parliament is highly ineffective in this regard, while at the local level, electors and local councils expect their notables to obtain favours for them from the administration. The dominant notable is at the centre of everything, accumulating offices and posts and relying on faithful colleagues who have been recruited or chosen by him. The press has typically been less than effective as a watchdog. The temptation to use the power of the state for personal objectives – in terms of policy, personal power or party advantage – has thus been considerable, as revealed by large-scale corruption scandals in recent years (Frears, 1988; Mény, 1992, 1996). As for party finance, before 1988 donations were prohibited and direct public funding unavailable, so French parties raised money increasingly through illegal methods – both for political ends and personal enrichment. Reforms since the late 1980s have imposed a strong regulatory system, setting campaign spending limits, preventing political campaigning on television, limiting private and corporate contributions and introducing strict rules of disclosure on income and spending (Drysch, 1993; Avril, 1994).

Germany, on the other hand, is a country where it was long assumed that a professional civil service and a strong sense of public morality restricted corruption to a few notorious cases. A low level of tolerance for infringements of this code has meant that what are seen as acceptable parts of the political process elsewhere are considered to be grave political scandals (Glees, 1988). However, Blankenberg *et al.* (1989) argue that the 1980s were a decade in which the German political system became like any other. One scandal, in which a leading businessman was alleged to have paid bribes to all parties except the Greens, exposed the limitation of German regulations on party finance: parties had long been dependent on donations from foundations set up explicitly in order to evade the tax laws, and clientelistic relations between donors and politicians lent themselves to outright bribery. Meanwhile, the *Neue Heimat Co-operative* affair, which involved the trade unions and a long string of public works and construction scandals in Berlin, implicating both Social Democrat and Christian Democrat mayors, revealed that Germany was far from immune to corruption. More recently, there has been further confirmation of corruption in public works, involving airport construction in particular. But, unlike in France and Italy, there has been no public outrage or process of cathartic change, and reform has been inadequate. Attempts to eliminate abuses in party financing since the mid-1980s have failed to close many loopholes, including the immunity of MPs from prosecution for bribery, the existence of tax deductible donations alongside poor disclosure rules, and extensive direct donations to politicians which, unlike those for parties, remain unpublished and beyond scrutiny.

Austria also experienced a number of spectacular scandals in the 1980s and, as in Germany, this led to new legal regulation (Klee 1993). Parties have been required to list and report donations higher than a certain threshold since 1984, but this is so high that transparency has hardly been increased. This has fostered a general public distrust of all kinds of party donations. Unlike Sweden and Holland – where self-regulation has underpinned a high level of propriety in party funding – cross-party collusion in Belgium, based on close relationships between political families, has allowed illicit practice to flourish. Judicial investigations may also have been restrained because of this 'consociational' defence mechanism. As elsewhere in this group, there is much evidence of routine corruption involving public works officials and ministers (Frognier, 1986).

The 'Quite Corrupt': Spain, Italy and Greece

In the southern European countries, while the state has taken on the appearance of modernity, its late development alongside the emergence of parties meant that it was founded on particularistic, personalised social structures (Heywood, 1996, p. 127). In both Spain under Franco and Greece under the colonels (1967–74), authoritarian rule did not eliminate these practices, but rather institutionalised them. In Italy under the long period of Christian Democratic hegemony between the late 1940s and the 1970s, clientelism became the very essence of party – and therefore state – power, and systematic corruption the essential strategy for any party (notably Bettino Craxi's Socialist Party) that sought to challenge that hegemony (Hine, 1996; Rhodes, 1997).

The Italian case is by far the most spectacular, not just in Southern Europe but across the Continent as a whole. The history of Italy's postwar Republic is studded with corruption scandals and massive evidence of the abuse of power. What in the late 1940s amounted to a straightforward struggle against communism by the Christian Democrats (DC) with the backing of the Americans and the Catholic Church had, by the 1980s, become a cynical conspiracy by those occupying the most important parts of the state apparatus to perpetuate their hold on power and exploit the public sector for the enrichment of themselves and their parties. The struggle for control of the state became more intense after the mid-1970s, when the success of the socialists at the polls gave them 'coalition blackmail' power over the DC, and a relationship with the traditional rulers of the country based less on political compromise (under Craxi the socialists drifted firmly to the centre-right) than on 'graft' – the distribution of the spoils of office. In the process, large parts of the public sector – including nationalised companies and broadcasting – became party 'fiefdoms'. A 'market-place' for illegal transactions became established, and the politicians, bureaucrats and party professionals who could operate most effectively in this market wielded the greatest power. The relationship between these actors became quite instrumental and totally divorced from the normal conventions of democratic government. The scale of the funds involved was enormous – in one year alone in the late 1980s it is estimated that some L 3,400 billion (£136 million) in illegally obtained funds flowed into party coffers (Rhodes, 1997). Since 1992 – when the details of systemic corruption first emerged – hundreds of politicians, bureaucrats and industrialists have been put on trial and the web of corruption found to be so extensive as to incriminate the entire established political class. Bettino Craxi – probably the most despised member of that class – faces a countless number of indictments and, living in exile in north Africa, has been named as a fugitive from justice.

Elsewhere in the region, corruption scandals have been less spectacular, but illicit forms of governance none the less extensive. From the 1970s, Spain found itself confronted by a sudden growth and modernisation of the economy, together with increasing state intervention, alongside pre-modern economic rules and ethics (Lamo de Espinosa, 1997). This was also true to a large extent of Italy, despite being a founder member of the EC, and of Greece. Only in the 1980s were modern fiscal systems introduced in Spain and Greece, or consolidated, in the case of Italy. Until then, tax evasion was considered to be normal practice, insider trading was legal and routine, stock market activity was based on privileged information, and shareholders were poorly protected – if at all – by legal regulation. In all three countries, modernisation – and 'Europeanisation' (implying a certain spread of 'Protestant' norms and values) – have caused a 'clash of cultures' and created pressures for a more rational–legal administrative structure, greater discipline in party financing, and a more rigid division between public power and private interest.

The corruption scandals that have hit these countries since the late 1980s have much to with the modernising process and the clash between traditional and modernising elements (Koutsoukis, 1989). The socialist parties in these countries have embodied this tension, coming to power during a period of rapid economic change and carrying with them a burden of massive cultural, political and economic expectations at the very time when the resources available to them were being diminished by recession. Securing resources and consolidating power consequently meant exploiting the corruption 'opportunity structure' to the limit. But from a necessary evil, corruption can quickly become standard practice. It is for this reason that in Italy, Greece, Spain, and France as well, socialist parties have been tarred more than others with the brush of corruption, even if, in reality, they were no more culpable. But they were not only the victims of circumstance. None was prepared for reform, either on a political or ethical level. While the Spanish socialists managed their conversion more successfully than the others, Craxi's Italian socialists paid a heavy price for their abuse of power.

While all three of these countries are in the process of implementing reforms in public administration, those developments undermining the integrity of Northern bureaucracies are also creating more potential for corruption in the South. For example, privatisation processes in all these countries have multiplied the opportunities for personal enrichment at public expense. It will therefore be some time before it can be seen whether anti-corruption reform will be able to take root in this unstable environment. Party finances have also undergone important changes in one of these countries – Italy – while in Spain the existing system has been found to be highly inadequate and reform is on the agenda. In both these countries, the capacity of political actors to bypass or manipulate rules has been striking, providing a clear warning that corruption cannot be defeated by regulatory reform alone. Moreover, ill-considered or incomplete regulation will have perverse outcomes. In both countries, public subsidies were expected to contribute to a decrease in corruption, more control of lobbying, more equal opportunities in party competition, and some control of the cost explosion in election campaigns (Ciaurro, 1989; del Castillo, 1994). But both countries also placed unrealistic constraints on private (personal or company) donations and, while imposing few controls on electoral expenditure, failed to allow public resources to increase. The result was a system that encouraged irregularities and systemic corruption. New and extensive controls on party funding and spending (disclosure rules, advertising, media access) were introduced in Italy in 1993 and had a major impact on party behaviour in the 1994 and 1996 general elections (Rhodes, 1997). As in France, the opportunity structure has been modified substantially by regulatory reform, but entrenched social practices are likely to change only slowly.

The European Union: A New Transnational 'Opportunity Structure'?

All international organisations and programmes are susceptible to corruption and fraud. But the complexity of rules in the EU and the scale of the funds it deploys through a myriad of channels creates special cause for concern (Passas and Nelken, 1993). The opportunity structure for illicit practice is extensive: the EU has a bureaucratic system isolated from civil society, while the Council of Ministers and European Commission have created a culture of silence, secrecy and internal solidarity against external scrutiny (Van Outrive, 1993, pp. 131–2). The production of tens of thousands of regulations, including extensive amendments of existing ones, their complex interaction with the regulatory systems of member states, the transfer of vast sums from the agricultural support and regional structural funds budgets, and inadequate auditing procedures, have created a system that is easy to infiltrate and exploit but very difficult to monitor. Given the slow development of police co-operation and member state opposition to the harmonisation of criminal law, the prosecution of fraud and corruption on a pan-European basis remains difficult, regardless of innovations such as bilateral agreements against money laundering and the creation of a Community anti-fraud unit in 1988. The latter can do little in the absence of an independent legal base for enforcement which the member states, still jealous of their sovereignty, are highly reluctant to concede (Leigh and Smith, 1991; den Boer and Walker, 1993). The abolition of border controls can only increase the opportunities for illegality.

As Van Outrive (1993) points out, although fraud is often talked about in the EC, corruption as such is a taboo subject. Indeed, to date there has been no in-depth study of corruption in the European institutions as such. There is, however, sufficient evidence of the complicity of corrupt national officials in defrauding European programmes to suggest that European integration has added a new dimension to *national* opportunity structures. Moreover, national governments have failed in the past to prosecute EC fraud as thoroughly as fraud in their own countries. Official assistance is clearly a major factor, especially in parts of the EU where clientelism is still important in social and economic relations. But, as Passas and Nelken (1993) argue, this can also be the result of complicity via definitions of what constitutes a serious crime and how it should be pursued. For example, Britain has a 'value for money' approach (tantamount to turning a blind eye to small-scale fraud), while Germany prosecutes all fraud as a matter of course. Italy, although distinctive for its special law on EC fraud (and a national agency for investigating agricultural fraud), has lower penalties for defrauding the EC than its own institutions. France and Germany have very detailed anti-fraud laws and procedures, but large gaps in defining corporate responsibility. Most EU member states prefer non-penal solutions and out-of-court settlements. An absence of punishment means there is little deterrence in current laws against EC fraud, making it difficult even to provide a valid assessment of its extent and importance (Passas and Nelken, 1991).

Member state resistance has prevented a common, pan-European, strategy against corruption and fraud. But given the abolition of border controls and the expansion of European funding programmes, a significant move in this direction is essential, including EU penal legislation, greater judicial co-operation, a harmonisation of national anti-fraud laws, powers of investigation for EU's anti-fraud squad and a statute concerning the protection and penal responsibility of EU officials (see Van Outrive, 1993).

Conclusion

To sum up, recent West European experience suggests not only that 'illicit' governance is widespread – even in those countries traditionally assumed to be relatively free of such practices – but that there is no panacea or miraculous remedy. The fight against corruption has to be undertaken through a complex cocktail of measures involving legal proceedings (transparency, controls), institutions (separation of powers, strength of the administration), and structures (regulation methods, competition rules). Moving forward along all of these dimensions is imperative, not just at national level but also within the institutions, programmes and procedures of the EU. The latter is especially important, given the extent to which economic, ideological and institutional changes have already eroded standards of behaviour and introduced new, illicit, social practices into the member states. With the creation of the single market and the steady abolition of border controls, a new system of pan-European regulation is essential to ensure that *national* political opportunity structures become less, not more, conducive to corruption and fraud.

7

Electoral Systems and Voting Behaviour

MICHAEL GALLAGHER

In this chapter we shall focus on some of the most important aspects of elections in Western Europe. First, we shall examine the wide range of electoral rules under which people vote across the continent, and then we shall show that these different electoral systems can have quite pronounced consequences for the governance of a country. We shall also consider the evidence that European electorates are becoming disillusioned with conventional party politics, before going on to ask whether the growing significance of the role played in many countries by the EU creates its own problems of representation.

The Variety of Electoral Systems in Western Europe

In essence, electoral systems translate votes cast into election results. But this rather bland description obscures the important political effects that electoral systems can have. For one thing, different electoral systems may convert the same pattern of voting into quite different electoral outcomes. In addition, different electoral systems may result in similar patterns of preferences among the electorate being expressed in quite different voting patterns. This can happen because under some systems voters have no reason not to vote 'sincerely' (that is, in accordance with their true preferences), whereas under other systems they may have an incentive to vote 'tactically' – for example, by backing a candidate who is not their first choice so as to prevent the success of their least favoured candidate.

A conventional way of classifying electoral systems is to distinguish between PR and non-PR systems. PR stands for 'proportional representation', the principle that parties – or 'opinion' generally – is represented in proportion to its strength; in other words, if a party wins, say, 30 per cent of the votes at an election, a PR electoral system should award it something close to 30 per cent of the seats in parliament.

The method used to fill parliamentary seats in the United Kingdom is the archetype of a non-PR electoral system. The UK is divided into 651 territorial constituencies of (very approximately) equal populations, and within each constituency the seat goes to the candidate who receives the most votes, whether or not this represents a majority of the votes. This method of awarding seats can produce quite disproportional outcomes; for example, in the general election of 1992, the Conservatives won a majority (52 per cent) of the seats despite having received only 42 per cent of the votes, while the Liberal Democrats, with 18 per cent of the votes, not far short of half of the Conservatives' total, took only 3 per cent of the seats.

An archetypal PR system is that employed at elections in the Netherlands. Here, the lower house of parliament (the *Tweede Kamer*) consists of 150 MPs, and these are elected by a method of proportional representation from one 150–member constituency that embraces the entire country. Each party presents 'lists' of candidates, and the voters cast their votes by indicating a preference for one of the various lists. Once all the votes have been cast, a sophisticated mathematical procedure is applied to award each party (or at least, each one that wins more than the threshold of 0.67 per cent of the votes cast) its 'fair' share of the seats. Not surprisingly, elections in the Netherlands produce very proportional outcomes; the kind of disparities between vote shares and seat shares that are common in Britain are inconceivable under the Dutch electoral system.

Two aspects of the Dutch electoral system are more significant than they might appear at first sight: these are *district magnitude* (the number of MPs returned per constituency) and the *threshold* that a party needs to overcome before it will be represented in parliament. As a general rule, the larger the district magnitude, and the lower the threshold, the more proportional will be the election results. Indeed, district magnitude is often more important than the electoral formula in deciding how proportional an electoral system is (Taagepera and Shugart, 1989: pp. 112–25). Similarly, the threshold of representation (the share of the votes that a party must reach to have any chance of receiving some seats) can play a major role in determining proportionality; if, in the Netherlands, the threshold were raised from 0.67 per cent to, say, 20 per cent, the outcome of the election would be very far from proportional because (on past form) only two or three parties would meet this condition, and all the votes cast for the smaller parties would be wasted.

We can see the impact of these two factors when we look at some of the other electoral systems in operation around Western Europe. For example, Luxembourg employs exactly the same mathematical formula for awarding seats as does the Netherlands, but for electoral purposes the country is divided into four constituencies, each returning an average of fifteen deputies. This makes Luxembourg elections some-what less proportional than Dutch ones, and a less proportional case still is Spain, which is divided into fifty-two constituencies, which return on average only seven deputies each. The effect of this fairly small district magnitude is to make Spanish electoral outcomes much less proportional than their Dutch counterparts and to give the largest party a sizeable 'bonus' (the amount by which its share of the seats exceeds its share of the votes). The Spanish socialists (the PSOE) have been able to win a majority of seats in parliament with as few as 39.6 per cent of the votes, an outcome that seems more characteristic of a non-PR electoral system than of one described as PR. Small district magnitude, then, will have the effect of making an electoral system less proportional, and in practice most countries, unlike the Netherlands, do use subnational districts and thereby reduce the proportionality of their election result.

Similarly, the use of a threshold has the effect of reducing propor-tionality, by discriminating against those parties that fail to reach it, thus ensuring a seat bonus for the parties that exceed it. The threshold of 0.67 per cent that the Netherlands employs is exceptionally low, and in practice it has little effect; if a party fails to win this many votes, it is probably so weak that it would not qualify for any seats in any case. Every other West European country to set a threshold pitches this at a rather higher level. In Denmark, parties need to win at least 2 per cent of the national vote to qualify for parliamentary representation; in Greece, the figure is 3 per cent; and in Sweden, it is 4 per cent.

Most West European countries that use PR have adopted electoral systems with 'complex districting'; that is, with more than one level at which seats are awarded (for details see Gallagher *et al.*, 1995, p. 282; Mackie and Rose, 1991, pp. 509–10). For example, in Denmark the country is divided into seventeen constituencies, which between them return 135 deputies. This produces a reasonably proportional outcome, but inevitably some parties will be over-represented and others under-represented. To iron out these discrepancies, a further forty seats are held in reserve, and these are now awarded so as to give each party as close to its 'fair' share as possible (subject to the proviso that only those parties reaching the set threshold of 2 per cent of the national votes can receive a share of these forty seats). Essentially similar schemes, under which a first allocation of seats is made at constituency level and then a further round of seats is awarded at a higher tier so as to increase the overall proportionality of the outcome, operate in Austria, Belgium, Germany, Greece, Iceland, Italy, Norway and Sweden.

Of these, perhaps the best known case is the German electoral system, which returns 656 members to the Bundestag. The first allocation of seats is carried out in 328 single-member constituencies, employing the same first-past-the-post method as in Britain. Naturally enough, the great majority of these seats are won by the two main parties, the Christian Democrats (CDU/CSU) and the socialists (SPD). The remaining 328 seats are awarded on the basis of 'second votes' cast by voters for party lists, and these seats are awarded to the parties so as to make the overall result as proportional as possible. German election results are thus much more proportional than those in Britain, although their proportionality is tempered by the use of quite a high threshold for the 328 list seats: to qualify for a share of these seats, a party must either have won 5 per cent of the list votes, or have won at least three of the constituency seats. The system is thus very fair for those parties that overcome the threshold, though for those that fall below it (as the Greens did in 1990 before making a comeback in 1994, and as the liberal Free Democrats are often in danger of doing), it can seem harsh.

The German system is popular with electoral reformers elsewhere; it is seen as combining local constituency representation with overall proportionality, and the German record of postwar economic success – whether or not this can really be linked causally in any way to the electoral system – does its acceptability no harm. The German system has been adopted (by a referendum in 1993) in New Zealand, and its impact is seen in recent electoral changes in Japan and Russia, as well as Italy and several of the post-communist regimes in Eastern Europe.

In discussing PR, we have so far described *list systems* (so called because voters choose between the lists presented by the various parties). It is worth noting that these list systems vary in the extent to which they allow voters a choice of candidate: 'closed' systems, as used in Germany, Portugal and Spain, allow voters no such choice (the order in which the party places its candidates on the list determines their prospects of election), while 'open' systems, as used in Denmark, Finland and Switzerland, allow the voters to choose which of a party's candidates are elected. There is another variety of PR, the *single transferable vote* (STV), which extends the voters' choice a stage further by dispensing entirely with party lists. Voters rank all the candidates in a constituency in order of their preference, unconstrained by the candidates' party affiliations, and the counting process is designed to take into account not just their first preferences but also, in many cases, their second or lower preferences. STV is employed in two countries, the Republic of Ireland and Malta, and delivers results that are as proportional as those produced by other European PR systems (for a fuller description of STV as it operates in Ireland, see Sinnott, 1993).

Although virtually every West European country has adopted one version of PR or another, in two countries the electoral system is not based on PR principles. The British case we have described above, and the other exception is France, which uses a double-ballot method of election. At parliamentary elections, metropolitan France is divided into 555 single-member constituencies, and within each of these there can be two rounds of voting on successive Sundays. A candidate winning an overall majority of the votes cast in the first round is elected there and then, but if no candidate achieves this, the second round is held a week later. The second round is confined to those candidates who have reached a prescribed threshold (12.5 per cent of the electorate) in the first round (if fewer than two candidates reach this, the top two candidates from the first round proceed to the second round). In the second round, the candidate who receives the highest number of votes wins, regardless of whether this is a majority. French presidential elections are fought under similar rules, except that only the top two from the first round can contest the second round.

The Consequences of Electoral Systems

To describe every detail of any country's electoral system would take a great deal of space – in each case, it is clear that someone has spent a lot of time working out the precise method of converting votes into seats. Similarly, some political scientists have devoted much of their limited time to trying to assess the effects of different electoral systems. But are electoral systems really important? Are they really little more than technical aspects of a country's political system, or might the choice of electoral system have significant consequences for the whole of political life? Can we, in fact, decide which is the best electoral system?

That different electoral systems can have important political con-sequences is beyond dispute. This is apparent when we look at a cluster of separate (but related) aspects of election outcomes: proportionality, the number of parties in parliament, and whether governments are coalitions or not. Generally speaking, in countries with PR systems proportionality and the number of parties is higher – and coalition government is more likely – than in countries that do not use PR.

When it comes to proportionality, PR systems, hardly surprisingly, do indeed produce outcomes that reflect party strengths more accurately in parliament. There are various ways in which we might measure proportionality (Gallagher, 1991; Lijphart, 1994a, pp. 58–67), and they all tell the same story: non-PR electoral systems generate more disproportionality (Lijphart, 1994a, pp. 96–7). As we would expect, given the above discussion, proportionality is the highest of all in those countries that use a PR system and large district magnitudes, such as Austria, the Netherlands and Sweden.

Similarly, parliaments elected under non-PR systems contain on average more parties than those elected under PR (Lijphart, 1994a, p. 96). The reason is that smaller parties, provided they reach any threshold in operation, can expect to be treated reasonably 'fairly' under PR, while under non-PR systems they can expect to be underrepresented. For example, the British Liberals and Social Democrats won 22.6 per cent of the votes in the 1987 general election and received just 3.4 per cent of the seats, returning to Westminster as an insignificant group in a small corner of the opposition benches; in the Finnish election of the same year, the Social Democrats won about the same share of the votes (24.1 per cent), yet they not only received 28.0 per cent of the seats in the new parliament but also emerged as the leading party in the coalition government formed forty-five days after the election. Small parties suffer doubly under non-PR electoral systems. Not only does the electoral system convert their votes into seats less fairly (since they do not finish first in many constituencies and hence most of their votes are wasted), but, in addition, this very fact is known to voters and, precisely to avoid casting a wasted vote, some people will vote for the candidate they least dislike among those perceived as having a realistic chance of winning the seat. As with proportionality, not all PR systems deliver identical outcomes: in some countries (such as Belgium, Denmark, Finland, the Netherlands and Switzerland) parliamentary strength is spread widely among many parties, none of them especially strong, while in others (such as Austria, Germany, Greece, Malta, Portugal and Spain) parliamentary strength is little more fragmented than in Britain or France.

Coalition government is more common in countries that use PR than in those that do not. It is very rare in Britain, where one party usually wins the majority of the seats. This parliamentary majority is almost always brought about by the bonus awarded by the electoral system to the large parties; the last time any party succeeded in winning a majority of the votes was in 1931. With a PR electoral system, coalition government might well be the norm in Britain. In a number of PR-using countries, in contrast, all (or virtually all) governments are coalitions: this is true of Belgium, Finland, Germany, Iceland, Italy, Luxembourg, the Netherlands and Switzerland. However, some countries with PR systems have experienced long spells of single-party government, whether majority or minority; examples include Austria, the Republic of Ireland, Malta, Norway, Spain and Sweden. Moreover, many would argue that all governments are coalitions – even a single-party government is in practice a coalition of different groups, views, and interests.

Finally, we should note that it is by now well established that PR systems lead to parliaments that are more socially representative of the people who elect them than are parliaments elected under other methods. This is most obvious when we look at the number of women in parliaments around Europe (Randall, 1987, pp. 140–2). In the mid-1990s, the average number of women in parliaments in European countries using PR was 20.2 per cent; in Britain and France it was 7.7 per cent (Gallagher *et al.*, 1995, pp. 290–5). Of course, explanations for the number of women in parliament go much deeper than the electoral system (see Chapter 16), but undoubtedly PR facilitates the election of women because of the incentive it gives to parties to present a 'balanced ticket' within each multi-member constituency. In a 10-member constituency, for example, it would be extraordinary if a party list of candidates did not reflect a gender balance and, more broadly, did not contain representatives of ethnic, linguistic and any other minorities from whom the party hoped to win votes. In single-member constituency systems, in contrast, women have tended to find it difficult to be selected as the sole candidate of one of the major parties. The effect of PR is apparent when we look at countries whose electoral systems have a single-member lower tier and a PR higher tier. In the Italian election of 1994, for example, women won only 9 per cent of the single-member constituency seats but they took 34 per cent of the list seats (Katz, 1996, p. 48).

Having looked at some of the consequences of various electoral systems, we are left with the question: which electoral system is best? At one time, academic supporters of different systems used to argue rather polemically for their favoured method; in recent years, the literature on electoral systems has been much more concerned to pin down the effects of electoral systems in specific contexts than to make a case for or against a particular system. Even so, a number of writers have concluded that the evidence does point clearly in one direction – but unfortunately for those wanting to know which electoral system should be adopted, there is no consensus as to what direction the arrows are pointing.

For some writers, one essential point is that PR is better than the alternatives. In a broadside against the single-member plurality system in Britain, Finer (1975 – see also Lakeman, 1974) argued that the existing electoral system promoted adversary politics; ensured that the single-party government of the day was unduly influenced by extremists within its own ranks; created discontinuity in national policies since one party in government pulled down what the other party had done while in power rather than build upon it; and did not generate governments that were either stronger or more stable than those that would be elected under PR. Had S. E. Finer been writing twenty years later, he would no doubt also have highlighted the fact that the Conservative Party was able to achieve overall majorities at four elections in a row, thus entitling it to govern alone for eighteen years, without ever winning more than 44 per cent of the votes – not to mention the problem of democratic legitimacy brought about in Scotland and Wales as a result of their rule by a Conservative government with little electoral support in either country. The much-vaunted close link between voters and their MPs in Britain has also been questioned: Crewe (1985, p. 54) shows that a 1972 survey found that most voters knew little or nothing about their MP, almost half being unable even to name him or her. For Finer and E. Lakeman, the advantages of PR are overwhelming; for I. Crewe, one of the main advantages claimed for first-past-the-post proves to be a myth.

In contrast, Norton (1992) argues that the present British electoral system offers a reasonable balance between effectiveness and consent, and that PR would threaten this 'delicate balance'. While the present system ensures the accountability of governments to the voters, a PR system would be likely to lead to a coalition government that nobody voted for, that was put together by post-election horse-trading, and that might give undue power to a small party that occupied a key bargaining position. Whatever the merits of these arguments, the fact that the government of the day will usually owe its majority status to the existing electoral system is a powerful factor militating against the likelihood of the adoption of PR in Britain.

For most of the rest of Western Europe, the basic argument over PR or not PR was settled early in the twentieth century, or at the end of the nineteenth century, when country after country moved away from the single-member plurality system to one method or another of proportional representation (Carstairs, 1980). The question of which precise method to adopt is generally seen as being more technical than the fundamental issue of whether PR should be implemented in the first place, but the distinction between party list versions and STV is sufficiently significant to generate some heat. A major reason for the adoption in most of Europe of a list system is that these systems guarantee a close relationship between each party's share of the votes and its share of the seats, whereas STV, because votes are cast for candidates and preference orderings can cross party lines, does not. In practice, though, elections held under STV represent parties as accurately as those held under PR list electoral systems. Proponents of STV maintain that it gives the voters more power than list systems, because they can award preferences to candidates on the basis of whatever factor seems most important to them, and that STV 'enables the wishes of voters to be given effect, whatever these wishes may be . . . For that reason, it is the most democratic and therefore the fairest of the various systems of proportional representation' (Bogdanor, 1992, p. 20; see also Lakeman, 1974, pp. 111–50). However, STV is often seen as an 'Anglo-Saxon' variant of PR, and it is unlikely that any country currently using a list system will switch to it.

France is the only country to use the double ballot system, and this method of election is sometimes seen as an oddity of little wider interest. However, G. Sartori, while acknowledging that no electoral system is 'best for all seasons', concludes that 'if there is a "best" electoral system, this is the double ballot system in its wide range of adaptability, of possible formulations' (Sartori, 1994, p. 75). He argues that PR, even if it delivers representative government, is less likely to deliver responsible government, while the single-member plurality system compels voters to take a 'shot in the dark'. Under the double ballot, however, the voter has two shots, and the second time he or she shoots 'in full daylight', in full knowledge of the options and preferences of other voters (Sartori, 1994, p. 63). While the double ballot may increase the power of the voter compared with the first-past-the-post system, it is capable of producing results that are every bit as disproportional. In the French election of 1993, the two main right-wing parties, the RPR and UDF, succeeded in taking 80 per cent of the seats despite having received only 38 per cent of the votes. If this produced responsible government, it was achieved at a high price in terms of representativeness.

The fact that electoral systems are usually more easily manipulable than other parts of the institutional or constitutional framework means that they are inclined to become prime targets for those who want to 'reform' a political system, or to confer some partisan advantage on themselves, or indeed to achieve the latter under the guise of the former. In Britain, as we have seen, PR is advocated by those wishing for a more representative and participatory style of government; it is backed most strongly by the Liberal Democrats, who would gain most from its introduction, and resisted most solidly by the Conservatives, who would probably lose most. In the Republic of Ireland, the largest party, Fianna Fáil, twice attempted to abolish PR in favour of the first-past-the-post system, under which it stood to be in government almost permanently, but the proposal was defeated on each occasion in a referendum. The manipulation of the electoral system has been carried furthest in France and Greece. In the French election of 1951, the government even imposed different electoral systems in different parts of the country, in an attempt to weaken the communists and Gaullists as much as possible (Cole and Campbell, 1989, pp. 78–85). After the establishment of the Fifth Republic, the double ballot was employed, until in 1986 the socialists, fearful about the likely scale of their losses under this system, introduced PR. The incoming right-wing adminis-tration promptly reintroduced the double ballot, which it knew would make life much harder for the Front National, its competitor for conservative votes. In Greece, successive ruling parties have made the electoral system either more proportional or less proportional, depend-ing on what they expected to suit them best at the following election (Dimitras, 1994).

When things seem to be going wrong in the politics of a country, changing the electoral system sometimes appears to be an easy way to fix them. The Italian political system has long been known for a high degree of corruption, and matters finally came to a head in the early 1990s, when the parties that had dominated the country's government for many years, principally the Christian Democrats (DC) and the Socialists (PSI), began to collapse in the face of a newly-unleashed public disgust. The electoral system was seen by many reformers as a major culprit, for two major reasons: because of its highly propor-tional nature (which allowed a profusion of parties to enter parlia-ment); and because of the power that it gave to voters to award preference votes to candidates on their chosen party's lists. The latter, it was felt, engendered unhealthy competition among candidates of the same party and led to clientelistic practices. In 1991 a referendum reduced to one the number of preferences that voters could express, and for the 1994 election a whole new electoral system was devised, under which three-quarters of the seats were filled by a first-past-the-post system in single-member constituencies, and the remaining quarter by PR using closed lists. Something of an unsatisfactory mishmash, this was widely seen as only an interim option, with many reformers wanting the adoption of either the British or the French electoral systems and the complete abolition of PR – just the opposite of what Britain's 'reformers' want!

Electoral systems should be given their proper weight when we are assessing a country's political system as a whole. It is all too easy to use an electoral system as a scapegoat for a general malaise, and to imagine that by abolishing (or introducing) PR, or by raising (or lowering) a threshold so as to make the system a bit less (or more) proportional, or by introducing (or removing) choice as between candidates so as to give voters more (or less) power to choose their parliamentary representatives and to generate (or remove) competition among candidates of the same party, one can at a stroke put right everything about a political system that is giving cause for dissatisfaction. Matters are rarely if ever this simple. Electoral systems do not explain every aspect of a country's political system, and problems of democratic legitimacy, such as those suffered by Germany's Weimar regime or the Italian political system in the early 1990s, usually run much deeper than the electoral system and cannot be solved merely by changing a few of the rules.

However, as we have seen, electoral systems should not be looked upon as mere technical details without political consequences. PR systems lead to more proportionality of representation, to a greater number of parties, and to an increased likelihood of coalition government. They lead to more broadly-based and representative government, which should ensure that policy outputs will enjoy greater consensus than the outputs from governments elected in non-PR systems on less than half of the votes. However, Italian experience emphasises that PR alone cannot bestow democratic legitimacy on a regime. Whether the greater representativeness of governments elected under PR is achieved at the cost of responsibility is a moot point. Opponents of PR have sometimes argued that coalition governments are likely to be internally divided, inclined to think in the short term, and impossible to hold accountable, since each component party can disclaim responsibility for policies that prove unpopular. On the other hand, studies of the economic consequences of electoral systems have concluded that differences in electoral systems are not related to differences in economic performance (Lijphart, 1994b, pp. 7–8; Rose, 1992). The answer to the question of which electoral system is best depends entirely on what we want from an electoral system, and this is essentially a political rather than a technical question.

Non-Voting and Political Disillusionment

Electoral systems convert votes into seats, but one striking feature of European voting is that there is less and less of it as time goes on. In many European countries, turnout is steadily declining, leading to talk of the 'disappearing voters' (Flickinger and Studlar, 1992). For example, whereas 90 per cent of electors cast valid votes in the German election of 1972, this had fallen to 78 per cent in 1994, while turnout in Portugal fell from 92 per cent in 1975 to 68 per cent in 1991. In addition, turnout at elections in the postwar communist countries of Eastern Europe has generally been low. Hand in hand with this diminishing participation in the most important event in the conventional political calendar has gone what is often said to be a steady decline in membership of political parties (Katz, 1990), which is especially marked in such countries as Denmark, the Netherlands, and the United Kingdom. Even if the picture is not entirely straightforward – with membership figures reportedly picking up in Belgium, Finland, Germany and Malta, for example (Gallagher *et al.*, 1995, pp. 245–6) – there is still a general sense that party organisations are much less vibrant between elections than once they were, and that even where the absolute number of members has not fallen, the activity of these members has.

The reasons for a decline in party membership and/or activism are not hard to identify. Once upon a time, in the golden age of the archetypal 'mass party', political parties were able virtually to cocoon their members from the rest of society. In the early years of the century, a party such as the German SPD constituted almost a state within a state. The party had its own newspaper, which its members read and discussed, and its branch offices across the country were centres of social activity, running sports teams, outings and so on. It ran its own health service, financed by members through a health insurance scheme, and in 1906 founded a training school in Berlin for the political education of members. In addition, many members were further immersed in a party subculture by working in factories alongside other party members and belonging to trade unions associated with the party.

It is not hard to see why this kind of hold over substantial sections of society is no longer possible for political parties. The rise of the welfare state made the parallel health schemes operated by parties obsolete, and the decline of large-scale industrial production cut much of the ground from underneath the mass party of the left. Most party newspapers have not survived in the era of television, and the rise in leisure outlets diminished the appeal of the local party hall as a venue for socialising. In addition, there is no great political role for members to play within parties any more. Although parties sometimes launch internal 'great debates' between elections, giving the members at least the illusion of having something worthwhile to decide, it is generally the case that parties in government take little notice of the outcome of such debates. For example, the Spanish Socialist party engaged in a massive exercise, involving almost a million people and 15 000 debates, between 1987 and 1990 to draw up a new programme, but once the programme was formally adopted little more was heard of it and the socialist government went its own way regardless (Heywood, 1993; Gillespie, 1993, pp. 93–4). With parties more and more inclined to gear their activities towards success at the following election, the incentives to become or remain a party member, especially an active one, are ever harder to identify.

Declining turnouts and a fall-off in party activism could be seen as clear proof of disillusionment with the political system, yet matters are not necessarily quite so simple. For one thing, such developments can be seen as part of a widespread withdrawal from the 'public' into the 'private' world: a disinclination to spend time becoming involved in the formal institutions of the political system rather than an explicit disillusionment with them. In addition, the apparent decline in the centrality of parties in political life is related to an upsurge in the number of alternative channels of participation. A whole variety of new social movements have sprung up to press for political and social change in other ways, for example by lobbying policy-makers or by direct action. Single-issue interest groups concerned with environmental issues, for example, are more appealing to many as vehicles for participation than are political parties, which may be seen as overly bureaucratic and more concerned with the attainment of power for its own sake than with the achievement of a few clearly defined goals. Similarly, since the 1970s the feminist movement has emerged as, among other things, a rival to parties for the energies of some of those concerned with changing gender relations (see Chapter 16). In Denmark, for example, one of the countries where the drop in party membership has been most pronounced, it is said that although 'participation through the established and conventional channels has declined . . . this has been compensated for by a corresponding increase in less conventional political channels' (Togeby, 1992, p. 6).

In addition, those dissatisfied with a political decision are increasingly turning to the courts for redress of perceived grievances, and the courts in a number of European countries are finding themselves drawn increasingly into making decisions on the legality or constitutionality of the decisions of political authorities (see Chapter 6 above; Gallagher *et al.*, 1995, ch. 4; Volcansek, 1992). In other words, a decline in turnout and in narrowly-defined 'political' involvement may have as much to do with the growth of other opportunities for participation as with disillusionment with participation *per se*.

None the less, even when making due allowance for these factors, it is hard to avoid the impression that a sense of disillusionment with many aspects of the traditional political and party systems is widespread in a number of West European countries. One manifestation of this is the often unpredictable appearance of 'anti-party' parties, capitalising on a disparate range of grievances about corruption, stagnation, unemployment or racism (see Chapter 17). Another is the increasing sense of vulnerability felt by some of the most powerful parties across Europe (see also Chapter 8). The disbandment of the Italian DC, the largest party in the country for almost fifty years, in 1993–4 is still exceptional, but several other long-standing pillars of the establishment are aware that their foundations are not entirely secure. The Dutch election of 1994 saw the combined vote of the two main parties, the PvdA (Labour) and the Christian Democratic Appeal, fall below 50 per cent for the first time ever. In Austria, the two main parties, which between them regularly received over 90 per cent of the votes in the 1970s, were reduced to fewer than two-thirds of the votes for the first time in 1994, and fared little better in the 1995 election. The British Labour Party, which in the 1940s and 1950s often polled close to half the votes cast, was reduced to 28 per cent in the 1983 election. Ireland's Fianna Fáil, long accustomed to ruling in single-party majority governments, fell back in 1992 to its lowest share of the votes since 1927. Real earthquakes are still rare, but the sound of underground rumbling is certainly audible in quite a number of countries.

Problems of European Representation

One reason for an increased disillusionment, if this indeed exists, with national politics may be the increased complexity of relationships between purely domestic politics and politics at the level of 'Europe', especially the European Union. In the early 1980s, Gunnar Sjöblom suggested that people were suffering from 'information overload': they were confused by a never-ending stream of stories in the media about proposals, decisions and speculation, and were finding it increasingly difficult to be sure what was happening and who was responsible (Sjöblom, 1983, p. 385). Such confusion is heightened for citizens of the fifteen member states of the EU, who can hardly be blamed if they are unsure whether a particular policy emanates from their national government or from the EU and, if the latter, whether their government supported or opposed the policy. Holding the decision-makers accountable is particularly difficult when one does not know who they were.

The main mechanism supposedly providing some degree of democratic accountability within the EU is the European Parliament (EP), which, since June 1979, has been regularly directly elected for five-year terms. However, EP elections were soon branded 'second-order elections' (Reif and Schmitt, 1980) – that is to say, while national parliamentary elections were seen as the most important contest ('first-order elections'), EP elections, along with local elections, regional elections and by-elections were perceived by voters as of much less significance. In all second-order elections, the tendency is for turnout to be lower, and the vote for protest parties to be higher, than in first-order elections. In the 1994 EP elections, for example, little more than a half of the electorate across the EU turned out to vote, and in the Netherlands, Portugal and the UK turnout represented only about a third of the electorate. The main parties add to the air of apathy by presenting bland and indistinguishable manifestos (Irwin, 1995, pp. 192–3).

There is little evidence that EU citizens expect to have a particularly close relationship with any of their MEPs (see Bowler and Farrell (1993) for a discussion of this relationship). In eleven of the fifteen member states of the EU, EP elections are held under a national list system, under which the whole country is one large constituency – a similar electoral system to that which the Netherlands uses for domestic elections, as described in the first section of this chapter. This increases the proportionality of the outcome, but is not conducive to fostering links between citizens and MEPs. Belgium is divided into two constituencies, the Republic of Ireland into four, and Italy into five. Britain is divided into eighty-four single-member constituencies, each containing about 660 000 people, and Northern Ireland returns a further three members, elected under STV. One consequence of Britain's use of the first-past-the-post electoral system is that the size of the various party groupings within the EP itself is distorted. At the 1994 EP elections, for example, the Labour Party's share of the votes would have entitled it to only about 37 MEPs if a highly proportional electoral system had been used; in fact it won 62. In contrast, the Liberal Democrats would have won about fourteen seats but actually took only two. The distortion of representation in the EP caused by Britain's use of the single-member plurality system is one factor leading to pressure for the adoption of a common electoral system for future EP elections.

The likelihood that future EP elections will generate much more interest than past ones does not seem high. It is true that the power of the EP is growing – virtually every major landmark in the integration process, such as the Single European Act of 1986 and the Maastricht Treaty of 1992, has increased the influence of the EP. In many cases, though, this growth in influence is achieved by such byzantine methods (for example, the co-operation procedure or the co-decision procedure, both of which give the EP slightly more power to clip the wings of the Council of the EU) that they are quite unknown to the public. Indeed, the European public already has an inflated assessment of the power of the EP, and yet nearly half of all EU citizens do not turn out to vote in EP elections. Ironically, if people became better informed about the workings of the EU, they would learn that the EP is less powerful than they imagine, and thus they might be even less likely to vote (Irwin, 1995, p. 184).

Far from EP elections advancing in the public consciousness to become 'first-order elections', in fact, it may be more plausible to envisage domestic parliamentary elections slipping back to become themselves more like second-order elections. Voters may come to sense that policy is increasingly made by someone other than national governments; by the institutions of the EU, for example (conveniently summed up as 'Brussels', at least by all non-Belgians), or by global economic forces. National governments, especially in the smaller countries, may be perceived as being unable to do much more than tinker at the edges of policy. In addition, the vague and general nature of many party promises at election time, and (in many countries) uncertainty as to the likely composition of the next coalition government, all increase the likelihood, as Sjöblom puts it, of 'casual' parliamentary majorities – that is, majorities in parliament for policies on which the electorate has never passed judgement. The harder it then becomes to interpret an election result in terms of directives as to future policy guidelines, and thus the less the parties regard themselves as being bound by election outcomes, and so it becomes ever more difficult for the voters to hold public decision-makers accountable (Sjöblom, 1983, pp. 395–400). If this were to occur, we should expect national elections to start displaying the standard features of second-order elections, with turnout dropping and traditional major parties finding it increasingly difficult to retain the loyalty of their supporters in the face of an upsurge of activity by new parties. The fact that this describes reasonably accurately just what is happening in a number of European countries suggests that the provision of genuine democratic accountability will be a major problem in the years ahead.

8

European Party Systems: Continuity and Change

HERBERT KITSCHELT

The debate about the stability or change in contemporary Western European party systems is characterised by a cacophony of contradictory voices. On one side are those who see still the same old blocs of parties on the left and the right, large and small party machines, and dominance of parties' parliamentary and government leaders over the party membership. On the other side, some see a dramatic process of restructuring in European party systems with new parties, profound shifts of power and strategy within established parties, and novel forms of party organisation. Many of the seemingly contradictory views can be explained by distinguishing different types of party system change. I will first provide a simplified sketch of conventional post-Second World War European party systems and then turn to the changes in European polities since the 1960s or 1970s.

The Basic Structure of European Party Systems

In the late 1960s, Lipset and Rokkan (1967) explained the divisions and forces that shaped European party systems from their inception in the second half of the nineteenth century to the interwar period. The term 'cleavage' is the cornerstone of their analysis. Cleavages are lasting divisions (disagreements of interest or orientation) between social or political groups that may give rise to open conflict (Rae and Taylor, 1970, pp. 1–21). Cleavages can be based on the traits of individuals belonging to a group (socioeconomic position, race, religion, language), attitudes to which group members subscribe, and their joint group activities, that is, organisation and protest mobilisation.

Cleavages are strong when all three elements – traits, attitudes and activities – converge to shape the lines of conflict (Bartolini and Mair, 1990, pp. 213–20).

According to Seymour Martin Lipset and Stein Rokkan, societal divisions underlying party cleavages in European development derive from the national and industrial revolutions. The building of nation states pitted administrative centres, which attempted to extend extractive capacities (taxation) and build cultural identities over large territories of military rule, against peripheral, locally rooted elites. These processes gave rise to ethnic and regionalist centre–periphery conflicts later on. Further, the national revolution also placed the Catholic Church, as an international organisation, in conflict with state- and nation-building elites, triggering a religion–secularism or a Catholicism–Protestantism line of conflict. The industrial revolution first produced sectoral conflicts of interest between agriculture and industry, and later class conflicts between blue-collar workers and owners of capital.

How such social divisions translate into party alignments depends not simply on social development, but also on the ability of elites to craft alliances and co-opt groups. It would be wrong, therefore, to see Lipset and Rokkan's analysis simply as a sociological modernisation theory, applied to party formation, or as a 'sociology of politics' that treats political actors and institutions as the dependent variables. On the contrary, their comparative analysis focuses on the effect of elite interaction on the shape of emerging party systems (see Sartori, 1968). Class cleavages, dividing working class parties from parties representing farmers, small businesses, and salaried employees were an almost universal phenomenon by the late nineteenth century. Even here, elites were decisive in crafting the shape of the coalitions framing the class conflict. In some countries, elites who invoked Catholic social doctrine were able to split the working class and organise some workers into cross-class religious 'people's parties'. The emergence of religious cleavage lines, in turn, depended on ways in which the conflict over the reformation was settled among the elites in the seventeenth century and the extent to which Catholic concerns could be co-opted into conservative political parties, or left room for the independent mobilisation of Catholic lay activists (often against the express will of the Church). In a similar vein, whether the urban–rural division led to party alternatives representing the conflicting sides depends on the interweaving of socioeconomic change and elite action. Independent farmers' parties were more likely where medium-sized, independent family farms predominated, as in parts of Scandinavia or Switzerland.

In other countries, however, conservative elites, representing clerical interests, the large landlords, and bureaucratic layers of pre-democratic authoritarian states pre-empted the left or peasant parties from capturing the issue of land reform and engineered reforms under conservative auspices.

Up to the 1970s, descriptive accounts of European party systems identified six party system cleavages (see Lijphart, 1984, ch. 8). Along with class, religious, cultural–ethnic and urban–rural cleavages, such studies singled out conflicts over support of liberal democracy (with communists and fascists opposing it) and over foreign policy (national isolationists versus international integrationists). One may also divide European party systems more simply into three basic types of party system. The key to distinguishing these systems lies less in identifying the number of cleavages in each of them but rather in assessing how cleavages are interrelated. If two cleavages, say class and religion, pit the same groups against each other and are thus reinforcing, they create only one dimension of competition. In contrast, if one cleavage internally divides the groups that another cleavage pits against each other, we obtain cross-cutting cleavages and two-dimensional competition. For example, if all workers are secular and all business people and the self-employed are religious, competition is one-dimensional, although based on two cleavages. In contrast, if workers are divided into religious and secular groups, and business is divided over religion as well, we have two dimensions of competition.

The first type of party system in Europe embodies unidimensional left–right divisions in which the class cleavage over property rights and income distribution is structurally most salient. Parties run the gamut from the extreme left (communists, where significant) to the moderate left (social democrats) to centrist, and more or less moderate right-leaning pro-business parties (parties with the labels liberal, conservative, centre or people's parties). The first type of party system has only minor cross-cutting cleavages around the urban–rural divide, the religious dimension, or ethno-linguistic minorities. Cross-cutting is marginal, because on economic left–right issues, these cultural parties usually find themselves in the right or 'bourgeois' camp. Britain, Denmark, Finland, Norway, Sweden and most Mediterranean party systems (France, Greece, Portugal, Spain) are examples of this type of party system. Among the new post-communist party systems, the Czech Republic is likely to fall into this category (Kitschelt, 1995a).

The second type of party system combines two varieties of cleavage – class and religion – which crystallise around three party camps, yielding a triangular relation among parties in one and a half competitive dimensions. This system can be found in all those European countries where the Wars of Reformation were intense and where Catholic, Protestant and secular divisions are entrenched, such as in Austria, Germany, the Netherlands and Switzerland. Later, Italy joined this group, primarily because of the competition between the Pope and secular nation builders in the nineteenth century. In Eastern Europe, Hungary, Poland and some of the Baltic countries appear to be poised to join this group.

In the second type of party system, we encounter three large party families. First, there are secular socialist and communist parties. Second, there are secular bourgeois parties of different stripes. Third, there are strong religious parties that cross-cut the class cleavage and usually had overcome intradenominational divides by the early 1980s. Christian democratic parties often take a 'centrist' position on economic issues and thus become pivotal coalition makers between the forces of the economic left and right. From the time of the Second World War until the early 1990s, Christian Democrats in Italy, the Netherlands and Switzerland were never in the opposition and were pivotal for government coalition building. In Italy and the Netherlands, the Christian Democrats sometimes allied with the left and sometimes with the secular right.

The third type of party system is a residual category of true multidimensionality, sometimes generated by ethno-cultural conflict. Among European countries, Belgium is the single party system with more than one-and-a-half dimensions of competition. Here the tripolar division of liberal, Christian and socialist party camps familiar from the second type of party system is supplemented by a cross-cutting ethno-linguistic division that generated its own parties and eventually divided the conventional three-party families into Flemish and Walloon organisations. One might be tempted also to include the Republic of Ireland in this third category. There, class divisions are overlaid and muted by national divisions originating in the war of independence against Britain. It is likely that many post-communist party systems of Eastern Europe and the former Soviet Union with sizeable ethnic minorities will develop multidimensional competition with ethno-cultural cleavages.

Had there been no change in European party systems, we would expect the basic camps or 'blocs' of parties in each of the three types of system to have remained the same from the end of the Second World War to the present. In the famous conclusion to their essay of 1967, Lipset and Rokkan asserted as much, at least for the period 1945–65. The freezing of party systems is built on mechanisms such as the identification of voters with a party, based on their own repeated support for that party, or their parents' support, and the parties' ability to 'encapsulate' large segments of the electorate through party membership or participation in affiliated civic organisations (unions, churches, cultural associations). Lipset and Rokkan's freezing hypothesis accommodates change in parties' issue appeals and change in the party labels, as long as the basic blocs and divisions remain the same.

Three Ways of Thinking about Party System Change

It is least controversial to argue that party systems change by changing appeals of existing parties. Parties adapt their message and organisational form to appeal to new constituencies and voter preferences (this I will refer to as 'level I change'). This change leaves the basic party alternatives and lines of division in place. More controversial is the extent to which party systems have a propensity to create new parties that displace the existing competitors. In this regard, we can distinguish two further modes of change. Either the ideological 'blocs' in which parties compete remain the same, but old party organisations are replaced by new organisations ('level II change'), or new parties appear precisely because the main alternatives can no longer be accommodated in existing ideological blocs. The change of competitors coincides with a change of cleavage structures and competitive dimensions ('level III change').

There is general agreement that level II change (new parties, but old issues and alignments) is a fairly marginal phenomenon. Level II change tends to occur when existing parties make strategic mistakes in their electoral appeals and precipitate factionalisation and ultimately the split of parties. For example, in the late 1970s, the British Labour Party embraced a left agenda calling for unilateral disarmament and the nationalisation of corporations. As a consequence, moderate social democrats founded their own party, most of whose members eventually joined the British liberals. This example also teaches us that new parties can be sustained only if they have a distinctive issue appeal on a dimension of competition neglected by the dominant parties (Harmel and Robertson, 1985).

The significance of level III change in European party systems where new issues spawn new parties is controversial among political scientists. Sometimes old parties can co-opt new issues, but more often than not they face trade-offs that cannot easily be overcome. In order to get voters driven by new issue appeals, they may have to give up voters in their core electorate who oppose the new appeals. For example, appeals to environmental protection and feminism enable social democrats to attract young, educated and female voters, but tend to reduce loyalty among older, male, blue-collar constituencies. Similarly, Christian Democrats may win racist voters if they advertise tighter immigration laws, but they may lose their Christian–humanist educated constituencies. Hence, level III changes of party systems are not simply a consequence of unresponsive politicians in established parties. These politicians are rational, informed, calculating beings – but sometimes they face hard choices with trade-offs forcing them to sacrifice voters to new competitors. In addition, of course, institutional features of the settings in which parties operate may facilitate or constrain the occurrence of level III change. Electoral laws are one obvious, but often overstated constraint on party system change. Plurality and majority laws make it harder, but not impossible, for new parties to establish themselves, compared to the ease with which new competitors can enter systems of proportional representation. Also, the internal organisation of the existing parties matters. The more conventional parties are tied to mass organisations with networks of clientelism and patronage, the more internal status quo interests may silence innovative politicians who could widen a party's vote base.

Societal Forces Promoting Party System Change

Socioeconomic and political achievements of the 1945–73 period provide the backdrop against which the subsequent impact of markets and political institutions on political cleavage structures can be assessed. I do not wish to suggest a one-to-one correspondence of social changes and party system changes. Socioeconomic transformations, however, are catalysts prompting strategic politicians in conventional parties to alter their appeals. Where such efforts fail, the door is open to new parties. Because conventional parties often do adjust their appeal to new constituencies, it is likely that changes in party system formats (level III changes) are considerably slower and more muted than are socioeconomic changes.

Setting aside the sometimes substantial cross-national variations within Europe, the post-Second World War period is characterised by the rise of the Keynesian Welfare State (KWS) (Offe, 1983) (see Chapter 4 above). In this era, international trade gradually became more competitive, although capital flows were still constrained by domestic market regulations. Because businesses could not easily leave a country, they had considerable incentives to bargain with labour in order to accomplish a positive-sum compromise of interests. This compromise entailed labour's abstention from calls for the redistribution of property and income, and from militant labour action, in exchange for capital's concessions on rising real wages, an almost unconditional reinvestment of profits, and acceptance of a comprehensive social safety network, including retirement pensions and health and unemployment insurance.

In most countries, governments provided a range of other public services and benefits (housing, child care, education subsidies, and so on) in the 1960s and 1970s. Rising real wage costs were offset by increasing labour productivity that accompanied mass production systems relying on economies of scale and scope. Bolstered by this mix of technology, international trade relations and class co-operation, parties staked out marginally different stances on the extent of the 'mixed economy' and its mildly redistributive implications. They competed primarily along an economic left–right dimension, but within an overall centripetal dynamic. In contrast, three changes in the societal parameters that impinge on the mobilisation of political demands and party choice characterises the period from the early 1970s to the present.

First, in the technological arena, the electronic revolution has partially displaced mass production systems with flexible specialisation. This has triggered a continued fall of the ratio of production workers to service workers (business, personal and social). This in turn has led to an increasing demand for better skills and a decreasing demand for unskilled or semi-skilled labour. Moreover, falling transportation and communication costs exposed more economic sectors to international competition. All these trends increased demands on educational systems. Second, international competition in manufacturing markets became fiercer as newly-industrialising countries emerged. This depressed wages in all European industries facing new competitors. Where European producers tried to escape competition by moving up-market to more refined products, they called for more sophisticated human capital and reinforced the demand for a more skilled labour force. What is likely to have been even more consequential for political change, however, is the gradual opening of capital markets (banking, stock markets, direct foreign investment) that allowed business to exit from countries where the labour–capital compromise had yielded below-average profit rates. The internationalisation of capital flows thus led to a shift of bargaining power away from labour to capital and thus to a containment of wages and pressures to stabilise or reduce the 'social wage' component required to finance the welfare state.

Third, welfare states underwent considerable change after the mid-1970s. On the one hand, they expanded further, as an ageing population, higher unemployment and the entry of women in the labour markets enticed many governments to extend benefits and to employ more public-sector workers. On the other hand, the rigours of international competition limited further welfare state expansion, as did the increasingly controversial social and moral consequences of the citizens' dependence on public services.

The expansion, the overhaul and the occasional retrenchment of welfare states are mediated by political institutions and party struggles for power (Esping-Andersen, 1990). In a similar vein, the evolution of technological production regimes and economic governance structures, such as the internationalisation of trade and finance, are embedded in political–institutional contexts (see Piore and Sabel, 1984; Scharpf, 1991). Conversely, these changes in technology, international competition and welfare states affect politics, exposing a growing number of sectors to international competition, by increasing the demand and supply of education, by expanding client-interactive jobs, and by expanding, and later contracting, public employment.

International competition and welfare state expansion reinvigorated economic left–right divisions. Now, however, the conflict is less between classes than between sectors. Private business, management, and employees exposed to international competition tend to opt for a greater containment of redistributive measures and to be more concerned about containing production costs than about people working in protected industries or in the public sector. At the same time, the spread of higher education and the expansion of social services boosted the importance of a second dimension of political competition. Well-educated people working in client-interactive and cultural-symbol-producing jobs generally value individual autonomy and egalitarian participation in collective decision-making; that is, a 'libertarian' organisation of society that enhances cultural and political diversity. In contrast, less-educated people working in manual labour or clerical jobs tend to favour conformity, authority and cultural homogeneity; that is, a more 'authoritarian' political–cultural organisation. The division between libertarians and authoritarians became salient in the context of changing gender roles, public demands for environmental protection and technology regulation, conflicts over the arms race, and Europe's changing demographic profile with the influx of foreign workers and political refugees.

An overall view of the emerging landscape of political preferences shows a general shift towards more pro-capitalist, market-orientated views (because of intensified international competition more than the collapse of the communist world empire), and libertarian views on life-styles (because of higher educational levels, changing occupational profiles and gender relations). At the individual level and in the distribution of preferences within each country, however, libertarian views tend to go together with more redistributive 'left' economic views. Highly-educated individuals in client-interactive jobs tend to be employed in sectors that are insensitive to international competition (such as the welfare state or private personal and social services). Conversely, authoritarian views tend to be more commonly expressed by those who also endorse economic pro-market rightist views. Right-authoritarianism is more common among small businessmen and farmers. Less-educated blue-collar workers and clerical workers tend to turn to right-authoritarian political agendas when their traditional vehicles of political representation, such as communist or social democratic parties, cater too much to libertarian demands.

The distribution of popular political preferences in the 1980s and 1990s has had important consequences for political parties that used to compete almost exclusively on economic bread-and-butter issues or on religion, a waning independent cleavage division everywhere in Europe. Because of a shrinking blue-collar constituency (particularly of un-skilled workers) and increasing international competition, left parties have little choice but to favour more pro-market policies, containing welfare state spending and deregulating business activities. Otherwise, they tend to fare badly, especially among younger and more highly-educated white-collar employees and skilled technicians. In contrast, traditional leftist blue-collar constituencies who vote on economics have no alternative to conventional left parties, even if the latter support moderate policies. Such voters, however, may give less salience to economic issues in the new social environment and instead vote on non-economic issues. This brings to the fore the most difficult dilemma for left parties: if they champion libertarian demands (for women's emancipation, ecology, disarmament or, multiculturalisation), they attract more highly-educated white-collar employees and more young women, but they are likely to lose blue-collar workers, particularly among young male workers expressing little identification with left parties and labour unions, and of working-class retirees who dislike libertarian themes. If social democrats stick to conventional leftist themes, they risk losing voters who are mobilised by the political–cultural agenda. This opens the door for the rise of a new 'left-libertarian' cohort of parties that run under left socialist (Scandinavia, Netherlands in the 1970s), green or ecological (Austria, Belgium, France, Germany, Italy, the Netherlands, Sweden, Switzerland), or radical labels (Italy, the Netherlands in the 1970s) and over-proportionally draws on women and public-sector professionals.

Moderate rightist parties, such as Christian Democrats and liberals, face a dilemma that mirrors that of the left. In economic terms, such parties have an unambiguous incentive to move towards the pro-market right. In political–cultural terms, however, they may choose between more moderate positions and a pronounced anti-ecological, anti-feminist, national and ethno-centrist agenda. If they choose the former, the losers of the economic modernisation process, unskilled and semi-skilled workers, and white-collar employees disaffected with social democracy, also small businesses, farmers and retirees formerly close to the conventional moderate right, may turn to new right-authoritarian parties that run under labels such as the National Front (Britain, France, Wallonia) or the Progress Party (Denmark, Norway). In other countries, the labels, and sometimes the appeal, as well as the electoral support coalition of the new right diverge to a certain extent from the right-authoritarian ideal type, but they still incorporate some of its essential elements. This applies to Austria's Freedom Party, the Flemish Vlaams Bloc, Germany's Republicans, Italy's Northern League, the Dutch Centre Party and the Swiss anti-ecological Automobilists' Party (Kitschelt, 1995b). If moderate conservative parties choose a more radical right-authoritarian appeal, however, they risk losing voters in the political centre, such as highly-educated business professionals, engineers, technicians, and also a large proportion of younger women who may endorse a pro-capitalist policy, but are closer to libertarian political–cultural orientations.

Which strategy is optimal for moderate right and left parties depends on (a) the distribution of voters over economic and political–cultural issues; (b) the competitive situation in a country as characterised by the number and location of competing parties in the left-libertarian versus right-authoritarian space; and (c) the parties' strategic objectives. Where parties seek government office above all, they may choose to sacrifice voters to more radical left-libertarian or right-authoritarian parties, provided that puts them in a better position to control pivotal voters and obtain a strategic bargaining position in which no government can be formed against them. As a consequence, where the left is in office, left-libertarian parties increase their chances of making electoral inroads. Conversely, where the right is in office, and particularly where conventional leftist and rightist parties have converged in their policy positions, new right-authoritarian challengers face favourable opportunities.

The general model of change presented here does not forecast that conventional parties configured around traditional economic or waning religious cleavages will uniformly decline everywhere. Differences in the development of economic relations, welfare states, cultural interpretations and the strategic configurations of party systems are too great. On average, though, three hypotheses ought to hold true. First, wherever significant new parties have made inroads in the party systems of European democracies since 1970 (level III change), they belong to the left-libertarian or to the right-authoritarian party families, but not to other party families (hypothesis 1). Second, where in the 1960s the party systems were differentiated by a high number of effective parties, existing parties could more readily absorb new political issues by altering appeals (hypothesis 2). Third, where party systems in the 'golden age' of the Keynesian welfare state thrived on patronage, clientelism and highly segmented sub-societies, conventional parties have experienced a steep decline in the ensuing decades caused by a triple dynamic (hypothesis 3). These parties have great difficulties in altering their popular message because a conservative party rank-and-file constrains the leadership's strategic mobility. Moreover, a highly-educated, independently-minded electorate in the 1980s and 1990s perceives clientelist networks as a fount of corruption and lack of fairness. Finally, private enterprise associates clientelism and corruption with an increase in the cost of doing business and has been more opposed to it as international competition has increased.

The Emergence of New Parties and Changes in the Competitive Space of European Democracies

If the first hypothesis is correct, we can expect level III change to be moderately strong and to yield only left-libertarian and right-authoritarian new parties. As far as left-libertarian parties are concerned, just about all of the larger established European democracies, with the exception of Britain, now have parties of this family. They command between 4 per cent and 15 per cent of the electorate. In Austria, Belgium, Finland, France, Germany, Italy, the Netherlands, Sweden and Switzerland, these parties run under 'green' or 'ecology' party labels. The 'greening' of former left-socialist, workerist, radical-liberal or even communist parties pre-empted the rise of ecology parties in Denmark and Norway and, to a lesser extent, in Italy and Sweden. A hybrid case is the Netherlands, where small left socialist, left Catholic, and even communist parties joined hands and formed a 'Green Progressive' party. Moreover, in the Netherlands a liberal reformist party of the 1960s, Democrats '66, has moved energetically into the left-libertarian political sector (see Müller-Rommel, 1989).

Government participation by social democrats reduced their strategic flexibility *vis-à-vis* new libertarian issue challenges and facilitated the rise of these parties (see Müller-Rommel, 1982). The existence of encompassing labour unions tightly linked to social democratic parties and by corporatist labour relations also limited the flexibility of the conventional left (Kitschelt, 1988). Only in the Netherlands were social democrats able to fend off the left-libertarian challenge, but they did so at the price of going, with one brief exception, to the parliamentary opposition benches from 1977 to 1989 (see Kitschelt, 1994, pp. 149–54).

Right-authoritarian parties have also arisen in a number of countries. They have been especially successful in Belgium (Vlaams Blok, National Front), France (National Front) and Switzerland (Automobilists' Party and the former National Action), and to a lesser extent, but also in Denmark (Progress Party) and Norway (Progress Party). In all these cases, party activists and electorates combine the elements of the right-authoritarian disposition: pro-market economics and authoritarian, anti-ecological, ethno-centrist orientations. Other parties that are often lumped together with the pure right-authoritarian parties are more mixed cases, as they combine a spectrum of demands broader than the right-authoritarian core. This applies to the Austrian Freedom Party, a formerly liberal party, and the Italian Northern League. These parties thrive on the decline of the highly segmented, pillarised and clientelistic Christian democratic and socialist parties, and attract broader strata of voters with generalised anti-party and anti-state appeals.

In other countries, right-wing extremists have either not adopted the winning right-authoritarian electoral formula necessary to attract a substantial electorate, or the competitive configuration has been unfavourable to the extreme right. Although the policies of Germany's conventional left and right parties converged in the 1980s and thus offered favourable conditions for the rise of a right-authoritarian party, German unification and the inability of the extreme rightists to combine ethno-centrist and authoritarian appeals with a free market message limited their success in attracting a stable, lasting constituency. In Britain, the Netherlands and Sweden, the continued polarisation of left and right parties throughout the 1980s made conditions unfavourable for the rise of an extreme right. In Britain, the first-past-the-post electoral system is often blamed for the lack of left-libertarian and right-authoritarian parties. That system, however, did not prevent the return of the liberals, the surge of social democrats after 1982, or the electoral growth of the National Front in the first half of the 1970s before Margaret Thatcher incorporated a nationalist–populist rhetoric in the Conservative Party's strategic appeal.

My first hypothesis about party system change rules out significant level II change; that is, the emergence of new parties within the existing cleavage structures and dimensions of competition. Do European political systems sustain this part of the argument? There is only a single country, the United Kingdom, where a new party, the Social Democratic Party after 1982, achieved moderate success by situating itself on the conventional economic left–right axis. The party grew from the split in the Labour Party after its sharp turn to the left in 1979–81. The social democrats soon joined forces with the liberals, but the electoral support of the new alliance was squeezed in the 1987 and 1992 general elections by the gradual return of the Labour Party to a more centrist position. In none of the other larger European democracies have new parties been able to establish a substantial and persistent following by appealing to established cleavage lines.

A search for other new parties not located on the left-libertarian–right-authoritarian axis yields a similarly negative result. Even ethno-regionalist parties, such as those of Flanders and Wallonia, have been unable to sustain the temporary electoral surge they enjoyed in the late 1960s and early 1970s. Conventional parties co-opted their issues and electorates, or ethnic parties transformed themselves into right-authoritarian parties (for example, Vlaams Blok).

Overall, developments in European party politics provide evidence for level III change. Is this, however, enough to speak of a radical transformation of European party politics? Or are those who see continuity correct in their assessment that conventional parties have shown astounding robustness and demonstrated the longevity of 'frozen' cleavages? After all, new parties have siphoned off only 10 per cent to 20 per cent of the votes from conventional parties since the 1960s (Mair, 1993). My answer is yes and no. The rise of the new parties is only one of many changes in the programmatic appeal, strategic posturing, and electoral coalitions configured around all parties in European party systems, including the conventional parties. For this reason, it is more important than the limited shift in electorates to the new contenders may indicate. Advocates of the continuity thesis ignore the substantial changes in message and appeal initiated by conventional parties. One should add, howerver, that this change would not have taken place had it not been for the challenge created by new left-libertarian and right-authoritarian parties.

The Resilience of Conventional Parties

Even where we observe only muted level III change, there is still substantial level I change in the appeal and electoral coalitions of conventional parties. On the left, communist, socialist and social democratic parties have had to cope with the shrinking base of blue-collar workers and a larger, heterogeneous base of white-collar ones. Depending on the seriousness of the left-libertarian challenge and the strategic situation of parties on the right, social democrats have either sacrificed votes to maintain their hold on government, or competed for left-libertarian votes and gone over to the opposition. In some instances, they were bogged down by a stalemate between labour unionist and left-libertarian factions, and therefore could not follow any consistent strategic response.

Christian democrats, on the moderate right, had to deal with the progressive secularisation of societies that enabled liberal parties in some countries to compete for their voters with increasing success (such as in Belgium and the Netherlands). Just as social democrats in the 1980s and 1990s are often haunted by close linkages to labour unions, Christian democrats are particularly vulnerable to decline where they are entrenched in clientelistic and patronage relations between state and party, which is true of Austria, Italy and, to a lesser extent, Belgium. Where clientelistic patronage systems were weaker or quickly dismantled in the 1960s, Christian democrats declined little, which was the case in Germany and the Netherlands after 1980. As international market competition has become more salient, socio-economic change has benefited secular liberal and conservative pro-market parties. This, in turn, has fuelled their efforts to open markets further in order to solidify their advantages. Whether their fortunes have improved, however, depends on the strategic choices of Christian democratic and new radical rightist party politicians. Liberals and conservatives were most successful when they polarised politics around economic issues and Christian democrats joined in their stark, free-market stances. Right-authoritarian parties failed electorally where a strong liberal free-market party dominated the conservative spectrum. This is true of Britain, Belgium, Denmark, the Netherlands and Sweden in the 1980s.

In the Scandinavian countries, liberals and conservatives also fed off of the decline of agrarian centre parties. To win new voters in the 1970s, the latter tried to adopt the libertarian themes of political decentralisation and environmental protection. These efforts, however, split the parties' old, culturally conservative constituencies from the new constituencies they sought to attract. Moreover, when centre parties entered coalitions with liberal and conservative partners, the libertarian agenda had to be abandoned. System change at level I also characterises changes in party organisation. In most countries, as measured by member–voter or member–electorate ratio, mass party organisations across the political spectrum have eroded gradually. This change, however, is not the most telling indicator of organisational transformation (see Katz and Mair, 1992). More important is the change in the relationship among activists at different levels within parties.

Within the left-libertarian parties, new 'stratarchal' organisational patterns have emerged to create national and regional party leaders who are relatively independent of local party activists (Kitschelt, 1989). Social democratic and socialist parties that also succeeded in creating a relatively autonomous leadership by shedding mass party organisations and simultaneously empowering rank-and-file members and activists at the local level, appear to have been most strategically flexible in the 1970s and 1980s. At least, where left-libertarian challenges were strong, they were able to protect their electoral market share (Kitschelt, 1994, ch. 5). Based on thorough comparative research, Mair (1994, p. 15) finds similar changes at the top and the bottom of European party organisations: 'the somewhat curious pattern that is developing, therefore, seems to be one in which the party in public office is afforded more power or more autonomy; in which the party in central office is becoming more professionalised; and in which, at the same time, through enhanced democratisation, the ordinary members themselves, albeit sometimes fewer in number, are being afforded a greater role'. Although grassroots democratisation is sometimes a ruse leaders use to have members acclaim pre-structured decisions or to weaken the influence of meddlesome middle-level activists who wish to control the party leadership, more often than not the new structures reflect the strategic quandary of party leaders and their need for input from below at a time when clear ideological roadmaps are no longer available.

What enables conventional parties to hold on to electoral market shares? On average, parties that had more than 5 per cent of the parliamentary seats in the decade of the 1960s, or in the election closest following 1960, lost 11.2 per cent by the decade from 1985–94, or 14.3

per cent when compared to the election closest to 1994 (see Table 8.1). Countries which had more party system fragmentation in the 1960s indeed show a greater resilience of the conventional parties in the 1980s and early 1990s, but the correlations are weak. The existence of powerful patronage and clientelist networks in party politics, as they existed in Austria, Belgium, Italy and to a certain extent in Switzerland in the 1960s, however, is a very strong determinant of the decline of conventional parties. Whereas the conventional parties of the other eight countries listed in Table 8.1 declined on average by 9.2 per cent between 1960 and 1994, conventional parties in the four countries with clientelist patronage structures experienced a loss of no less than 24.5 per cent. This finding strongly suggests that clientelism increases the strategic immobility of parties and makes them prey to new competitors.

'Europe' as a Cleavage Line and Dimension of Competition in Party Systems?

Although an increasing range of policy issues is determined by negotiations at the level of the European Union and although the European Parliament has gradually gained some power over legislation, the budget, and the governing personnel of the EU, there is little evidence of a European cleavage dimension either in national or in European elections themselves. Is there a chance that the European integration will trigger party system change at level I, even at level III (new parties around a cross-cutting pro- versus anti-European cleavage), as European policy-making becomes more important?

Up to now, European elections have attracted far lower turnouts than have national elections in countries where voting is not compulsory. Voters attribute little salience to European issues, and politicians generally use European elections as a foil for domestic purposes (Lange and Davidson-Schmich, 1995). European elections are typical 'secondary elections' (Reif and Schmitt, 1980) that work much like American mid-term elections. More often than not, they generate a backlash against the nationally governing parties. They are favourite forums for ambitious political entrepreneurs to test the electoral pull of new parties. Many left-libertarian and right-authoritarian parties in Europe savoured a first success in European elections. Nevertheless, there is some cross-national variance in the significance of European integration as an issue in national party competition. For this reason, it is worth while speculating about the salience that conflicts between

TABLE 8.1 *The decline of established parties from 1960 to 1994*

	Strength of established parties in national elections (in %)			
	Closely following 1960	In the period from 1960–69	In the period from 1985–94	Close to 1994
Austria	96.4 (1962)	96.4	74.0	62.6 (1994)
Belgium	94.0 (1961)	91.7	83.1	77.6 (1991)
Denmark	92.7 (1960)	93.8	81.6	84.8 (1994)
Finland	92.2 (1962)	94.3	81.3	81.1 (1991)
France	87.9 (1962)	92.7	80.8	73.5 (1993)
Germany	94.3 (1961)	95.1	88.1	85.0 (1994)
Italy	97.2 (1963)	95.0	76.6	70.0 (1992)
Netherlands	87.5 (1963)	85.4	87.6	81.6 (1994)
Norway	89.4 (1961)	90.6	89.9	90.1 (1993)
Sweden	95.5 (1960)	93.2	84.3	82.6 (1994)
Switzerland	90.3 (1963)	90.6	76.5	69.6 (1991)
United Kingdom	87.5 (1964)	88.7	74.4	76.0 (1992)

Note:

Parties included:

Austria: People's Party and Social Democrats, Freedom Party only in the 1960s.

Belgium: Liberals, Christian Democrats, Socialists and Flemish People's Union.

Denmark: Conservatives, Liberals, Radicals, Social Democrats, Socialist People's Party.

Finland: National Coalition, Swedish People's Party, Liberals, Agrarians, Social Democrats and Communists.

France: Gaullists, Independent Republicans, Socialists + Allies, Communists.

Germany: Christian Democrats, Social Democrats and Free Democrats.

Italy: Italian Social Movement, Christian Democrats, Liberals, Social Democrats, Socialists and Communists.

The Netherlands: Religious Parties later combined in the Christian Democratic Appeal, United Freedom Party, Democrats '66 and Labour Party.

Sweden: Conservatives, Liberals, Centre and Social Democrats.

Switzerland: Catholics, Radicals/Liberals, Swiss People's Party, Independents, Social Democrats.

United Kingdom: Conservatives and Labour Party.

supporters of national autonomy and advocates of further European integration acquire in different European countries.

First, domestic opposition to European integration may be particularly vocal in countries with exceptionally large or small welfare states.

Large and redistributive welfare states prompt anti-European feelings among supporters of the economic left, who fear that integration will require a levelling-down of social benefits and protection to near a European norm in order to enable domestic industries to stay competitive. Conversely, in countries with small welfare states, the economic right may see integration as an inflationary source of demands for new entitlements. The contours of these divisions are clearest in the Scandinavian countries with large welfare states, and Britain with an exceptionally weak welfare state.

Second, European integration may be controversial in countries that are large net contributors to the European Common Agricultural Market and the Structural Fund. Particularly in countries that are net contributors to these schemes of subsidisation, the economic right might oppose further European integration for fear of further political intervention in markets. Third, beyond these economic factors, countries' foreign-policy trajectories – whether or not they are NATO members or had a colonial empire – may affect national politicians' willingness to support European integration. Fourth, European integration tends to be more politicised within countries deliberating entry or having recently entered. In the original member states, further European integration tends to be a valence, not a positional issue that divides parties.

Taking these four variables, the Benelux countries, France, Germany and Italy have the least potential for political mobilisation around European integration on more than a single-election, single-issue basis. The same applies to countries that are major beneficiaries of EU largesse (Greece, the Republic of Ireland, Portugal and Spain, for example). Here, politicisation might only intensify if the accession of East Central European countries to the EU were to syphon off subsidies now going to Southern Europe. As countries with a high potential for a party politicisation of the European issue this leaves the Scandinavians (including the non-member Norway), Britain, Austria and the non-member Switzerland. Austria is far too integrated into the German economy to make Europe an issue. In Scandinavia, the main opposition to European integration now comes from the left, where anxieties about dismantling the welfare state are a concern. In Britain, with a small and residual welfare state, the right opposes further European integration because the Conservatives believe that Britain, now a significant net contributor to the EU, should not also be forced to expand its welfare state. In Switzerland, finally, opposition to European integration is likely to come from the right and the left. The left is concerned about abandoning the country's neutrality and the right is wary of new social policy burdens and large net contributions to the European budget.

Despite having the potential for creating domestic conflict, it is unrealistic to expect Europe to emerge as a major salient issue in the near future. Much of European legislation is of a highly technical nature, with few broad redistributive implications. Moreover, the principle of subsidiarity guarantees that many of the issues that divide left-libertarians from right-authoritarians will remain on national, if not on subnational, levels of policy-making.

Conclusion

Is there change in European party systems? Or were Lipset and Rokkan correct when they emphasised the essentially 'frozen' nature of European party alignments in the 1960s? As this overview shows, there are no easy answers. There is little doubt that socioeconomic change has brought about profound level I change in party systems. The conventional parties have to cater to changing electoral constituencies and coalitions. In the course of this process, they have also been swept up in a reform of organisational party structures that has eroded the old mass party model. At level II, where new parties within established political cleavages and competitive dimensions appear, there has been only negligible change since the 1960s. At level III, where new parties coincide with the change of cleavages and competitive dimensions, moderate change has taken place. A net decline of conventional parties amounting to an average of 14 per cent electoral support since 1960 may not sound like much. It is, however, in part causally responsible for what change has taken place at level I. Conventional parties would have lost even more votes had they not responded to new-left-libertarian and right-authoritarian challengers by adopting new messages and strategies.

What characterises both level I and level III changes, however, is the move away from parties that resemble assembly lines and department stores, offering everything to everyone, to parties that are more akin to craftshops and boutiques, catering to more sophisticated and discriminating customers. In most party systems, and particularly in those that were least fragmented in 1960, or governed through clientelism and patronage, the effective number of parties has increased. In a more crowded field, parties have been compelled to tailor their products more closely to the constituencies they intend to target. In this sense, the opposite of Kirchheimer's (1966) expectation of 'catch-all' parties appears to have taken hold in European politics. Moreover, even where large encompassing parties persist, they have experienced pressures to change their organisational form to respond more flexibly to the demands of specific constituencies. Flexible specialisation is thus not only the key word for post-Fordist production systems, but also for change in West European party systems.

9

Organised Interests and the State

COLIN CROUCH AND ANAND MENON

Any group, where its members perceive that they share certain interests and could promote these interests further by some organised action – in particular, action aimed at some level of political authority – may be regarded as an interest group. Therefore, the range of issues with which groups are concerned, the means they use to advance them, and the power that they wield can all vary enormously. In this chapter we shall be concerned mainly with functional interests in Western European societies: that is, those groups based on the performance of some function within the economy, though some references will be made to such promotional or pressure groups as environmental organisations. For reasons of space, we shall largely neglect local and regional action (see Chapter 11), concentrating on the diverse range of interest groups at the levels of the nation-state and the European Union.

Patterns of Organised Interests

This diversity – and the impact of changes in it occurring under the pressure of economic globalisation – will be surveyed here in terms of five broad types of pattern of organised interests: pluralism, elitism, *étatisme*, neo-corporatism and consociationism.

First, *pluralism* describes a situation in which a wide range of organised interests represent their members and lobby on their behalf. The state rarely initiates policy collaboration with the organisations, and the organisations accept little responsibility for policy outcomes. This model of organised interests in many respects describes the US polity and is less dominant in Western Europe, apart from the United Kingdom. Pluralism is closely associated with liberal political arrangements, where barriers to system entry are low and governments unlikely to be pro-active. One might also expect pluralism to be dominant where there are large numbers of actors who have not aggregated their interests (provided there are no hindrances to associational formation), as in relatively new or rapidly-changing sectors, such as advanced electronics and computer industries (Cawson, 1994), geographical areas in rapid growth where settled community networks have not yet developed, or small businesses in unregulated sectors.

Pluralist analyses have been criticised by proponents of other approaches. In response, pluralists formulated a 'neo-pluralist' analysis (Dunleavy and O'Leary, 1987, ch. 6), making particular use of the concept of 'policy network' which demonstrates that, in certain circumstances, interests can form relatively stable and consistent relationships with parts of the state machinery. A network can be defined as an 'identifiable group of interacting bureaucrats, interest group representatives and (to a lesser extent) politicians whose purposes are sufficiently interdependent to seek to co-operate in achieving them' (Hayward, 1995, p. 235). The notion of network enables us better to describe the forms of interaction which link the state to organised interests. While a defining feature of policy networks is their stability, they can vary widely according to membership and degrees of integration, from relatively loose and open issue networks to closed and highly collusive policy communities. While policy network analysis has developed within pluralist theory, there is no reason to assume that such networks always exist under conditions of easy and open access to participation; they can be found among any of the forms being discussed here.

Indeed, one has to be careful that pluralism is not used loosely to refer to situations in which only a very partial selection of interests is organised. For example, if employers are easily able to organise, but not employees; or businesses, but not customers; polluters, but not environmentalists, we should not really speak of pluralism but of a second form of system: *elitism*. Elitism is a form of interest system in which a restricted range of interests gains a monopoly of access to the state. This might happen because the barriers to entry for collective organisation are high and skewed, or because potentially opposing interests are too weak.

Third, under *étatiste* regimes the state takes the leading role in allocating functions to organised interests and in choosing its partners in policy networks. This contrasts with both pluralism and elitism in that the state is here strongly pro-active. It contrasts further with pluralism, though not with elitism, in that the number and range of interests the state wishes to make use of is likely to be small. As the use of a French word for the phenomenon suggests, such systems have been associated historically with the French state, which throughout the nineteenth century developed a strong steering role in the modernisation of its society. Its main mode of action for this was regulation. Sometimes groups would organise in order to resist or try to amend regulation, leading to oppositional associations very different from the kind of chosen media for communication with social interests established by the state itself; for example, manual workers, small businesses and farmers. Similar patterns are sometimes found in countries which in part imitated French central administrative practices: Italy, Belgium, and to some extent Spain, after its release from dictatorship.

Fourth, *corporatism* describes a form of organisational behaviour in which associations, while representing the particular interests of their members, also discipline them in the interests of some wider collectivity. To behave in such a manner, organisations need a well-articulated, hierarchical structure. There must also be a smaller number of organisations than under pluralism – more similar to elitist and *étatiste* situations. If members are to be disciplined by their representative organisations, it is important that they do not have alternative associations to choose from. This limitation to competition refers only to alternative associations for members with a single interest: for example, employers' associations. Corporatist structures do not necessarily inhibit competition between organisations representing opposed or different interests.

Within Europe corporatism has mainly been associated with Germany, Austria and Scandinavia. In the case of Germany and Austria, the growth of the modern state took the form of an association between the state and certain producer interests – very different from either the *laissez faire* model of Britain and the USA, or the more state-centred French model (Crouch, 1993, ch. 10). Originally, the range of interests admitted to such structures was narrow, but in the postwar democratic period it has extended to cover employee interests.

Scandinavian systems developed mainly under the pressure of very strongly organised employer and employee interests that during the interwar years had been locked in bitter conflict. Within these small economies on the fringe of Europe this had been considered dangerous during the difficult interwar years, and patterns of joint regulation on a corporatist basis developed. In neither Scandinavian nor German corporatism is the state necessarily very active, provided associations are regulating matters in what the government considers to be a satisfactory way.

Some sectors tend to be corporatist, whatever the overall pattern within the country. Agriculture is the most outstanding example (Keeler, 1987). This is a sector which, in industrial societies, is nearly always subject to some kind of price and production regulation, the vagaries of harvests being difficult to integrate with precise calculations of supply and demand, while it is difficult even in a strong *étatiste* system of the French type to achieve regulation without the co-operation of a large number of producers.

Corporatism might enable the various participants in a market economy to achieve a high level of co-operation and perhaps serve a wider public interest, despite the fact that they are also in competition with each other. Since associations of economic actors might normally be expected to pursue their collective interests at the expense of the wider public – for example, by forming special-interest lobbies and protectionist cartels – associations will act in a corporatist way only under certain specific situations of organisational design (Olson, 1982; Crouch, 1993, chs 1–3).

Finally, *consociationism* is a term of more specific application than corporatism. At the same time, it is broader, being used to describe whole systems of politics and not just organised interests. It describes a situation in which large groups sharing important and politically relevant characteristics are able to co-operate with other groups having different, even opposed, characteristics. Co-operation is possible because, although members of the groups live rather segregated lives, the leading elites co-operate in the management of the system as a whole. The concept was developed to describe the way in which potentially conflicting religious communities in the Netherlands (Catholics, Calvinists and agnostics) produced a co-operative, peaceful society (Lijphart, 1977). It has been extended to other examples where religious, ethnic or other deep cultural divisions within societies are managed through organisations embodying some mix of mass segregation and elite co-operation.

Consociationism might be regarded as a special type of corporatism, as both make use of organisations to represent the special interests of a membership while also restraining those members in the pursuit of a wider interest. The main difference is that corporatism tends to be concerned with rather specific, economic, producer interests, while consociationism relates to wider cultural identities. These may, however, come together where social class, in its strong sense as both an economic and a cultural identity, is concerned. Elements of consociational practices can be seen within corporatism when a wider range of cultural, sporting and leisure interests become organised around the core of interest representation. There have been important instances of that in Scandinavia, Germany and, above all, Austria. Similarly, through a kind of elective affinity of organisational practice, the original model of religious organisation of the Netherlands was later used for that country's corporatist interest organisation in the producer arena.

Changes since the 1980s

A variety of pressures has acted on these various forms of organised interest:

(a) Moves towards a global economy, paradoxically linked with the growing prominence of the individual firm;
(b) Economic policies of liberalisation and deregulation;
(c) A weakening of labour markets resulting from the return of high unemployment or unstable employment; and
(d) The growing importance of the EU as a focus for interest group activity.

Globalisation and the Firm

The meaning and significance of economic globalisation has been discussed elsewhere in this volume; here we must examine its implications for different forms of interest group organisation, and, first, to relate it to the role of the firm.

Disturbed product markets and intensified competition have led individual companies to seek maximum freedom in finding new competitive niches. For larger companies this includes seeking multinational locations for their activities and forging strategic alliances with potential competitors from other nations or continents. In doing so they establish rules of co-operation quite autonomously from the rules of governments. These firms are therefore removed from the framework of constraints established by earlier needs to base themselves primarily in one country.

Coincidentally, the main model of successful development of recent years has been Japan, where large firms develop internal cultures. Attempts at imitating this – translated through the perspectives of US business schools that remove from the account the associative networks that also link Japanese firms with each other and with the state – have led many Western firms to seek autonomy from all external pressures, whether from state regulation or associational membership.

Globalisation thus leads firms to take up certain distinctive positions in relation to governmental and associational frameworks. They have an incentive to try to shrug off not only state regulation, but also business associations that exist to represent their interests. Very large firms have the additional incentive of themselves 'going global' and transcending national frameworks of government and associations.

This is likely to be exceptionally damaging to neo-corporatist and consociational arrangements, which depend very heavily on specific national (or sometimes subnational) institutional networks. These signs of strain can be seen strongly in Sweden, whose economy is particularly dominated by multinational corporations which now have only a minor part of either their production or consumption in the country. This has been a major factor influencing the explicit decision of Swedish business organisations to pull out of a neo-corporatist form of action in favour of one of pluralist (or rather elitist?) lobbying.

Tendencies of this kind have been weaker in Germany, partly because, at least in the labour field, German neo-corporatist industry-level collective bargaining arrangements already allow considerable scope for company autonomy through works councils. However, in the mid-1990s there has been some evidence of German firms pulling out of employers' associations because of the constraints they are considered to exercise over firms' autonomy. Similarly, the strong regional corporatism in association with the country's powerful level of *Land* (regional) government has come under strain as global firms loosen their ties with their regional economy.

There are, however, counter-tendencies. Small and medium-sized enterprises – which in some sectors have become increasingly important as a consequence of unpredictable markets and frequent change – often benefit from support from national or local policies or associational networks that protect them from some of the vagaries of intensified competition – a phenomenon often referred to as the 'embedded firm' (Grabher, 1993). Such facilities as help with research and development, association with local universities, co-operative patterns of industrial relations, and co-operation among the networks of small producers themselves, have all been important props to competitiveness, supporting innovation and enterprise. They are all forms of corporatism (sometimes very informal), or *étatisme* (provided some licence can be allowed to that term to extend to subnational levels of government). Examples can be found in Denmark, parts of Germany, central Italy and specific regions of France and Spain, as well as such areas as Silicon Valley and in other parts of the USA.

Sometimes the networks linking such firms to each other and to public services are informal and elude corporatist interest organisations, but in other cases formal bodies have been important in orchestrating the whole process. There is in particular an interest contrast between Denmark and Sweden here. The precarious state of neo-corporatist structures in the latter country was described above. Meanwhile, in Denmark, after a period of crisis in the early 1980s, the entire neo-corporatist industrial relations system has been restructured in a way that permits a wide degree of company autonomy within a prevailing national framework (Due *et al.*, 1994). It may be significant that, in contrast with Sweden, the Danish economy is characterised by its large number of small firms.

Étatiste systems also have difficulties with globalisation and the search for company autonomy, as large firms shake themselves free from the authority of individual states, not least because, in a world of internationalised business activity, the state has less to offer in the way of knowledge about or control over often distant markets and the location of potential manufacturing activity. The French and Italian states gradually relinquished much of their formal tight regulatory role during the course of the 1980s, though two caveats have to be entered here. First, it is difficult to disentangle globalisation as such as a cause of this from the overlapping but distinct process of neo-liberal deregulation to be discussed below. Second, in both countries the shift away from a strong state role took the form partly of a move towards more corporatist structures. In Italy, this mainly occurred at regional and sectoral level within the collective bargaining system. In France, there was a clear attempt at imitating certain German institutions.

Pluralist organised interest systems are affected in a different way by these pressures. First, among business interests there is a rise in direct and specific lobbying by firms, and a decline in work by associations for entire industries or areas. This has long been an element in French business interest representation, but it has now spread more widely. A leading case is Britain, where many trade and employers' associations weakened and lost members during the 1980s; in several cases these disappeared altogether (Purcell, 1995). But the fact that firms 'go global' and lose dependence on a particular government's jurisdictions does not mean that they cease to be interested in lobbying that government. For example, a firm choosing between a number of potential locations for a new investment will be interested in discussing with the various governments the tax concessions, subsidies and relaxation of regulations that they are prepared to offer in order to attract the investment. Major government decisions become the objects of intense lobbying by powerful companies empowered by their increasing mobility, such as the pressure exerted on the Swedish government by Volvo, under the threat of relocation, to enter into the EU.

To the extent that this process takes place, the relationship between business interests and the state changes from being one concerned with the optimal conditions for the success of a particular branch of industry within a national environment, to one of special favours for individual firms. To the extent that this leads to an increase in the number of contact points between the government and the interest, there may be a growth in pluralism. On the other hand, the pluralism might become increasingly elitist, with a growing predominance of capital over labour interests. This happens, first, because globalisation extends the choice of labour markets from among which employers can choose employees without similarly increasing the range of employers open to choice by employees. Second, whereas corporations can organise themselves internationally relatively easily, it is very difficult for labour to do so; businesses need only to develop systems of co-ordination and monitoring; labour has to develop real connections of solidarity. Third, the growing importance of the individual company sometimes, though not always, means a decline of labour organisations – a question that will be considered further, below, when the labour market is considered more specifically.

Neo-liberalism and Deregulation

Neo-liberalism refers to a combination of economic policies which include the decline of Keynesian demand management, growing reliance on unconstrained free markets, the reduction of taxation, and a roll-back of the welfare state. Deregulation is an aspect of this, involving a reduction in the constraints imposed on free markets by such government measures as those to protect inefficient industries, sustain quality standards beyond those demanded by the market, protect the environment, or safeguard working conditions. It is difficult to distinguish neo-liberalism and deregulation from responses to globalisation, since a major motive in deregulation in Western Europe is to attract investment from firms which might otherwise move to parts of the world where regulatory burdens are light. In turn, globalisation benefits from deregulation, as the breakdown of trade barriers enables firms to locate their facilities wherever they like without fearing import tariffs. However, neo-liberalism and deregulation have implications for systems of interest representation that are rather separate from those discussed above as consequences of globalisation itself.

First, deregulation has been ambiguous. There has certainly been a relaxation of trade barriers; for countries within the EU there has been an important shift in regulatory level from nation states to Europe, which will be discussed below. There have been moves to reduce levels of, for example, labour protection in some countries, but there have been increases in regulation in other areas of society: environmental concerns, rights for women and ethnic minorities.

This has important implications for interest organisations. Political debate over regulation creates work for interest organisations. A world without regulation would be one in which pluralist and elitist groups had less need to lobby governments, the level of *étatisme* would have diminished automatically, and corporatist and consociational organisations would have less business. In principle, deregulation means weakening the world of organised interests. However, the process itself involves intense political struggle and, if anything, a demand for more lobbying and organised interest services. Which regulations should be abolished? Which retained? What should take the place of regulations being amended? This has been the state of the regulatory game over recent years, and its consequence has been an intensification rather than a weakening of lobbying processes.

Lobbying over regulation can occur under all system types – pluralist, elitist, *étatiste*, corporatist, consociationist – but it is the territory par excellence of pluralist and elitist action, as the definitions of these forms early in this chapter made clear. Participation in the administration of existing regulations is an activity largely restricted to corporatist and consociationist systems; it is that participation that often provides the framework for the associations to share in public business and to discipline members while at the same time keeping members' dependent on the organisation. Pure *étatiste* systems virtually by definition have no use for such participation. Pluralist systems are not equipped for such a process, and if an interest group in such a system does participate in administration it becomes a problem case of regulatory capture. Therefore, if deregulation does in fact take place, corporatist associational systems lose functions, members become less dependent on the associations, and the associations move towards a more lobbying role.

How far to travel down such a road remains a major unresolved issue for German firms. To accept such a logic suits their deregulatory mood, but possibly at the expense of destroying their economy's great capacity to produce collective goods for business. Meanwhile, in France, Italy and Spain representative systems capable of playing something of a neo-corporatist role to replace previous mixes of étatisme and clientilistic lobbying have only recently been constructed. Will the logic of deregulation lead to their early abandonment? Again, the issue is complicated by the shift of regulatory activity to the European level and the consequent question whether any re-regulation at the European level would continue to operate through very diverse national mechanisms.

The neo-liberal agenda also includes a reduction in the role of interest organisations in general, as these are regarded as cartels likely to restrain free trade, serving the interests of their members in conspiracy against the public interest. Nevertheless, so long as there is a multiplicity of states, globally mobile businesses will engage in bargaining with and lobbying of governments over the conditions on which they will invest in countries; in this way, global liberalisation increases rather than reduces the amount of politicking and non-market behaviour taking place in the economy. If the general neo-liberal project succeeds in gradually reducing the role of interest organisations, this elite lobbying process will move fully to the level of individual firms, with paradoxical implications. Neo-liberal economics requires level playing fields and open competition; neo-corporatist associations representing entire economic sectors are more likely to produce such conditions than is special pleading by individual firms.

The Weakening Labour Market

Contemporary labour markets are vulnerable to considerable fluctuation and uncertainty. The aggregate level of employment is no longer safeguarded by national governments' demand management. Changes in both technology and international competition produce frequent changes in the identities of occupations and the numbers of people practising them. As part of the freedom from constraint being demanded by firms, employers seek less regulation by law or collective agreements of their relations with their workforces. An increasing number of employees are engaged on temporary or otherwise insecure terms.

The main implication of this for the politics of organised interests is a decline in the bargaining power of labour, in particular of trade unions. Also, the decline of manual employment has reduced the size of the workforce most likely to join unions; when non-manual workers do form unions, they are less likely to develop broadly based soldaristic ties.

This last characteristic has particularly important consequences for neo-corporatist and consociational interest systems. The stability of Scandinavian neo-corporatism depended for a long time on the solidarity and authority of a national movement able to act in a class interest that, for several decades, more or less coincided also with perceptions of a national interest. There had been an element of consociationism in the Scandinavian systems, in that a manual workers' subculture was being represented as well as a more rationalistic economic interest. As the ranks of non-manual workers rose, the relative size of manual federations declined, while non-manual unions were either not members of federations or were grouped in federations that lacked the central authority of manual ones. The overall cohesion of corporatist bargaining systems was severely strained.

Of course, many aspects of organised interest politics do not involve labour. Business interests transact many other issues. It is only where labour market issues have been fundamental in sustaining the system of organised relations among businesses that a decline of organised labour threatens neo-corporatist business organisation as such. This had been the case in Britain, and possibly in Sweden, but was far less evident elsewhere. Similar arguments will apply to *étatiste* systems.

Pluralism is considerably challenged by weakening labour markets, as it requires a range of actors representing diverse interests. Given the weakness of consumer organisation, a decline of labour means virtually no challenge to business interests, and a consequent shift towards elitism.

However, market weakness does not necessarily cost labour its place in relations with government and organised interests. Workers are also citizens, and problems of social order might in fact increase during a period of labour market weakness as a result of growing uncertainty and insecurity. Trade unions might then ironically become valuable to governments as potential allies in avoiding social turbulence; and the fact that they are weak in the labour market may make unions grateful to have some other symbol of significance while being unable to exact an expensive price for their co-operation. Current labour market insecurity therefore has indeterminate implications for the place of unions. The outcome depends on political perceptions of the existence of any social threat.

In a number of countries there has, for varied reasons, been anxiety over the stability of the social order. Three southern European countries (Greece, Spain and Portugal) have only recently emerged from dictatorship and have fragile economies still in the process of modernisation. In Greece and Spain, unemployment is very high; in Spain there is also anxiety over regional separatism. Governments of various colours in these countries have been anxious to sustain at least a formal appearance of co-operation with union leaderships (Crouch 1993, ch. 7). France and Italy also continue to experience bouts of major labour turbulence; in these countries too governments have been anxious to incorporate unions among the forces supporting orderly conduct, and the years of labour weakness have actually seen new initiatives to do this (ibid.). Tendencies towards strengthening the interest organisation structure have also been in progress in these countries (and in Spain) as part of a programme of moving away from an *étatisme* which has been seen as outmoded both during the neo-corporatist heyday of the 1970s and during the subsequent years of neo-liberalism.

In these cases, the idea of organised labour co-operating in the pursuit of order is more an aspiration for the future than something based on past experience. In a number of other countries the past strong record of the industrial relations system as a component of national economic success serves to sustain labour representation. This is the case in the Netherlands and Scandinavian countries. The systems have frayed considerably in recent years, but elites still tend to look to means of repair rather than destruction, though, as noted already, Sweden is a partial exception to this, in that an unusually globalised business sector and the parties associated with it have been more willing to turn their backs on the national model. However, social-democratic and other parties do not share this approach. Austria and Germany have even stronger legacies of industrial relations success, while in addition memories of the prewar past make political leaders unwilling to take risks with social order. Political elites in small countries have additional grounds for sustaining national unity in a period of uncertainty and globalisation. In cases where the consociational or other base for this has become fragile (for example, Belgium and the Netherlands), we see an incongruous strengthening of *étatisme* within a prevailing neo-liberalism in order to shore up the interest representation system.

All these tendencies lead, not just to attempts at sustaining the organised interest network, but at encouraging a weak form of neo-corporatism in particular – with elements of consociationism if they exist. Governments are not particularly interested in sustaining organised labour's power to lobby in a pluralistic way, but to have its support in sustaining social order. Governments and employers would often prefer to make a few compromises to win the agreement of organised labour on the introduction of elements of a neo-liberal agenda rather than risk major conflict by forcing through such an agenda in full. Within most European states – and, as we shall see, at the level of the EU itself – an institutionalised neo-liberalism, and a negotiated, weakly corporatist, form of deregulation are emerging.

Britain stands outside this generalisation in not seeking any negotiated, institutionally embedded approach to the introduction of the deregulationist programme to which it is strongly committed. None of the criteria that seem to explain the institutional approach elsewhere (past record of success of the system; fear of social division; small country) apply. Also, since 1979, Britain has been governed by a single party, the Conservative Party, which has virtually no connections with organised labour. In every other European country there has been government by social democratic or Christian democratic parties, all of which have both the need and the opportunity to make use of links with union leaders, and/or multi-party governments that include at least some parties with such contacts.

The European Level

The final pressure on forms of interest intermediation has been the heightened salience of the EU. The increased activity on the part of both national and transnational interests in Brussels since the mid-1980s has been marked. It has partly been the result of the transfer of many functions of economic governance away from the nation-state (see ch. 2). The Single Market initiative is the clearest example of this. This trend has been reinforced by some aspects of globalisation, linked to the impact of new technologies, which have undermined previously national monopolies, such as the supply of energy or telecommunications services, and the increasing international mobility of both capital and (linked to this) firms across national borders, which undermines the efficacy of national regulation (Menon and Hayward, 1996). The transfer of economic functions precipitates an increased interest on the part of those actors affected in the supranational level. Thus, large telecommunications firms have become increasingly dependent on decisions taken in Brussels, as evidenced recently by the debate within the Commission in May 1995, as to whether to authorise the joint operation of Deutsche Telekom and France Telecom, or the interest shown by the advertising industry in the Commission's broadcasting proposals of the mid-1980s.

Linked to the increase in the functions performed by the EU is the fact that, under the influence of EU action, states find their own competencies reduced. Deregulation and privatisation, brought about through a combination of the effects of globalisation and pressure exerted from the European level, have arguably limited the amount of direct control that states can wield over businesses, which increasingly seek funding from the international capital markets. In terms of macroeconomic policy, the convergence criteria of the Maastricht Treaty and EU competition policy have reduced the ability of states to provide funds for business. Perhaps more strikingly, progress towards economic and monetary union has been marked by the granting of independence to most central banks (see Chapter 2). Given the fact that, historically, 'tripartite corporatist bargaining has typically involved the government's use not only of fiscal but also of monetary policy instruments' (Streeck and Schmitter, 1991, p. 157), the (at least nominal) reduction of state control over monetary policy significantly reduces its ability to satisfy interest group demands. Finally, the ability of the state to satisfy demands has been reduced by territorial shifts partly caused and partly facilitated by European integration. The increased freedom of manoeuvre enjoyed by regions – in those countries where regional governments have some political autonomy – has undermined the central role of states in regional provision and empowered the latter to become important interests in their own right at the European level (Chapter 11).

The relative decrease in the role of the state and increase in EU performance of key economic functions is a necessary but not a sufficient condition for the growth of lobbying activity. As important in this regard is the willingness of the EU (and in particular the Commission) to foster and maintain contact with organised interests. The European Round Table of Industrialists (ERT) has found itself in a position not merely of seeking to influence Commission policy, but also of having its input actively sought by Commission officials (Cowles, 1995). Perhaps more noteworthy than the influence of big business (a feature at both national and EU levels) is the way in which the Commission has fostered links with the kinds of pressure groups which often find themselves somewhat marginalised at national level, such as environmental, women's and consumers' organisations (Hine *et al.*, 1996).

Such behaviour serves a practical purpose: contrary to popular myth, the Commission is a relatively understaffed institution, heavily reliant on outside interests for technical information. In highly technical sectors such as research and development policy, the consultation of outside experts is an indispensable element of policy formulation. This has also been true of links with, for example, the ERT.

Second, consultation with interests provides a means of achieving legitimacy, both the technical legitimacy referred to above and, more broadly through links with environmental and other pressure groups, the popular support for Community actions that has so often been lacking. A final factor is that the EU institutional framework provides many points of relatively easy access for groups wishing to engage in dialogue. Apart from the relative openness of the Commission, the European Court of Justice can prove to be a crucial ally for lobbyists, especially on environmental or gender equality issues, while the perceived importance of the European Parliament as a target for interests is also increasing (Mazey and Richardson, 1993, pp. 15–16).

The rise of the EU as a focus for interest-group activity has affected, though to differing extents, national patterns of interest intermediation. In some cases, previously closed and collusive policy communities have lost their sole influence over policy as EU initiatives have opened up the area to a welter of new actors, as, for example, with the British water industry (Richardson, 1996). On a broader level, while pluralist systems have not been altered fundamentally by the impact of the EU, more *étatiste* systems such as the French are increasingly experiencing the need for far wider consultation with interests than was previously the case. Ministerial advisers now routinely consult with interest groups upon receipt of a Commission proposal, while these groups are also provided with an opportunity to affect policy-making at the implementation stage (Lequesne, 1993, pp. 33, 53).

However, none of this has led to the development of a single model of interaction between the central institutions and private interests, and practices vary widely between sectors and over time (Greenwood and Ronit, 1994). This can be accounted for in several ways. First, different institutional decision-making procedures exist at EU level for different sectors (note the residual powers the Commission enjoys over coal and steel, stemming from the ECSC), while common policies exist for some policies such as agriculture, but not for others.

Moreover, some scholars have argued that EU-group relations cannot be characterised in terms of stable policy networks (Kassim, 1994) because of the continued institutional adaptation which occurs at EU level; the institutional targets of lobbyists may change over time, as evidenced by the increased importance of the European Parliament after the Single European Act and arguably after Maastricht.

Corporatist arrangements are further unlikely to develop at the European level because of the relative weakness of peak organisations, and perhaps more important because these organisations, and particularly the employers' federation, UNICE, are far from united. Firms from different member states of the EU do not necessarily share the same interests. Thus, for example, German firms may support the idea of increasing social costs in Germany's partners so as to enhance their own comparative advantage, and so will not necessarily share the stance of the British Confederation of British Industry (CBI) over EU social policy. For the reasons discussed above, transnational workers' co-operation is difficult to achieve.

While, as pointed out, there has been an increase in lobbying at EU level, it would be a mistake to equate this with a proportional increase in the importance of the EU as a focus for lobbying activity. Much interest-group activity at the Brussels level is concerned with simple fact-finding concerning a little-known institution. As major companies become more familiar with the workings of the EU, it would seem likely that such activity will decline. Institutional complexity also helps to account for this lack of stable patterns. Lobbying the EU involves the need to hold discussions at a number of levels and in a number of different locations at the Brussels level. Thus for the electrical group, Philips, lobbying on the subject of High Definition Television (HDTV) required maintaining contact not only with the Dutch ministries of economic affairs and transport, but also with (directorates General) DG III (Internal Market), DG IV (Competition), DG X (Audio-visual Affairs, Information, Communications, Culture) and DG XIII (Telecommunications). It also led to a realisation of the flaws in a strategy that ignored the European Parliament and consequently allowed consumer organisations to wield significant influence through this institution (Verwey, 1994).

It would also be wrong to equate the increasing number of groups active at Brussels with a concomitant move away from national-level interest intermediation. There is no zero-sum game here between the nation-state and the EU as targets of interest-group activity. Groups still need to lobby domestic authorities in order to achieve their ends. This is partly a question of competence. While macroeconomic and industrial policy initiatives have implied a shift of authority over many crucial functions away from the nation-states, this has not happened in some other areas, such as welfare provision or education. Indeed, the existence of entrenched interests at the national level, often involved in cosy relationships with the state through policy communities, can impede the transfer of competence to the European level (Jones, 1996).

More fundamentally, the nature of EU decision-making processes also accounts for the continued importance of the national level.

Lobbying in national capitals is necessary even to achieve results in Brussels, given the central importance of the Council of Ministers in the legislative process. Interests not only lobby at the national level in order to achieve their ends in terms of national policy, but may also find lobbying national authorities an effective way of affecting policy developments at the level of the Union. Clearly, certain trends at the EU level will have an impact on the efficacy of such strategies, not least the increased use of Qualified Majority Voting, which undermines the ability of single state to block a policy proposal. The response of groups to such developments may, however, involve putting pressure on other member states rather than a shift to lobbying exclusively at the EC level.

Conclusions

There are contradictory processes at work. In some respects one can identify a distinct weakening of neo-corporatist and above all of consociational and *étatiste* forces, and, within pluralism, a shift towards elitism and towards company rather than associational lobbying. This is all convergence, and convergence on an American pattern. On the other hand, we have seen some continuing advantages for a thin corporatism – both where it already exists with a successful past and where there is anxiety over social order. The struggle for advantage among different kinds of system is therefore unresolved, and it is possible that, except in cases where corporatist systems seize up completely and are abandoned as useless, there will continue to be national differences, alongside a fair amount of re-engineering to make systems more decentralised and company-sensitive.

Essentially, the global shift leaves neo-corporatism very much at a disadvantage. Corporatist structures exist only where there are strong, disciplined organisations which become involved in a dense web of interactions. This cannot take place at the world level. It happens to some extent at the level of the European Union, where interest organisations play a part in the formulation of policy. However, European associations of business and labour have a very weak capacity for self-discipline over national affiliates, and are rarely part of substantial neo-corporatist relationships. Euro-corporatism remains a very weak, diluted phenomenon – at national level in many countries, thin corporatism seems to have a curious viability.

The European Commission tends to attract interest organisations into relationships as it extends its own influence. A type of exchange resembling corporatism in form but concerning primarily symbolic business takes place. The Commission and the associations exchange legitimacy: the Commission can grant an association a voice at an important level of decision-making, which is particularly important to trade unions at the present time; the associations can help the Commission acquire some of the attributes of a national state. This is similar to what is going on in relations between associations and national governments where the latter fear threats to social order: weak associations are grateful to be taken into the circle of those consulted by the state; and states want to demonstrate their centrality and stability to groups who might challenge them. This takes us away from the main interest that business management might have in neo-corporatism: but these essentially political criteria may well be important in shaping the context within which business operates. Tendencies of this kind counteract the trend otherwise dominant for industrial relations, whether corporatist or not, to move down to company level and to become technical and non-political.

PART THREE
Public Policy

10

Capitalism versus Capitalism in Western Europe

MARTIN RHODES AND BASTIAAN VAN APELDOORN

Globalisation and European integration are having a profound impact on Europe's socio-economic order. Other chapters in this volume discuss the implications of these developments for macroeconomic management and welfare states. This chapter focuses more precisely on their consequences for Europe's 'models' of capitalism. It argues that while there is still considerable diversity among the national 'capitalisms' in western Europe, both globalisation and integration are eroding national particularities, if not – as yet – pitching them towards full convergence. Their relative strengths provide them comparative advantage in different sectors; they therefore remain in competition and the outcome of that contest is yet to be determined. But opposition between competing models of capitalist development is also manifested at the transnational level where opposing forces pursue similarly diverse strategies. After examining the diversity of European 'capitalisms' below, we consider the arguments and evidence concerning their contemporary transformation. But beyond the changes occurring in national 'capitalisms', there is also a question of what kind of socio-economic order, or 'model of capitalism' is emerging within the supranational regime of the European Union (EU).

The Diversity of West European Capitalisms

It is often maintained – especially in the debate over industrial policy and free trade – that companies, not countries, compete (e.g. Krugman, 1994). This argument may have some sense when it comes to opposing the simplistic view that a nation's industrial strategy should seek to emulate those of its competitors. But it discounts the fact – now backed by substantial analysis – that a country's institutional context is critical, not just in shaping the environment in which firms operate, but in creating a national 'variety' of capitalism in which firms are embedded as complex, corporate and *social* organisations. In turn, although this is an even more controversial argument, the institutional context and national character of corporate organisation will influence the performance of the firm and create comparative advantage for the economy. The conventional economist's conception of 'the naked firm' – which competes as an independent, 'decontextualised' market actor – is untenable. So, at least for the time being, is the argument that globalisation has swept away the national distinctiveness of both firms and their national systems of innovation and support. Nevertheless, as we argue below, important tensions are now emerging between national systems and the 'extra-national' sphere of multinationals and global finance. Bit by bit, globalisation – and the new domestic pressures and coalitions it generates – are beginning to unravel the cosy relationships between government, banks, companies and unions that underpinned national socio-economic orders. This process is neither creating 'naked firms' nor destroying national distinctiveness. For even multinational firms and global banks must comply with national and increasingly international regulations (Kapstein, 1994); and the 'historically rooted trajectories of growth' created by national institutional relationships are not susceptible to rapid transformation or demise (Zysman, 1994). But significant changes are occurring in Europe's national capitalisms. And many of those changes indicate a degree of convergence on a new 'hybrid' model, pragmatically combining elements of different systems.

But what are these systems, and how do they differ? Various attempts have been made to categorise capitalist systems, providing important insights into institutional distinctions and the ways they affect the functioning and performance of firms. Albert (1993) draws a distinction between 'Atlantic' (Thatcherite/Neo-American) and 'Rhenish' (German or Rhineland) capitalism. While the former prioritise individual success and short-term financial profits, the latter promote collective achievement, consensus and long-term results. We will investigate these distinctions shortly, but the principal differences derive from contrasts in corporate governance: while the key characteristics of the Atlantic model are arms-length relations between the sources of finance and firms, the supremacy of shareholder interests and little restriction on predatory behaviour (via mergers and acquisitions), those of the Rhenish model derive from the concept of 'stake-holder' capitalism – the location of the firm and its management within a network of interests, including banks and workers. The purpose is a collective one: the pursuit not of short-term profit but of the long-term interests of all. While noting that in Europe only Britain and Germany conform, respectively, to these ideal-types, France, argues Albert, lies somewhere in between – the result of its long legacy of state intervention. Other countries also fit imperfectly. Regini (1995) and Bianco and Trento (1995) argue that Italy is quite distinct from either model – because of a mix of regulatory systems (one for small and another for large firms) and a highly specific form of corporate governance. However, other authors – De Jong (1995) and Moerland (1995a) – specify an all-inclusive continental brand of 'network-oriented' capitalism – as opposed to Anglo–Saxon 'market-oriented' systems (Britain and Ireland) – and divide it into two sub-varieties: the Germanic or 'social market' type (Germany, Benelux, Denmark) and the Latin or 'pragmatic' type (Italy, Greece, Portugal and Spain). France, again, is an awkward customer, as is Belgium. While De Jong places them both in the 'social market' group (although France only since the mid-1980s when the state began to withdraw from widespread industrial and financial ownership), Moerland considers them members of the Latin family since they conform, by and large, with its principal features: the importance of family control, financial holdings, cross-shareholdings among companies and extensive state ownership. We accept this categorisation for Table 10.1.

Quite apart from definitional problems, an objection can be made that *regional* differentiation of economic governance within countries renders even the concept of national – let alone cross-national – regimes of capitalism too abstract. This is especially true of France, Germany and Italy which have quite distinct regional economic arrangements (see Chapter 11). Nevertheless, regional economic differentiation occurs *within* national systems and the latter will influence even strong regional economies: the dynamic German regions discussed by Cooke *et al.* clearly benefit from the positive features of the national system, including that country's patient capital markets and well-developed training systems (Rhodes, 1996b). For all their limits, attempts to discover more or less distinct systems of economic governance in Europe are useful for understanding how economies function, how they compete and how they are changing. Tables 10.1 and 10.2 present the essential characteristics of these systems, the first outlining the 'external' environment of firms, the second the system of 'corporate governance', i.e. the nature of firm internal organisation

TABLE 10.1 *Characteristics of market and network-oriented systems: external environment*

Institutional context	Market-oriented Anglo–Saxon	Network-oriented Germanic	Latin
Role of the state	Shift towards a minimal state since the 1980s	A regulatory rather than interventionist state	Extensive public ownership
Co-operation between social partners	Conflictual until the 1980s; now minimal contact (Ireland maintains corporatism)	Extensive at the national level till late 1960s. Revived in the 1980s/1990s	Social pacts in Italy and Portugal in 1980s/1990s; problematic in Spain and Greece
Labour organisation	Union membership high till 1980s; fragmented organisation	Union membership density high; strong centralised unions	Union density generally low: significant decline outside public sector
Education and training	Fragmented training system; poor skills provision	High level of participation in vocational and professional training	Lower levels of participation in fragmented training systems
Labour market flexibility	Poor internal flexibility due to poor skills; high external flexibility	High skills allow internal flexibility, external flexibility more restricted	Lower internal flexibility (lower skills); external flexibility also restricted
National innovation system	Low levels of R&D weak regional innovation support system	Higher levels of R&D regionalised innovation support systems	France excepted, R&D national and regional support weak
Finance for innovative small firms	Explosion of venture capital companies, but regionally concentrated	Lack of venture capital for new high-tech start-ups	Venture capital weak; access to regional banks for small firm finance

(the role of management, employee influence) and its relations with shareholders and institutional sources of finance.

These characteristics reveal substantial differences between the models. The most important differences are between the Germanic countries and the rest. For while the former provides a generally productive support environment for firms – with high levels of education and

TABLE 10.2 *Characteristics of market and network-oriented systems: corporate governance*

Corporate features	Market-oriented Anglo–Saxon	Network-oriented Germanic	Latin
Employee influence	Limited; Japanese FDI promotes shop-floor collaboration, 1980s/1990s	Extensive through works councils on organisation of work and training	Strong shop-floor influence until early 1980s; now minimal
Role of banks	Banks play a minimal role in corporate ownership	Universal banks play an important role in corporate finance and control	Bank holdings and participation in France and Spain only
Role of stock exchange	Strong role in corporate finance; 70% of top 100 companies in UK listed	Publicly listed corporate firms limited; stock exchanges small	Stock exchanges relatively undeveloped; closed ownership
Shareholder sovereignty	Widely dispersed share ownership; dividends prioritised	Number of freely traded shares limited; dividends less prioritised	Shareholder sovereignty recognised but shareholders rights restricted
Family controlled firms	General separation of equity ownership and management control	Family ownership important in small and medium-sized firms	Family ownership and control extensive, exercised through holdings
Market for corporate control	Scope for hostile take-overs 'corrects' management failure	Take-overs restricted; managers under direct stakeholder influence	Take-overs restricted; little external challenge to management
Management boards	One-tier board system: includes executive and non-executive managers	Two-tier board system: supervisory and executive responsibilities separate	Administrative board combines supervisory and executive duties
Managerial labour market	Incentives (e.g. stock options) align management with shareholders	Performance-linked compensation limited: 'equality' important	Incentives more important (e.g. stock options in France)

Source: Adapted from Rhodes (1993, Table 2) and information in Moerland (1995a; 1995b) and De Jong (1995).

R&D (research and development) support – the Anglo–Saxon and Latin countries are much less well-endowed in both respects. The Anglo–Saxon system may be establishing some comparative advantage with its higher level of labour market flexibility (the low level of constraints on employers both inside firms and in their ability to hire and fire) but by and large this is offset by the lower levels of education and skills in the British work force, certainly by comparison with German, and, although to a lesser extent, France.

What, then, are the negative and positive features of these different types of system? In the *Anglo–Saxon, market-oriented system*, it is generally thought that the advantages stem from the dynamism imparted by both the external threat to poorly performing managers from hostile take-over and the incentives given them by performance-related compensation. The sovereignty of the shareholders is assumed to provide another check on management since the large shareholders can, in principle, replace them. If managers are also the largest share-holders, however, this constraint is clearly reduced (Moerland, 1995a, 1995b). The disadvantages are several: the absence of long-term contractual relationships with suppliers of capital and workers may encourage short-term, quick-profit oriented strategies; mergers and acquisitions – which have accelerated in recent years – may distract management from long-term corporate strategy, prioritise 'paper en-trepreneurialism' ('get-rich-quick' schemes) and encourage asset-strip-ping and empire-building, without necessarily adding to productivity or the enduring viability of firms; and the priority given to the share-holder interest may militate against the interest of employees, for not only are management–employees relations less institutionalised and productive in the Anglo–Saxon firm, but employee remuneration as a proportion of net value added is much lower. But perhaps the most damning indictment of the market-oriented system (at least in the British case) is its poor corporate performance. For although short-term profits are higher than in the Germanic system, the long-term survival of Anglo–Saxon corporations is in doubt: while in 1970 they accounted for over one third of the largest 180 European firms, by 1992 their share had fallen to less than a fifth (De Jong, 1995).

This almost certainly has as much to do with the less than productive general environment of the firm as its particular form of corporate governance. The most important weaknesses are a poorly developed and fragmented training system, which the introduction of a system of national vocational qualifications and a new training system based on employer-run training and enterprise bodies (TEC) has still fundamen-tally to tackle; short-termism in finance (highly centralised, in addition to its international vocation, the financial sector fails in providing local finance where detailed local knowledge, risk assessment and commitment and commitment to longer-term investment is required); and persistently lower levels of spending on R&D than the European average, except in defence, despite one of the highest rates of profit growth in Europe in the 1980s (Walker, 1993). This reflects a system of corporate governance oriented to shareholder – and, increasingly, executive – remuneration rather than longer-term investment and growth.

The *network-oriented systems* of the European continent also have advantages and disadvantages, the latter generally receiving much less publicity and attention than the former – especially among British exponents of the 'social market' system (e.g. Hutton, 1995). Among the advantages generally attributed to network-oriented, 'contractual' corporate governance are the benefits of close and long-term relationships between firms and strategic capital suppliers. Often with board representation (as in the German supervisory board system), banks will, at least in theory, be well informed about managerial behaviour and performance and provide a more 'constructive' form of control than the Anglo–Saxon 'market' for corporate control – i.e., the threat of take over and dismissal. At the same time, a better institutionalised and similarly longer-term relationship between management and employees should allow an ongoing process of conflict free organisational adjustment within the firm, especially in the adoption of new technology and the associated redeployment of workers. This process of adjustment is facilitated, in turn, by the nature of the external environment, with its strong support in terms of transferable skills and regionalised R&D facilities in centres of education and research. In certain German regions (e.g. Baden-Württemberg), this support network has been bolstered by a regional government commitment to consolidating the links between state, industry and science (see Chapter 11).

But what of the negative aspects? As Moerland (1995a) points out, there are two major *potential* disadvantages. The absence of an active external market for corporate control means that managerial failure may not be corrected, especially in those countries where the positions of managers and employees are strongly protected. At the same time, the strong 'insider' role of capital suppliers (the famous *Hausbanken*) in the German case creates an information gap to the disadvantage of 'outsider' smaller investors. One can add that in Germany, but even more so in France and Italy, the intimate relationships between capital suppliers and managers are often consolidated by membership of a relatively closed elite (e.g. the incestuous network of graduates of the prestigious Ecole Nationale d'Administration in France; the restricted membership of Italy's so-called *salotto buono*, the select club of leaders of the largest traditional companies and financial organisations). While this facilitates contractual relationships and may in some ways enhance industrial adjustment (by creating joint strategic orientations on the part all those involved in corporate governance), covert cross-share-holdings may also create a degree of collusive complacency, allowing bad decisions to remain unchecked and, in the worst cases, encouraging corruption. Recent corporate disasters in Germany (Metalgesellschaft, Schneider, Bremer–VulKan), corruption investigations in France (Lyonnais des Eaux, Général des Eaux) and judicial investigations into corporate practice in Italy (Fiat's Gemina financial holding) all provide evidence of this problem. The relative weak equity (stock) markets in these countries compounds the problem, for management is often over-protected from the influence of system 'outsiders': the fund managers, small and foreign investors who are excluded from the contractual system but are now struggling hard to make their voices heard.

At the same time, not everything is rosy in the external environment of these systems. First, as mentioned in Chapter 4, there is a problem of escalating social costs linked to the high level of welfare spending that is typical of these systems, and its dependence on funding from employers – and employees – contributions. This creates a growing non-wage labour cost problem. The relocation issue has become an increasingly salient one, given shifts of lower technology industry to the Asia-Pacific (the German BASF chemicals company has recently announced the transfer of its world-wide leather and textile chemicals' division to Singapore after the shift of most of its German customer companies to the region) and medium-technology firms to Britain (where the ratio of profit to labour costs for new projects is eleven times higher than at home) (*Financial Times*, 11 July 1996). These developments have generated a lively debate in Germany as to the future of *Standort Deutschland* – Germany as a location for industry. Within Germany itself there is little evidence of any substantial shift from medium- into high-technology sectors, indicating a structural problem of economic adjustment. As in France, this is the conse-quence of a number of factors, including a poorly developed venture capital sector and an innovation system locked into traditional sectors and technologies (Keck, 1993; Chesnais, 1993). As Streeck (1995a) warns, rising unemployment and a lack of technological dynamism may mean that the German system of knowledge production and diffusion has lost touch with changing markets and that the virtues of the system in the past – its training system, cost structure, pattern of product and process innovation – may become liabilities in a globalised economy.

System Transformation: Convergence or Parallel Evolution?

This brings us to the challenges posed by globalisation. The threat is two-fold. The first challenge is to established and cosy systems of corporate governance as globalisation places a premium on two alternative strategies: 'going global' and becoming a player in rapidly changing international product markets (e.g. large car manufacturers which have developed the 'world car' based on standardised components sourced internationally but customised for particular markets); or 'locking into the local' and serving specific market niches. The former strategy accentuates the breach between companies and their domestic corporate environments already opened by the traditional multinational. The second challenge partly derives from the first, but is compounded by intensified international competition: not only are the ties that bind the corporate organisation to the domestic environment area strained and sometimes broken, but the national company infrastructure of training, education, research and development need to be constantly upgraded as process and product innovation accelerates and newly industrialised countries – with lower costs, well-educated work forces and more flexible institutional systems – move into higher technology markets.

Globalisation of finance and the internationalisation of firms have different but often related effects. For while retail banking remains largely nation-bound and its competitiveness derives from being 'locked into' local networks (it serves particular local and regional customers, is dependent on carefully constructed networks and hemmed in by still nation-based legal systems) corporate banking and bond and equity transactions have 'gone global'. The most dynamic European banks are now becoming international operators. Two of the three large German banks (which, in their close relations with firms, have constituted the core of the German corporate finance system) are engaged in the current rush to build global investment banks capable of challenging the dominance of the giant US firms like Goldman Sachs. Both Deutsche Bank (which operates in the City of London through its subsidiary Morgan Grenfell – which has all the characteristics of an American firm) and Dresdner Bank (which has purchased London investment banker Kleinwort Benson) are considering reducing their industrial shareholdings in Germany (although this is restricted by the 60 per cent capital gains tax they would have to pay on such sales). At the same time, driven by the need to raise funds internationally to develop an international presence in medium and especially high-technology sectors, companies are both engaging in joint ventures with other transnationals or seeking citation on Anglo–Saxon stock markets in London or New York. These are much larger and more efficient than their relatively under-developed counterparts in the 'networked economies' in Paris, Frankfurt or Milan. Hence, alongside the *Standort Deutschland* debate, there is another, equally concerned discussion about the future of *Finanzplatz Deutschland* – Germany as a financial centre.

Although such debates are also being conducted in the other 'network' economies, Germany is witnessing the most spectacular changes and threats to its traditional system of corporate governance, in part because it is Europe's most successful economy and has some of Europe's most dynamic companies. Whether banks or industrial groups, these will not be slow to exploit the new opportunities arising in the global economy and this will have knock-on effects on domestic business and financial organisation. The general 'academic' consensus is that dramatic results should not be expected from such changes, despite the prediction of Albert (1993) that, although less successful in terms of reconciling profits and social justice, the Anglo–Saxon model would triumph due to its cosmopolitan character and its linkage to the media globalisation of Anglo–Saxon culture. As far as corporate governance is concerned, it is assumed that the fundamental characteristics of the continental 'network' systems will persist, with some shift towards Anglo–Saxon methods, while the Anglo–Saxon 'market-oriented' systems will gradually take on some 'network' aspects (e.g. Carl Kester, 1992: Schneider-Lenné, 1994). Zysman (1994, 1995) argues strongly against the presumption that national systems can be eroded by 'globalisation' (a term he also contests). However, Moerland (1995b) predicts convergence along several dimensions of corporate governance:

- banks will become more important in market systems as the universal banking model becomes more widespread, while the power of banks in network systems will be reduced, in line with growing opposition to banking power, especially to the German bank practice of owning large blocks of equity in firms;
- network systems will increasingly accommodate the Anglo–Saxon characteristic of channelling capital flows to corporations through

investment funds, pension funds and insurance companies, while managers will identify more closely with stock price behaviour as more companies seek stock market quotation and managers' remuneration is tied more closely to performance (through stock-options, for example);
- while the Anglo–Saxon market for corporate control will become less ferocious (as corporate raiding, hostile take-overs and asset stripping lose favour), management in 'network' countries will become increasingly subject to the influence of shareholders, the result of a combination of growing shareholder pressure and new EU regulations (see below).

The net effect of these changes will be to reduce the distinctiveness of national systems rather than undermine their basic principles. However, if we observe the dynamics of how certain small changes produce much wider repercussions, we can predict a turbulent time ahead, especially for the 'network systems', for the 'market' systems already conform with, rather than resist, the new global pressures. In fact, several dynamics are at work in destabilising traditional 'contractual' relations in these countries.

- The first is the effect of globalisation on employee influence in the Germanic firm. Quite apart from the issue of non-wage labour cost competition, there is the pressure that the changing nature of the global corporation will place on the tradition of social consensus. First, German employers – like their counterparts in other 'organised' capitalist countries like Denmark and Sweden – have been decentralising bargaining to the level of the firm to tailor costs more precisely to its needs (see Chapter 9). Solidarity among workers is consequently diminished. In addition, as 'networked' firms 'go global' and embrace new methods of business organisation and new forms of finance, the traditionally greater share of net value added they distributed to workers in the past will be challenged by the growing power of institutional shareholders – both domestic (including newly liberated pension funds) and foreign.
- This leads to a second point. Germany, France, Italy and the other continental economies have all witnessed an increase in the domestic presence of foreign – especially American – investors, attracted by the opening up of European markets and the lucrative business generated by the privatisation programmes launched by all governments in recent years. Now while the nature of privatisation differs from country to country (in some, like France and Italy, companies

are often secured from foreign take-over by continued government stakes or shareholder pacts between core investors), its net effect has been to undermine traditional relationships. This is not just because foreign (Anglo–Saxon) investors have different expectations from 'stakeholders' with a longer-term interest; but because newly privatised national companies will expand the size of the domestic lobby opposing traditional, and privileged, contractual relations. Take France, for example, where large parts of the extensive public industrial and financial sector (built up by the Socialist government in the early 1980s) is now being privatised. While certain large corporations will remain under state control – especially non-commercial financial institutions such as the mutual banks, the Caisse d'Épargne savings bank network, the Crédit Agricole and the Post Office – the way that they operate will have to change substantially as the result of an onslaught by the expanding commercial sector on their special lending rights and subsidies. Long seen as a central part of a 'socially-oriented' banking system, the latter are now seen as 'competitive distortions'.

- Some of the French commercial banks will fall under Anglo–Saxon corporate control as large foreign banks pick off the most profitable among them. Foreign financial services companies have expanded in the European market and their American business methods have been pushed aggressively, influencing the ways in which domestic companies also do business, given that, until recently, financial intermediaries in most European countries have been as hidebound and conservative as their stock markets. American business culture is being spread throughout Europe by the growing presence of US institutional investors, consultancy firms and credit agencies like Standard & Poors which exercise considerable influence over the direction and nature of investment. One obvious way that the foreign lobby is influencing corporate governance is by encouraging the spread of shareholder sovereignty in the 'network' systems. In France, Germany and Italy, lobbying by shareholder groups for greater management transparency and responsiveness has been backed by foreign shareholders and fund managers frustrated by the interlocking elite relationships that still dominate these systems.

As already stressed, none of this means that continental corporate governance will be transformed overnight. Indeed, there is considerable resistance from companies – including multinational companies – to a wholesale adoption of Anglo–Saxon practice. But just as the external firm environment is gradually being changed by globalisation, corporate governance will gradually shift towards the 'market' model, producing new 'hybrid' varieties of European capitalism.

The European Dimension: A Transnational Model of Capitalism?

As we stated in the Introduction, the opposition between competing models of capitalism is also manifest at the European level where a similar struggle has occurred. As a result, a novel supranational socio-economic order or 'model of capitalism' is taking shape. Four ideological and strategic orientations have been in contest: European social democracy; neo-mercantilism; neo-liberalism; and embedded neo-liberalism:

- *Pan-European social democracy* is promoted by social democratic political forces and the European trade union movement, and was spurred on by the former European Commission president, Jacques Delors. To the extent that it promotes both a European 'social dialogue' and a Commission-led industrial policy for 'Euro-champion' firms, it is a hybrid of the German 'social market' model and the French 'interventionist' model (Ross, 1993). For Delors (1992), as for other social democrats, a united Europe offered an opportunity to protect the European 'social model' – the mixed economy and extensive social protection – against globalisation and neo-liberalism (see Chapter 4). Following Delors' departure, this project has lost significant momentum and has been sidelined by European business.
- *Neo-liberalism* is the ideological outlook of global financial capital (based primarily in the City of London), but also of some (mainly British) multinationals. This strategic orientation favours European integration only in as far as it leads to freer markets, i.e. less regulation and fewer barriers to trade. The European region must be wholly subordinate to the world economy and exposed to what are seen as the beneficial forces of globalisation.
- *Neo-mercantilism* is the dialectical opposite, oriented instead towards a strong regional economy through industrial policy and the promotion of Euro-champions (if necessary protected by European tariff walls) as a bulwark against global competition. Its advocates are certain European firms which, although producing on a transnational scale, nevertheless primarily serve and are dependent on the European market.
- *Embedded neo-liberalism* is the preferred option of the truly global transnationals (TNCs) which produce, market and sell their goods in

all three of the world's macro-regions – Europe, North America and Asia (Ohmae, 1985). Most explicitly advocated by German firms, it is clearly committed to a free trading Europe that is fully open and adapted to the global economy. It is premised on a strong belief in the free market and supports neo-liberal policies of deregulation and flexibilisation. Nevertheless, it falls short of the orthodox neo-liberal model as promoted, for example, by Thatcherism, for its advocates recognise that the free market must be embedded in a regulatory framework which fosters both competitive business and social consensus (Holman, 1992; Hodges and Woolcock, 1993).

The Emergence of a Transnational Business 'Ideology'

The struggle between these rival strategies has partly shaped the course of the European integration process since the beginning of the 1980s, as illustrated by the case of the European Roundtable of Industrialists (ERT), a transnational business forum consisting of some 40 top executives of European TNCs. The ERT played a major agenda-setting role in the relaunching of the European integration process (see Sandholtz and Zysman, 1989; Holman, 1992; Cowles, 1995 for accounts of this role), and is unique both in representing large sections of European business at the highest level and in transcending the conventional forms of EU corporate lobbying. We can detect all three basic business orientations outlined above in the evolution of the ERT and its strategy.

In the 1980s, the main dividing line within European transnational business was between 'neo-mercantilists' and 'neo-liberals', and 'embedded neo-liberalism' was borne as a synthesis from this struggle. During its first five years (1983–8), the ERT was clearly dominated by the 'neo-mercantilists' and a protectionist regionalisation strategy. Thus, although the Roundtable's first priority was to 'relaunch Europe with an industrial initiative' by creating the European internal market, a protectionist attitude towards global competition could also be detected. In this respect there was a partial convergence with the social democratic project. As noted above, Delors himself wanted to promote a 'Euro-champion strategy'. But attempts by parts of the Delors Commission to establish a European industrial policy along those lines failed, partly because in the end the companies concerned were unwilling to cooperate. In fact, collaboration with non-European partners became a primary goal, precluding any 'Europeanist' solutions beyond existing and limited co-operation programmes such as ESPRIT or EUREKA – which soon included US firms themselves (Wyatt-Walker 1995). By the time the Delors Commission relaunched the idea of Euro-champions to help the ailing European electronics sector, the TNCs, as well as other import-competing firms, had abandoned their neo-mercantilist strategy (Ross, 1993).

It is in this light that we have to understand the subsequent gradual shift towards a more neo-liberal orientation on the part of a majority of the Roundtable's members. The globalisation process (global sourcing and global alliances) accelerated in the 1980s and European economic integration became part and parcel of that process. The 1992 pro-gramme made the European economy more open to international trade and investment flows and therefore precluded mercantilism (Grahl and Teague, 1990). Defensive regionalisation, as pursued by the ERT's original membership, was no longer viable. Thus, the ERT shifted gears in 1991 and produced a blueprint for the future of Europe which Holman (1992) calls a 'catch-all strategy'. This could be viewed as a first step towards an eventual synthesis (first fully expressed by the ERT in its 1993 reports) between neo-mercantilism and neo-liberalism. An open world economy was now seen by a majority of ERT members as essential for the flourishing of European industry. However, in this view, a mere opening up of national economies should not be the only goal of European integration; there should also be a supranational framework to provide coherence and stability and help co-ordinate *national* efforts to promote economic expansion through investment in infrastructure and R&D. It is in this sense that the ERT's neo-liberal-ism is embedded: it is embedded in both the national and supranational institutions of the EU.

The strategic orientation of 'embedded neo-liberalism' served as a rallying point for both political and social forces at the transnational level and helped prepare the ideological ground for the Maastricht Treaty. For this reason, the Maastricht compromise represented neither a triumph for Thatcherite neo-liberalism nor the construction of a neo-mercantilist Europe. Rather it expressed the synthetic concept of 'embedded neo-liberalism'. Monetary union – the central part of the treaty – and its convergence criteria most clearly reflect the neo-liberal orthodoxy (see Chapter 2). But aspects of the Rhenish 'network' model can be found in the Maastricht chapters on 'Trans-European [infra-structure] Networks' and 'Research and Technological Development' (reflecting a German-style industrial policy or *Ordnungspolitik*) and in the appended Social Protocol and Agreement which sets out proce-dures for bargaining between European trade unions and employers.

All these elements of the treaty (apart from the Social Protocol) had in fact figured prominently on the policy-agenda promoted by the European Roundtable (Apeldoorn, 1996).

Competing Capitalisms and the Regulatory Framework of Embedded Neo-Liberalism

But how precisely is this new regulatory framework interacting with the competition between capitalist models? To the extent that much of the European regulatory project allows 'mutual recognition' – i.e. competition between rules – European-level initiatives as such should have little effect, in theory, on the particular characteristics of 'network' or 'market-oriented' systems. Thus a European 'embedded neo-liberal' *Ordnungspolitik* should accommodate national diversity rather than erode it. But what is the evidence to date? Chapter 2 has already discussed the character of the new European regulatory system for competition policy and financial services. It was pointed out that, although that system derives from a free-market rather than 'neo-mercantilist' vision, in most cases a 'two-tier' regulatory structure is being established in which a degree of slack is permitted for national distinctiveness. Thus, Europe is set to remain a regulatory mosaic, regardless of the greater uniformity that is also being created by pan-European rules.

In financial services – an area of regulation with far-reaching consequences for European corporate governance – EU directives have already altered business conduct, by introducing new standards of capital adequacy and risk assessment and increasing transparency. Old practices – insider trading, the monopoly status of traditional brokers, unregulated 'gentleman's' agreements on conduct – have been swept away, and parochial stock exchange activities have been revolutionised by organisational change, computerisation and – in the German case – a centralisation of securities, futures and options trading and a privatisation of the Frankfurt exchange. The recently introduced (January 1996) Investment Services Directive (ISD) and its sibling, the Capital Adequacy Directive (CAD), set new minimum standards for markets and traders and will help remove the last vestiges of 'nationalism' from Europe's stock markets. But as with the Capital Movements and Second Banking Directives (see Chapter 2), scope for some national diversity is maintained. While it is no longer possible for governments and stock exchanges to prevent competition across their borders – for investment firms regulated in their own countries can acquire a 'passport' to operate in others and trade on foreign exchanges using remote access – host countries cannot take away the passport of 'visiting' companies (which may have been awarded it in a country with more relaxed standards) and capital adequacy standards will remain diverse, given that a *minimum* rather than a uniform level is required. At the same time, governments may continue to protect their markets, as evidenced by the problems of insurance companies gaining access to Germany and mortgage issuers in penetrating France (*Financial Times*, 16 February 1996).

As far as business regulation is concerned, there are considerable gaps in the European framework and in some respects the struggle between 'global' neo-liberalism and 'embedded' neo-liberalism goes on. Thus, while the battle over state-aids continues (as in the 1996 case brought by the European Commission against the German region of Saxony for subsidising a new Volkswagen plant), VAT rules are still unharmonised (in part because of the difficulties in bringing corporate tax rates together – an essential step in preventing lower tax countries from enjoying unfair advantage) and bankruptcy laws remain nationally specific. The clearest case of struggle between the 'global' and he 'embedded' European perspectives has been over the proposed pan-European company structure – the *Societas Europaea* (SE) – which could replace national systems of incorporation for many companies. The key obstacles to a single European company statute are, once again, competing tax regimes and the national specificities of existing company law. But the role of employees within the firm is the most controversial issue. The present draft proposal includes provisions on workers' information and consultation which the British want removed and the Germans want strengthened to include participation in management – as in their supervisory board system which allows for employee representation. Removal of this clause might satisfy the British government. But true to their global orientation, certain large British firms are opposed to a European statute altogether, advocating a mix of national and international governance, and a harmonisation of rules for company behaviour through the International Accountancy Standards Committee.

Of course, the issue of workers' representation has repercussions well beyond corporate governance and alerts us to the fact that the firms' external environment still differs substantially from country to country, posing serious problems for the construction of a European 'social regime'. The Anglo–Saxon neo-liberal 'social model' has met with considerable resistance in continental Europe where strongly rooted (institutionalised) traditions of social protection are well-entrenched.

However, even though the victory of neo-liberalism in the European Union is not total, there is no reason to anticipate the construction of a supranational Rhineland capitalism. In the first place, it must be realised that – in spite of all the rhetoric about a 'social dimension' to the internal market – the programme embodied in the Maastricht Treaty still falls far short of any European *social* market economy. The social chapter of Maastricht was in fact reduced to an annex of the treaty (as the UK refused to sign it) and even the implementation of this minimalist programme has arguably gone little further than symbolic politics, something that is unlikely to change under the present Commission (see Rhodes, 1995b). This is the clearest evidence that the social democratic project for Europe has failed.

If Maastricht reflects any elements of Rhineland capitalism, then, it is a very watered down version of that model, especially with regard to its social component. One reason for this is that the strength of German labour (and the trade unions in other 'social market' countries) is not mirrored at the European level, where organised labour plays only a marginal role in a policy-making process dominated by European business (Streeck and Schmitter, 1991; Traxler and Schmitter, 1995). Europe's transnational capitalist class regards even the very weak EU social dimension with suspicion. The creation of a supranational Rhineland capitalism – replicating significant elements of the German model at the EU level – would be a very daunting task, even if the political will were there. As Streeck (1995b, pp. 55) argues, any Europeanisation of the German model would be 'limited to those German institutions that make or accommodate markets, at the exclusion of complementary institutions, equally central to German capitalism, that socially embed and correct such markets'.

European integration will continue to be primarily a process of market integration. This supremacy of the market is 'softened', however, in so far as the single market is still embedded by old institutions at the national level as well as – albeit minimally – by new European institutions. This form of embeddedness seems to be more geared to the interests of transnational industrial capital – with EU policies oriented to promoting the global competitiveness – than to the creation of a social consensus for the European project. In this respect, the embeddedness of neo-liberal Europe is located primarily at the national level. However, to the extent that the emphasis at the European level will be increasingly on mere market integration rather than European state-building, national embeddedness may also be hollowed out.

Conclusion

Whether embedded neo-liberalism will prove to be a stable *European* model of capitalism remains to be seen. Much seems to depend on whether the power of global financial capital, which is the least interested in any form of embeddedness, will be reined in by the interests of industrial capital, whose longer-term success requires supportive social and political institutions. If the Anglo–Saxon model of finance gains more ground on the European continent, then the social and political structures of European capitalisms may also be eroded and move towards the more minimal provisions of the market-oriented systems. Nevertheless, there are good reasons to expect that while systems of corporate governance may converge, the external support networks of the Germanic – and, to a lesser extent, the Latin firms – will be remodelled rather than abandoned, given the manifest failure of Britain's 'disembedded' model. Indeed, if the latter does not begin to converge with the continental model by rebuilding its systems of training, education and innovation support, then that country's economic decline will continue, while its European competitors continue to invest in the broader institutional structures of comparative advantage. Whether the latter succeed, of course, is quite another question.

11

Regional Economic Policy and a Europe of the Regions

PHIL COOKE, THOMAS CHRISTIANSEN AND
GERD SCHIENSTOCK

Today, the number one factor for competitive advantage is innovation. With the changes brought about in global economic relations by the rise to prominence of the East Asian economies and the demise of Fordism as a model of industrial and wider societal regulation (see the Introduction to this volume), new approaches to creating competitive advantage have emerged. Increasing attention is paid to this imperative in European economic development measures and programmes.

Among the most challenging of these interventions are efforts to build systems of innovation in support of business competitiveness on a regional scale. These complement more established systems of innovation that operate at the national level – as analysed in Chapter 9 – by seeking to integrate industrial linkages within a given regionally administered area. Recently, European Union policies have shown signs of moving from a piecemeal to a more systemic approach to innovation support for business enterprises. The dynamics of the Single Market and the growing significance of European regional policy have led to the emergence of a novel, tripartite system of multilevel policy-making in Western Europe: regions and the European institutions are now working alongside national governments in promoting regional growth.

Evidence of systemic regional advantage began to emerge in the 1980s. Studies began to show the existence of innovation networks linking firms, intermediaries, research institutes, government agencies and technology bureaux, especially in regions with many small subcontracting firms. Classic examples in Europe include Baden-Württemberg, Emilia-Romagna, Tuscany and (small-country) Denmark. These economies are developing the interactive innovation practices that have

190

also been associated with competitiveness in Japan, Singapore, Korea and Taiwan. In such cases there are also strong signs that such networks are associated with clusters of industries. The specialised industrial districts of North–Central Italy, the integrated chains linking suppliers and producers in Baden-Württemberg and the high technology complexes of Rhône-Alpes have all pointed to the arrival of a new kind of innovative, specialised economic region with competitive, global reach. These have led to a process of institutional and business imitation in other regions. To some extent, EU policy has sought to encourage the emulation, with appropriate regional and local adjustments, of these dynamic regions.

However, other regions are not developed around industrial districts or business clusters, and the various regions have different problems. These range from the need to build up competitiveness (for example, regions in Ireland), restructure the existing economy, as in Baden-Württemberg, or replace existing industry as in many (Objective 2) regions undergoing industrial restructuring. There is a widespread need for adjustment because of new global conditions, even though each region's economy has its own unique history and circumstances. Even the strong regional economies referred to above have not been immune to the pressures of global competition. Increased unemployment, rising social tension, firmer controls on environmental degradation, fears of declining competitiveness and major exchange-rate turbulence have proved problematic (see Chapter 2). A continuing climate of 'global monetarism', the pursuit of low inflation and balanced budgets by governments, implies a new period of institutional and policy innovation.

Thus all regions in Europe face the need for adjustment; accepted models are themselves no longer exemplars. So every region must develop its own response shaped by its social context. This raises several questions: are regional innovation systems (not to mention regions) becoming more convergent or more divergent because of 'institutional borrowing'; are these matters of globalisation, competitiveness, innovation and economic clustering being played out at the local or regional level in the EU member states; and, finally, is a distinctive *regional* economic dimension emerging within the EU?

The New Economic Role of Regions

The increasing globalisation of markets has changed the environment of European companies drastically. They are confronted with intensive price, time and quality competition not just abroad but also at home. To stay competitive, European companies have to restructure their whole business organisation, including their innovation activities, as well as consumer and supplier relationships. Companies anticipate more success in regaining global competitiveness if they benefit from the specific advantage of their environment. Those that have reacted specifically to different environments have been more successful than others who believed in 'one best way' of organising business (Aichholzer and Schienstock, 1994).

Because of intensive global competition, companies are forced to look for the most supportive environment worldwide. Their restructuring is therefore directed by the concept of 'product specialisation'. This is not only true for larger companies but also for medium-sized firms. New transport and information technologies facilitate the global organisation of companies' production and innovation processes. Moreover, as production becomes more science-based, advantages such as a developed research infrastructure, a highly-qualified workforce or an innovative culture are becoming more important than natural resources, which means that a supportive environment for innovative companies can be created deliberately. To become attractive for companies, regions and localities can set up specific institutions to support their innovation strategies. In this respect, it may be that 'region-states' are now more appropriate for designing supportive environments than are nation-states (Cooke, 1996). Ohmae (1995), for example, argues that in an increasingly borderless world the nation-state is becoming dysfunctional: the 'region-state' is the 'natural' economic area, since it represents genuine communities of economic interest and can take advantage of true linkages and synergies (economies of scale and agglomeration) among economic actors. Regions have to seek competitive advantage by mobilising all their assets, including institutional and governmental ones where these exist, or demand them where they do not (Cooke, 1995).

Although it has been suggested that regional economies are becoming more important, there is little consensus on how to define a region. It is important to mention that a regional classification is an intellectual concept. It exists only in terms of the criteria by which it is defined. Four criteria are often used to define a region: (i) a region must not have a limited size; (ii) it should display homogeneity in terms of specific criteria; (iii) it may be distinguished from bordering areas by a particular kind of association of related features; and (iv) it must possess some kind of internal cohesion. It is also important to mention that the boundaries of regions are not fixed once and for all; regions can change, new regions can emerge and old ones can perish. Therefore to analyse a region, criteria must be found that define a functioning unit within a specific time.

The concept of 'industrial cluster' may be used to define a region from an economic perspective (Porter, 1990). Clusters are dense networks of economic actors, interacting closely and with intensive exchange relationships. All economic actors who contribute directly to the dominant production process of a region are partners in this network, including manufacturing and service companies, and supply and marketing companies. Financial institutions, research institutes and technology transfer agencies, economic associations and unions, training institutions, the regional government and even informal associations are also included. Well-established industrial clusters are not found in all regions, while regions displaying cluster-like economic features may have more than one economic cluster. Regions may differ in their closeness of co-operation and in some regions the local authorities may be rather weak. In others it may be difficult to find a well established supportive institutional set-up at all, in which case national institutions may be more important than regional ones, if they exist at all. Therefore it is important to distinguish between different types of region in seeking to find out how they function and how well they perform. It is also important to analyse how national and regional systems are related.

The economic criterion for defining a region became less reliable as large corporations restructured their activities to serve their own internal, company divisions of labour. Cultural homogeneity, too, is less powerful than it once was, cases such as Catalonia and, for example, Flanders/Wallonia notwithstanding. A tendency towards pragmatism, especially in the European context, where administrative boundaries at subnational level increasingly double as designations of regions has, for the present, taken the lead in the field. In instances such as the German *Länder* or even the Spanish and Italian cases, some degree of regional distinctiveness based on the effects of regional economic and other policies seems to be emerging. And among the policies which seem to have some influence in creating a new regional distinctiveness are those which support innovation within regional economies.

Innovation Systems and Regional Development

The concept of innovation is used in connection with the analysis of processes of technological change. Technological change is seen conventionally as having three different stages: invention, innovation and diffusion. Invention is defined as the stage of production of new knowledge; innovation as the first application of the existing knowledge to production; and diffusion as the broadening use of new technologies. This is a 'trickle down' or 'cascade' model; the extent of fundamental research substantially influences the opportunities for technological innovation within a territory, which in turn determines the economic growth rate. In the case of an adequate distribution of resources to fundamental scientific research, technological progress makes it possible to initiate a process of economic growth. However, in reality it is rarely possible to find such a sequence of clearly delineated stages (Lundvall, 1992). Rather, innovative activities can be both stimulus and result, consequence and prerequisite. Therefore a broader definition of innovation is now increasingly being used, which includes all activities of the process of technological change: problems of awareness and definition, the development of new ideas and new solutions for existing problems, the realisation of new solutions and technological options as well as the broader diffusion of new technologies.

It is also important to bear in mind that innovations are not exceptional or large-scale phenomena; on the contrary, they can take place at any time, incrementally and in all areas of the economy (Lundvall, 1992). Using such a broad definition, it is useful to focus on the process of learning through which knowledge and new technologies are created, distributed and used in specific areas. Learning is defined as a collective process shaped by the existing structure of production, by organisations and by institutions. The characteristics of such a learning system are central to questions of growth, employment and competition. In this context it is useful to distinguish between different processes of learning: learning in a broader sense such as searching and exploring (which takes place within the production process); and learning in the narrower sense such as learning-by-doing, by using and by interacting in relation to normal production activities (Johnson, 1992). Searching and discovering are more complex learning processes, including activities of problem definition and problem solution, which take place in specific institutions. Searching means a process of deliberately choosing and recombining existing knowledge to develop new products and processes. Searching therefore takes place within specific technology paradigms (Dosi, 1982). Exploring, on the other hand, means the production of new knowledge for newly-defined problems rather than producing knowledge capable of direct technological application.

On this conceptual basis it is a matter of increasing policy concern to the European Commission, notably its Directorates General (DG) XVI (regional policy), XII (science and technology policy) and XIII (information technology), to seek both to maximise the innovation potential of firms in its leading technology-intensive regions, and to integrate and stimulate related innovative activities among firms in less-favoured regions (Landabaso, 1993). Of paramount importance to the future development of such thinking and policy-preparation is the notion of 'system'. This is because, in the past, EU policy in support of innovation among firms has been piecemeal. Now there is an interest in supporting efforts to make innovation measures more systemic, through pilot initiatives such as Regional Innovation and Technology Transfer Strategies (RITTS) and Regional Innovation Strategies (RIS). This suggests the beginning of a convergence in the stylised picture EU policy-makers have of innovation processes (interactive, networked and reflexive) and regional development processes (linkages between firms and among agencies, partnership, learning and monitoring). This gains particular weight where regions have relatively powerful administrations capable of delivering industrial policies with a strong and, to the business community, popular, innovation dimension.

Towards Regional Productivity Coalitions

In the literature on innovation the meaning of the term 'system' is not yet analysed in great detail. Some general definitions of a system of innovation exist (Nelson, 1993). For example, Lundvall (1992) defines a system of innovation as constituted by elements and relationships which interact in the production, diffusion and use of new and economically useful knowledge. An innovation system is therefore a social system: innovations are the result of social interaction between economic actors. And it is an open system which interacts with its environment.

But this system approach only provides an analytical framework, not a theory. Other concepts allow us to explore the connection between social and institutional structures and techno-economic change, and therefore the nature of a regional innovation system. Perez (1987) emphasises the importance of this connection for economic growth and international competitiveness in specific territories. Mismatches occur between new technologies and the old social model of production. As old institutions and cultural patterns correspond to the requirement of the outdated technological system, they have to change if the new paradigm's productivity potential is to be fully exploited. In this context, Grabher (1993) argues that certain forms of development may lead to political, structural and cognitive rigidities, which then become a hindrance to the search for a new technological paradigm. In an economic crisis, however, there are opportunities for learning to carry out major changes, as it becomes clear that surmounting the crisis will be impossible within the traditional path of development. The requisite institutional change will involve all of the following: work organisation and management practices as well as to the education system, the financial system, the industrial relations system, the governance and regulatory systems and so on.

Successful learning systems can be found in the strong regions where responsible self-management underpins regional productivity coalitions. These are the concrete expression of the kind of interactive, systemic learning found increasingly in the world of innovation, translated, as it were, into the regional arena of civil society and civic politics. It reaches its highest form in 'reflexive regions' (that is, regions that can 'think' and act strategically) such as Baden-Württemberg and Emilia-Romagna (Cooke and Morgan, 1994a, 1994b; Cooke 1996a). Such regions have become something of a template for new thinking among DGs XVI, XII and XIII about the nature of the economic development process and the measures appropriate for promoting regional productivity coalitions in less-favoured regions. An increasing share of regional policy instruments seek to stimulate intra- as well as interregional network relationships in order to qualify for, let alone implement, European regional innovation and related economic measures.

Understanding how these regions work is assisted by two further concepts: industrial districts and governance. The concept of industrial districts (see, for example, Pyke and Sengenberger, 1992) describes the characteristic patterns of successful regions by pointing to the following elements: the existence of a strong small and medium-sized enterprise (SME) sector, intensive horizontal co-operation between companies, a highly-qualified workforce and flexible work structure, a dense infrastructure of supportive institutions and organisations, and an innovative regional culture as well as an active regional government. The concept, however, distinguishes between 'high road' and 'low road' regional strategies, which means that an innovative system can be created deliberately by economic actors. As for governance in these systems, this can be conceived as a shift from a traditional 'state-regulation' mode to a 'self-regulation' mode of operation (Latniak and Simonis, 1994). Self-regulation refers not to a neo-liberal notion of individual self-reliance but rather to the self-management of society by responsible groups or associations (see Hirst, 1994).

Thus, typical members of such regional productivity coalitions – based around industrial districts and 'self-regulation' – will be, to one extent or another, regional ministries, regional development agencies, chambers of commerce, training agencies, technology-transfer agencies, research institutes, universities, private companies, consultancies and relevant voluntary or business associations. Not untypically, such coalitions will stimulate and promote the conduct of periodic commissions of inquiry into perceived crisis situations in regional economies. During the 1990s this has been the case for Baden-Württemberg (Future Commission), Emilia-Romagna (President's Commission), Wales (Institute of Welsh Affairs '2010' Commission) and numerous others. But such instances of 'institutional reflexivity' are by no means ubiquitous. The EU is seeking increasingly to encourage such activity on a wider regional canvas.

The Enabling Role of EC Structural Funds

The general move towards reflexivity and indigenous growth on the regional level has been further accelerated by the process of European integration since the mid-1980s. There are two main aspects to this process, which have had a strong bearing on regional economic policy: for the less developed regions in the Community, the 1988 reform of the 'Structural Funds' provided new stimulus and additional support; for the better-off regions, the opportunities afforded by the Single Act and the 1992 programme increased regulatory competition for direct investment and provided incentives for interregional co-operation.

The new structural funds have aimed at providing a framework not only for the redistribution of financial resources, but also for a management of regional policy to enable regions themselves to take charge of economic development. Besides the doubling of the EC capital available, and the introduction of so-called Community Initiatives, there were four main aspects to this structural fund reform – concentration, programming, additionality and partnership (European Commission, 1993).

While the amount of money spent on regional development has been increased significantly – the funds were doubled in 1988 and again in 1993, and at the time of writing stand at Ecu 142bn for the current five-year period – it is now also less widely distributed. A number of key parameters for EU regional policy have been defined – the conversion of regions in industrial decline, the structural adjustment for regions lagging behind, and the development of rural areas – as a means of concentrating funds. The bulk of the money goes to the 'Objective 1 regions' which are by definition below 75 per cent of the EC average of GDP per capita. EC regional funds are now spent on multiannual 'Community Support Frameworks' (CSFs) in which the parties involved in the running of regional policy agree on a number of priorities and goals (Programming). On the basis of these two-to-five-year framework documents, management committees in the regions then choose individual projects for funding. These committees include local and regional representatives as well as national and Commission officials. Although often cumbersome, the CSF preparation and implementation procedures ensure that EC regional policy avoids a previous tendency to 'fly the European flag' by financing one-off projects with little or no connection to the problems and opportunities present in specific regions (Wise and Croxford, 1988).

Both the preparatory and the implementation stage of CSFs demands substantial input from local and regional actors. Obviously, the European Commission is not in a position itself to judge the development needs of often remote and peripheral regions; and it has been keen to involve regional actors in policy-making and avoid reliance solely on member state representatives for input and know-how. The idea of partnership is to ensure that all levels agree on a common platform for policy-making. National governments still have a major say in policy formulation and in designating the regional actors that can participate; but the policy process now firmly includes representatives from the levels most concerned with the substance of decision-making (Marks, 1992). At the same time, the Commission convened a new consultative body of regional and local authorities to advise on the regional implications of Community policy-making. While initially marginal to the policy-process and internally divided, this body was the foundation for the Committee of the Regions, which the Maastricht Treaty introduced to the Union structure, and which is a much more substantial contribution to the presence of regions at the European centre (Christiansen, 1996b).

The most controversial reform, additionality, has two aspects: co-financing and preventing the substitution of national by European funding. Co-financing stipulated that the funding of CSF development projects should not come solely from the EC, but should be matched by national, regional, local and even private money. This is intended to ensure that actors at all levels, especially the local level, share a belief in the viability of the project and its usefulness for regional development.

The requirement of matched funding is probably the best guarantee of this commitment, while also providing an effective filter against symbolic or unwarranted project submissions. There is also a multiplier effect: not only is more European money aimed at specifically designated areas, but these regions themselves are now spending more money on development. Second, the structural fund money going into a member state's region must be *additional* to the flow of national public spending into the region. There have been numerous accusations from local and regional actors, as well as from the Commission, that member states are not complying with additionality – a concept the Commission has found tremendously difficult to supervise and enforce (McAleavey, 1993). Ill-feeling on all sides has resulted from the lack of transparency in this matter, and, at least at one stage, the British government and the European Commission were close to a European Court case.

The Commission has only had sufficient information and freedom of action to pursue additionality properly in the Community Initiatives. These initiatives, which have a separate budget line, account for about 10 per cent of the total structural fund budget and are designed to deal with specific problems: the conversion of coal-mining areas (RE-CHAR); of steel-manufacturing areas (RESIDER); of areas affected by the decline of defence spending (KONVER); of textile areas (RETEX); and assistance for cross-border co-operation (INTERREG) (European Commission, 1994a). Their greater flexibility in decision-making and financial management made these initiatives very attractive to regions, and it is here that one finds the best example of a clear and direct relationship between the EU and regions.

The structural fund reform has clearly assisted the emancipation of the less-developed regions, perhaps changing less their financial or economic situation than their culture of dependency on transfers from the centre. The actual achievement of cohesion or increased convergence among the regional economies remains questionable (Begg and Mayes, 1993; Rodríguez-Pose, 1994). But the importance of the structural funds should rather be sought in their enabling role: by transforming administrative cultures and promoting greater self-reliance in economic development, they are assisting regions to exploit the possibilities that now exist for innovation and flexible specialisation.

Competition for Foreign Direct Investment and European Funds

Beyond the lagging regions or those in decline, those with higher growth levels have been affected by other reforms in the Community since the mid-1980s (Begg, 1985). It is now widely recognised that the implementation of the 1992 programme has been one of re-regulation rather than deregulation (Majone, 1989). With Europe providing the regulatory framework to ensure the 'four freedoms' of the Single Market (of capital, labour, goods and services), member states and, increasingly, regional governments have had to respond by preparing their regulatory systems for competition for capital investment, skilled labour, know-how and access to core markets in the European Economic Area (Cooke, 1992).

The mechanism for this dynamic relaunch of 'Europe' was provided by the principle of mutual recognition: that products complying with the regulations in one member state and fulfilling minimum standards under EU legislation, must be allowed to be traded in all other member states (Dehousse, 1989). The indirect assault on non-tariff barriers to intra-EU trade meant that national and regional regulatory systems were now in competition to provide the best environment for the production and export of goods and services. The more traditional competition for foreign direct investment, which was heavily influenced by national variables, has increasingly become a competition between regulatory systems, including those of individual regions. As national non-tariff barriers to trade have gone, the significance of factors that are contextual to production, such as infrastructure, industrial relations, workforce skills, quality of life and so on. – factors that often are, or could be, influenced by regional authorities – has increased.

As a result, the pattern of inward investment in the EU is increasingly seen in *regional* rather than purely national terms. Japanese investment into the UK since the mid-1980s, for example, is widely seen as investment into Wales and the North-East of England, because of the specific regulatory conditions that are provided there. With this realisation – which is of different intensity in different national systems – has come the drive among regions actively to influence the pattern of inward investment. This trend towards pro-active attraction of investment includes both 'domestic' and 'foreign' activity. Within the region, there are attempts to harness local potential, to speed up the land use planning process, to improve the infrastructure and communications situation, and to match the demands of investors with the provisions for vocational training and higher eduction. Beyond their borders, regional authorities have taken to representing and promoting the region abroad, both by maintaining a permanent presence in Brussels and other international capitals, and by lobbying on the region's behalf at international fairs and conferences, or in bilateral meetings with potential investors (Mazey and Mitchell, 1993). In many cases, the dynamics of regulatory competition and the demands of lobbying have led regions to establish independent agencies or private law firms that have the task of ensuring the co-ordination of domestic and external investment efforts.

A combined result of regulatory competition and flexible specialisation is the trend of 'specialised' regions to engage in interregional co-operation (Borras Alomar, 1995; European Commission, 1994b). Faced with too great a diversity in their national context in the search for co-operation, exchange and joint ventures, better-off regions frequently find partner regions in other member states. Ventures such as the 'Four Motors of Europe' (a cross-frontier collaboration involving Baden-Württemberg, Rhône-Alpes, Lombardy and Catalonia) are a way for regions to compete for both European funds and private international capital, by joining others with similar economic characteristics and utilising the combined strength of, in this case, considerable experience in technology transfer.

On the whole, the impact of European integration on all regions in the EU has been considerable. The opportunities afforded by the Single Market and the reformed structural funds have not only led to changes in long-lasting development patterns in many regions, but have also, and crucially, transformed their administrative and regulatory systems. As a result, the relationship between national and regional level decision-makers has changed: the Europeanisation of policy-making means that regions both can and have to take more responsibility for their socioeconomic destiny, a trend that has been identified in most countries. To the extent that this, in turn, requires greater autonomy in political decision-making powers at the regional level, the European influence on West European territorial politics has therefore been substantial. While scepticism remains about whether there is indeed the rise of a 'Europe of the Regions' (see, for example, Anderson, 1991; Borras Alomar *et al.*, 1994), the changes occurring are clearly fundamental. This has led authors in recent years to analyse the regional issue in the EU in terms of 'multilevel governance', arguing that we now have to consider the EU as a complex polity, based on multiple levels and power relationships between supranational, national, local and regional authorities (Marks, 1993; Christiansen, forthcoming).

The Relationship between the 'Global' and the 'Local'

However, the notion of a 'Europe of the Regions' remains rather nebulous, and the emphasis above on regional pro-activity does not signify an uncritical attachment to it. There are clearly some tendencies towards member-state 'hollowing-out' (Held, 1991) – the shift, that is, of policy-making to the EU level and demand for, or advantage taken of, greater regional economic powers at subnational levels. Sovereign parliaments are losing powers, especially over economic matters, as many of these become the subject of Council of Ministers and other European institutional determination (see Chapter 2). But other matters of political interest may rise up to fill the space that used to be occupied by economic (or, for that matter, foreign affairs) debates. Family affairs, child abuse, crime and legal matters are amongst the issues that seem to be more pronounced on the agendas of national assemblies in the 1990s compared to, say, the 1960s. As for the shift of power downwards to the regions, the situation is very uneven. Spain is the apotheosis of this. The Basque government raises taxes, keeps 70 per cent and sends the rest to Madrid to run defence and foreign affairs. The Basque police are separate from the Spanish, and the economic ministries pursue many distinctive policies. Linguistically and in terms of the media, Basque culture is well-represented. Yet Extremadura has virtually none of these characteristics, despite being a region within the Spanish state system. In principle, a region such as this can call down such powers if and when the need for them is given political expression. But its regionalisation is, for the present, latent.

This variability is also true of the member-states themselves. We only have to compare Belgium and Britain to see the extremes of full federalism operating in the former – at member-state level – and fairly full centralism in the latter. Except for reinstating local government representation for London, a city of quasi-regional scale, an incoming British Labour government in the second half of the 1990s would only contemplate establishing regional 'chambers' of nominated representatives. Wales and Scotland would be given more; but then it is arguable that they are in any case, nations rather than regions. So what is new at the regional level? Interestingly, it is the regions rather than the nation-states that often implement the EU's new initiatives and programmes; and this returns us to a question posed earlier in this chapter as to whether regional economic policies in the EU are tending to converge or diverge.

On the one had it is extremely hard to argue that they are diverging significantly, even where, as in the case of Britain, there is a notable degree of Euro-scepticism and sometime reluctance readily to accept EU funding. Even in English 'regions', Structural Fund investments in roads and other infrastructures, Science and Technology for Regional Development in Europe (STRIDE), Strategic Programme for Innovation and Technology Transfer (SPRINT) and many others are to be found operating. The operation can be marginally distinctive when it comes to implementation, but, as with Community Support Frameworks, comparable broad categories of activity are funded and action plans must fit the criteria without enormous latitude being displayed. But on the other hand, it is clear that distinctive 'policy cultures' influence greatly the translation of EU policies into national contexts.

Selecting the STRIDE Community initiative – which seeks to strengthen capacity of lagging regions for research, technology and innovation – as the lens through which to observe this process, Nauwelaers (1995) concludes the following. In France's Objective 2 regions, STRIDE projects had 'a clear bottom-up character . . . rooted in their local environment' (ibid, p. 12), in line with their local development mission but with little transparency or openness between projects and regions. Networking and consensus building at *local* level were real achievements in consolidating public technology transfer infrastructures but less adequate in relation to the private sector. In contrast, STRIDE in Wallonia (Belgium) was targeted directly at SMEs, with the aim of improving their 'innovation culture' from inside through training. The global character of the innovation process was recognised, extending support well beyond the merely technological, and inter-enterprise networking was stimulated though, as in France, less systematically than was anticipated. The emphasis on public-sector-led provision and innovation promotion in France is a product of French policy culture in this field and produces a linear (one-way) and bureaucratic rather than co-operative approach. But in the strongly federal system operating in Wallonia, the regional administration was able to work directly with small firms, rather than with yet another level of bureaucracy.

This case illustrates the more general argument that one of the advantages of regionalised industrial policy is that the agency responsible may be expected to be more in touch, sensitised to and sensitive of the needs of regional firms (O'Doherty, 1994). Although it is still difficult to incorporate the business sector fully into specific programmes – even where these are designed to help them – nevertheless, direct access is clearly facilitated where the delivery mechanism is closer to the market. Also, where a regional approach is possible there is less likelihood of policy delivery being disadvantaged by attachment to an outmoded theory of the processes at which intervention is aimed. In the Wallonian case, the more global view of technological application and innovation culture suggests strongly the presence of an 'interactive learning' approach to innovation, as discussed above. In contrast, the

French state apparatus, with the centralised assets of a well-developed national system of innovation, has predictable problems in developing a co-operative innovation model.

To round off this discussion of the relationship between the 'global' and the 'local' in an EU context, the nature of EU policy-making in this should be mentioned. Here the concept of 'policy networks' within the Commission becomes important (Cooke, 1996b). By policy networks we mean the individuals, groups, organisations or institutions that interact around specific policies or projects. The stability of such networks derives from the establishment of trust and reliability, reputation and customary rules that members adhere to. The networks have access to resources and influence in pursuing projects considered important. The nature of the project dictates the configuration of the network: if regional innovation is the policy, then individuals of consequence to both aspects will comprise the network.

The Commission operates as a multi-organisation (Cram, 1994) in which 'purposeful opportunism' (Klein and O'Higgins 1985) takes the form of a battle between DGs to head the Commission policy agenda. Cram (1994) notes that, in the innovation field, the Commission's multi-organisational nature is particularly complex, with competing and overlapping competences as well as complementary ones among DGXIII (on which she focuses) for Information Technology, DGXII (Science and Technological Research), DGIII (Industrial Policy), DGIV (Competition), to which we would add DGXVI (Regional Policy) and even DGXXIII (SMEs). Promoting innovation policy itself has therefore to be a sensitive, co-operative process of interactive learning and policy entrepreneurship.

Regional innovation policy has of late been the product of an uneasy alliance between DGXII, DGXIII and DGXVI. Put crudely, DGXVI has the money and the other two have the responsibility for innovation. DGXVI, under the reformed Structural Funds, is seeking a broader definition of infrastructure investment than its traditional road-building and related remit. Telecommunications, still in the sense of hardware, has moved up the policy agenda, not least because of its capacity for integration. The information superhighway is seen as a vital economic growth instrument, bringing peripheral, lagging economies closer, in principle, to the key points on the networks. So, information technology and innovation-related hard and, crucially, *soft* infrastructures (technology-transfer centres; science exploitation centres; Business Innovation Centres) are but a short step away. Though these are the remit of DGXIII, it does not have sufficient resources to ensure their construction. DGXII, meanwhile, with its research remit and foresight function has an important role in communicating innovative ideas and prospective policy areas which may assist DGXIII to spend some of DGXVI's money (Landabaso, 1993). Avoiding the overlaps and duplications of the past will be assisted, in part, by the new Community Support Frameworks. DGXVI has now adopted a more systemic approach and needs to bring in the other DGs to ensure a more integrated end result. This is not to say that the approach works perfectly but, in general, regional innovation has itself proved an integrative policy area within as well as outside the Commission.

Concluding Remarks

In this chapter we have argued that regional economic policy, particularly regional innovation policy, is increasingly being seen as a useful adjunct to the improvement of the innovation capacity, and hence competitiveness, of European companies. The rise of a globalised economy in which firms operate strategically by entering each other's markets not merely in terms of sales but also in production, processing and conducting command, control and research functions in host economies, has introduced a clear change in the level of competitiveness required if European firms are to survive.

The question of whether, as a result of globalisation, the efficacy of nation-states has been compromised with respect to economic policy must, in the European case, be answered positively. So much of strategic economic policy-making and, in particular, requirements for budgetary, fiscal and monetary control have moved or are in process of moving to the European level, that 'national' economic regimes protecting national 'champion' companies by tariffs or industrial subsidies are unquestionably on their way out, if not already a thing of the past. This 'hollowing-out' of the state has been a striking feature of the EU member states in the closing decades of the twentieth century.

But, as the supranational level has accrued powers at the expense of the member states, have the regions also lost policy influence? The answer here seems to be in the negative. Most EU states have at least as strong, and often stronger, regional powers than was the case in, say, the 1960s. Some leading regional economies have displayed high annual growth rates and low unemployment with innovative regional industrial policies, particularly with regard to enterprise support for small and medium-sized firms. This is no accident, for the new economic order is one in which the synergies between small firms themselves, and between them and large firms, are themselves sources of competitive advantage. This clustering phenomenon, often focused at the regional scale, is seen as a key element of economic dynamism, from the industrial districts of Northern Italy to the financial services of the City of London. A decentralisation of industrial policy has been occurring.

Of particular importance here is that a new model of interactive learning and systemic innovation is capable of being operated successfully at the regional and local level by global corporations. That is why firms such as Sony from Japan locate their R&D centres in regions such as Baden-Württemberg where they can take advantage of the externalities in skill and expertise stimulated in part by judicious regional governance.

The European Commission seeks to promote network forms of interactive learning and systemic innovation through the policies of DGXVI, DGXIII, DGXII and others. To some extent, the dynamic, networked regional economies are a template for such measures and there is some convergence in the kind of innovation infrastructure to be found increasingly in richer, and some less-favoured, regional economies. This process is also having interesting effects upon the internal workings of the European Commission, whose directorates, at least in the field of regional innovation, can also be seen to be influenced by the idea of economic growth through the pursuit of co-operative advantage.

12

Foreign, Defence and Security Policy

PHILIP GUMMETT

With the end of the Cold War, the old security policies and structures that served the countries of Western Europe have been called into question. In the heady days of 1988 and 1989, there was talk of massive disarmament and of a substantial 'peace dividend'. Events since then, in the former Yugoslavia and elsewhere (including post-Mikhail Gorbachev Russia) have dampened that early optimism. Nevertheless, the basic questions remain of what West European defence and security policy is for, and within what framework it can best be pursued.

This chapter sets current debates within the context of a brief history of post-Second World War security developments. It looks at developments in Europe's two nuclear states, France and the United Kingdom, but considers also recent events in a wider range of countries. It ends by reviewing present thinking about security and foreign policy structures.

The Early Postwar Context

In seeking a new defence and security framework, Europe is in the late 1990s repeating an exercise last attempted at the end of the Second World War. To understand current debates, it is important to appreciate certain features of the history of this policy domain.

In 1945, Western Europe was divided between the 'victorious powers' (principally Britain and France) and the defeated (Germany and Italy), but for all of them the economic position was dire. Of the leading European 'victorious powers', Britain was devastated industrially, and France was still primarily agricultural. Yet both still considered themselves to be Great Powers: they had been at the meetings at Potsdam and Yalta where the terms of the postwar settlement had been agreed; they were on the Security Council of the newly-formed United Nations; and they remained imperial powers, albeit fading ones. As late as 1951–2, Britain was spending as much as a half of what the USA was spending on research and development into the new field of guided weapons. There was also no question but that Britain would have its own atomic bomb programme. It was some time before there was widespread appreciation of how decisively the war had signalled the industrial, as well as the military, supremacy of the USA over the European powers. The USA, in fact, had had a 'good war', doubling industrial production, and was hungry in 1945 for markets to maintain this level of output. This was one of the factors behind Marshall Aid to Europe, announced in June 1947.

Defeated Germany, meanwhile, had been partitioned. The USA, together with Britain and France, occupied the western part, and imposed a constitution which restricted Germany's scope for rearmament. The Soviet army held East Germany (Berlin, located, of course, within East Germany, was subject to special partitioning between the Western powers and the Soviets), together with Eastern and Central Europe. Yet the USSR was by no means universally seen as an 'enemy' by European states until late 1947. The height of the 'Cold War' came with the Berlin blockade – and the consequent Allied airlift – of June 1948 to May 1949, and with the forcible take-overs of power by communist governments in much of Eastern Europe.

In security terms, Western European states responded to the new climate partly by the formation of new alliances, and partly through national means. In March 1948, Britain, France and the Benelux countries formed the Brussels Treaty Organisation (BTO). The central concern of this alliance initially was Germany. With the Berlin blockade, however, concern about the USSR intensified. Talks began between the BTO powers, the USA and Canada about a North Atlantic security agreement. These led by April 1949 to the signing of the North Atlantic Treaty (and establishment of the associated Organisation – hence 'NATO') by Belgium, Canada, Denmark, France, Iceland, Italy, Luxembourg, the Netherlands, Norway, Portugal, the United Kingdom and the USA (but not Germany). NATO built a collective planning and decision-making structure that gave it more significance than the BTO. The latter withered, but maintained an active parliamentary assembly, and survived in a somewhat moribund state, later adding Germany and renaming itself the Western

European Union (WEU), before finally enjoying an unexpected rea-wakening some forty years later (see below).

The period 1950–4 saw serious consideration among the Six of aligning NATO with the emerging European economic institutions. The idea developed of a European Defence Community (EDC), which would involve Germany. This seemed particularly attractive when the Korean War (1951–3), and the fear that it could spark another global war, made the Soviet threat loom larger in Europe. German rear-mament within the framework of collective decision-making would mean that Germany could strengthen European security against the USSR, while itself being constrained from aggression against its still nervous neighbours. This scheme appealed also to integrationists, since the EDC treaty, which was signed in 1952, envisaged a European army, centralised procurement, and a high degree of collective decision-making. This would have represented a substantial addition to the functionalist logic of the Common Market, ECSC and Euratom.

But the EDC treaty was not ratified in the French National Assembly, partly because Britain would not join, thus increasing French fears of German domination. Moreover, with the end of the Korean War, and the death of Josef Stalin (both occurring in 1953), the Soviet threat receded. In addition, two groups hostile to the EDC, the Gaullists and the communists, strengthened their position in the Assembly between 1950 and 1954, so that the treaty, when presented in 1954, failed. The usual lesson drawn from this is that defence is not a suitable vehicle for European co-operation. Taylor (1984) suggests, however, that the record is less clear: the EDC was ratified in the Benelux countries and in Germany; Italy was expected to ratify; the French Assembly had also approved the principle in 1950. There was therefore nothing inevitable about its failure. This is worth recalling when, later in this chapter, we review the current state of debate in Europe on these very same questions.

With the failure of the EDC, a different solution to the German question had to be found. German rearmament was therefore effected in 1954 through the incorporation of Germany, and Italy, into the BTO/WEU, and on terms that effectively subordinated the WEU to NATO. Germany was specifically bound to eschew nuclear, chemical and biological weapons, restrict the production of other types of weapons, and accept WEU inspection of compliance. Membership of NATO followed in 1955.

NATO itself, meanwhile, had been building an elaborate political and military structure, headquartered in Brussels. Member states exercised political authority through permanent ambassadors to the

North Atlantic Council. Unanimous decisions were required, thus avoiding any ceding of sovereignty. Planning committees were set up to oversee policy with respect to nuclear and conventional weapons, and a military command structure, initially organised on the basis of geographical regions (Atlantic, Channel, Continental Europe) put in place the means to mount actual operations, drawing upon forces committed to NATO by member states. Behind this appearance of equality of sovereign states, however, it was clear from the outset that one state, the USA, was dominant: Western Europe was in no position to guarantee its own security in the early 1950s.

This position was acceptable for the first decade or so of European reconstruction. The special authority enjoyed by the former General Dwight Eisenhower, Europe's liberator, as US president in the 1950s, further eased the arrangement. Nevertheless, France at least became increasingly unhappy with it, especially after the USA refused its support for the Franco-British invasion of the Suez Canal in Egypt in 1956. This unhappiness was part of what lay behind the French decision of 1958 to develop their own atomic bomb, as well as their decision of 1966 to withdraw from the integrated military structure of NATO (though not from the treaty itself). Even into the 1990s, the US military commitment to Europe was massive. Thus, at the start of that decade, the US posted 300 000 troops (and families) in Europe, and supplied most of the nuclear weapons. The US has also traditionally supplied NATO's Supreme Allied Commander in Europe (SACEUR).

If NATO's dependence on the USA has been an issue in the politics of some European states, so also has it in the USA itself, as expressed in the debate over 'burden-sharing'. Indeed, the USA tried in the 1960s to transform the Alliance into a more equal partnership. From this episode emerged the phrase the 'European pillar' of the Atlantic alliance, which included proposals (never implemented) for a NATO Multilateral (nuclear) Force. Soviet reaction against this idea, which it saw as putting German fingers on a NATO nuclear trigger, became a key driver of the Nuclear Non-Proliferation Treaty of 1968. The idea of a European pillar has, however, resurfaced recently (see below).

Nuclear policy has been a key, and controversial, element of NATO thinking. Underlying it has been the unwillingness of NATO members to match Soviet troop numbers. In 1952 it was agreed to increase NATO's army strength from twenty-five to ninety-six divisions within two years, Soviet divisions at the time being thought to number 140–170. But this would have meant a massive increase, with the costly political price of a sharp rise in levels of conscription. As the Korean war ended, and the fear of a wider war subsided, the goal dropped to thirty divisions, and emphasis switched to the introduction of nuclear weapons as a way of offsetting what has always officially been declared to be massive Soviet conventional superiority. We return later to a discussion of European security questions at inter- and supranational levels, but first we review developments at the national level in Europe's two nuclear-armed states.

The Nuclear States

Britain

Britain's nuclear programme began quite independently from – and, indeed, in part as a reaction against – that of the USA (the Manhattan Project), in which it had participated during the Second World War. Subsequent decisions led to the development of the first British deterrent – the V-bomber force; to Britain's abortive attempt to build its own intermediate-range ballistic missile, Blue Streak; and then to a policy of dependence on the USA for the delivery of British-made nuclear weapons. This policy began unhappily with a plan to buy the air-launched Skybolt ballistic missile, and, when this was cancelled by President John Kennedy in 1962, by the purchase of Polaris submarine-launched ballistic missiles. This missile, with various subsequent improvements, became the basis of the UK nuclear force, augmented by a decreasingly effective bomber force (Freedman, 1980).

The life-expectancy of the submarines meant that if there was to be a successor to Polaris, the decision would have to be made around 1980. This issue, coinciding with the 1979 NATO decision to deploy Cruise and Pershing-II missiles in Europe, fanned massive controversy. The debate was partly technical, about what sort of system should be acquired. The choice quickly settled (for reasons of invulnerability) on a submarine system, and on ballistic missiles as the delivery vehicle. There was also a strategic debate, concerned with what the system was *for*. Arguments turned on the view that a British bomb, within NATO, increased Soviet uncertainty by presenting it with a 'second centre of decision making'; that the bomb would constitute a distinctive 'UK contribution to NATO'; and that it was a 'last-ditch UK weapon of ultimate resort' (an awkward argument to use without giving the impression of not trusting the commitment of the USA). In addition, there were *military* arguments, concerning the value of naval and other links with the USA; and *political* ones, concerning Britain's place in the world, and its access to the 'nuclear high table'.

Although counter-views existed to all these arguments, which were expressed vigorously during lengthy public protests and intellectual debate, there was never any real question but that the Thatcher Government would go ahead with a Polaris replacement and economics drove in direction of purchasing a US system, Trident-I. The plan was for four to five UK-built submarines, each with sixteen US Trident missiles equipped with eight independently targetable warheads. Unlike Polaris warheads, each Trident missile could attack eight distinct targets, and to much greater effect. Opponents tried to argue that a force of this power meant that Britain was preparing not merely to deter, but actually to fight, a nuclear war. Controversy increased when the USA announced its intention to replace this missile with the larger, even more accurate, Trident-II which the Thatcher Government decided was the more cost-effective choice, even if its capabilities exceeded UK requirements.

With the end of the Cold War, and mutual declarations that Britain and Russia are no longer targeting each other, the ministry of defence stated that it would not deploy more warheads than it would have done under Trident-I (a maximum of 128 per submarine); and then, in November 1993, that each submarine would carry no more than 96 warheads. At the same time, the government resolved another nuclear debate, over whether (and how) to replace the Tornado-carried nuclear bomb. After failing to persuade a sceptical Treasury of the need for a new air-launched cruise missile to carry this bomb, it was decided instead to use some Trident warheads in a tactical mode (SDE, 1993, para. 128; SDE 1994, para. 303 and p. 19).

Production and deployment are at the time of writing well under way, with two of the submarines already accepted by the Navy by early 1995. The Labour Party, after adopting a unilateralist position in 1980s, now proposes to eliminate UK nuclear forces through multilateral negotiations, so that a change of government in the near future would not immediately affect the programme.

France

In the case of France, the lines of postwar defence policy took a little longer to clarify. Although France, like Britain, had contributed to the Manhattan Project, and so had nuclear experts with knowledge of the US programme, the extent of this was less than in the British case, and the economic and industrial capacity to act on that knowledge was even more constrained. The initial French nuclear programme was more ambiguous than that of the British. It aimed to develop a general capability in nuclear technology, without any immediate commitment to weapons. Nevertheless, by the time a decision was made, in 1958, to build and test a bomb by 1960, a substantial infrastructure had been built up, and the goal was readily achieved. As in Britain, this decision owed much to a determination to maintain independence from the USA, fitting centrally into what came to be called Gaullism – national control over the armed forces, high priority to French nuclear weapons and reliance on French-made military equipment, coupled with energetic arms exports (Menon, 1995) – even though the decision to proceed with the bomb was taken just before Charles de Gaulle became president in 1958. Concerned with US domination of NATO, and with maintaining industrial and technological independence, the French have also built a more extensive capability than Britain's. In addition to nuclear armed bombers, France had until recently nuclear-armed intermediate-range ballistic missiles. Its arsenal at the time of writing includes submarine-launched ballistic missiles, and an air-launched missile (ASMP) which at one stage it had hoped to sell to Britain. The submarine force is larger than Britain's, comprising five submarines, each with sixteen multiple-warhead missiles.

French nuclear policy has traditionally been less contested than in Britain, and there has been no equivalent to the British Campaign for Nuclear Disarmament (CND). But there has recently been more doubt than in the past. President François Mitterrand and others began to talk somewhat enigmatically from late 1991 about the possibility of French nuclear forces in some way becoming dedicated to European rather than merely French defence. This theme returned in 1995 as part of President Jacques Chirac's attempt to regain the public relations initiative during the furore provoked by the resumption of French nuclear tests in the South Pacific, although none of France's European partners responded warmly.

Interest has, however, grown in recent years in some form of Franco-British nuclear co-operation. At the time of writing, discussions are understood to be taking place on nuclear strategy and on the possibility of an integrated policy over submarine patrols. This theme was addressed by Prime Minister John Major and President Chirac in October 1995, when the two countries undertook to 'pursue and deepen' their nuclear co-operation. Both countries are finding it increasingly difficult politically to justify their nuclear forces in the face of proposed cuts by the USA and Russia under the second Strategic Arms Reduction Treaty, their support in 1995 for the indefinite extension of the Nuclear Non-Proliferation Treaty, and their commitment to a Comprehensive Nuclear Test Ban Treaty.

Another nuclear-related area for possible Franco-British, or wider, co-operation arises with respect to anti-missile defences. France, like other European states bordering the Mediterranean, places more emphasis than does Britain upon the desirability of defences against any future military threat from Africa or the Gulf region. In similar vein, but fuelled also by French concern about the continued reliability of US support, can be mentioned French interest in developing a European satellite observation and monitoring system, independent of that of the USA to which Britain, at least, has long enjoyed privileged access.

NATO Nuclear Policy

Nuclear politics in Europe has, as already shown, extended beyond the two nuclear weapons states to embrace the wider field of NATO's nuclear policy, and to draw in a range of states who do not have their own nuclear forces, notably Germany, Italy and the Netherlands.

A problem arose in the late 1970s over the growing obsolescence of a particular element of the NATO (read US) nuclear forces devoted to the defence of Europe, namely the F-111 bombers. For the military, the question was, how to replace the F-111s? For the politicians, the question was, how to ensure continued US coupling to Europe? At the same time, there was concern about the strategic significance of a build-up of a new class of Soviet intermediate range ballistic missiles (IRBM), the 3-warhead SS20, which governments seized upon as a convenient symbol in terms of which to justify modernisation plans. In December 1979, NATO took its so-called 'dual track' decision. The first element of this decision was to deploy, by the end of 1983, 108 highly-accurate Pershing-II IRBMs, and 464 mobile ground-launched Cruise missiles. These were chosen because they were available, affordable, relatively invulnerable (because mobile), and supposedly 'reassuring' to the public in Europe because of their visibility. The second element of the decision comprised an offer not to deploy these new missiles if the USSR removed all its SS20s from the western part of the USSR. This, however, was a confusion introduced by the politics of the controversy. The military said they needed to replace the F-111 regardless of the presence of the SS20. But governments, seeking a simple argument, had chosen to present the issue to their people generally in terms of the need to counterbalance the SS20, and were subsequently hoist by their own *pétard*.

Hundreds of thousands of protestors took to the streets. The debate caught some wider resonances, including concern expressed about the revival by the the US president, Ronald Reagan, of Cold War rhetoric, accompanied by a big arms build-up, and concern in some quarters (rightly or wrongly) that the Cruise and Pershing missiles would invite pre-emptive attacks upon Europe, in part because their considerable accuracy was said to make them 'war-fighting weapons' rather than deterrents. Deployment of the new weapons did, in fact, begin (for example, at Greenham Common in the UK), but they quickly became the subject of arms control talks once Mikhail Gorbachev took power in Moscow. The issue was subsequently resolved, though not to the satisfaction of the military, through the Intermediate Nuclear Forces treaty of 1987, which eliminated the whole class of intermediate-range nuclear weapons. The treaty was remarkable not only for being the first to eliminate a class of nuclear weapons (as opposed to merely setting limits to growth in numbers), but also for its agreement upon an extraordinarily intrusive verification system, necessary if there was to be confidence that weapons were really being destroyed.

That such a verification system could be accepted (permitting each side to witness the destruction of missiles) was itself a sign of the changed times, and from this flowed other important initiatives, notably the treaty on Conventional Forces in Europe of 1992. When fully implemented, this treaty, together with the post-treaty break-up of the Warsaw Pact and then of the Soviet Union itself, would leave NATO forces in Europe with conventional superiority over Russia. This overturning of the position that underpinned NATO's resort to nuclear weapons to redress the conventional imbalance would further call into question the grounds for any form of nuclear weapon on European territory, although by late 1995 doubt had arisen over whether Russia would implement the treaty fully because of the problems that troop reductions would cause it in Chechenya and other border areas.

The End of the Cold War

Until the late 1980s, the size and shape of European defence activities reflected the specific geopolitical circumstances of the Cold War. Since then, the defence sector has suffered a loss of demand and coherence. The military strategies and force structures pertinent to possible massed attacks from the east lost their relevance, but it became less clear how to organise military forces in response to the more diffuse set of risks that then emerged. This was true in relation both to the possibilities of threats from weapons of mass destruction, and to the use of national armed forces in multinational coalitions, such as the burgeoning United Nations' interventions. At the same time as military power was devalued, so economic power increased in significance, and Germany, especially once it had absorbed the costs of reunification, took centre stage in that respect. Further change on a broadened security front was presaged by debates about enlargement of the European Union to the east, with tricky problems of both economic and military security to be resolved. In addition, to the west, the USA was retreating, and uncertainty over US commitment to Europe increased sharply after the 'Gingrich revolution' which led to Republican Party dominance in the congressional elections of November 1994.

The difficulty that all countries face is that of identifying aims and requirements in a coherent fashion, and then of finding the necessary funds at a time of public pressure for cuts. When 'the threat' came clearly from the Soviet Union, it was possible to plan fairly straightforwardly. Moreover, because of the scale of forces assembled to deal with that threat, lesser defence problems could be managed with some configuration of forces drawn from the large total. But the single large threat has now been replaced by multiple smaller, but less clear-cut, 'risks'. Not only is it difficult to know what to plan for, but with smaller forces than in the past, there will be less scope for withdrawing elements of the total to meet particular eventualities. If each country could count on meeting all conceivable eventualities in the company of the same fixed set of allies, then a division of labour might be agreed. But even this seems implausible at present. Hence the profound uncertainty that grips defence planners and those responsible for maintaining the defence industrial base.

Gradually, new positions are emerging. For most countries these have involved sharp reductions in spending and in manpower, and rather more mixed impacts on equipment spending. Data on overall budget and personnel reductions, comparing 1985 (the year of Gorbachev's assumption of power) with 1994, are given in Table 12.1. The overall position is clear: sharp reductions in both budget and personnel in all the larger West European defence spenders, and, for comparison, in the USA.

There has also been considerable rethinking, nationally and at the levels of the NATO alliance and the WEU, of military strategy appropriate to the reduced Russian threat, and to the types of military intervention in which European forces are increasingly finding them-

TABLE 12.1 *Defence expenditure and military manpower, 1985 and 1994, selected countries*

Country	Defence expenditure ($m, 1993 prices)		Numbers in Armed Forces (000s)	
	1985	1994	1985	1994
France	42918	42724	494.3	409.6
Germany	46330	34848	478.0	367.3
Italy	22576	20632	385.1	322.3
Netherlands	7814	6901	105.5	70.9
Spain	9900	7416	320.0	206.5
Sweden	4194	4818	65.7	64.0
UK	41891	33861	327.1	254.3
USA	339229	278730	2151.6	1650.5

Note: UK and US forces unlike those in most other countries listed, are entirely professional – that is, no conscripts (compare, France, 51% professional; Germany 52%).
Source: IISS (1995) pp. 264–5.

selves engaged. NATO has adopted a new strategy which features reduced forces along the line of division between East and West; a strong, highly mobile, and heavily-armoured multinational 'rapid reaction force' capable of being moved quickly to areas of tension; and other forces held further back, in the form of relatively-rapidly mobilisable troops and others kept in reserve. NATO has also had to engage, with mixed success so far, in designing political and military command structures for operations outside the traditional NATO area. This requirement, resulting from the UN intervention in the former Yugoslavia, has been further complicated by the need to find ways to incorporate Russian troops into the UN force, without them coming under NATO command (a problem 'solved' by putting them under the command of the US officer who happened also to be the commander of the NATO forces).

At the national level, we can illustrate recent changes with a few examples:

Britain
Has gone through a major analysis of its defence policy (the 'options for change' exercise), and now defines it defence objectives as to ensure the protection and security of the United Kingdom and its dependent territories, even when there is no major external threat, an objective that the ministry of defence argues is ultimately guaranteed by the nuclear deterrent; to insure against major external threat to the UK and its allies – the NATO commitment on land, sea and air – and to contribute to promoting Britain's wider security interests through the

maintenance of international peace and stability. This includes support for NATO, WEU and UN operations, notably peace-keeping tasks, as in the former Yugoslavia. Accordingly, Britain has continued with the Trident nuclear force; has withdrawn its existing tactical nuclear weapons, and abandoned the plan for a tactical air-to-surface nuclear missile; and is in the throes of major reductions in the armed forces and in equipment spending. But it remains broadly committed to all-round capabilities, and is continuing with most of its major projects, including the Eurofighter 2000 aircraft, in collaboration with Germany, Italy and Spain. Additional cuts announced in July 1994 aimed to yield savings of £750 million per year in 1996–7 and more thereafter, together with job losses of 18 700 in the armed forces and support services, but without reducing further the equipment programme.

France
Has sought to maintain a similarly wide range of forces, capable of supporting not only its interests in Europe but also of projecting force into areas of French interest in Africa, the Pacific and elsewhere. This commitment came increasingly into question, however, in the years after 1989, years in which France, almost uniquely among Western nations (but see Sweden in Table 12.1), tried to maintain level spending on defence, and in which it also had to begin to come to terms with the realisation (driven home during the Gulf War of 1991) that its expensive indigenous weapons programme had produced equipment that was in many respects inferior to that of the USA, and even the UK. Accordingly, Prime Minister Edouard Balladur set in train what purported to be the first comprehensive review of French defence policy since 1972, but was in fact highly conservative, although it did suggest that defence issues needed to be moved on to a more European plane. In terms of cuts, the French army fell from 300 000 men in 1983 to 240 000 in 1994; the navy reduced its warships from 175 in 1981 to 113 in 1993; and the air force reduced the number of combat aircraft from 450 to less than 400 over the same period. But France has cancelled hardly any major new programmes, though it has abandoned short-range nuclear missiles. More than any other European nation, it is building up its effort in space, and has announced the formation of a joint military force, the 'Eurocorps', with Germany and others. The election of Jacques Chirac as president, however, has brought a new review of defence policy, and a very much tougher budgetary line, which is making substantial inroads into force sizes and equipment programmes.

Germany

Is making the most substantial manpower cuts of the larger countries, and this against a background of reunification (thus inheriting troops of the former GDR). It is experiencing also the consequences of the withdrawal of former Soviet troops and reductions in numbers of NATO troops stationed in Germany. Between the end of the Cold War and the mid-1990s, over 800 000 troops will have disappeared from German soil, the majority of these from former Soviet and East German forces, but with significant reductions in NATO forces also. Germany dramatically drew international attention to the depth of its defence cuts with its decision of July 1992, later reversed, not to proceed beyond the development phase of the European Fighter Aircraft, although the future of German commitment to this, its largest current defence project, continues to remain uncertain. At the same time, with the end of the Cold War, Germany has at last felt able to begin to take on a wider military role. Hence, in 1994, the Constitutional Court ruled that German forces can now be used outside Germany itself, provided this is at the request of the UN, and on missions with a peacekeeping or other humanitarian purpose.

Sweden

To refer finally to a non-NATO, indeed neutral, country, Sweden faces a different problem: it now has to come to terms with the meaning of non-alignment in a post-Cold War world. Against a background of postponed material acquisitions in the 1980s, and a re-evaluation of requirements to meet new demands arising from possible Swedish association with NATO and international peace-keeping operations, Sweden is in the throes of a five-year (beginning 1992) expansion of defence spending which is scheduled to level off in the second half of the 1990s.

Towards a New Security Framework?

Alongside these national developments, the search is on for a new security framework for Western Europe, comparable to that which NATO has provided since the late 1940s. NATO itself continues to be one candidate for that framework, not least in the attraction which it holds for countries of the former Warsaw Pact. Yet the very sensitivity of admission of those countries to full membership, with the security guarantee to which the other members would thereby be bound, not to mention the implications for relations with Russia, complicates considerably such a step. In addition, account has to be taken of the arguments about the wisdom of continued reliance on the USA for the guaranteeing of Europe's security, not to mention arguments also voiced to the effect that NATO had a specific role in relation to a specific threat that no longer exists; and that to maintain NATO, therefore, is to maintain an outmoded Cold War security structure.

An alternative potential framework is the European Union. The Maastricht Treaty of 1992 introduced a foreign and security policy pillar alongside the other pillars of the single market/economic union. Specifically, it called for the establishment of a common foreign and security policy (CFSP) which, in the carefully chosen words of Article J.4 of the treaty, 'shall include all questions related to the security of the Union, including the eventual framing of a common defence policy which might in time lead to a common defence' (Treaty on European Union, C 191, 29.7.92, Article J.4). The treaty further requests the WEU, as an 'integral part' of the development of the EU, to elaborate and implement decisions and actions of the Union which have defence implications, while at the same time not prejudicing the obligations and commitments of certain member states under the North Atlantic Treaty.

This was evidently a compromise between those (led by France) who wished to develop the WEU as the defence arm of the EU, independently from NATO and the USA, and those (led by Britain) who were willing to accept the WEU as the European arm of NATO but argued that the latter was the only European-based military structure with any operational capability. The compromise was only possible because of the happy chance that the membership of the WEU constituted, at the time, an almost perfect (European) subset of the members of both the EU and NATO (see Figure 12.1).

Developments in this field since Maastricht have been extremely complex, but key features include the following. In 1992, the WEU agreed to identify European military units for use by the WEU 'when not required for NATO tasks', and to set up a Planning Cell (but of only forty military officers) to consider operational plans. The joint French–German–Belgian 'Eurocorps' was to be so identified, with Spain likely to join, the aim being to be able to commit 40 000 troops by 1995. Other already existing multinational forces, such as a joint UK-Dutch naval amphibious force, and some other UK and NATO forces currently based in Germany, were similarly defined. This step, together with others since agreed, began to give some semblance of an operational capability to the WEU, but is still at an embryonic stage. Not only does the WEU lack a real military capacity, it also, as France

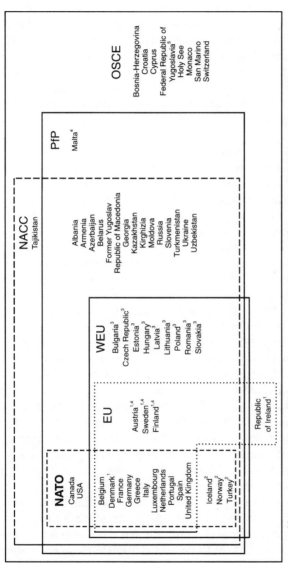

NATO
Canada
USA

Belgium
Denmark[1]
France
Germany
Greece
Italy
Luxembourg
Netherlands
Portugal
Spain
United Kingdom

Iceland[2]
Norway[2]
Turkey[2]

EU
Austria[1,4]
Sweden[1,4]
Finland[1,4]

Republic of Ireland[1]

WEU
Bulgaria[3]
Czech Republic[3]
Estonia[3]
Hungary[3]
Latvia[3]
Lithuania[3]
Poland[3]
Romania[3]
Slovakia[3]

NACC
Tajikistan

Albania
Armenia
Azerbaijan
Belarus
Former Yugoslav Republic of Macedonia
Georgia
Kazakhstan
Kirghizia
Moldova
Russia
Slovenia
Turkmenistan
Ukraine
Uzbekistan

PfP
Malta[4]

OSCE

Bosnia-Herzegovina
Croatia
Cyprus
Federal Republic of Yugoslavia[5]
Holy See
Monaco
San Marino
Switzerland

Notes
1. Observer in the WEU.
2. Associate Member of the WEU.
3. Associate Partner in the WEU.
4. Members of PfP may attend NACC Meetings as Observers.
5. Membership suspended.

FIGURE 12.1 *Membership of international organisations as at 1 April 1996*

continually points out, lacks the satellite observation and monitoring capability that modern military engagements require.

It was also agreed in 1992 to support conflict-prevention and crisis-management measures under the direction of the WEU, and subject to UN or CSCE (now the Organisation for Security and Co-operation in Europe – OSCE) resolutions; and that all EU members should be eligible to join the WEU. This last point has evident implications for the enlargement of the EU, because of the linkage between WEU membership and security guarantees. Indeed, the additions to the EU since Maastricht of three neutral states (Austria, Sweden and Finland), the last of which shares a lengthy border with Russia, already illustrate the point well.

There have also been various attempts, intensified since Maastricht, to develop an armaments policy and an armaments agency (to manage common projects and procurement) under the aegis of the WEU. These attempts should be seen against the background of attempts dating from the mid-1980s to rationalise the European arms market. National protectionism, short production runs – since these are based largely on national orders – and therefore considerable diseconomies of scale, all result in high prices compared to those available from larger US firms, based in the larger US market. At the time of writing, these plans seem to have reverted to a Franco-German initiative to begin by pooling certain of their arms interests in the hope of making some progress, with Britain having committed itself also to participation.

NATO and the WEU, meanwhile, have felt obliged to respond to overtures for membership from former Eastern Bloc countries. They have done so first through the formation of a North Atlantic Co-operation Council (NACC) and then through the introduction of a new category of 'associate partner' in the WEU, followed by the establishment of Partnership for Peace (PfP) agreements (see Figure 12.1). These arrangements have drawn countries of East and West into joint discussions about defence and security affairs, and opened the way to various forms of military co-operation.

At the NATO summit of January 1994, US President Bill Clinton succeeded where his predecessor had not in persuading the Europeans (and especially the British) that the USA welcomed the development of a stronger European defence identity, and that this would not lead to a US withdrawal from Europe to below the 100 000 troop commitment that had already been promised. The summit also laid down the basis for further articulation between the WEU and NATO in the form of plans for a new NATO command structure, designed as to enable the WEU element to detach itself and its troops for independent European action in the form of what were named 'Common Joint Task Forces' (CJTF).

Indeed, NATO has demonstrated forcefully in Bosnia that it, and its American leadership, remain crucial to military action in and around Western Europe, and that neither the WEU nor the EU have yet been able to take its place. The WEU had very little direct part in the land and air operations designed to keep the peace and supply humanitarian aid in Bosnia. It did have responsibility for enforcing the maritime dimension of the UN arms embargo and trade sanctions against the former Yugoslavia in the Adriatic, but was unable to operate effectively until US surveillance information was made available to it. The Dayton Agreement of 1995, and the establishment of the NATO-led Implementation Force (I-FOR), with its substantially higher troop numbers (including US forces) and greater powers to use force, further emphasised the relative operational weights of the two organisations. Nevertheless, the experience of I-FOR will be important for the development of the CJTF idea. The construction of this force, even though it includes US personnel on this occasion, is seen by military experts as a model of what the CJTF concept is intended to achieve in terms of its capacity to draw upon the forces of several countries, with full use of NATO command, control, communication and intelligence facilities. If I-FOR succeeds, therefore, it could have the incidental effect of providing useful experience of how to organize the kind of temporary lessening of forces from NATO that the WEU is seeking. This path may also become easier to tread following the French decision of late 1995 to re-enter most of the military planning structures of NATO, since this step will reduce the level of US–French suspicion that has also impeded the CJTF concept.

What Role for the European Union?

It is worth recalling that the European Community was conceived in the aftermath of the Second World War with the aim of making war in Europe inconceivable. But the goal of military security was to be achieved indirectly, through non-military forms of co-operation. Thus, the Common Market, and the agreements to co-operate in the three industries of coal, steel and atomic energy, were seen not as ends in themselves but as the means of binding the member states into a union within which war could have no part. As the Community expanded to twelve, and then fifteen, member states, the same approach has been followed. The resulting taboo on direct involvement with defence issues has, however, inhibited a common European approach.

Article 223 of the Treaty of Rome formalised the Community's exclusion of defence from its joint responsibilities by permitting member states to keep the Commission at bay on matters that they regarded as being of security importance. Only in cases where trade in dual-use (civil and military) items distorted the operation of the (civil) common market could the Commission step in; and even here there has been reluctance because of the sensitivity attached by member states to this area. The Commission proposed the abrogation of Article 223 under the Maastricht Treaty, but this was unacceptable to key governments, including the British and French.

Nevertheless, the European Commission has been building its own capability in the field of foreign and security policy. It has sought to co-ordinate policy on OSCE and on arms control and disarmament, including nuclear non-proliferation. It has also been working to develop a regime covering export of armaments and dual-use items from the Single Market that would allow elimination of national systems.

Believing, moreover, that leaving policy on the CFSP to the (intergovernmental) Council will not achieve much, the Commission is also pressing to enhance the capacity of the Union to think and act in this field. It is proposing that there be established a staff to work continuously in the field of foreign and security policy, drawn mainly from officials of the Commission, the Council and the WEU, and serving all three bodies. Second, the argument is being put that the six-monthly rotation of the presidency of the Council would not lend sufficient continuity to the external representation of the Union's foreign and security policy, and that a new role needs to be created for this purpose, somewhere between the political and the administrative spheres. Third, it is proposed that the Chiefs of Staff of the national armed forces should meet regularly to seek to define common policies, from which could flow common equipment requirements. This would also help with another of the Commission's aspirations, namely, to give a better sense of direction to the Union's defence, industrial and technological base in order to assist the survival of at least the minimum core which is needed to underpin the CFSP.

That base is currently highly fragmented because of its division between so many national markets. This makes it extremely vulnerable to the large American firms which, with the sharp recent decline in their home market, are now hungrily eyeing the European market and the markets around the world to which European defence firms have traditionally exported. Given their scale (the largest US defence firm, Lockheed Martin, after its January 1996 acquisition of Loral, has an annual turnover equivalent to the sum of total British and French government annual defence equipment spending), the US firms pose a formidable threat to the survival of their European competitors, unless European governments choose to protect their own firms – at high cost to their own taxpayers, or a pan-European arms market is created. This, while still smaller than the US market, would at least be of comparable size and so would permit economies of scale of the same order as those available to US firms.

Here, then, is an area which, while still intensely political, at least comes sufficiently close to some of the Commission's responsibilities (those for industrial and technological policy, for ensuring coherence between the three Maastricht pillars, and for regulating international transfers of dual-use technologies) for it to attempt some modest initiatives even before the larger questions concerning CFSP are addressed.

Those larger questions will be addressed during the Inter-Governmental Conference (IGC), which began in Turin in 1996, on the future of the Maastricht Treaty. They will therefore be addressed in a heady political atmosphere, stirred by a series of sensitive debates over federalism, monetary union, and revision of the Union's institutions and voting procedures in the face of enlargement. It remains to be seen at the time of writing whether significant progress will be made on CFSP, which, of course, raises further sensitivities of its own, or whether a more general paralysis of the European project will set in. If the IGC drags on, however, it may start to overlap with the planned review in 1998 of the 1948 Brussels Treaty, which will present a further occasion to re-evaluate the EC-WEU relationship. One thing is certain: the issue of a European defence identity, raised over forty years ago, is still with us. Its resolution depends, ultimately, on what form and intensity of integration European states seek to achieve. A real foreign and security policy, if history is any guide, requires in the end military force to back it up. The question is, does 'Europe' see itself as the kind of political actor that requires a real foreign and security policy?

13

Environmental Policy and Politics

UTE COLLIER AND JONATHAN GOLUB

In the mid to late 1980s, few books on European politics and policy would have talked about environmental issues, let alone devoted an entire chapter to environmental policy. Now, environmental protection has become an integral part of policy-making in most of Western Europe. This chapter discusses recent developments in environmental policy and politics in Western Europe. The first section shows how national approaches to environmental problems have varied, allowing a broad distinction between 'green' and less 'green' countries. This is followed by an examination of how national, international and EU policies have become increasingly intertwined, the latter taking on particular significance in recent years. This section also discusses the impact of the subsidiarity debate and the difficulty of accommodating national and subnational environmental policies within a coherent European framework. The third section focuses on some of the recent challenges presented to policy-makers, such as sustainable development and the emphasis on economic instruments.

National Environmental Policy and Politics

In Western Europe, some countries are considered much more environmentally pro-active than others, both in terms of their domestic policies and their involvement in EU and international policy developments. Although a clear classification is fraught with difficulties, this section discusses the different shades of green found among European countries. For purposes of comparison, the states of Western Europe may be classified into roughly three groups.

The leaders of the pack – Germany and the Netherlands

The environmental profiles of the green leaders in Western Europe share a number of characteristics. Widespread awareness of environmental problems and highly active environmental pressure groups have generated a substantial demand for domestic legislation. Governments in these states have responded to this demand by introducing ambitious pollution reduction efforts across a wide range of environmental areas, allocating considerable financial resources to pollution reduction, and by integrating environmental considerations into many other policy sectors. Environment ministries are well staffed and resourced. In both international forums and in EC policy-making these countries have initiated many environmental proposals which have become binding laws and yielded substantial environmental improvements throughout Western Europe.

No environmental policy analysis can ignore Germany, Western Europe's most populous member state and its strongest economic power. At the outset a distinction must be made between the environmental record of the former Federal Republic of Germany (FRG) (for convenience referred to here as Germany) and that of the former German Democratic Republic (GDR). Since the early 1980s, Germany has actively pursued an image as a leader in environmental policy in Europe and has been the key member state driving the EU environment policy forward. The discovery of large-scale damage to German forests was the catalyst for strict legislation on emissions from power stations and cars and has been instrumental in introducing legislation in these areas at EU level. More recently, Germany has developed an ambitious, if somewhat ill-fated, recycling policy and has set itself the toughest carbon dioxide (CO_2) emission reduction target globally (25 per cent by the year 2005). Overall, Germany spends a significant amount on environmental protection, 1.7 per cent of its GDP, and by 1992 had amassed a special environmental fund of DM 263 billion.

German environmental policy has been dominated by legislative measures which are based on the principle of *Stand der Technik* ('best available technology'), as well as the precautionary principle (Weale, 1992). This has had some impressive results, with Germany decoupling economic growth from the flow of several major pollutants: German sulphur dioxide (SO_2), nitrogen oxide (NO_x) and CO_2 emissions were reduced by 71 per cent, 17 per cent and 10 per cent respectively between 1980 and 1991, a decade of rapid and steady economic expansion. The reduction in NO_x emissions, most of which comes from cars, was achieved despite a 30 per cent increase over this period in both traffic volume and number of vehicles. Water pollution, energy intensity and per capita waste generation have also decreased.

Even as an environmental leader, Germany still faces a number of obstacles to sustainable development. Germany's continued prosperity depends on the performance of inherently polluting industries, such as large chemical and automobile plants which formed the basis of its postwar economic reconstruction, and the increase of CO_2 emissions from the transport sector continues unabated. Furthermore, unification has presented some formidable challenges to environmental policy with the former GDR pollution legacy. The GDR had a per capita level of SO_2 emissions which was almost four times that of the former FRG, and consumed a vast quantity of energy compared with its European neighbours. It also had the lowest ground water and surface water potential in Western Europe, with 30 per cent of its water 'ecologically dead' and 45 per cent completely unusable even after treatment. Finally, at least 90 per cent of waste disposal sites failed to meet EC standards, while the country sold disposal space for West German hazardous waste. The OECD estimates that environmental 'reconstruction' in the former GDR will require in the neighbourhood of DM 250 billion, much of this directed towards waste water treatment. Additionally, unification, and the general economic costs associated with it, have pushed environmental concerns down the political agenda.

The Netherlands has also played a role as a leader state, both domestically and at the EU level. By 1992, the Netherlands ranked top among West European countries in terms of membership in environmental organisations, issue salience and government expenditure on environmental protection (1.9 per cent of GDP, rising to 2.7 per cent in 1995). The government's National Environmental Policy Plan defines both general goals (such as achieving sustainable development within one generation) and ambitious quantitative targets with deadlines, as well as describing broad measures to reach these targets, including the integration of environmental policy into other policy sectors (Collier, 1994). An indication of its commitment has been government efforts to relieve environmental pressure in the transport sector; significant Dutch investment in public transportation and construction of cycle paths kept the growth of the road network and traffic volume lower than in any other Western European state during the 1980s. The development of the plan has also reflected the Dutch political culture which involves the consultation of a variety of interest groups in the policy process, in an effort to reach a consensus.

However, as the OECD highlights in a recent evaluation of Dutch environmental policy, emissions in sectors such as agriculture and transport, the two main pillars of the Dutch economy, remain far in excess of sustainable levels. Furthermore, the consensus approach has been criticised for allowing certain vested interests such as agriculture and the refinery industry (in particular Shell) to shape policies in their interest (Van Straaten and Ugelow, 1994).

Apart from Germany and the Netherlands, Denmark, Austria, Finland, Switzerland, Sweden and Norway rank among Western Europe's most environmentally pro-active countries. All have well-elaborated environmental policy frameworks and have at various times taken the lead in international environmental agreements. Environment ministries are generally well funded and staffed. In all, a number of positive environmental trends can be identified. Denmark has been successful in reducing its SO_2, mainly through large improvements in energy efficiency. But traffic is a big area of tension, especially as the controversial bridge link to Sweden is expected to create substantial growth. Meanwhile, Sweden is struggling to reconcile the decision to shut down nuclear power stations with the aim of reducing CO_2 emissions.

Ambivalent Countries – Britain and France

These two states are a step behind the leaders. Despite some differences in national circumstances, they have in common a fairly low salience of environmental protection, a low proportion of the adult population participating in environmental groups, scattered and inconsistent pollution reduction efforts, and infrequent environmental initiatives at the international or EU level. In addition, environmental ministries often remain underfunded and relatively weak.

The UK used to be known as the 'dirty man' of Europe, mainly because of its refusal to reduce sulphur emissions in the early 1980s and its adherence to 'dispersal and absorption', a pollution control philosophy which took advantage of Britain's island status and its highly resilient ecosystem. However, by the mid-1990s, SO_2 emissions were on a clear downward trend and CO_2 emissions are projected to fall by between 4 and 7 per cent by the year 2000. Water quality has seen substantial improvements, and recycling activity has much increased. The passage in 1990 of the Environmental Protection Act strengthened environmental protection and promised substantial 'greening' of all departments and policy areas.

Green consumerism has established itself and, recently, the anti-roads lobby has had first successes, resulting in cuts in the government's road building programme. Environmental policies have become very important at the local level, with many local councils employing environmental co-ordinators. However, there are some major inconsistencies in government policies, with, for example, rail privatisation likely to lead to a further shift to car travel on top of the 67 per cent increase in traffic volume during the 1980s, and an increase of the already climbing levels of NO_x emissions. Green consumerism also has its limitations: the amount of waste produced per capita in the UK grew more than in most other states during the 1980s, and recycling levels still remain relatively low compared to the leader countries.

At the EU level Britain has taken a more active role in the development of policies, but whether this represents a form of greening remains unclear. In the cases of volatile organic compounds and integrated pollution control, for example, Britain's leadership has been an attempt to set the agenda in accordance with its preferred approaches to pollution control, much as Germany managed to do throughout the early years of EC policy. In some cases there can be little doubt that the British proposals would improve environmental standards across Europe, but in others they have been designed to maintain the traditional dispersal approach, which many countries have criticised as being environmentally inadequate (Golub, 1996a). Furthermore, as discussed below, Britain has led the campaign against the carbon tax and a number of other EU policies, arguing that they should be scuppered or scaled back in accordance with the subsidiarity principle.

France has not seen the same growth in environmental awareness as Britain. To some extent this can be explained by the fact that, because of low population densities, environmental problems are often not as acute there as, for example, in the Netherlands. The environmental movement is not well organised in France, except in response to certain local problems, and issue salience remains low. For such a highly-developed country, France spends very little on environmental protection (less than 1 per cent of its GDP), reflected, for example, in its relatively low levels of sewage treatment. However, the government has drawn up a National Environmental Policy Plan, and, whatever its potential environmental shortcomings, the government's devotion to nuclear-generated electricity helped reduce SO_2, NO_x and CO_2 emissions in the 1980s. Efforts have been made to implement the 'polluter pays' principle, with a number of pollution taxes, and the government is pursuing a partnership policy, encouraging local councils as well as industrial companies to draw up environmental charters or plans. However, as with similar British initiatives, participation is entirely voluntary, comparing unfavourably with the Dutch 'covenants', which are legally enforceable. At EU level, France has rarely been a major opponent of environmental measures, except over small car emissions and recently in the case of the energy/carbon tax.

The Laggards – Italy, Greece, Spain, Portugal, Ireland

Although these countries sometimes differ, each exhibits a number of similar characteristics which indicate a strong ambivalence towards concerted environmental improvement. Since the early 1980s there have been scattered improvements in all of them, but in each case these must be viewed against the fundamental obstacles still facing environmental policy.

In contrast to opinion surveys which indicate support among their general populations for action to improve the environment, polls designed to test relative issue salience and low levels of membership in green groups reveal a pervasive lack of environmental awareness and concern. While in the late 1980s the number of small environmental groups grew dramatically, reaching 700 in Spain and Italy, and membership of major groups expanded, with Greenpeace opening offices in Spain, Portugal and the Republic of Ireland, involvement in major green groups remained drastically lower than in the rest of Europe (Heijden *et al.*, 1992). A contributing factor to these low levels of membership, and to low levels of environmental awareness in general, has been the relative lack of media coverage devoted to environmental issues.

While spectacular environmental disasters, such as the 1976 dioxin spill in Seveso and the 1986 Chernobyl nuclear accident, may generate awareness, referendums and occasional government responses – for example, the 1986 Environmental Policy Act in Greece – environmental policy in each of these states remains superficial and highly reactive. Global economic competition has forced some large industries to undertake greater environmental protection in order to gain access to foreign export markets, but for the vast majority of small to medium-sized firms, environmental improvement still depends much more on domestic regulations, which are frequently lacking.

A clear indication of this has been the relatively insignificant amount of money – often well under 1 per cent of their GDP – spent by these states on environmental improvement. Starved of funding, many environmental programmes are not carried to completion and existing facilities fall into disrepair. As of 1990, for example, Portugal, Greece and the Republic of Ireland could afford to treat less than one-fifth of their sewage waste water; and while this proportion was officially higher in Spain and Italy, 60 per cent of Spanish sewage treatment involves only the most rudimentary technology, and 80 per cent of Italian sewage treatment plants were found to be defective. In lieu of long-standing national environmental traditions, many of the environmental actions that have been taken in these states are a direct result of international environmental agreements, particularly EC laws. But international pressure will need to be matched by domestic changes; the OECD estimates that in order to meet its EC obligations, the Portuguese government, found to have the worst environmental record in Europe, would have to double its current level of environmental spending for ten years (OECD ongoing).

Another substantial barrier to environmental improvement, common to all countries but particularly severe in these states, arises from fragmentation of government policy. Fragmentation originates from two sources: the dispersion of responsibility across many government departments, and the relative weakness of environmental ministries. Unfortunately, the recent creation of such ministries, or large ministries which include the word 'environment' in their name – Italy 1986, Portugal 1990, Spain 1993 – has not reduced fragmentation. In practice, these new ministries, like those established previously in Greece and the Republic of Ireland, continue to share authority for environmental policy with a range of other departments and agencies whose primary aim is improved economic performance, although the situation in the Republic of Ireland and Italy shows some signs of improvement, with the establishment of Environmental Protection Agencies in 1991 and 1994 respectively.

In addition to widespread interministerial conflict, intraministerial conflict arises in the 'superdepartments' where an overwhelming proportion of staff are responsible for issues such as public works rather than the environment. While this problem plagues environmental ministries throughout Europe, the intensity of the economic growth imperative and relative absence of post-materialistic values makes it somewhat more pronounced in these states. Successful environmental improvements achieved by individual environment ministers such as Giorgio Ruffolo in Italy (1988–92), and Antonis Tritsis and Kostas Laliotis in Greece (1981–4, 1993) are exceptions.

In Italy and Spain, fragmentation is exacerbated by the sharing of environmental competence between central and regional government. Intended to lend legitimacy and efficiency to environmental policy-making, the result has often been ambiguity, a severe lack of co-ordination, and a heightened risk of agency capture by local economic interests (La Spina and Sciortino, 1993; Aguilar-Fernández, 1996).

A third obstacle to improved environmental policy in these states is widespread non-compliance with environmental laws. This has been attributed to the 'Mediterranean syndrome', whereby deeply rooted aspects of political culture – which one Italian observer characterised as a lack of public interest, frail public ethics and basically premodern political values – prevent the effective provision of public goods (La Spina and Sciortino, 1993). Scepticism of imposed obligations and the expectation that non-compliance is 'the rule of the game' undermines the application of environmental laws; and, in many instances, non-compliance is so extreme that the distorted incorporation of directives can in fact nullify the impact of EC laws. They also have the dubious honour of consistently topping the list for violating them.

The Significance of Green Parties

To some extent, then, there is a North–South divide, although even some Northern countries are more ambivalent towards environmental protection than others. The question arises whether environmental policy leadership is related to the electoral fortunes of Green parties. As Table 13.1 shows, Green parties are represented in the national parliaments (second chamber) of a number of West European countries.

In general, the greens remain a marginal force in politics. This is not surprising in countries such as France and the UK, where the environment has never been a priority and where majority voting systems

TABLE 13.1 *Green party representation in national parliaments*

Country	Year of last election	Party	Percentage of vote	No. of seats (out of total)
Austria	1995	Die Grünen	4.8	9 (183)
Belgium	1995	Agalev/Ecol	8.4	11 (150)
Finland	1995	Vihreät	6.5	9 (200)
		Ecology Party	0.3	1 (200)
Germany	1994	Die Grünen	7.3	49 (662)
Italy	1995	I Verdi	2.5	6 (630)
Netherlands	1994	Groen Links	3.5	5 (150)
Sweden	1994	Miljöpartiet	5	18 (349)
Switzerland	1995	Grüne Partei	5.0	9 (200)

Source: Keesings Contemporary Archives 40 (4, 9, 10); 41 (5, 12); 42 (4), *Electoral Studies* 15/1 (1996).

make the entry of small parties virtually impossible. Yet, in some countries, which are generally considered to be 'green', such as Denmark and Norway, there is no Green Party representation despite a proportional voting system, while in the Netherlands, the green left got fewer seats than the General Association of Elderly People. Meanwhile, Belgian greens received the largest proportion of the vote, but this has had no apparent effect on the environmental positions of the major parties, leaving the country fairly ambivalent overall (Rihoux, 1995). Italy is the only Southern state to have green deputies, but its environmental record surely does not rival that of Denmark or Norway.

There are a number of different reasons why Green parties are more successful in some countries than others. In Denmark, for example, other small radical parties, as well as the socialists, have adopted environmental issues as a priority area, leaving no role in an already crowded party system for the greens. Furthermore, within individual countries, the greens' fortunes may vary from one election to the next but not necessarily reflecting the varying salience of environmental issues. The German greens lost the 1990 election in Germany mainly as a result of internal squabbles, while the Swedish greens re-entered Parliament in 1994 partly because they promoted themselves as a 'conventional' political party and because they opposed EU entry (Bennulf, 1995). The German greens are something of a case apart, having clearly made the transition from a protest movement/party to a coalition partner. By the mid-1990s, they had effectively become the third strongest party in German politics, as the Liberal Democrats have declined.

Overall, Green parties have probably had only a limited influence on environmental policy formulation. Environmental awareness is a necessary but by no means sufficient condition for their support; and they are neither a necessary nor sufficient condition for environmental awareness or a successful environmental policy! Until they occupy positions in ruling coalitions, the success of Green parties should be measured by their ability to force policy reorientation within the major political parties, for this remains the crucial determinant of environmental improvement in each state.

Multi-level Environmental Policy

Looking at the nation-state tells only part of the story. Some environmental problems straddle national borders and require supranational solutions. Since the 1970s there has been an explosive growth of environmental activity at both international and EU levels. International agreements have been reached on a whole range of issues (see Table 13.2).

The negotiation of such agreements can be a long process. In some ways, the Framework Convention on Climate Change was quite unusual in that it only took two years of negotiation until its signature at the Rio summit. However, the text of the convention is extremely vague, avoiding the mentioning of targets. The First Conference of the Parties in 1995 yielded a commitment to draw up a binding protocol with targets by 1997, although it is not clear whether this can be achieved. But the example of the ozone convention shows how subsequent specific protocols can render an initially vague convention very effective, in this case resulting in a phase-out of CFC production by all industrialised nations by 1996.

Critics often point to the lack of enforcement powers in international agreements, yet as Haas *et al.* (1994) have shown, levels of compliance can be good. By convening high-profile meetings of government representatives at regular intervals, these international agreements focus public attention and bolster domestic pressure for environmental improvement. Certainly, with regard to sulphur emissions, CFCs and the pollution of the North Sea, much has been achieved. In Europe, action required by international conventions has generally been preceded, or indeed superseded, by more specific and stricter EU legislation.

Since the early 1980s the European Community has become perhaps the most important source of environmental policy in Western Europe. Although environmental policy was not mentioned in the original treaty, Community action was taken first on the grounds that national measures could act as trade barriers and disrupt the functioning of the

TABLE 13.2 *Selected international environmental agreements*

Name of convention	Year agreed
Ramsar Convention on Wetlands of Internal Importance	1971
Oslo Convention on the Prevention of Marine Pollution by Dumping	1972
Convention on International Trade in Endangered Species (CITES)	1973
Convention on Long Range Transboundary Air Pollution	1979
Vienna Convention for the Protection of the Ozone Layer	1985
Basle Convention on the Control of Transboundary Movements of Hazardous Wastes	1989
Framework Convention on Climate Change	1992
Convention on Biological Diversity	1992

Common Market, and second because environmental problems were of such a scale that they required a co-ordinated response (Hildebrand, 1993). Community powers were enshrined in the 1986 Single European Act (SEA), and subsequently expanded in the 1992 Maastricht Treaty (TEU). Since its inception in 1973, EC environmental policy has grown steadily, comprising hundreds of directives and five environmental action programmes.

One consequence is that the primary decision-making centre for all states has shifted to Brussels. The power of individual states to formulate autonomous national policy has been eroded, particularly after the institutional changes of the SEA and the TEU replaced unanimous voting and the threat of national veto with widespread qualified majority voting in the Council (Golub, 1996b). The guiding frameworks and narrowly-drafted standards produced in Brussels take priority over previous or conflicting national legislation. For the states in Southern Europe the EC has been a particularly powerful force; the entire regime of EC directives, complete with quantitative reduction targets and deadlines, had to be transposed into national systems with little or no pre-existing legislation. While there have sometimes been serious problems in transposition and enforcement, national laws have been put in place in response to EC pressure, two notable examples being the 1985 Italian Galasso Act and the 1990 British Environmental Protection Act.

The mechanics of the multi-tiered EU decision-making process are highly complex. The supranational level sometimes brings with it potential costs and unwanted constraints on national action, but also potential gains in solving collective action problems and overcoming domestic resistance.

Although officially the Commission retains a monopoly over EC legislative initiatives, owing to its tiny staff, resource dependencies on national ministries and pressure groups are created, becoming the actual sources of almost all EC proposals. A general feature of EC decision-making has been for individual states to advocate their own domestic standards as Community directives, thereby avoiding competitive disadvantages by forcing other states to make similar environmental investments. Clear examples of this phenomenon were German pressure for the Large Combustion Plant Directive and tighter car emissions standards through the use of catalytic converters (Boehmer-Christiansen and Skea, 1991). The threat of a single state going alone and erecting trade barriers to environmentally unfriendly products has also prompted the Commission to issue Community-wide standards. In other cases, green groups, often deprived of national access or influence, utilise the openness of the Commission to push forward proposals (Mazey and Richardson, 1993). With a wealth of proposals on the table from the policy initiation phase, the complex bargaining dynamics of the Council then play a crucial role in the Europeanisation of environmental policy.

Concentrating on the bargaining dynamics in the Council helps to explain the sometimes puzzling phenomenon whereby EC environmental directives ratchet up pre-existing national standards. Until 1987, prior to the SEA, each state effectively exercised a veto over all environmental legislation in the Council. And it might have been expected that consensual decision making would yield only lowest common denominator results, with no state willing to incur the costs of regulation. While such outcomes certainly did occur, and many directives were drafted so vaguely that only minimal changes to national practice were in fact required, standards were often dragged upwards because of the nature of Council decision making and the ability of states to secure their perceived national interests. Four types of mechanism deserve particular attention, although in practice they often occur simultaneously, with cumulative effects.

Manoeuvrability of Green Ministers

Insulated from domestic constraints, negotiations in the Council allow some opportunity for national environmental ministers, especially those from Southern Europe, to strike bargains which might not be supported at home. This increased manoeuvrability becomes a weapon in both intra- and interministerial domestic conflicts. Manoeuvrability also arises from the opportunity of green ministers to adopt laws whose implementation and cost occur far in the future, when the current negotiator or government will not suffer the repercussions. For countries with frequent government turnover this lag effect plays an even greater role. Such manoeuvrability has proven decisive on several occasions. It produced drinking water standards that were tougher than those that existed in any of the member states, including Germany, and facilitated the imposition of many EC standards throughout Southern Europe.

Issue Linkage

Negotiations in Council are marked by frequent trade-offs between various national objectives, so that states expect to link sacrifices in one area with gains in another. Sometimes linkage takes the form of exchanging one environmental policy for another, as was the case when Germany made concessions on car emissions in order to secure agreement on the Large Combustion Plants Directive. But linkage can also occur between specific policies and the more general goal of continued European integration, with all its expected payoffs. During negotiations over water and air pollution controls, there were several instances where countries opposed the content of a directive but nevertheless supported its adoption to demonstrate their credentials as 'good Europeans' (Haigh *et al.*, 1986; Bennett, 1991). For the Southern states, the cost of EC environmental legislation was out-weighed by the economic advantages of continued Community membership, particularly when accompanied by substantial payments in the form of the Cohesion and Structural Funds. A proportion of these funds was specifically designated to offset the cost of implementing environmental obligations; but the vast majority has gone towards infrastructure development and other environmentally damaging projects.

Limitations of Intergovernmentalism

Further, Council deliberations do not always produce lowest common denominator outcomes because of the inherent limitations of inter-governmental bargaining. For example, no country can afford to veto every proposal it finds undesirable. Inevitably, compromises will be made, and standards will sometimes rise. The introduction and extension of qualified majority voting for environmental laws may accelerate this process. Also, directives often produce unforeseen consequences. The results can be extreme: during negotiations over various EC water standards, Britain did not expect to make significant changes to its existing practices but recently discovered that in order to meet these standards it may have to invest £34 billion (Golub, 1996a; OFWAT, 1993). Similarly, Spain was willing to take on the full range of EC environmental obligations to prove its European credentials, but has recently tried to relax some standards and deadlines after discovering the real costs of meeting them (Aguilar-Fernández, 1996).

Consequences are often unforeseen or out of the control of the Council because actors not party to the original bargains become involved in devising or applying the rules. The European Court of Justice has played a leading role in ratcheting up standards when interpreting the specific directives which originally appeared innocuous to some member states, as in rulings against Britain for bathing and drinking water violations. The European Parliament, while it cannot force the adoption of laws, has played a role in raising standards whenever possible, the most famous example being the 1989 car emission directive (Judge, 1993). At other times, a simple lack of information on the part of a specific member state facilitated agreement, as was often the case with Spanish and Italian representatives, whose ministries could not afford to conduct rigorous cost-benefit analysis on proposals and sometimes could not even afford to attend meetings where policy details were formulated, arriving only at the last moment to sign the final version.

Expected Non-Compliance

In some cases, government representatives signed EC environmental laws with little or no expectation of enforcing them. Many of the original member states, particularly Britain, did not take the process seriously. The creation of a legal service within DGXI and the arrival of determined environmental lawyers such as Ludwig Krämer did much to re-educate these states. There is evidence that the endemic non-compliance of the Mediterranean states was sometimes recognised and even assumed by their ministers at the bargaining stage.

The Subsidiarity Debate

The 1992 Maastricht Treaty injected further complexity into the process of European environmental policy-making by placing 'subsidiarity' at the centre of political debate. Under the subsidiarity principle, political responsibility and decision-making authority should be devolved to the lowest appropriate level, whether national or subnational. This has raised doubts about the desirability of European-wide environmental standards and focused attention on the capability of regional actors to tackle environmental problems adequately (Golub, 1996c; Dubrulle, 1994).

A major concern to many environmentalists has been that under the subsidiarity principle many EU environmental laws might be repealed; and certain states compiled 'hit lists' of legislation which, in their opinion, interfered unnecessarily with national sovereignty. Despite strenuous resistance from the European Parliament, the Commission eventually surrendered to pressure from several of them, most notably the UK, and removed various proposals from the agenda.

With the entire body of EU environmental law open to re-examination, the Commission and member states are now struggling to define their respective roles. While there is general agreement that EU action remains indispensable in certain cases, the form of this action remains a hotly contested issue. To provide the maximum possible discretion to each state without sacrificing the environment, the Commission is redrafting many of its laws as framework directives, setting common objectives but allowing differentiated solutions.

While many states may applaud the apparent reining-in of Brussels bureaucracy, their enthusiasm may be short-lived because subsidiarity is a double-edged weapon which might actually undermine national sovereignty by empowering subnational actors. Local and regional authorities have long been important actors, in both policy implementation and design. Enhancing their role will be less of a problem for federal countries such as Germany and Belgium, but will pose difficulties for traditionally unitary states such as France and Britain, and for Spain, where the federal division of power is ambiguous and in a state of flux.

The potential demise, or at least scaling back, of European-wide environmental standards might allow pro-active leader states or regions to forge ahead, free from EU constraints; but it may also threaten environmental improvement. As mentioned above, EU policies were conceived in part to remedy the dismal environmental record of many national governments; and many achievements at the national level were the result of direct EC pressure. Returning policy control to these states, or their regional governments, bodes ill for the future, especially in Southern Europe, where subnational economic disparities result in fierce competition for employment and inward investment, leading to frequent agency capture and policy implementation failure.

New Challenges and Opportunities

Until the mid-1980s, environmental problems were dealt with mainly in an *ad hoc* fashion. Often, their effects rather than their causes were addressed. Since then, the concept of 'sustainable development' has become a major influence on policy, and was the major theme at the United Nations Conference on Environment and Development (Rio Summit) in 1992 (Brenton, 1994). In an important departure from the 1970s and early 1980s, when many environmentalists rejected growth in any form, discussion now centres more on the quality of growth rather than growth *per se* (Collier, 1995). A novel element of reconciling environmental protection with growth has been the argument that investing in the former may stimulate the latter. By reducing their consumption of raw materials and seeking 'lean production', firms may gain long-term competitive advantages over their less efficient rivals. Additionally, trade in pollution abatement technology has become a sizeable market in which green firms can gain first-mover advantage and reap substantial profits.

An equally important aspect of sustainable development involves improving environmental protection without increasing the regulatory burden on industry. New policy instruments, including flexible tools such as market-based instruments or voluntary agreements, are replacing traditional forms of command and control regulation. The use of market-based instruments has been much discussed within the context of climate change, in particular the carbon tax. The energy and transport sectors are the main culprits of emissions but as CO_2 removal and disposal is technically difficult, emissions have to be reduced through greater energy efficiency, new forms of transport, and shifts in fuel production and use. Higher prices for carbon-based energy are likely to bring about reductions, but there is considerable disagreement about the exact level of such a tax.

At EU level, proposals for a carbon tax have faced insurmountable difficulties (Collier, 1996a). A proposal was made for a combined carbon/energy tax, so as not to benefit unduly other energy sources, in particular nuclear energy, which have dubious environmental benefits. However, this caused strong French opposition, because France relies heavily on nuclear energy. Furthermore, the potential threat to competitiveness provoked the unanimous opposition of industry. Finally, the UK opposed the tax on subsidiarity grounds. Meanwhile, some Western European states have already implemented a CO_2 tax. But such measures often exempt industry, which accounts for 30 per cent of all CO_2 emissions.

States throughout Western Europe are also experimenting with a wide variety of new environmental instruments. Voluntary agreements with industry to reduce emissions, also called 'environmental covenants', have a long history in Denmark and the Netherlands. There has also been a promotion of green consumerism through ecolabels or energy efficiency labels on products, or publicising the results of company eco-audits. Ecotaxes on energy use, packaging, waste disposal and other environmentally damaging activities are also becoming more widespread, the revenue being used to subsidise investment in clean technologies, remedy existing environmental damage, or provide new government income. Many states are also considering a complete overhaul of their tax systems by offsetting ecotaxes with tax cuts in other areas. A number of studies suggest that such fiscally neutral measures would boost employment and facilitate growth, while also making polluters pay for their environmental damage.

The EU has adopted directives on eco-audits, energy efficiency and ecolabels, and is considering framework legislation on ecotaxes to co-ordinate national actions and prevent divergent national tax regimes and market distortions. But this needs to resolve questions over the appropriate use of the revenue thereby generated, and whether such taxes violate EU competition laws. One example which highlights the need for EU rules is the Italian tax on plastic shopping bags, which has been heavily criticised because foreign exporters of plastics to Italy are taxed and the money given to Italian companies, while Italian exporters of plastics are tax exempt.

Economic instruments might facilitate environmental policy-making but are not a panacea. To guarantee pollution reduction, a regulatory framework will have to establish quantitative goals, monitor progress and provide enforcement mechanisms for these measures. Furthermore, sustainable development will still require substantial investment by firms, and changes in consumer behaviour, each of which will encounter widespread opposition.

Conclusions

Environmental protection has ascended the political agenda, bringing significant progress against many forms of pollution. However, there are still many unresolved problems, and new ones have recently appeared. Amongst them, climate change presents a particularly difficult challenge, as it requires action in the energy and transport sectors, where policy-makers are only slowly taking the environment into account, and where the opposition of vested interests is particularly strong.

The environmentalist political movement is likely to remain marginal. Green parties have established themselves in a number of Western European countries since the early 1980s but have had a limited impact. Their fortunes oscillate considerably from one election to the next and they have problems transcending their single-issue image. Nevertheless, in many countries they have managed to force a 'greening' of the major parties.

Environmental protection is a multilevel policy issue and naturally raises questions of power within and between states, between national and supranational authorities, and between government and industry. Although sustainable development has established itself as a goal, the traditional tension between environmental protection and economic growth remains a central issue for all levels of government and for industry. Understandably, each of these actors claims the authority and ability to adjudicate between competing priorities. Policy makers are thus searching for ways of achieving both, through deregulation and the use of new instruments.

While the salience and effectiveness of environmental protection still varies among states, Europeanisation and globalisation has done much to raise standards. The collective nature of EU policy-making will continue to link the environmental fortunes of all West European states. Expansion of the EU to include the environmentally pro-active Northern states, and the new power of the European Court of Justice to levy fines for non-compliance could well lead to even higher standards. Alternatively, political decentralisation and the possible expansion of the EU to the less green states of Eastern Europe may increase fragmentation, and produce spectacular successes alongside dismal failures. In sum, environmental policy will remain important in Western Europe but its future is somewhat uncertain.

PART FOUR

Politics, Ideology and Future Challenges

14

Beyond Liberal Politics?
European Modernity and the
Nation-State

NICK RENGGER

This chapter seeks to examine the thesis that contemporary European politics is undergoing a profound change. This thesis argues that the central institution of European politics over the past 500 years – the nation-state – is being radically transformed and so too are many of the aspects of politics most associated with that institution – notions of sovereignty, of civil society and its relation to the state, political economy and the nature of representative, liberal democratic politics. But are these transformations imagined or real? What are their implications for the evolving practices of European politics? What do they presage, if anything, for politics more generally?

The Emergence of a Postmodern Politics?

To start with, let us examine some of the arguments that make this case, in varying ways and to differing degrees. Although it is a contentious term, it might make sense, at least for the purposes of this discussion, to call this cluster of arguments 'the assumption of the emergence of postmodern politics'. It should be noted that the term 'postmodern' is an enormously contested one. In modern social and political theory it is usually used to refer collectively to a group of in fact very disparate thinkers such as Michel Foucault, Jacques Derrida and Jean-François Lyotard who argue in varying ways and to different degrees against 'modern' Enlightenment-derived notions such as reason, rationality and universality. This chapter is not concerned with

247

these wider concerns and 'postmodern' refers only to the set of assumptions about contemporary politics that are being discussed (see Rennger, 1995, ch. 2). Of course, the arguments that make up this cluster are very heterogeneous. Thus, what is discussed here is something of a composite picture, taken from a wide variety of sources, many of whom would disagree profoundly with one another. None the less, for all that, when taken together they do add up to a fairly clear view of the evolution of European modernity, which sets them apart from more usual or traditional views. Let me outline this assumption first, before going on to consider what its advocates think follow from it.

Perhaps it is best to start with the arguments of Bauman (1992a, 1992b). Zygmunt Bauman claims that there are four basic types of postmodern politics to be contrasted with more traditional (let us say 'modern') politics. These types are as follows:

The Rise of a 'De-territorialised' or 'Tribal' Politics

What Bauman has in mind here is perhaps best symbolised by the growing significance of ethnic, national and, more generally, 'particularist' loyalties. Whereas modern politics was, pre-eminently, a politics of rational interest (class interest, for example, or more general material interests such as economic prosperity), postmodern politics is a politics of 'tribal loyalties', where the primary loyalty is not to some fixed territorial entity (a state, in other words) but to an ethnic group (the Basques, the Serbs, the Kurds), a way of life (travellers, for example), or even perhaps a lifestyle (think of the politics of gay and lesbian liberation). Of course it is important to emphasise that neither Bauman, nor other writers who similarly emphasise these developments (see Connolly, 1991 and 1995; and Walker, 1992, for example) suggest that these forms of politics have completely replaced more traditional 'modern' politics. On the contrary, their argument is rather that this newer form of politics is becoming more important, co-existing with older forms, and thereby creating an uneasy transitional situation they call 'postmodern' (or, in the case of Connolly, 'late modern') politics. The most important assumption linking these phenomena is said to be the decreasing significance of 'territory'. One might add here, although Bauman does not mention it, the rise of the use of television, fax machines, tape cassettes and the Internet in aspects of modern politics (think of the role of the media and the fax machine in the overthrow of communism in Eastern Europe, or the ability of the Ayatollah Khomeini to distribute his message in Iran via tape cassettes prior to his return). By definition, these things are 'transborder' phenomena, thus also displaying the decreasing salience of territory.

The Emergence of a Politics of Desire

This type of postmodern politics has to do with the rise of forms of politics in which personal enhancement and lifestyle issues are particularly emphasised. It is also important to see it, Bauman thinks, as a corollary to the third type of postmodern politics – the politics of fear and risk (see below). Of course, the rise of lifestyle politics has been emphasised by more traditional political scientists as well (Inglehart, 1977, 1992). However, rather than this politics simply being the evolution of traditional materialistic politics of class or well being into a new politics of 'postmaterialism', the politics of desire contains elements of cultural, affective and emotional wants and needs, and (again) is seen as being intimately related to the increasing powers of technology and the new social and informational forms it is producing. It is into this area that the work of many other so-called postmodern theorists often fits (Baudrillard, 1988; Baudrillard, 1993; Virilio, 1990). Among the most significant and perhaps potentially important aspects of politics to be informed by this logic are, for example, the politics of gay and lesbian groups. Here the 'deterritorialised' issue politics discussed above is combined with a politics of desire in the most direct sense – the ability to choose a 'lifestyle' (in this case one governed by a particular sexual orientation) without fear of discrimination in its pursuit.

The Politics of Fear and Risk

This type of postmodern politics goes hand in hand with the one already described. Just as postmodern politics emphasises a politics of desire, so it also is especially aware of the risks and fear inherent in the technological and informational revolutions of 'late modernity'. Perhaps the best-known development of this theme has been in the work of the German social theorist, Ulrich Beck, whose argument that we live in a 'risk society' has become increasingly influential (Beck, 1986). The theme has been picked up by many writers, among the best known of whom are Anthony Giddens and Scott Lash (see Giddens, 1993; Lash and Urry, 1993; and Beck *et al.*, 1994). The basic point of Beck's argument is that postmodern societies contain growing areas of unlimited risk. For example, we may live next to a nuclear power station and risk a higher incidence of leukaemia or cancer; we may be eating food that is contaminated by a hitherto unsuspected or un-confirmed disease (BSE, for example); we may be unwittingly or unknowingly damaging aspects of the food chain, or allowing pollutants in our streams or rivers poison our own water supplies and fertile land and so on. This type of postmodern politics naturally goes hand in hand with both former types in that such a politics of risk is both obviously deterritorialised (think of Chernobyl) and the converse of the politics of desire and lifestyle enhancement. A corollary to this type, however, is the rising importance of the issue of trust in contemporary politics. Many have perceived a decreasing sense of trust, in governments, in corporations, and in aspects of civil society, and worry that this lack of trust is undermining other important aspects of politics. What price democracy, for example, if there is no trust? (For discussions see Dunn, 1992; Giddens, 1991; Baier, 1993; Fukuyama, 1995.)

This aspect of 'postmodern politics' is also often intertwined in the politics of desire discussed above. For example, increasingly open and aggressive gay movements both might and have led to increasingly vehement (and sometimes violent) reactions by others against these lifestyle choices, who perhaps find such choices or such lifestyles threatening in various ways. Or, to give a different example, a lifestyle choice giving full reign to one's sexuality in terms of engaging in sex with a large number of people (especially if certain sexual practices that are much less safe than others are involved), whether the individuals concerned are heterosexual or homosexual, might put both the chooser and others in danger from sexually transmitted diseases such as hepatitis and AIDS. The politics of this clash might involve difficult choices about liberty, from social pressure on the one hand and the importance of public health on the other. The point is not to highlight this issue alone but to emphasise how the politics of desire and those of risk and fear might go together.

The Politics of Certainty

This final type of postmodern politics again overlaps with the others. What it amounts to is an ever-increasing need to affirm the rightness of given choices. If we opt for a certain lifestyle, we must be sure that it is the right choice, at least for us. Of course, this can take a wide variety of forms, from the hysterical to the relatively mild. However, Bauman's point is to emphasise that in a world characterised by the growing interpenetration of postmodern politics, and given the fragmentations and dislocations they will inevitably involve, it is only to be expected that the quest for at least some level of *certainty* will become equally urgent.

Of course, as I have already indicated, other versions of the rise of postmodern politics put things slightly differently. For William Connolly, the crucial aspect of 'late modern' politics is the condition of radical pluralisation it brings with it and, in turn, the rise of new fundamentalisms. This is remarkably similar to Bauman's final three types of postmodern politics – and is a development that few of the advocates of the rise of postmodern politics consider to be entirely positive. The problem would appear to be that in the conditions of 'late modernity', certainty is an increasingly contested concept. Traditional modes of authority (religion, the political establishment and so on) appear to be losing the general respect that could give their pronouncements real weight. Those alternatives that have arisen tend to proclaim 'certainty' in a particularly strong, even sometimes, harsh manner (think, for example, of the new-found certainty of many of the Christian right in the USA or of versions of radical Islam in the Middle East and elsewhere). In politics more generally, at least in liberal political systems, such claims tend to be treated with considerable suspicion. Yet, political systems need some level of 'certainty' if they are to work at all. Again, this is where the question of trust seems especially relevant. If we cannot have even putative certainty, then surely it places an even greater weight on the phenomenon of collective trust. If I am not certain about what lifestyle to choose, whether to eat beef or not, or whether to welcome further integration of my nation in the European Union, those 'entrusted' – a key term – with representing me, governing me and so on, must have my trust, otherwise I will be twice as suspicious as before. A political system where trust is completely absent is one reduced to the lowest common denominator of all: fear of superior force. If this is not yet our fate, some postmoderns seem to feel that the politics of certainty and of trust must be central concerns for the twenty-first century.

What are the implications of this view for European politics? Obviously, there are many, but for the purposes of this chapter I want to emphasise and discuss two very general ones. The first set consists of what we might call 'macro' questions, to do with the general 'architecture' of politics, while the second consists of rather more 'micro' questions, to do with its content.

The first area can be broken down fairly neatly into three sub-areas which we shall look at in turn: the implications for the state; the implications for the process of European integration; and the wider implications for Western Europe as a whole. For the last three hundred or so years the central political and institutional unit of European politics has been the nation-state. Politics has been widely perceived internally as the process of administration and institutional form within such units, and externally of the interrelations between them. The internal forms of administration and conflict have evolved, especially since the late eighteenth century, around certain general norms; for example, class, material prosperity and access to the institutional and legal forms of political power. Between such states, the governing form has been hostility and tension, and the threat, if not always the actuality, of war. However, if the advocates of the rise of postmodern politics are right, this central dichotomy between internal and external, as well as the forms each have taken in the modern period, are increasingly problematic. If politics is becoming 'deterritorialised' then the glue that bound the territorial units – the nation-states – together (that is, the doctrine of sovereignty tied to territory) is dissolving. And if that is true, then the division between internal 'domestic' politics and external 'international' politics is also dissolving. If the kinds of politics increasingly dominated by questions of desire, and of risk and fear, are truly becoming more significant, then traditional questions (class and so on) and traditional distinctions (domestic/international) are doubly in question.

None of this, of course means that 'states' as administrative and bureaucratic units are going to disappear overnight. It does, however, mean that something very precious for the nation-state's self image – and its ability to sustain itself in the manner of that self image – will have been lost, probably for good. That precious item, which we might call the 'spiritual' character or aspiration of the state, is its legitimacy as the sole or major source of its citizens/subjects' loyalties and political obligations. It was this sense of the state as the 'good society', the 'society of societies' as it were, that made states worth fighting for and dying for. Without it they become simply large-scale providers of goods and services, and, as Stephen Clark has said, 'who would die for the water board?' (Clark 1989). Since, at least on the Weberian definition, part of what made a state a state was 'control of the legitimate means of violence', and what made it legitimate was its unique character, anything which destroys that goes some way towards destroying the state itself.

As far as the project of European integration goes, the assertion of the rise of postmodern politics has equally stark implications. In the first place, it undercuts almost completely the 'debates' – if that is quite the word – between the so-called federalists and supporters of state sovereignty. Support for state sovereignty, of course, falls at the hurdle just discussed. However, federalism, in its European sense, fares little better. The assumption on which the integration process rests (that institutions, legal processes and norms can gradually and effectively be homogenised and standardised across the member states of the EU) would clearly be undermined by the politics of desire and by the politics of risk and fear. The whole project of European integration, moreover, rests on a series of logics that the rise of postmodern politics, if true, undercuts. For example, the desire to secure the states of Europe by binding them together irrevocably into an 'ever closer union' clearly rests on the logic of 'external' competition that is in any case undermined by the types of postmodern politics. Or, to take another example, the logic of much of the internal politics of the EU depends upon the logics of traditional 'modern politics' (think of the Common Agricultural Policy (CAP) or the emerging welfare provisions of the EU such as the Social Chapter and the Social Protocol and Agreement). Yet if the advocates of postmodern politics are correct, these forms of politics, while unquestionably important, are being compromised by the newer forms in such a way that they will never perform the tasks that the original and evolving design of the EU laid out for them.

As for the wider implications for Western Europe, one of the hallmarks of contemporary European politics in the West (and increasingly elsewhere) is the assumption that a healthy democracy, and therefore a healthy state or confederation of states, rests on a healthy civil society. The notion of civil society is indeed one of the most heatedly debated but also one the most important notions within contemporary politics (Cohen and Arato, 1992; Seligman, 1992). Very roughly, it might be said to symbolise the network of clubs, associations, corporations and so on that make up a modern society but that are not part of the 'state' in a formal – or even an informal – sense. Thus cricket clubs, universities, churches, trade unions, professional associations and so on are all part of civil society. The problem is that the rise of postmodern politics is deeply ambiguous for civil society. On the one hand, it might allow spaces for such civil society to expand and might allow it greater freedom from state governance, institutions and processes than at present. On the other, many of the forces associated with the rise of postmodern politics are dissolving the bonds of civil society as they are the bonds of the state itself.

One of the obvious implications of this, emphasised by many of its advocates, is the dangers it poses for established patterns of democracy: how can the evolving practices of democracy cope with the rise of postmodern politics? This concern is shared by other analysts of

contemporary politics, who may not share postmodern prescriptions
and diagnoses. For example, for Barber (1995), the contemporary
political scene is best understood as a clash between the forces of what
he terms 'Jihad' and 'McWorld', understood respectively as the forces
of more or less radical particularism, parochialism and so on (religious
fundamentalism, ethnic nationalism and other forms of tribalism) and
the forces of exponentially increasing global capitalism (the information revolution, globalised financial markets, multinational media
empires and so on). The difference between Barber and the 'postmoderns', however, is revealed by the fact that both 'Jihad' and
'McWorld' are inimical to democracy because they both undermine
those practices and institutions that have been, however imperfectly,
the best and safest carriers of democratic ideas – that is, those
associated with the nation-state. While Barber accepts that democracy
is not necessarily wedded to such states (after all, it was born in the
Greek *polis,* certainly not a nation-state), he does think that to all
intents and purposes democracy requires something like the institutions and rule/law-governed character of modern states to be
practicable. And this is precisely what is under threat in the era of
'Jihad' and 'McWorld'. As we have seen, the advocates of postmodern
politics are far less wedded to the institutions and practices of the
nation-state. None the less, they too are concerned that at least some
aspects of postmodern politics might undermine practices of civil
society which support and sustain a commitment to radical 'otherness'
and plurality.

This point is not dissimilar to that made by a number of other writers
who are by no means advocates of postmodern politics in the sense
described here. The work of David Held and Daniele Archibugi on
'cosmopolitan democracy' is a case in point (Held and Archibugi, 1994;
Held, 1995). But there are critical differences between these writers and
their 'postmodern' counterparts.

In some respects these differences parallel wider differences between
'postmodern' thinkers and those who are either reluctant to abandon
completely aspects of modern politics (such as Barber) or who (like
Held) think that we should not, because 'the modern' remains to be
completed. Held echoes the concerns of perhaps the most influential
contemporary critical social theorist, Jurgen Habermas, who has
bitterly criticised allegedly postmodern thinkers such as Derrida,
Foucault and Lyotard for abandoning 'modernity' and, along with
it, the capacity to judge and act in politics (Habermas, 1989). The
general debate would take us too far away from our main concerns
here, but to signal its importance, we might term thinkers such as Held

and Archibugi (and also Barber, though he is less clearly Habermassian in his sympathies) 'cosmopolitan democrats', and the advocates of postmodern politics who emphasise similar themes, but in different ways, 'agonistic democrats', because of their emphasis on what William Connolly has called an 'ethos of pluralisation'.

For all their differences, however – and they are profound – all these writers suggest that the contemporary shape of world politics is such that the likeliest casualty in the short to medium term will be democracy itself, unless we evolve real responses to the developments that I have characterised here as the rise of postmodern politics.

The second set of implications has to do with less grand but equally important areas of modern politics such as the character and role of parties within democracies and, perhaps, most critically, the traditional division of politics into 'conservative' and 'progressive' forces, between right and left. For many advocates of postmodern politics, the rise of these kinds of politics means that such labels as 'conservative' or 'progressive' (or, indeed, 'socialist') no longer have any clear meaning. Such terms depended for their force on notions of politics that accepted, in principle, at least the ideological assumptions built into the notion of 'progress', that is to say history as a story moving from a (worse) beginning towards a (better) conclusion. This was the story that, traditionally, liberals and socialists wanted to tell, and that conservatives denied. This accounts for the similarity on this point between conservative and some postmodern accounts of politics, which have been noted and picked up by a number of writers. However, conservative views fare little better, since the point of postmodern politics is to challenge the possibility of any fixed positions, including the traditional ones that conservative politics usually appeal to. The terms 'left' and 'right' therefore have little relevance to advocates of postmodern politics. However, there is, of course, an irony here, since most of those who do advocate postmodern politics are, to a greater or a lesser extent, identifiably on the existing political left.

Assessments

Just how seriously, then, should we take these arguments? To begin with it seems fair to say that it would be unusual – to say the least – if the changes and developments since the 1970s were not having a profound effect on the shape and character of politics. But are the specific types of politics described by the advocates of postmodern politics the best ways of understanding these effects?

It is true, I think, that, at least in important ways, politics is becoming deterritorialised, if by that term it is meant that territory as a simple fact matters less today at the end of the twentieth century, than possibly at any other time in recorded history. Many of the uses for which territory was a prerequisite in the past are now available without owning a particular territory or, to put it another way, putting territory together with capacity is no longer a function of control over territory, merely access to it. Japan – to give just one obvious example – now has far more access to 'territory' than the country ever succeeded in acquiring through conquest. Of course, this is a feature of politics that has been evolving at least since the mid-nineteenth century; but it has certainly received a powerful boost from the information revolution since the 1980s, and is increasing ever more speedily.

However, the key question is surely the rate of this evolution and what it implies for forms of politics that are predicated *upon* territory. The most important of these is, unquestionably, the nation-state and its associated institutions – among the most important of which, as we have seen, is democracy. Is it true that the nation-state is under threat, or that these developments presage a threat to democracy? In part, the answer to this question depends on what we mean by 'nation-state under threat'. If this means simply that the idea of hermetically sealed, internally homogenous and legitimate political units, gathered under the twin banners of sovereignty and nationality, is becoming decreasingly plausible as a description of the world in which we live, then it seems to me that this is both true and very much to be welcomed.

Such a view of the state, though encouraged both by states themselves and by many analysts, has always been at best a simplification. State boundaries have always been contestable and permeable – even in the case of authoritarian regimes – and the manner in which states have drawn their legitimacy from their simple possession of territory problematic (think of the conflict between the state and other forms of authority which continued well into the nineteenth century).

If, however, it means that the administrative structures, institutional forms and political processes associated with 'nation-states' in the modern world are likely to disappear overnight, then this is clearly incorrect. The point is surely to agree that those aspects of postmodern politics that are clearly visible among the lineaments of contemporary life are scrambling the traditionally accepted categories of politics (domestic/international; economic/political/cultural and so on) but also to explore the ways that those categories were always rather too tightly drawn for their own good. It suited the evolution of the political elites of modern Europe to suppose that power should be centralised around a single legitimate core (the sovereign) and that relations between political associations should be channelled through that core. However, it was not really until the twentieth century that the technology began to exist to allow them to police that claim; and as the technology evolved, so the possibility of actively policing it began to recede. The sociocultural form of modernity – to use an almost endlessly contestable term – is in a state of almost constant change. But the way we understand and respond to such continual change will depend upon the mood we match it with; and that will, of course, depend on the particular perspective we adopt (Rengger, 1995).

Of course, the real concern expressed by Barber and others is that without the glue that has traditionally been provided by the nation-state, and by the institutions of civil society supported by and sustaining of the nation-state, democracy as a mechanism of genuine accountability and citizen participation will dissolve. However, I think that on this point the 'postmoderns' may have an advantage over 'moderns' such as Barber. It seems to me that there is no reason to suppose that the nation-state is particularly a friend of democracy, and considerable reasons for supposing the opposite (Rengger, 1996). So the fact that the state might in some sense be evolving and losing aspects of its traditional powers and roles is not necessarily something to be worried about. However, the fact that civil society may also be losing its ability to sustain itself is something to be very concerned about indeed. For if we are to sustain democratic practices of however minimal a kind in the face of the evolution of postmodern politics, then we have to have ways of relating to one another and combining in ways that are not simply tied to interest (which is hardly likely to disappear as a political concern), risk, fear or desire. There exist already many intimations of what a society based simply around these might be like, and none of them is pleasant.

This leads me to a further point. The rise of postmodern politics as I have sketched it so far has emphasised the pressures on the nation-state. Advocates of this view do not necessarily suppose that 'government' will cease. Indeed, quite the contrary. Many would argue that in the new situation created by the rise of 'postmodern politics', government will become more difficult to map because more invisible: 'governance' will be far less transparent and, as a result, less accountable. Again, this brings advocates of postmodern politics into discussion with some other theorists who, without subscribing to a full-blown postmodern politics, do suggest that powerful and profound changes might be going on. For example, the American scholar, Alexander Wendt, has suggested that we are witnessing the gradual emergence of what he calls an 'international state' (Wendt, 1994). For Wendt, this 'state' contains many of the functions of traditional states, but shorn of the language of full loyalty and obligation – what I call their 'spiritual' character – and without a clearly defined sense of territory. Wendt is here drawing on the emergence of institutions such as the EU, but also the group of seven so-called 'leading industrial countries' (G-7), and the increasingly multilateral character of a good deal of political decision making at all levels (Ruggie, 1993). The point here, of course, is that, since most democratic institutions work at the state (or the local) level, such a development does indeed threaten democracy. Of course, many 'postmoderns' would want to push this point much further than does Wendt (Walker, 1992; Der Derian, 1992; Walker, 1994). However, once again there is some commonality of view between what we might call a critical modernist approach and a postmodern one.

In this respect, it seems to me that there are good reasons for supposing, first, that something akin to postmodern politics is indeed becoming more important, and second, that it will pose considerable problems for what we might call the architecture of European politics in the twenty-first century. However, does this hold true also for the 'softer' aspects of politics touched on above? Inasmuch as the tradi-tional 'left–right' division of European politics had to do with ques-tions such as class and/or industrial or economic prosperity, then it is clear they are not the same as they were, say, in the 1930s or the 1970s. However, it still seems reasonable to talk about 'left' and 'right', if by these terms is meant attitude towards, and perspective on, the political/economic establishment and elites of a given society or societies. By and large, the 'left' is suspicious of such elites, even if (or when) it is part of them, while the right is supportive of them. However, in so far as new issues, especially social ones (abortion, the effect and implica-tions of genetic engineering and new technologies and so on) are increasingly the kinds of issue that can be subsumed under the second or third type of postmodern politics then, of course, traditional 'left–right' distinctions will not be much help in orientating oneself towards them.

In sum, although potentially powerful, the implications of postmo-dern politics are that they are not materialising at the same rate or in the same way. In other words those 'postmoderns' who think that the point about the contemporary situation is its fluidity and transitional character (Connolly and Bauman, for example) seem to me to be closest to the mark. Overall, then, and if the foregoing point is borne in mind, it seems that there is much to be said for at least part of the assumption of the rise of postmodern politics. The next question, however, is how we should respond to it in the context of contemporary European politics.

Responses

Here, I think, we find ourselves navigating perilously between Scylla and Charybdis. On the one hand there is the obvious temptation, succumbed to by some, to be swept up (and possibly away) by the supposed benefits of many of the aspects of 'postmodern politics': the opportunities for new forms of democracy (electronic town halls and the like), the rise of the Internet and so on. There is also the temptation to view such developments in even greater terms, whether optimistically or pessimistically. Arguments like Fukuyama's 'End of History' thesis (Fukuyama, 1992), or Huntington's 'Clash of Civilisations' thesis (Huntington, 1993) are examples of these. On the other hand, there is the equal temptation – and this is perhaps a majority view among many political scientists and political actors – to dismiss such claims as absurd, or, at best, hugely inflated. As I have suggested above, I think both these responses would be mistaken. The changes highlighted by the claim of the rise of postmodern politics are real enough, and attempts to ignore them simply will not work. However, merely 'accepting' them (or even welcoming them) will not work either. The reason should by now be obvious. The rise of postmodern politics is an ongoing process, and, moreover, it is not a linear one. It will require human agency however it actually develops. We need, therefore, to think about what kinds of agent we are, what kinds of goal we should aim at, and how we should seek to achieve these goals.

My starting point is the postmodern claim concerning particularity and plurality. This claim, I suggest, has two aspects. It is both a description and, at least in a sense, a normative claim; that is to say, a claim that this is a good or a desirable state of affairs. It seems to me, however, that the second aspect depends upon the way in which the first is manifested. It may well be true that diversity/otherness is to be cherished in and of itself, and not simply as a projection of ourselves. However, we can only take this view, I think, if we have societies which allow us to see difference in this light, which means societies in which *fear* of difference is not meaningful. Modern Western European states, however, have very considerable difficulties with this. To begin with, they are committed, at least publicly, to forms of liberalism which *deny* or *reject* the claims of difference and of particularity. For modern

European (and, indeed American) liberal democracies, rights, for example, are 'universal' and 'individual', and the claim that we should see groups (or, indeed, individuals) in a radically *plural* way is deeply problematic: it is assumed to undermine the 'general equal treatment of all' that modern liberal democracies are held to rest upon. This is doubly true if we think of the evolution of the institutions of modern Europe in general, and especially the growing emergence of the 'international state' that is the EU. Here, the whole process rests upon the assumption of convergence; of economic criteria, of political systems, and (though not usually explicitly) of the practices of individuals within the Union. Radical plurality is widely perceived as being a threat to the whole process.

The implications of this, however, are that a sensible response to the rise of postmodern politics is to be suspicious of the process of 'European integration', not because it is draining sovereignty from sovereign states but because it is showing absolutely no sign of taking seriously the emergence of the new forms of politics and all they will bring with them. The problem is that, as Barber suggests, continued inattention to the increasingly obvious tensions between particularity and stipulative and often over-mechanistic universality will result in growing political crisis and disenchantment. However, the usual alternative (that is, the strengthening of nation-states, and a refusal to cede 'more sovereignty to Brussels') is equally illusory and probably worse in terms of its likely effects. The politics of risk and fear feeds on the assertion of a 'strong state', and greater attempts to prevent the erosion of sovereignty are only likely to produce a more hostile reaction from those in whose interests it is that the integration process proceeds as smoothly as possible (these now include the vast majority of the European business elite, whose closeness to the European political elite hardly needs emphasising). We appear, then, to be in something of a quandary; neither of the most heatedly debated alternatives for the overarching architecture of Western European politics looks likely to be capable of coping with the rise of postmodern politics.

Barber (and indeed Bauman, Connolly and many others) are therefore quite right in pointing to the centrality of civil society as an agent whereby these tensions might be accommodated. Of course, simple appeals to the notion of civil society are clearly not enough. It requires work and sustenance, and there is considerable evidence that, in Europe generally, and especially in the UK since the early 1980s, quite the opposite process has been at work (if 'there is no such thing as society', there clearly cannot be a civil version of it!). None the less, among the more important tasks we might give our attention to as citizens and political actors is the support and extension of civil society, both within particular countries and, perhaps most importantly, across Europe as a whole. Of course, there are many social movements that are doing just this and have been doing so for a long time. But given contemporary conditions, such efforts need to be redoubled.

However, even the existence of a strengthened civil society is unlikely, of itself, to allow effective responses to the rise of postmodern politics. In fact, among the most important responses we can make to the rise of postmodern politics, is not institutional at all. It is simply to recognise that the traditional understanding and practices of politics we have developed over the past five hundred or so years will have to be substantially rethought if we are to have a chance of re-energising our civil society and, as a result, reformulating our democracies to cope with 'postmodern' challenges. Many writers, certainly not all of them 'postmoderns', have recognised this in varying ways since the 1980s. It is a recognition present, for example, in the work of Alasdair MacIntyre as much as it is in that of any postmodern thinker (MacIntyre, 1987). The problem with such a claim, of course, is its lack of specificity. However, if it is true that what we need to do is to rethink our practices, our understanding and our institutions, it is hardly surprising that we cannot instantly give an institutional recommendation. It is over the forms that such rethinking should take, of course, that the various writers and scholars whose positions have often dovetailed previously and from which I have drawn here are most likely to go in different directions.

My own view is quite simple. We have to understand that we are situated, contextual and particular beings. Only if we do so, do we have any chance of also reaching beyond our situation, our context and our particularity, and understanding and appreciating other forms of situation, context or particularity. Europeans have such ways of thinking about politics available in their intellectual and political traditions: the Platonic and Aristotelian traditions, for all their differences, agreed on this, as did that of the early Christians. These are not, however, the traditions that have been dominant in the shaping and evolution of modern European politics. But perhaps therein lies our opportunity. If the advocates of the rise of postmodern politics are right, to whatever extent – and I have tried in this essay to suggest that they are – then the transitional period they detect is surely a good time to begin the process of rethinking our conceptions of politics. Much of that rethinking will, of course, be new, as the 'postmoderns' and many others suggest. For some of it, however, we might be well advised to look deeper into the traditions we already have available to us.

Whatever is the case here, however, such rethinking in general, as well as the reframing of our political practices, seems to be central to the task of coming to terms with postmodern politics in Western Europe. Of course, it is still far more likely that the debates will continue in the same old way between the federalists and the champions of sovereignty, advocates of the European elite, and the increasingly disenchanted and disenfranchised majority. If that is so, then something very precious will indeed have been lost with the rise of postmodern politics; but we shall not be able to blame the postmoderns for losing it: it is the rest of us who will have ignored the message.

15

The Media and Politics

RAYMOND KUHN

This is the age of the media in Western Europe. Virtual saturation has been reached in the number of households equipped with radio and television, while a sizeable proportion also have a video-cassette recorder and many subscribe to multichannel cable or satellite broadcasting as well. This is also the age of media politics. The media play a vital role as a channel of communication between political elites and the public. Television is the single most important source of political information, especially for national and international news. Its pervasiveness and emphasis on visual imagery have convinced many political actors that it has an almost magical capacity to shape public opinion. As a result, they crave access to the small screen, stage events for the cameras and, depending on their power, seek to influence, co-opt, manipulate, control or censor television coverage for their own partisan purposes. With the election in 1994 of the telegenic, image-conscious media mogul, Silvio Berlusconi, as Italian prime minister, the 'mediatisation' of West European politics attained unprecedented heights.

The central role of the media in the political communications process has made their organisation and functioning key issues of contemporary policy debate. Ownership and control of media companies, media funding and the regulation of content are now staple items on the policy agenda. Moreover, these issues are no longer confined to the national political context: they have also assumed a supranational importance with the European Union (EU) seeking a higher profile in policy-making. This is clearly part of the wider strengthening of EU powers *vis-à-vis* national governments (see Chapter 3). But it is also a response to the technological and economic changes which have made nation-state boundaries increasingly permeable to cross-border media flows (for example, via satellite transmission) and strengthened the presence of transnational companies in the media of different national systems.

Media Diversity in Western Europe

Are the media in Western Europe a coherent entity about which one can make meaningful generalisations? There are certainly many problems in doing so. For example, 'the media' embrace a variety of mass communication and associated technologies – newspapers, magazines, radio, television, video, cable and satellite, as well as books, theatre, cinema and advertising. Even an analysis confined to a single national political/media system would need to distinguish between these media in terms of their structure, functioning and effects. More significantly for the purposes of this chapter, there exist clearly discernible cross-national differences among West European political/media systems, before one even begins to take account of important subnational particularities.

First, there is an impressive variety on the supply side, with contrasting levels and types of media provision from one country to another.

Second, media consumption patterns differ. For example, there are wide disparities in the extent of newspaper readership. Spain and Portugal are at the bottom of this particular league table, followed by Greece, Italy and France. In contrast, in Germany, the United Kingdom (UK) and, above all, the Scandinavian countries, newspaper readership figures are high. In addition, whereas in some countries (for example, the UK) national newspapers enjoy the largest circulations, in others (for example, France and Germany) local/regional papers dominate the market.

Third, variable patterns of ownership both within and across media sectors are evident within national systems. For example, in Spain in the early 1990s, the top two press groups had only 24 per cent of the daily newspaper market as measured by circulation, while in Ireland the corresponding figure was a staggering 76 per cent (Commission of the European Communities, 1992, p. 31). Levels of private-sector ownership in the broadcast media differ from country to country, as does the extent of cross-media holdings.

Fourth, contrasting frameworks of media regulation are apparent. Rules governing permitted levels of monomedia and cross-media ownership vary enormously. For example, in France and Italy the merger of press groups is prohibited if their combined newspaper circulation exceeds a certain market share (in France 30 per cent, Italy 20 per cent). In the UK and Germany there are no such specific constraints, but there are thresholds which may trigger an examination by competition authorities. In the other member states of the EU in 1994 there was no specified limit on newspaper holdings (Commission of the European Communities, 1994, p. 65). In broadcasting regulation, cross-national differences are evident on issues such as independent production quotas, the televised screening of feature films, and political advertising on television (Lee Kaid and Holtz-Bacha, 1995).

Fifth, financial arrangements for the media also differ across Western Europe. For example, some countries provide state aid to the press (including France, Italy, Spain, Norway, Sweden and Austria) while others do not (including the UK, Ireland, Germany and Denmark). In Spain the public-sector television channels receive a large amount of their revenue from commercial advertising, while in Britain the British Broadcasting Corporation (BBC) still does not have advertisements on its domestic radio and television services. In Germany, the state was largely responsible for funding the country's cable infrastructure, while in the UK this was left to the private sector.

Sixth, there are disparities in the level of media politicisation. In some systems (for example, Gaullist France, Francoist Spain, Portugal during the Salazarist dictatorship, and Greece under the Colonels) a practice was established that broadcasting was a *de facto* part of the executive branch of government. Despite reforms, the weight of this legacy has never been fully shaken off. In other systems, such as in Germany and Italy, political parties in power at either the regional or national level became accustomed to securing a measure of partisan political control of television. In Germany some regional public broadcasting corporations are dominated by the Christian Democrats (CDU/CSU) and others by the Democratic Socialist Party (SPD) (Humphreys, 1994). In Italy in the 1980s the three channels of the public corporation, the RAI (Radiotelevisione Italiana), were divided up between the Christian democrats, the socialists and the communists respectively in a sharing out of political spoils (Sassoon, 1985). Whether dominated by the state or political parties, such systems have tended to exhibit the following characteristics: key media appointments made on political rather than professional criteria; news coverage politically controlled; and the lack of a concept of broadcasting as a public sphere enjoying a high degree of autonomy from partisan politicisation.

In the Netherlands the broadcasting system was originally conceived on the basis of different social and political groups running their own stations – a system known as 'pillarisation', which complemented the political structures and practices of consociational democracy (Brants, 1985). In other systems, such as in Britain, there has been a well-entrenched tradition of broadcasting independent from day-to-day control by politicians. This has allowed broadcasters to develop a legitimacy based on their professionalism rather than their political sympathies, even if the reality has not always matched the public service rhetoric (Negrine, 1994). In Scandinavian systems too 'the general aim was to keep parties at a distance and minimise the direct involvement of politicians in broadcasting' (McQuail, 1995, p. 150).

Finally, there are cross-national differences in media product. Most obviously, much content reflects explicitly national concerns such as politics, crime, culture, sport and weather. In addition, there are sometimes significant cross-cultural differences regarding what is acceptable. For example, explicit sexuality in media advertising may be tolerated in one country, but problematic in another. Moreover, even where content is exactly the same (for example, the same programme being broadcast on different Western European television channels), there will often be cross-national differences in audience response. The same media 'text' may be decoded in quite different ways as a function of the nationality of the audience.

Common Media Policy Issues in Western Europe

Yet despite important aspects of cross-national difference, there are also significant common elements in West European media (Siune and Truetzschler, 1992). The newspaper sector of the press is generally in decline, even in those media systems where the level of newspaper readership is still high. The number of titles has shrunk during the postwar period, total circulation figures have fallen, and the share of media advertising expenditure taken by newspapers has dropped. Across Western Europe, albeit with peaks and troughs in demand, general information newspapers are losing out because of competition from the broadcasting media and specialised magazines.

In contrast, the broadcasting media are expanding. The growth in the number of radio stations and television channels, particularly since the start of the 1980s, has irreversibly changed the audio-visual landscape across Western Europe. As a result, the amount of audio-visual output available to audiences has increased enormously. Moreover, this expansion has been accompanied by a shift in the balance of power away from public-sector ownership and towards privately-owned media. Whereas at the beginning of the 1980s there were only four commercial television broadcasters in Europe, by the beginning of the 1990s there were fifty-eight (Collins, 1994, p. 146).

There are certainly clear elements of similarity as far as the key issues on national media policy agendas are concerned. These include:

- the impact of technological change, as new forms of programme transmission such as satellite broadcasting and cable television become commonplace, while technological convergence breaks down established policy boundaries between broadcasting and telecommunications;
- concentration of ownership both within and across media sectors;
- transnationalisation, as powerful media companies operate increasingly across national boundaries; and
- the regulation of the audio-visual media as traditional regulatory regimes are modified to cope with increased commercial competition.

At the same time, the supranational nature of some of these developments combined with wider changes in the balance of power between member states and the EU has resulted in another contemporary trend:

- the 'Europeanisation' of the media policy agenda.

Technological Change

One of the most notable developments in West European media since the early 1980s has been the impact of technological change. In the newspaper industry, the introduction of new technology, often bitterly opposed by the workforce, has revolutionised the production process and labour practices. But it has not led to a growth in diversity, whether measured in terms of ownership or number of titles, as market entry costs for daily newspapers remain high.

It is in the audio-visual field that technological change has had the greater impact. In radio, the combination of FM frequencies and satellite transmission has helped the growth of radio provision, including local stations catering for small geographical communities and ethnic minority groups. In television, two new means of delivering programmes to households have come to rival the traditional method of terrestrial transmission. While cable and satellite have had a differential cross-national impact in terms of audience share, everywhere they have had a powerful influence on the media policy agenda, throwing established broadcasters on to the defensive (Dyson *et al.*, 1988). These new programme delivery systems have altered the parameters of broadcasting distribution, and therefore also the audio-visual media debate, in three important ways.

First, they have smashed the previously binding technical constraint of a finite airwave spectrum in broadcasting. Previously the limited number of available frequencies meant that broadcasting supply had to be rationed. A free market in broadcasting was technically out of the question. In practice, this usually meant that the state was responsible for the allocation of broadcast frequencies and normally these were given to a public-sector broadcaster which often enjoyed a monopoly in programme provision. This technical limitation is no longer applicable. Fibre-optic cable has the capacity to deliver multichannel television to households (Negrine, 1985), while digital compression of broadcast signals opens up the possibility of numerous television channels using traditional terrestrial (and satellite) frequencies.

Second, satellite broadcasting allows signals to be transmitted across national boundaries. Of course, television signals have never been strictly confined to national territories. In frontier regions and in smaller European states (such as the Benelux countries), television programmes from neighbouring national systems have been available for a long time. However, for the inhabitants of larger countries who are not living in frontier areas, the traditional programme regime was that provided by the national broadcaster(s). This is no longer the case. Through satellite (either direct to households or via cable systems) audiences across Western Europe can watch programmes beamed in from outside the national territory, either from the broadcasters of other national systems, or from new pan-European and global channels such as MTV and CNN (Negrine, 1988). The main barrier to transfrontier television flows is no longer technology or geographical boundaries, but language. Or to put it another way, cross-border television is no longer a problem of distribution but of reception. One possible consequence may be that supranational linguistic communities rather than national populations will provide the broadcasting markets of the future in Western Europe.

Third, new technological developments have resulted in a process of convergence, whereby previous distinctions between media in terms of technology (for example, telephone and television) and function (interpersonal versus mass communication) have become blurred. Cable is an excellent example of such convergence. Originally it was employed as a means of programme distribution by terrestrial broadcasters in areas where off-air reception was poor. Then at the start of the 1980s the development of broadband cable networks opened up the possibility of multichannel television, challenging the control of the terrestrial networks. The supporters of cable argued that the main initial attraction for households to subscribe to the new medium would be the expansion of the number of television programmes available. In West Germany, for example, cable received the backing of the CDU federal government in the 1980s in part because it allowed commercial channels to enter the television market (Porter and Hasselbach, 1991, ch. 2).

However, for government policy-makers and telecommunication agencies, cable had much wider implications than merely the extension of television programme supply. Instead, the combination of fibre-optic cable and star-switched systems allowed the construction of sophisticated information networks which would carry a wide range of interactive communication services. It was largely on the basis of its industrial and economic potential as an information and communications medium that the socialist government in France in the early 1980s formulated an ambitious project to cable the nation. Cable was part of an industrial strategy that would give France a leading edge in the electronics sector at a time when traditional manufacturing industries, such as steel and textiles, were in decline (Kuhn, 1995, ch. 8).

Technological convergence has led to new actors becoming involved in the media policy field. In the UK, for example, British Telecommunications (BT) is actively seeking a stake as a cable network operator and provider of information and entertainment services. While the conservative government has allowed cable operators, many of whom are owned by American telecommunication companies, to offer telephone services to subscribers in addition to television programmes, it has so far largely kept BT out of the cable market. But this may soon change, since the British Labour Party has promised to allow BT to enter this market in return for the company linking up schools and hospitals to the information superhighway when it returns to office. In France the telecommunications company France Télécom has taken a leading role in planning cable infrastructure since the early 1980s, while more recently water companies have become major cable operators and terrestrial television shareholders. In Germany, where broadcasting has been a postwar responsibility of the regions, cable investment by the Bundespost in the 1980s allowed the federal government to enter an area of policy from which it had been excluded by the postwar constitutional settlement.

In short, a multimedia revolution incorporating different but compatible technologies is changing the way in which information and entertainment services are produced and exchanged. Cable is thus an integral part of a communications leap forward, the impact of which is being felt far beyond the realms of television programming. The question that policy makers across Western Europe are still wrestling with is how all this will affect the regulation of both telecommunications and broadcasting.

Concentration of Ownership

The issue of media ownership and control features high on national policy agendas in response to a discernible trend towards monomedia and multimedia concentration (International Institute of Communications, 1996). In particular, with the decline in the newspaper industry and the expansion of commercial broadcasting, press groups such as Rupert Murdoch's News International in the UK, Hersant in France and Springer/Kirch in Germany have sought to secure a stake in the audio-visual media, thereby provoking concern about oligopolistic control of information (Tunstall and Palmer, 1991). National patterns of cross-media ownership have become more complex as companies have diversified their media holdings across different sectors. Many have also engaged in a process of vertical integration and acquired a stake in the production, programming and transmission of media product.

The problem for policy-makers has been reconciling the desirability of ownership pluralism and content diversity with the economic arguments in favour of critical mass size and cross-media synergy. They have also had to take account of the fact that leading national media companies operate increasingly in international markets. Ownership restrictions which may promote desirable competition within national and subnational markets may prevent media companies from competing effectively at the European and global levels.

In general, ownership regulations governing the press are less evident than those dealing with the audio-visual media. This reflects the traditionally less open conditions for market entry into broadcasting. The general trend across Western Europe is towards the liberalisation of cross-media ownership restrictions. In France, a complex set of rules introduced in 1986 allows for a considerable concentration of cross-media power. Germany's 'new broadcasting legislation is conspicuously 'relaxed' with regard to cross-media ownership' (Humphreys, 1994, p. 324). In Italy, proposals to restrict ownership concentration in private television and force Berlusconi to divest some of his media interests were defeated by referendum in 1995. Meanwhile, in the UK the Conservative government proposed to liberalise existing provisions by introducing new thresholds for market share, both within and across different media sectors (Department of National Heritage, 1995).

Transnationalisation

The role of powerful transnational companies raises questions about national identity and cultural preservation. The most economically powerful media groups tend to be those which have a strong national domestic base from which they have infiltrated foreign media markets. These include the Bertelsmann publishing group (Germany), Berlusconi's Fininvest company (Italy), the Canal Plus pay-TV company (France), and News International (UK).

Some companies have largely confined their interests to Europe, while others operate across the globe. Murdoch, for example, has interests in Australia, the USA and South-east Asia in addition to Britain, while the UK-based Pearson Group has holdings in Hong Kong, the USA and Australia, as well as in France and Spain. The Bertelsmann Group was in the early 1990s the world's second biggest media company, with extensive media interests in the USA. In contrast, Silvio Berlusconi's Fininvest has tended to confine its activities to continental European systems such as France, Spain and Germany in addition to its home base in Italy. Similarly, while Canal Plus has a stake in pay-TV in Francophone Africa, its main markets are in Western Europe, including Spain and Germany. Small countries tend not to produce big transnational media players, though Luxembourg is exceptional, because its geographical position and liberal approach have made it an attractive base for commercial media companies (Dyson, 1990, ch. 5).

Media Regulation

Regulation has been an important media policy issue as broadcasting regimes based on public service ideals have been modified to cope with increased commercial competition. While the concept of public-service broadcasting is a difficult one to define precisely, it usually comprised the following elements: the provision of a nationwide service; public funding, normally through a licence fee; a balanced programme schedule, containing information and education as well as entertainment; programmes to reflect national cultural values and regional diversity; and a commitment, not always honoured in practice, to balance and impartiality in news output. This West European public-service model of broadcasting contrasts with the explicitly more commercial approach adopted in the USA and the overt state-controlled model of Eastern Europe and authoritarian societies.

This 'old order' was undermined by the expansion in audio-visual media during the 1980s (McQuail, 1995). New technology was one destabilising factor. Another was financial problems caused by licence fee saturation against a background of rising production costs. Ideology also played a key role in some political systems. Many West European conservative governments were seduced by new right ideas emanating from the USA, which called for greater deregulation and liberalisation of service provision, a reduced role for the state, to include the privatisation of public utilities and increased emphasis on the market for the allocation of resources. Many of these ideas were applied in the media policy field, with the result that the status of broadcasting changed from that of a public to a private good. This was frequently accompanied by an economistic approach to policy-making in the audio-visual sector, replacing the previously dominant cultural paradigm.

In the UK, for example, the government-commissioned Peacock Committee published an influential report in 1986 which placed the concept of consumer sovereignty at the heart of its analysis as part of a radical libertarian reform of broadcasting (Peacock Committee, 1986). In Germany, CDU/CSU regional governments were primary actors in facilitating the entry into broadcasting of private-sector companies, initially through the new media of cable and satellite (Holtz-Bacha, 1991). In Portugal, the ruling centre-right Social Democratic Party abolished the state monopoly in broadcasting in 1990, introduced commercial competition and paved the way for what one commentator has described as a 'savage deregulation' of the television system (Traquina, 1995). The Greek broadcasting system was opened up to commercial broadcasters at the end of the 1980s, ushering in an era of competition between new private channels and the public sector (Tsaliki, 1995).

Even governments nominally of the left were affected by the ideological *zeitgeist* which championed liberalism and consumerism. In France, for example, the socialist government abolished the state monopoly in 1982 and introduced two commercial terrestrial channels in 1986. The privatisation of the main public sector channel, TF1

(Télévision Française 1), by the Jacques Chirac-led conservative government in 1987 was the culmination of a move away from public service and towards commercial values in broadcasting provision. In Spain too it was a socialist government that allowed the establishment of commercial television in the 1980s (López-Escobar, 1992).

In Italy the questioning of the public service ethos in broadcasting was accompanied by a full-scale deregulation of private-sector radio and television provision in contrast to the top-down, controlled liberalisation of most other systems. Radical change took place in Italy in the late 1970s (earlier than elsewhere in Western Europe) as a result of a decision by the Constitutional Court that the state monopoly entrusted to the public-service broadcaster, the RAI, was no longer enforceable at the subnational level. Hundreds of radio stations and television channels began to transmit programmes in conditions of uncontrolled anarchy. The political elites were divided as to how to respond, and a policy vacuum was created. As a result, Berlusconi was able to impose his economic dominance on the newly-created private sector by eliminating or taking over rival channels (Mazzoleni, 1991). By the time the Italian government passed legislation to re-regulate broadcasting in 1990, a new equilibrium had established itself between the RAI and the Berlusconi channels, in which the former had been driven down-market in the search for audiences.

The eventual emergence in Italy of a public sector in broadcasting more heavily regulated than the private competition was parallelled in the experience of other West European countries. The route taken may have been different, in that no other system went through the total deregulation of the private sector as Italy had done. In Britain and France the government retained a significant degree of control over the deregulation process which was marked by legislative initiatives such as the 1990 Broadcasting Act in the former and the 1982, 1986 and 1989 audio-visual statutes in the latter. In Germany, with its strong tradition of judicial interventionism in media policy, the Constitutional Court played an influential role in approving new forms of regulation while still striving to preserve the overall postwar emphasis on pluralism.

Within national broadcasting systems there is now generally at least a two-track system of content regulation, with tougher rules being applied to public-sector channels than to commercial ones. As a result, across Western Europe there is a greater shared sense of identity and mission among public-sector broadcasters on the one hand (for example, the BBC, France Télévision, ARD (Arbeitsgemeinschaft der Rundfunkanstalten Deutschlands), RAI) and commercial broadcasters on the other (for example, ITV, TF1, RTL plus (Radiodiffusion-

Télévision Luxembourg), Canale 5) than between the representatives of these two groups within any single national system.

The economic liberalisation of broadcasting has expanded consumer choice among different programme outlets. Specialist subscription channels (for example, in sport and film) have increased the range of output for devotees of these genres. But for defenders of public-service values, greater competition may also lead to lower programme standards, heavier reliance on American production, a reduction in diversity of opinions, a loss of cultural identity, the unacceptable commercialisation of programming aimed at children, and the possible loss of an educative and informative public sphere in mass communications (Blumler, 1992).

The 'Europeanisation' of Media Policy

The development of new media technologies, the emergence of transnational media companies and the drive towards closer European economic and political union have combined to bring about a limited 'Europeanisation' of media policy since the early 1980s. In the audiovisual field the EU has focused its attention on three distinct but interdependent sectors: hardware (notably the setting of common standards for satellite television transmission); software (the establishment of a programme of support for audio-visual production and distribution); and regulation (the harmonisation of certain provisions to establish a single broadcasting market) (Collins, 1994, p. 21). In the press sector it has examined the question of state aid to newspapers and recently it has investigated concentration of ownership across media sectors and national boundaries (Commission of the European Communities, 1992, 1994).

The single most notable achievement of the European Community in media policy was the 1989 Directive 'Television Without Frontiers'. The supporters of this initiative had two goals: 'to ensure that the circulation of broadcast signals and services emanating from member states was not impeded in other member states; and to harmonise Community broadcast regulation so that competition between signals and services took place on a fair and equal basis' (Collins, 1994, p. 58). The provisions of the Directive included the regulation of television advertising and programme sponsorship, a European content quota, steps to promote independent production and distribution companies, measures to defend the European cinema industry, and regulations to protect minors from violent or pornographic programmes. Most important, the Directive inhibited member states from restricting retransmission on their territory of television broadcasts from other member states (Collins, 1993, p. 13). Though the Directive contained some interventionist provisions (for example, on content quotas), its thrust was essentially liberal and anti-protectionist: the creation of a single market (Negrine and Papathanassopoulos, 1990). Moreover, its interventionist aspects (for example, the rules on European production quotas) were weakened by the injunction that they were to be met 'where practicable', and so were difficult to enforce.

The other two EU audio-visual initiatives have been essentially interventionist. The first had two aims: the establishment of common satellite transmission standards across the EU as a step towards the establishment of a satisfactory market for European consumer electronics industries; and the development of a European High Definition Television standard to protect Europe from Japanese and American competition. This initiative has failed in part because its scope did not include lower-powered telecommunications satellites which have, in fact, become major deliverers of television services: the Astra satellite which transmits the channels of BSkyB to British audiences is a notable example. More importantly, technological progress has outpaced the attempts of policy-makers to impose a unified, coherent and up-to-date technological standard across the EU.

The second initiative is the MEDIA programme to support the production, distribution and financing of film and television. It aims to support the audio-visual industries of small countries whose cultures are perceived to be threatened by the single market. But no matter how worthy its intentions, or whatever its specific successes, MEDIA is unlikely to counter the European dominance of Anglophone producers.

The ideological conflict between free market supporters and interventionists has assumed an institutional dimension within the EU, pitting Directorates General (DGs) of the Commission against each other. However, this conflict is only one of the impediments to a coherent EU audio-visual policy. Another is the continuing power of national actors. National governments, regulatory bodies and media organisations still dominate what is still largely a national policy-making process. Moreover, even when the policy forum is transferred to the supranational level, the policy debate often continues to reflect national concerns. Some governments have sought to use the EU as a larger playing field for promoting their own domestic policies (for example, France on programme quotas and hi-tech industries). As the General Agreement on Tariffs and Trade (GATT) talks in 1993 demonstrated, the French government has feared the consequences of an audio-visual free market for its own production industries and national culture, and has tried to promote a European audio-visual space protected from the perceived global threat of Anglo-American cultural imperialism. In contrast, other governments (for example, British and Danish) have sought to minimise the impact of European interventionism to protect their national sovereignty.

At the same time, linguistic and cultural differences across Western European audiences remain a crucial barrier to the creation of a fully-fledged single broadcasting market (Shelley and Winck, 1995). The strength of these differences has posed another problem for EU policy-makers as to whether the object of policy should be to promote cultural unity or reflect difference. There has been a move away from the 'melting-pot' approach, which promoted cultural homogenisation, towards an emphasis on Europe as a cultural 'mosaic', in which diversity and variety are prized (Robins and Cornford, 1994). This new discourse may be a recognition of the fact that as yet there is no single European audience. Attempts to create pan-European television channels, some of them backed by the EU, have largely failed, while pan-European advertising campaigns have not been successful. In contrast, in some countries such as Spain and Belgium, cultural, linguistic and political differences have given regional television channels an important role in serving the needs of subnational audiences (Garitaonandia, 1993).

More fundamentally still, apart from small countries whose audiences are accustomed to watching programmes from larger, linguistically consonant neighbouring systems (the Republic of Ireland is an obvious example – see Hussey, 1995, ch. 14), there is little audience demand for the television programmes of other EU member states. Paradoxically, products with cross-national appeal are likely to have been imported from outside the EU, usually from the USA. West European television audiences tend to prefer their own national products first, American second and those of other European broadcasters a distant third. They share the same programme tastes only as part of a much wider global audience, not as an integrated European one.

The 'Mediatisation' of West European Politics

The centrality of the media, especially television, in everyday life has had a notable impact on the political communications process. While the nature of that impact may vary from one system to another, aspects of the 'mediatisation' of politics are widespread. The influence of the media can be seen in party organisation, pressure group activity, policy presentation, leadership style, and the shaping of the political agenda. Government ministers, parties and pressure groups now pay at least as much attention to the packaging of their messages as to their content, in the belief that favourable media coverage is essential for policy and electoral success.

The following features of 'mediatised' politics are to be found to a significant extent in all West European states. First, the importance of the media as channels of communication between political elites and the public has increased. Acutely conscious of the media's role in shaping opinion, all political actors try to use the media to bolster electoral credibility, obtain support for policies and reinforce political legitimacy. The media also provide channels from the public to politicians, facilitating the expression of public opinion and acting as a watchdog on elite behaviour. Recently the media in various countries (including Britain, France, Italy and Spain) have helped to expose political sleaze and corruption (see Chapter 6).

The 'mediatisation' of politics has had an important impact on the status and behaviour of political parties. These have functioned traditionally as intermediaries in the political system, aggregating interests, recruiting to political elites, acting as channels of information between elites and public, and helping to mobilise the electorate (see Chapter 8). Some of these functions are in decline in the media age. For example, during election campaigns the media no longer just cover a campaign, but have become the campaign battleground, with contending political elites struggling to structure the media's election agenda. The media no longer simply report on politics; they have become political actors in their own right.

Second, political elites have had to make concessions to the media regarding the style and presentation of politics; consequently, the terms in which political messages are put across to voters have changed. All political actors have adapted their behaviour to ensure favourable television coverage, some more willingly than others. Many of the changes may appear trivial: from the correct modulation of voice tone to the acceptance of appropriate dress codes, from eye-catching party logos and symbols to the colour of the sets at party conferences – but all are designed to facilitate the viewer's reception of the political message (Scammell, 1995).

Third, this packaging of politics has given rise to a new set of political actors, vocabulary and practices. To help cope with the demands of the media age, political organisations employ a variety of people whose prime function is media promotion. Communications consultants, marketing advisers and opinion pollsters provide support and proffer advice to political parties and pressure groups on how best to present themselves. Novel expressions have entered into journalistic terminology and popular discourse to describe these new functions: 'spin doctors' put a gloss on the political message, which itself must contain 'sound bites' for easy media consumption (Jones, 1995). The 'walkabout' and 'photo opportunity' have been invented by election candidates purely for the benefit of the television cameras, while party conferences are stage-managed for the television viewers at home rather than the delegates in the hall.

Pressure groups have also adapted their techniques. The international environmentalist pressure group, Greenpeace, is a master of the constructed media event (Hansen 1993). In 1995, for example, it was involved in two high-profile protests (against the disposal of the Brent Spar oil rig, and the French nuclear tests in the South Pacific), during which it set up events for media consumption to influence public opinion and the environmental policy agenda. Greenpeace provides its own video footage for broadcasters to use – a practice which may lead sections of the media to abandon dispassionate reporting.

Fourth, the media age has influenced leadership styles. Television tends to personalise political debate and place greater emphasis on the public profile of political leaders. This is true whether the political system is presidential or parliamentary. Leaders now spend a considerable amount of time appearing on the media and communicating their policies to the electorate, which means they have to pay close attention to their public image. A weak or confused image is deemed to be an electoral liability. An image which combines strength of purpose and competence with caring qualities may be an asset (for example, Margaret Thatcher's 'Iron Lady' and François Mitterrand's 'Quiet Strength'). Image projection is seen as being increasingly important because traditional electoral cleavages such as class, religion or regional differences are being replaced by more volatile and consumerist voting behaviour (see Chapter 7).

The most stunning example of the impact of the media on political communications in Western Europe took place in Italy in 1994. In the particular circumstances of the implosion of the party system amid revelations of widespread political corruption, Silvio Berlusconi used his domination of private television to launch a new type of political party under his charismatic leadership. Many of Forza Italia's key personnel worked for Berlusconi's media holding company, Fininvest, and his television networks (Italia 1, Rete 4 and Canale 5) were ruthlessly exploited in the campaign to seduce voters (Mazzoleni, 1995).

The electoral success of Forza Italia led some media and academic commentators as well as the political opposition within Italy (notably the former Communist Party, the PDS) to criticise the partisan use that Berlusconi had made of his media interests. At the same time there was speculation that Forza Italia might be the forerunner of a new type of political party in Western Europe ('a media party') based on a subservient media supporting a telegenic leader – the ultimate in the 'mediatisation' of the political sphere. But while Forza Italia's success is part of an identifiable trend – the shift from catch-all parties to market 'niche' parties (see Chapter 8) – it is vital to retain a sense of perspective. One should not overestimate the media's impact on Berlusconi's election victory. Berlusconi won in part because he was able to exploit the political vacuum left behind after the collapse of the traditional parties. Moreover, it may well be that even within the particular conditions of Italy the Berlusconi phenomenon may prove to be a flash occurrence – a product of a transitional phase in Italian party politics. Nor should one extrapolate from the Italian experience. The Berlusconi phenomenon looks to be more of a one-off national event than the start of a dominant West European trend.

Conclusion

An overall evaluation of the relationship between the media and politics in Western Europe is not an easy task. In simple terms, there are two possible and contrasting assessments.

The first is essentially pessimistic. It argues that the commercialisation of the media has led to growing concentration of ownership and control in the hands of a few transnational, multimedia corporations. Commercial media outlets have turned politics into another branch of the entertainment industry by personalising and trivialising political debate, while in-depth investigative programming is being abandoned as public-service broadcasters adopt more commercial 'infotainment' strategies. Politicians have adapted to the demands of the media by emphasising image at the expense of substance, while still seeking to shape the media agenda and retain control of information for partisan ends. The media stand implicated in this critique because their power to shape opinion has been manipulated by elites to preserve vested interests and reinforce the existing distribution of power. In particular, the Berlusconi phenomenon reveals the potential for the personal manipulation of the media for economic and political ends.

The second assessment is essentially optimistic. The growth of the media has opened up new channels of communication between elites and the public. The media perform an important information function, raising issues of public concern and acting as a platform for competitive political elites to present their policies for scrutiny to the electorate. The media also fulfil a key watchdog function in West European polities, exposing corruption and malpractice. The result is that mass audiences are better-informed about politics than ever before, and can adapt their political and electoral behaviour accordingly. The media have helped to empower citizens and this is set to continue, as technological change increases the diversity of the media and makes it more difficult for politicians to control the supply of information. In short, the media are key agencies in the ongoing process of repairing the democratic deficit at both national and supranational levels.

Neither assessment is wholly convincing. Both contain elements of truth; but they also overstate their case. In general, the media are neither crude propaganda weapons controlling the masses nor are they enlightened agencies of information. This is not to deny the power of the media in shaping the political agenda and influencing the value systems and behaviour of audiences. The media may not tell us what to think: and their influence is filtered through a prism shaped by personal experience, socialisation by the family and education, and by sociological variables such as class, gender, ethnic status and age. But they do influence heavily what we think about. For this reason alone, issues such as the impact of technological change, concentration of ownership and regulation of content should continue to feature prominently on the policy agenda.

16

The Integration of Feminism into West European Politics*

JONI LOVENDUSKI

The contemporary status of women in West European politics varies considerably. Each country has its own mix of feminism, its distinctive patterns of women's political behaviour and its particular forms of gendered power structures. By the middle of the 1990s there had been at least two waves of feminism in most West European democracies. The women's liberation movement (WLM) of the 1970s and 1980s developed an agenda first established almost a century earlier when feminists first mobilised to achieve citizenship and, in some cases, legal personhood for women. New or second-wave feminism brought fundamental issues of rights and representation to the policy agenda. They also extended the ambit of women's demands as a women's studies movement emerged which questioned relations between the sexes, the accompanying division of labour, and the meaning of gender in social life.

First-wave feminists were divided about women's suffrage in most countries, but those who supported 'votes for women' believed that women had an interest to represent which their enfranchisement would secure. They believed that women's suffrage would bring more women into politics, would feminise political institutions, and change the nature of politics. By contrast, the WLM, where it appeared, had little faith in formal political institutions. Feminists in the 1970s commonly argued that the constitutional reforms won by earlier generations of the sisterhood had brought little tangible result for women. During the

---

* The data used in this article were prepared by Lucy Peake of Southampton University.

1980s those attitudes shifted as many feminists sought entry to political institutions and structures.

Meanwhile the ideas of feminism became more widely accepted, politicians were made aware that their futures depended upon changes in 'gender gaps' and portfolios of sex-equality policies. New institutions were established to implement sex-equality policy, which became part of the governing apparatus of most democracies.

As the dynamism of the 1970s WLM faded, the political integration of women advanced. The twenty-five years from 1970 to 1995 saw a steady increase in the presence of women in leading political institutions, a shift in policy agendas to include women's issues, and the development of state feminism in the new equality offices. These changes were the result of women's agency, of deliberate action by women to influence politics. Although ambiguities about working in the political mainstream (called 'malestream' in the UK and USA) persisted, feminists explicitly sought to change the formal politics of parties, governments, oppositions, interest organisations and other forms of public participation. Activity was directed at increasing the representation of women in the Nordic states from as early as the 1960s, and by the 1980s was apparent throughout Western Europe. International organisations such as the European Community and the Council of Europe were also sites of activity to improve women's representation.

These excursions into formal politics were campaigns in their own right and were also linked to core feminist interests in such issues as reproductive rights, sexual violence, child care and equal opportunities. The widespread mobilisations of women that ensued rarely took the form of a unitary national women's movement sharing a common politics. Feminists and other women disagreed about the issues, the priorities and the appropriate political behaviour of women. Women's political participation varied across and within the countries of Western Europe. A full consideration of the patterns of women's politics, or of feminist politics in Western Europe would take many books. Therefore this chapter will introduce some of the most striking components of women's politics in Western Europe. It falls naturally into three parts – behaviour, policy and institutions. After a discussion of patterns of political participation and representation I will consider the impact of feminism on public policy. This will be followed by a discussion of the evidence that a form of 'state feminism' has emerged in Western European political systems. In the concluding section I will consider whether increased women's representation has made a difference to West European politics.

Women, Feminism and Gender

As feminists and their critics frequently point out, we should not elide feminism and women's politics. However broadly feminism is defined, it is possible to find women who do not subscribe to it. Definitions of feminism vary according to the circumstances and outlook of those who make the definition. This is complicated by the fact that many who support equality for women and belong to women's organisations are reluctant to be called feminists because there is a social stigma and political disadvantage attached to such labelling. Inevitably, this complicates definition-making. Core terms and concepts such as feminism and gender must be defined, however. A useful, if somewhat arbitrary, definition of feminism is Drude Dahlerup's statement that it is those ideologies, activities and policies whose goal it is to remove discrimination against women and to break down male domination of society (Dahlerup, 1986, p. 6). Clive Wilcox has attempted to produce 'objective' estimates of support for feminism in Europe using results of Eurobarometer surveys. His analyses of support for sex equality and women's rights indicate that there are quite high degrees of feminist consciousness in Western Europe. He classifies more than a third of West European women as feminists, but there are extensive variations between countries: about half of the women in France and Italy but only a quarter of the women in Britain could be classified as feminists (Wilcox, 1991).

The terms 'sex' (and therefore woman) and 'gender' also present difficulties. There is no single agreed definition of 'gender', or of 'sex', which may be offered here. Political scientists often use 'gender' interchangeably with 'sex', but in feminist scholarship the terms are more loaded and complex. For the purposes of this chapter, the term 'sex' is used to refer to biological sex, and men and women are therefore biological males and females. 'Gender' will be used to denote the way relations between the sexes are produced and institutionalised. To put it another way, 'gender' is used to refer to the social consequences of biological differences between women and men.

Behaviour: Political Representation and Participation

Gender relations affect politics in different ways. First, gender relations traditionally have enabled men to dwell in the public sphere as a result of the work undertaken by women in the private sphere – a separation that has also tended to prevent important domestic issues from receiving public attention. Second, women have mobilised within political institutions to alter gender relations in both the private and public spheres; hence gender has been brought directly on to the political agenda by feminists. Third, feminist ideas about sex, gender and equality have found their way into fundamental debates about democracy and political representation, and into discussions of social policy. Patterns of political participation and representation were developed over generations in political institutions designed to institutionalise the dominance of the groups who founded and influenced them. Legislatures, governments, political parties, electoral systems and interest organisations were all designed to reflect the interests of men, and to institutionalise and regulate the patterns of competition between different groups of men. These organisations were not devised to exclude women because, with a few exceptions, none of their founders considered it to be an issue. But they *were* organised to exclude or to empower some men at the expense of others and to reflect some interests at the expense of others – factors which have led to organisational and cultural arrangements and values that have an impact on women. Different patterns of national development affected women's share of political power. Different organisations and institutional structures offered different opportunities to feminists seeking political influence for women.

Table 16.1 shows large differences in the presence of women in contemporary West European legislatures. A good part of the explanation for those variations is to be found in particular organisational and institutional arrangements, political cultures and patterns of women's mobilisation. Those countries with the highest representations of women (Sweden, Norway, Denmark and the Netherlands) have three prerequisites of political equality: (i) electoral systems based on proportional representation in which elections may be won and lost at the margins, thus forcing political parties to attend to new political groups; (ii) political cultures which place a high value on social equality; and (iii) significant sections of their women's movements mobilised to increase women's representation and have consistently worked within political institutions to promote women.

Those with the lowest representations (France, Greece, Portugal, the UK) are missing one or more of the three prerequisites. These patterns and explanations are well known and well documented, but other important patterns deserve more of our attention. Rapid changes in the representation of women in Germany and Italy indicate the importance of party competition, changes in the opportunity structure, and the

TABLE 16.1 *Women in selected European legislatures and governments at the beginning of the 1990s (percentages)*

Country	Date	Lower Chamber	Upper Chamber	Date	Government
Belgium	1991	9.4	10.9	1992	18.7
Denmark	1990	33.0	*	1993	29.2
France	1993–2	6.0	4.9	1993	10.0
Germany	1990	20.5	25.0	1992	17.0
Greece	1993	5.6	*	1993	8.7
Republic of Ireland	1992	12.0	13.3	1989	10.0
Italy	1992	8.1	9.6	1993	12.1
Luxembourg	1992	8.1	9.6	1992	8.3
The Netherlands	1989–91	22.7	28.0	1989	24.0
Portugal	1991	8.7	*	1991	9.9
Spain	1993	16.0	12.6	1991	11.1
UK	1992	9.2	6.5	1992	7.0

Note: * No upper chamber.
Source: European Commission (1993), *Network of Experts on Women in Decision Making*, DG-V.

significance of specific policies to enhance the representation of women. Many European political parties have introduced quotas to increase the proportion of women candidates. Complacent West German political parties were forced by the success of the Green Party in the 1980s into a competitive bidding for women's votes, and offered quotas of women candidates, special addresses to women's issues, and pledges to feminise party leaderships and parliamentary wings. Although the initial impetus slowed in the 1990s, the promises remained and, in a system in which electoral victories are won at the margins, it will be difficult for parties to abandon their pledges to women. In Italy, quotas of women became a constitutional as well as a party matter in 1994. At the insistence of the *Commissione Nazionale per la Parità e le Pari Opportunità* (National Commission for Equal Status and Equal Opportunity) – the equality agency attached to the prime minister's office – a rule was introduced into the electoral law requiring 'zip lists' to be prepared. Parties were required to list candidates in alternate order by sex on the proportional representation fixed lists (which may not be altered by a preference vote) (Guadagnini, 1995).

Such constitutional strategies are rare. More common is the mobilisation by women within political parties in strategies which combine attention to the norms of party membership with the goals of empowering women. To do this, women must first become members of parties, and the majority of members of most political parties are men. Party membership statistics are famously unreliable. Table 16.2 shows that between the 1970s and the 1980s, women were an increasing proportion of the members of political parties in France, Germany and Sweden, but their membership was static or falling in the UK. Political parties offer very different institutional settings to their members. Most West European parties have developed their structures and procedures over generations. Such variations condition women's access to the parties. Carol Christy has explained how party membership recruitment practices may be more or less favourable to women (Christy, 1994). Parties which recruit a high proportion of their members through unions tend particularly to over-represent men. Changes in the method of recruitment should therefore lead to changes in the proportion of women. Christy's arguments suggest that the modernisation of the British Labour Party will attract a greater proportion of women members. The massive drive to recruit individual members under the leadership of Tony Blair bears this out. Women represented 45 per cent of the individual members who joined the Labour Party in the first six months of 1995.

The methods of selecting party leaders and candidates also vary in their woman-friendliness. There appear to be three kinds of strategy

TABLE 16.2 *Changes in women's membership of selected West European political parties (percentages)*

Country	Party	c. 1970 % women	c.1990 % women		
France	PS	22	28		
	RPR	41	43		
Germany	SPD	19	27	20 ⎫	New
	CDU	15	23	39 ⎬	länder
	CSU	10	17	0 ⎭	only
	FDP	14	30	n/a	
	Green		33		
Sweden	Left	25	41		
	Social Democrat	27	33		
	Centre	29	54		
	Liberals	40	47		
	Conservatives	44	29		
UK	Conservatives	51	48		
	Labour	40	40		

Note: n/a = not available.
Source: J. Lovenduski and Pippa Norris (eds) (1993) *Gender and Party Politics* (London: Sage).

adopted by parties to bring more women into their leadership. These are rhetorical strategies whereby women's claims are accepted on campaign platforms, and party spokespersons make frequent reference to the importance of getting more women into influential positions; strategies of positive or affirmative action in which special training is offered to women, targets are set, and sometimes financial assistance given, to enable women to come forward for consideration; and finally, strategies of positive discrimination which make the representation of women compulsory, with reserved places for women on decision-making bodies. With few exceptions, West European parties have adopted rhetorical strategies, and many have taken up positive action. Positive discrimination is much less common and tends to be restricted to internal party offices.

In general, party ideology determines which of the three strategies a party employs. Social Democratic and Green parties are far more likely to intervene in the process of selection and recruitment for office than are other parties. The French Socialists, the British Labour Party, the Dutch Labour Party, and the German Social Democrats have all adopted quotas of women for various offices. Generally, once one party has initiated positive discrimination or positive action, other parties will either follow suit or pursue their existing strategies more vigorously. In Sweden, the Social Democrats were the first to set guidelines, setting 40 per cent as the minimum acceptable presence of both sexes in the 1960s. Other parties soon followed suit, leading to a convergence of trends across Swedish parties (Sainsbury, 1993).

Differences in women's and men's political behaviour (often called gender gaps) are complex and may require many levels of explanation. Institutional factors interact with attitudes about politics and gender, and attitudinal differences between women and men. Much of the behaviour that is associated with political leadership (ambition, dema-goguery, ruthlessness, competitiveness) is culturally accepted for men but not women. Women's child rearing and other family responsibilities leave them poorly placed to travel the long distances often required to participate in legislatures and to work the long hours that are associated with political careers. This would lead us to expect women to be represented more at local and regional levels of politics than men, but that is not always the case (see Table 16.3).

A further complication is that gender gaps in attitudes do not always follow established political faultlines. The main social determinants of political activism were derived by political scientists from observations of male behaviour and then applied to both sexes. But the political consequences of social status are different for women and men, for two

TABLE 16.3 *Women as a proportion of local and regional councillors/deputies*

Country	Date	Regional Council	Government	Date	Local
Belgium	1991	10.5	10.0	1988	14.3
Denmark	n/a	n/a	n/a	1989	28.1
Greece	n/a	n/a	n/a	1990	9.0
France	1992	12.1	n/a	1989	17.1
Germany	1990–1–2	23.5	24.9		No data
Republic of Ireland	n/a	n/a	n/a	1992	11.6
Italy	1990	6.7	3.5	1990	9.2
Luxembourg	n/a	n/a	n/a	1987	7.0
The Netherlands	n/a	n/a	n/a	1990	22.0
Portugal	1992–88	9.2	0	1989	9.9
Spain	1989–90–91	14.2	8.9	1991	No data
UK	n/a	n/a	n/a	1993	25.0

Note: n/a = not available.
Source: European Commission (1993), *Network of Experts on Women in Decision Making*, DG-V.

reasons. First, women and men have different places in important stratification systems, and second, the significance of the various social divisions are different for women, who do not translate their class or religious and other affiliations into politics in the way that men do. To make this point another way, women and men are not similarly distributed across classes. They have different patterns of religious allegiance. Women generally live longer than men, hence the distribution of women and men across generations is different. Although women's and men's life cycles seem to proceed along parallel lines, the different stages have traditionally had very different meanings for the two sexes.

Policy: Women's Issues

The notion of 'women's' issues has been criticised by feminists, who argue that there is no single universal female identity; that women differ by age, race, class, nation, sexuality, physical ability and preference. However, there are many issues that affect women and men differentially, a reflection largely, but not exclusively, of social rather than biological differences. For example, in Britain, women are more frequent users of public transportation than are men, hence decisions about bus routes, station lighting and so on have more impact on women's lives than men's. Some of these issues are especially acute and have been politicised by feminists, who brought policy on sexual violence, equal opportunities, reproductive rights, equal rights and representation into West European political agendas. One important feminist angle on policy derives from a central understanding that the good society will give reasonable priority to both mind and body. It follows that social life is a function of issues of the private and public spheres which are by their nature difficult to separate. Public life depends on private arrangements, which are present but largely unacknowledged by policy-makers. Here I will consider two examples – equal opportunities, and male violence towards women.

Equal Opportunities

Second-wave feminism is ambivalent about the state, a product of both divisions among women about engaging in formal politics and the very mixed attitudes of those feminists who engaged with the state in their work on behalf of women. There were women's movements in each West European country active in support of sex equality strategies and equal pay campaigns. These movements had origins in previous waves of feminism, received support from international organisations such as the United Nations (UN), the International Labour Organisation (ILO) and the Council of Europe. Prior to the WLM, they tended to use insider strategies such as working inside political parties and trade unions), lobbying and traditional pressure group politics to bring about legislative reform. During the 1970s and 1980s most West European states established what Dorothy Stetson and Amy Mazur (1995) refer to as 'women's policy machinery'; that is, formally con-stituted government structures charged with advancing the status of women. The European Union had women's policy machinery in the form of the Equal Opportunities Bureau in DG V of the Commission and the women's and equality committees of successive European Parliaments. Many of these lasted for only the duration of the establishing government and were replaced, reformed or otherwise altered when new governments took office (see Table 16.4).

The responsibilities of the agencies has changed over time and continues to vary between states. However, there is in each state an agency with responsibility for sex equality in employment. The pro-blem these agencies were devised to remedy is unequal pay between women and men. Unequal pay is seen as being a symptom of other

TABLE 16.4 *Women's policy machinery in Western Europe*

Established pre-1970

Austria	Department of Basic Questions Concerning Women, 1966 (1981)
Austria	Committee of Women's Employment, 1969
UK	Women's National Commission, 1969 (1992)

Established 1970–80

Austria	Equal Treatment Commission, 1979 (1991)
Austria	Equality Liaison Officers, 1978 (1980)
Belgium	Commission on Women's Employment, 1974 (1993)
Denmark	Emancipation Council, 1975 (1978) (1988)
Finland	Equality Council, 1972
France	State Secretariat for Women's Rights and Consumer Affairs, 1974 (1981) (1985) (1986) (1988) (1990) (1991) (1992) (1993)
Iceland	Equal Status Board, 1976 (1985) (1991)
Republic of Ireland	Employment Equality Agency, 1977
The Netherlands	Secretariat of State for Equal Rights, 1977 (1981)
The Netherlands	Inter-Ministerial Co-ordinating Committee for Equal Rights Policy, 1977
The Netherlands	Equal Rights Policy Co-ordinating Department, 1978 (1982)
The Netherlands	Inter-Ministerial Co-ordinating Committees, 1980
Norway	Equal Status Council, 1972 (1979)
Norway	Ombudsman for Equal Status between Women and Men, 1979
Norway	Equal Status Board, 1979
Norway	Local Equal Status Committees, 1975 (1977)
Portugal	Committee for Equality and Women's Rights, 1973 (1975) (1977) (1991)
Portugal	Committee for Equality at Work and in Employment, 1970
Sweden	Minister for Matters Concerning Equality between Women and Men, 1976 (1991)
Sweden	Inter-Ministerial Unit, 1980
Sweden	Equal Opportunities Commission, 1980
Switzerland	Federal Commission for Matters relating to Women, 1976
UK	Equal Opportunities Commission, 1975 (1992)
UK	Equal Opportunities Commission for Northern Ireland, 1976
UK	Advisory Committee on Women's Employment, 1973

Established 1981–90

Austria	Subdivision of the central division of the Ministry of Social Affairs for Basic Questions Relating to the Employment of Women, 1983
Austria	Office for Women's Affairs (Frauenreferat), 1982
Belgium	Emancipation Council, 1986 (dissolved in 1993)
Belgium	Advisory Committee on Disputes Relating to Equal Treatment for Men and Women in the Public Services, 1984
Belgium	Department responsible for the Cultural and Occupational Promotion of Women (French-speaking community), 1985
Belgium	Flemish Women's Consultative Committee (Flemish Community), 1990
Cyprus	Permanent Central Agency for Women's Rights, 1988
Finland	Ombudsman for Equality, 1987
Greece	General Secretariat for Equality between Women and Men, 1985
Greece	Council for Equality, 1989

inequalities, a diagnosis that has enabled women's policy networks to press for wide-ranging legislation.

There is general agreement that the most immediate cause of unequal pay is the vertical and horizontal segregation of the labour market by sex. Horizontal segregation refers to the separation of women and men into different industries, firms and sectors of the economy. Vertical segregation refers to the higher occupational status of women and men in the same areas of employment.

Analysis of European employment data indicates that women fare best relative to men in Sweden and Norway, that pay differences between women and men persist, and that rates of improvement over time vary but are generally disappointing. Equality of employment opportunity for women and men is a continuing feature of West European public policy. In the EU the policies are subject to minimum standards set by five Equality Directives enacted during the 1970s and 1980s.

Policies do vary, however, and are set in very different welfare state contexts. This is important, because sex equality employment legislation provides for formal equality but often ignores substantive inequalities between the sexes in the division of unpaid work. Such policy gender-blindness ignores the impossibility for the majority of women of entering the labour market on the same terms as men. Crucial here is the issue of policy on care, the main form of women's unpaid work. Variations in welfare state provision mean that European women are incorporated into their labour markets on varying terms, hence the sex equality strategies of different countries treat different problems. Widely cited is the example of Sweden which had no formal equal pay legislation before 1980. There sex equality strategies were part of broadly-conceived aims to achieve adult worker citizenship (Lewis, 1993).

Jane Lewis makes a useful distinction between countries which do and do not intervene in arrangements about unpaid work, offering a presumption that women do less well in states in which governments do not intervene. The Scandinavian countries have gone furthest with such interventions, with, for example, their generous parental leave systems, and it is there that women fare best materially over their life course (Lewis, 1993, p. 21). The relative lack of enthusiasm shown by Swedish and Norwegian women towards the European Union has been explained by reference to their fears that entry would mean equalising downwards, to the lower material standards of women in the EU countries.

TABLE 16.5 *The distribution of women's employment by status and sector in selected European countries (percentages)*

	1	2	3	4	5	6	7/8/9
Greece (1992)							
Primary	41	10	42	–	26	42	2
Secondary	25	8	54	50	66	36	22
Tertiary	46	17	53	38	44	6	6
The Netherlands (1993)							
Primary							
Secondary							
Tertiary	47	15	59	42	66	–	9
Norway (1993)							
Primary	33	50	60	67	33	26	–
Secondary	27	19	74	40	56	–	19
Tertiary	62	35	80	53	74	33	19
Portugal (1993)							
Primary	38	–	30	47	32	50	37
Secondary	19	23	36	55	44	42	33
Tertiary	36	53	55	60	69	19	37
Spain (1993)							
Primary	32	17	27	60	25	28	6
Secondary	20	7	52	23	45	15	14
Tertiary	53	17	54	49	60	5	12
Sweden (1993)							
Primary	17	–	57	31	74	25	22
Secondary	6	–	57	25	67	–	1
Tertiary	72	–	63	51	62	29	21

Notes:
Primary
Agriculture, hunting, forestry, fishing.
Mining, quarrying.
Electricity, gas, water.
Secondary
Manufacturing.
Construction.
Tertiary
Trade, restaurants and hotels.
Transport, storage and communication.
Financing, insurance, real estate, business.
Community, social and personal services.
Occupational status
1 Professional, technical and related workers.
2 Administrative and managerial workers.
3 Clerical and related workers.
4 Sales workers.
5 Service workers.
6 Agriculture, animal husbandry and forestry workers, fishermen and hunters.
7/8/9 Production and related workers, transport equipment operators and labourers.

Male Violence – I: Sexual Assault

The second feminist issue explored here is male violence towards women. The issue was also raised by first-wave feminists who, particularly in Britain and the USA, tended to regard alcohol as the cause and teetotalism as the solution, hence the exhortation to marry only men who had taken the pledge. Second-wave feminists developed more complex analyses, tending to see male violence to women as part of strategies of control and a reflection of women's relative lack of power. Their accounts acknowledge poverty and alcoholism as contributing factors, but underline the widespread incidence of such violence which is to be found in all social classes and ethnic groups. There are several issues in this category that have been brought to the political agenda by feminists, including rape and other forms of sexual assault, child sexual abuse and sexual harassment.

Although men are most often violent toward other men, and women sometimes assault men, sexual violence is defined by feminists as violence against women generated by the mere fact that they are female. Sexual violence issues have been raised throughout Western Europe, have been discussed in the European Parliament and have been the subject of Council of Europe conferences and reports. Control of definition is an important part of getting attention for a public issue. Feminists in some West European countries have succeeded in gaining acceptance for the view that such violence is, *inter alia*, a form of sex discrimination.

Feminist activity has had three main dimensions: information, campaigning and remedy. First, knowledge about sexual violence has been accumulated through research and publicised through women's movement networks. Second, widespread campaigns have sought to reform legal structures and implementation procedures dealing with sexual violence. Third, organisations have been developed to aid survivors of sexual violence, including refuges, rape crisis lines and survivors' groups. All the male violence issues are linked, hence all deserve attention. However, the outlines of their politics may be drawn from a discussion of sexual assault and sexual harassment.

Prior to feminist mobilisations about sexual violence, public knowledge of the issue was limited, often obscured by myths and social conventions restricting its discussion. Information, when it came, was shocking, because such violence was much more widespread than previously had been believed and because it was performed overwhelmingly by known men. Although many campaigns were sparked by high-profile rape trials which roused public anger, sustained feminist activity centred on gathering and publicising information, pressing for detailed legislative and procedural changes, and developing and offering services to survivors. Stranger rape, although horrific, is much less common than rape by known men – former or current partners, colleagues or 'friends'. Spouse abuse and rape have received close attention from European feminists. Refuge movements to provide shelter and assist with the remaking of lives of survivors are an established feature of all West European societies (Lovenduski, 1986; Kaplan, 1992).

In each case, an important part of raising the issue was to convince public opinion that such abuse was widespread, and that remedying this was necessary and urgent. The focus of legal reform strategies has been about changing definitions, criminalisation where the behaviour is not already criminalised, and implementation of policies by the police and courts. Legal and procedural reforms drew support from women and men across the political spectrum. In Britain, the campaign to criminalise rape in marriage began in the 1980s and culminated in a Law Commission recommendation in 1991. In Italy, where rape laws were defined in 1936 as an offence against public morality rather than an act of violence against individuals, reform attempts continue. In 1995, 200 000 women signed a referendum petition to secure consideration of a new law. In the UK, Belgium and Sweden, measures were taken during the 1980s to ensure the protection of rape survivors during the course of proceedings. In France, Belgium, Britain, Greece, Ireland, Italy and the Netherlands, procedures were revised to remove information about survivors' sexual pasts from admissible evidence, a measure that has not been followed uniformly by conservative judiciaries. Most new legislation of the 1970s and 1980s reflected feminist preoccupations to the extent that they redefined rape as criminal assault on individual dignity and a breach of the right to control a person's own body and sexuality. Some countries (Denmark, Spain, Germany, Greece and the Netherlands) introduced a new value to be safeguarded by law – that of sexual self-determination (Garcia, 1991).

Male Violence – 2: Sexual Harassment

Sexual harassment is a particularly interesting issue for analysts of feminist impact on policy. It combines equal opportunities and sexual violence concerns and is set in the workplace. The issue therefore highlights confusions about public and private issues. It is a relatively new issue which first began to get attention in the 1980s. Feminist activity around sexual harassment followed a similar course to that on sexual assault. Research was commissioned and its results publicised, campaigns were organised to alter laws, and help was provided for survivors. The campaigns were both lower-key and differently networked than the sexual assault campaigns. In many countries women worked through their trade unions, and equality agencies took up the issue. During the 1980s, research commissioned by governments or universities across Western Europe revealed very high incidences of sexual harassment (estimates varied between 30 per cent and 84 per cent of working women) and strong support from women for reform. Trade unions were often reluctant to take up the issue. Both perpetrator and victim were likely to be union members causing problems that officials were reluctant to address. However, unions did not want to share their workplace bargaining prerogatives, hence they gradually began to take up sexual harassment complaints (Garcia, 1991). Predictably, it is the unions with the largest and most active women's memberships that have given most attention to sexual harassment at work. The main response of officials has been awareness and information campaigns. In Britain, where the Equal Opportunities Commission had become very skilful at establishing case law on equality issues, the courts were closely involved. There was also pressure on the EC (now EU), but the results were disappointing for feminists. In 1991 the European Commission issued a recommendation on the protection of the 'dignity of women and men at work', rather than the directive for which feminists had lobbied.

There was considerable feminist grass-roots activity around antisexual harassment campaigns during the 1980s in the UK, France, the Netherlands, Portugal, Spain and Switzerland. But the law was often silent or, where it existed, was case law. Generally, sexual harassment is treated via criminal law and sometimes constitutional law. Only in Denmark, the Republic of Ireland and the UK has it been considered in terms of the anti-discrimination legislation. The question of how sexual harassment is dealt with in law has caused disagreements among feminists. Some argue that sexual harassment constitutes discrimination, is part of male strategies to control women, and should therefore be referred to explicitly in equal treatment legislation. The counterargument is that sexual harassment is a matter not of inequality, but of violence, and should be treated by laws prohibiting violence. Davernhas (1986) has pointed out that if a bi-sexual employer harassed women and men equally, s/he could not be prosecuted under equal treatment law because the activity would not be discriminating against women. This argument is difficult to dispute, but it should not obscure the fact that most sexual harassment at work is experienced by women and performed by men, and thus is a barrier to women's equality. The best legal remedy would treat it as both a matter of violence and of unfair sex discrimination. The problem with the law on violence is that it makes the individual responsible and ignores both the gendered nature of the crime and the isolation women experience in such circumstances. British case law has made employers responsible for sexual harassment in the workplace, leading to local agreements about good practice that appear to be quite workable, but are frequently ridiculed in the press as an unacceptable form of 'political correctness'.

Throughout Western Europe, policy on equal opportunities and violence to women was influenced by feminists during the 1980s. The influence was channelled through traditional political institutions which were utilised to carry feminist ideas onto the political agenda. The examples illustrate patterns of politics in which women mobilised politically over issues of special importance to women. Feminist activists linked with women organised in the mainstream political institutions such as political parties and trade unions which, mindful of the need for women's support, gradually took up the issues. These are not the only instances of feminist and women's politics, but they are particularly good examples of the influence of feminist ideas on public policy.

Institutions: State Feminism

A characteristic feature of feminism in contemporary democracies has been the establishment of new institutions charged with responsibility for women's concerns and the revitalisation of older structures, such as women's party organisations. Such change is apparent in many areas of feminist interest and has affected a considerable range of organisations. For example, police forces in Britain, Denmark and the Netherlands have instituted domestic violence units. Rape suites and clinics are now to be found in police stations and in some urban hospital systems. Women's refuges are important parts of local services. Women's committees and units operate at local or regional level in Germany, France, Italy, Spain, Norway and Britain. Often accused of marginalising the problems they seek to remedy, these institutions and facilities are important accomplishments of feminist politics, and they give institutional expression to areas of policy that previously went unaddressed by authorities. A variety of such agencies operate at national government level, the best established of which are those which implement or oversee policies on sex equality in employment.

The spread of European equality ministries and agencies is detailed in Table 16.4. These institutions indicate a presence of officials acting on behalf of officially-defined women's interests. They raise the question of whether their officials may be thought of as feminist political actors, of whether the agencies and staff may be thought of as 'state-feminist'. This question is important, because it allows us to hypothesise an institutionalisation of feminist concerns and to consider the possibility that networks of feminists have become established in state apparatuses. New research directed by Stetson and Mazur (1995) considers these questions in fourteen countries including Britain, Denmark, France, Germany, Ireland, Italy, the Netherlands, Norway, Spain and Sweden. They define state feminism as the institutionalisation of feminism in public agencies or women's policy machinery (Stetson and Mazur, 1995, p. 10). To determine whether women's policy machinery is feminist, they explore two of its aspects systematically. First, they examine the extent to which an agency influences the development of feminist policy, and second, the extent to which the agency enables feminists and women's advocacy organisations access to the policy process. Their approach has the advantage that feminism may be defined flexibly, in terms set by the culture in which it is located.

Thus feminist issues become the issues feminists have raised. Their classification of women's policy machinery labels Denmark, the Netherlands and Norway as strongly state feminist. These systems have agencies which have high levels of influence on feminist policy and facilitate high levels of feminist access to the policy process. The Republic of Ireland and Italy score low on both access and influence, hence are only minimally state-feminist. The remaining countries fall into intermediate categories. In countries where state feminism is well established, social democratic governments under strong pressure from moderate feminist groups created powerful offices with the authority to incorporate women's interests into central policy-making. These are countries which place high values on social equality, and operate within a broad consensus that the state is an appropriate overseer of equality strategies. Their women's movements included both the autonomous feminists of the women's liberation movement and the 'moderate' feminist caucuses typically found in political parties, unions and national women's organisations. Strong state feminism therefore appears to be associated with the constellation of factors that are associated with relatively high levels of women's representation.

Conclusions

The impact of feminism on West European politics has at least five manifestations. Since the end of the 1960s, the activities of feminist-inspired women's movements have increased the political visibility of women and women's issues. In most countries (i) the presence of women in governments and legislatures has increased; (ii) new policies have been developed in response to demands for attention to feminist-defined 'women's issues'; (iii) new institutional machinery has been established to implement the policies; (iv) that machinery has become a base for 'femocrats' who are at the centre of (v) emerging feminist policy networks. Thus in one sense the answer to the question about whether feminism makes a difference is simple and positive. Since the 1960s the social composition of arenas of political decision-making has become more female, the policy agenda explicitly addresses issues politicised by feminist ideas and activities, and institutional machinery has appeared to implement policy in areas on which many states have previously been silent. However, when we consider whether feminism has altered the architecture of West European politics, the answer is more difficult. The negative arguments seem strong and may be reduced to the contention that once in established political arenas, women, including feminists, soon begin to behave like the men they replace.

According to such arguments, party politics rather than feminist concern or gender difference explains much of the behaviour of women legislators. New political agendas are logical developments of social policy in welfare states, indeed they apparently vary more according to the type of welfare state than to the nature of feminist movement. New institutions are situated in and often reflect bureaucratic cultures which have been developed over generations – and they operate according to principles established to promote the interests of rising male groups. While they have been adapted by women's issues advocates it is difficult to pinpoint any special feminist characteristics in this adaptation. In addition, successful advocacy of feminist policies takes place according to well-established rules of the game. The main resource of feminism is information – a traditional resource of pressure groups – which is used to challenge and confront public opinion but also to persuade public officials. When the policy has been made, feminist expertise is incorporated as feminists themselves are co-opted into responsible agencies and organisations. Previously radical feminist ideas are sanitised as they become recycled for general use by the state. When they are established, feminist co-optees draw on movement resources to develop networks of influence which, *inter alia*, enable them to maintain and often to enhance their power. Even where feminists have made considerable inroads, it is difficult to argue that the rules of the game have changed.

Yet, even if all these points are conceded, it is possible to argue that feminism has made a difference. Ultimately the case turns on the achievements of its politics. True, these have been disappointing. Outcomes have rarely met expectations. Throughout Western Europe men, often after more than thirty years of sex equality policy, are better paid, better placed on occupational hierarchies, and more powerful than women. Nevertheless, gender gaps in employment are smaller than they used to be and this should be counted as a result. Sanitised feminist ideas are better than patriarchal ideas. Moreover, evidence of long-term change is to be found in Northern Europe. Dahlerup's accounts of women in Scandinavian politics indicate that increased membership of women in legislatures leads to more permanent changes in structures that make it easier for succeeding generations of women. Such 'critical acts', as she terms them, are the tangible results of increasing the presence of women in legislatures and cannot be explained in any other way (Dahlerup, 1988). The Nordic states have consistently run ahead of other European countries on matters of sex equality. They demonstrate that improvement is possible. Elements of their strategies are now to be found in other countries indicating that, in time, feminism may bring about the political integration of European women with beneficial consequences for gender relations.

17

New Challenges: Postmaterialism and the Extreme Right

PIERO IGNAZI

Since the early to mid-1980s, West European party systems have broadened their spectra to include 'new parties'. These newcomers are new in two different respects. First they are new because they have been founded (or have emerged from absolute irrelevance) in recent years; second because they do not belong to the traditional political families and pose an important challenge to them. The following analysis seeks to understand the origins of these new party families and to consider their significance. After an initial discussion of family membership, we proceed to consider their electoral performance and development, and several explanations for their initial appearance and subsequent growth: socioeconomic transformation and new social alignments; a crisis of democratic legitimacy; value change in society; and the failure of traditional political parties to respond to new demands and issues.

Defining the New Party Families

The new parties we are referring to in this analysis comprise basically the Green parties on the political left and the parties of the extreme right. Other 'new' parties also appeared in this period, including the Irish Progressive Democrats, the Italian Northern League, the Belgian Roussem and, very recently, the Italian Forza Italia, the French 'de Villiers list', and the Dutch 'pensioners' lists'. Most of these could be considered to be anti-establishment (Schedler, 1996) or anti-party parties, and they share some traits with the parties of the extreme right. But they do not fit the criteria for inclusion in this party family, and for this reason they will be disregarded.

In order to be a member of the extreme right family a party should fulfil three conditions: (i) it should be located at the right-wing pole of the political spectrum such that no other party is further to the right; (ii) it should express an ideal-ideological linkage with fascist mythology and principles; and (iii) it should express a set of beliefs that undermines the fundamentals of a polity. While the neo-fascist parties do not raise any problems of classification, the new right-wing parties of the 1970s and 1980s need a careful evaluation of their programmes, attitudes, beliefs and behaviour. Even if such parties do not openly advocate a non-democratic institutional setting, they nevertheless undermine system legitimacy by expressing distrust for the parliamentary system, the weakness of the state, the disruption of the traditional natural communities, 'unnatural' egalitarianism, and 'excessive' freedom. Their anti-system character is thus assessed on the basis of whether they display 'a belief system that does not share the values of the political order within which it operates' (Sartori, 1976, p. 133). Many new extreme-right parties do not share any nostalgia for the interwar fascist experience, and they even refuse any reference to fascism; but nevertheless they do express anti-democratic values in their political discourse.

As argued elsewhere (Ignazi, 1992, 1994) there is a gap between these *new* extreme-right parties – listed under the label of postindustrial extreme right parties in Table 17.1 – and conservative or bourgeois parties. This gap is expressed in their attitudes towards the representation mechanisms and the pluralist conception of the political system: while the conservatives are supportive of the system and never delegitimise these fundamentals, the extreme right expresses hostility and even rejection. The overlap on certain issues between the two families is more apparent than real: even where they share a common concern on themes such as law and order, moral traditionalism and immigration, these issues are dealt with in a completely different way. Not only do the extreme right parties invoke far more radical policies than their bourgeois counterparts, such policies are also qualitatively different as they spill over into questions of rights and entitlements. On a very salient issue such as immigration, for example, most of the *new* extreme-right parties demonstrate xenophobic and racist stances that are different 'in quality' from the conservatives' 'tough' positions because no extreme-right party has the principle of individual rights enshrined in its ideological genetic code. For them, the community (and the ethnos) or the state hold rights, not the individual, except in the economic field, where the new extreme-right parties support free-market against collectivist or statist approaches.

A borderline case is provided by the Danish and Norwegian Progress Parties. They do not deny the principle of individual freedom: in fact, R. H. Harmel and R. K. Gibson call them 'right-libertarian' and they use libertarian slogans against the social-democratic regime. But since these parties' political discourse is much more radical than that of the conservative parties, and their law and order stances quite strong, they could be included in the extreme-right family. The same applies to the Swiss Tessin League.

On the basis of these spatial, ideological and attitudinal criteria, we can offer a typology where parties further to the right of the political spectrum are categorised according to the presence or absence of a fascist heritage, and to the acceptance or refusal of the political system. If a party fits the ideological criterion – and, as a consequence, the systemic one – we can include it in the old, traditional, neo-fascist type. If a party is not linked to fascism but has an anti-system profile, we can include it in the new, postindustrial type. Table 17.1 sets out the parties in these two categories.

Returning to the distinction between extreme-right parties and the above-mentioned anti-establishment/anti-party parties, the commonalities between them can be considerable: many extreme-right parties are often included in this category, which is rather similar to the 'populist' one introduced by Betz (1994). It would be tempting to enlarge the range of the extreme-right class by including the 'anti-establishment' parties, but this operation would imply some 'conceptual stretching'. In fact, keeping in mind our first criterion – the spatial location – one can see that some anti-establishment/populist parties are 'mainstream parties' – that is, parties located in the middle of the political spectrum rather than on the right – which is the first, necessary condition of our typology. This is why, for example, one cannot include among the extreme-right parties an anti-establishment and populist party such as the Italian Lega Nord.

On the other side of the political spectrum, the new parties in the green family are more clearly grouped. But there are still some definitional problems. Green parties are not exclusively devoted to the protection of the environment but surround, and even justify, this concern with a broader set of issues, from pacifism to women's liberation, egalitarianism, minority rights and so on. Therefore, some authors distinguish between 'pure greens' and 'alternative greens' (Müller-Rommel, 1993, p. 16) while others have adopted the definition of 'left/libertarian' (Kitschelt, 1988) or 'New Politics' (Poguntke, 1989,

TABLE 17.1 *Extreme right parties in Western Europe*

A The old, traditional extreme-right parties

Italy	MSI/AN (Movimento Sociale Italiano-Italian Social Movement/ Alleanza Nazionale – National Alliance)
Germany	NPD (Nationaldemokratische Partei Deutschlands – Germany's National Democratic Party)
	DVU (Deutsche Volksunion-List D – German People's Union)
UK	BNP (British National Party) NF (National Front)
Greece	EPEN (Ethniki Politiki Enosis – National Political Union)
	KP (Komma Proodeftikon – Progressive Party)
	EK (Ethniko Komma – National Party)
	EP (Ethniki Parataxis – National Alignment)
The Netherlands	CP/CP'86 (Centrumpartij – Centre Party)
Portugal	PDC (Partido da Democracia Crista/ Christian Democratic Party)
Spain	FN (Fuerza Nueva/Frente Nacional – New Force/National Front)

B The new, post-industrial extreme right parties

Austria	FPÖ (Freiheitliche Partei Osterreichs – Austrian Liberal Party)
Belgium	VB (Vlaams Blok – Flemish Bloc)
	FNb (Front National – National Front)
Denmark	FRPn (Fremskridtspartiet – Progress Party)
France	FN (Front National – National Front)
Germany	REP (Die Republikaner – The Republicans)
The Netherlands	CD (Centrumdemocraten – Centre Democrats)
Norway	FRPn (Fremskrittspartiet – Progress Party)
Switzerland	AN/SD (Action National – National Action/Schweizer Demokraten – Swiss Democrats)
	AP (Autopartei/ Swiss Automobile Party)
	EDU (Eidgenössisch Demokratische Union/Federal Democratic Union)
	Lega dei Ticinesi – Tessin League
Sweden	NyD (Ny Demokrati – New Democracy)

1993a) in order to gather into the same category greens and other left-wing parties that are also concerned with the environment. A classical internal division in the group concerns the *realos* and the *fundis*: this distinction, borrowed from the internal debate in the German Greens (Grünen), divides the supporters of conciliation with the established parties to produce concrete results (*realos*) from the 'true believers' of political ecology, who plead for a more radical sociocultural alternative (*fundis*). The following analysis includes as members of the green family certain parties that others exclude, such as the Dutch Groen Links, the French ecological movements led by Brice Lalonde, the *realo* Swiss GPS, and the 'pure green reformist' Austrian VGO. However, the 'greening' Danish Socialist People's Party and Venstre Socialist Party are excluded, as is the communist-led Portuguese CDU, where the Os Verdes find (marginal) hospitality.

The Electoral Performance and Development of Extreme Right and Green Parties

Although both sets of parties began to emerge, with few exceptions, at the time of the first (1979) European elections, their major break-through occurred almost simultaneously in 1983–4. The German Grünen entered the Bundestag for the first time in 1983, striding over the 5 per cent threshold and taking twenty-seven seats. Even if their performance was not an absolute novelty in Europe – they were preceded by the two Belgian ecology parties (Ecolo and Agalev) which gained four seats in 1981 – the international importance of Germany meant that this event was seen as a turning point. The extreme right surfaced and gained both votes and international attention in 1984: the French Front National, under the leadership of Jean-Marie Le Pen, moved from 0.2 per cent at the 1981 legislative election to 11.2 per cent at the 1984 European elections. This represented the highest score ever achieved in a postwar nationwide election by an extreme-right party. At the same Euro-election, extreme-right parties gained sizeable votes in the Netherlands and Greece (where a Euro-parliamentarian was elected); but it is again the importance of the country, and the scale of the success that gives the French development significance. The sub-sequent 'imitation effect' produced by the French and German devel-opments is important: the spread and circulation of ideas, slogans and issues at the European level were inevitably supported by their affirma-tion in two geopolitically important countries.

Since the mid-to-late 1980s, both the greens and the extreme-right parties have gained in strength. If we compare the electoral outcomes of the European elections of 1989 with the preceding ones of 1984, it is clear that the take-off was located somewhere between the two. Dividing the period 1980–94 into two subperiods (1980–7 and 1988–94), both the greens and extreme-right parties increased their support between the first and the second (see Table 17.2). In national elections, the greens (excluding the UK, Greece, Norway and Portugal, where such parties are either absent or quite marginal) increased their average vote from 2.7 to 5.1 per cent; while that of the extreme right (excluding Finland, the Republic of Ireland, the UK and Spain for the same reasons) went from 3.3 to 7.2 per cent. In the case of the extreme right, Austria showed an increase of 12.2 per cent, Belgium 6.1 per cent (*five times* the earlier score), and in Switzerland and Norway the far-right vote more than doubled.

On the basis of electoral outcomes in 1988–94, extreme-right parties can be divided into four classes: *strong parties* with 10 per cent or more of the vote (FPO, FN, MSI/AN, FRPn); *medium-sized parties* with between 3 per cent and 6 per cent (VLB, FRP, NyD, Autopartei and AN/SD); *small parties* with less than 3 per cent (CD, FNb, Tessin League, EDU and the German Republikaner – which only score more than 3 per cent in European elections and have never elected a national MP); and *the irrelevant parties,* that is, those which have contested national elections but without success (the German NPD and DVU, the Norwegian 'Stop Immigration', the British NF and BNP, the Austrian NDP, the Spanish FN, the French and Belgian PFN, and the Greek EPEN, as well as other minor parties such as the Portuguese PDC, the Dutch CP'86, and the newly-born Finnish IKL).

As for the Green parties, the increase in 1988–94 is less dramatic because of their take-off before 1988. Finland, Belgium, and above all France, show the highest increase throughout this period. The green family can also be divided into four groups: the *strong parties* with above 10 per cent (the Belgian Agalev/Ecolo); the *medium-sized parties* with between 5 and 7 per cent (the German Grünen, the Finnish Vihreä Litto (Green League), the Austrian Gruene Alternative (created from the merger of VGO and ALO), the French Génération Écologie and Les Verts, the Swiss GPS (Grüne Partei der Schweitz) and the Swedish Miljöpartiet; the *small parties* with between 1.5 and 4 per cent of the vote (the Italian Verdi, the Dutch Groen Link, the Irish Green Alliance, the Swiss POCH/GBS (Grüne Bundnis Schweitz); and *the irrelevant parties* with less than 1 per cent (the Danish Miljöparteit, various Greek groups, the Spanish Los Verdes, the Norwegian Miljö-partiet de Grønne, the Dutch De Groenen and the British Green Party which, despite its impressive – but unrepeated – 14.9 per cent in the 1989 Euro-election, has always scored poorly in national polls, achieving just 0.5 per cent in the 1992 general elections.

While the proportion of votes going to the established parties was stable until the late 1980s (Mair 1993), it has decreased markedly during the 1990s. The Italian case is perhaps the most striking example of the downfall of a very stable party system. But the Republic of Ireland has abandoned the historical duopoly of Fianna Fail and Fine Gael, providing room for four new parties – three of them originating as splinter groups from the established parties – while Sweden and the Netherlands have both opened their parliaments to newcomers. However, much recent literature on volatility would suggest that such evidence is unrepresentative. Bartolini and Mair (1990) demonstrate that electoral volatility has been low and within right- and left-wing blocs rather than between them. Moreover, in the 1980s, mean volatility has decreased compared to the 1970s (Gallagher *et al.,*

TABLE 17.2 Electoral results Greens and extreme right parties (1980–94)

		1980	1981	1982	1983	1984	1984 Election	1985	1986	1987	1988	1989	1989 Election	1990	1991	1992	1993	1994	1994 Election
Austria	FP				5.0				9.7					16.6				22.5	
	Green				3.3				4.8					4.8				7.3	
Belgium	AD/UDRT		2.7					1.2											
	FN		–							0.1					1.0				2.9
	VLB		1.1				1.3	1.4		1.9			4.1		6.6				7.8
	Greens		4.5				8.2	6.2		7.1			11.5		10.0				13.8
Denmark	FRPn		8.9			3.6	3.5			4.8	9.0		5.3	6.4				6.4	2.9
	Greens									1.3	1.4			0.9					
France	FN	0.2					11.2		9.8		9.6		11.7				12.3		10.5
	Greens	1.1					6.7		1.2		0.4		10.6				10.8		5.0
Finland	Greens				1.4					4.0					6.8				
UK	NF																		
	Greens				0.2		0.6			0.3			14.9			0.5			3.2
Greece	Epen et al.		1.7		0.2			0.6				0.3	1.8	0.1		0.5			
	Greens						2.6					0.1	2.1	1.1					
Ireland	Greens						0.5			0.4		1.5	3.7			1.4			7.9
Italy	MSI				6.8		6.5			5.9			5.3			5.4		13.5	12.5
	Greens									2.5			6.2			2.8		2.3	3.2

Country	Party	Election results (%)
Germany	NDP	0.2 0.8 0.2 0.8 1.6 0.3 – 0.2
	REP	1.5 0.6 7.1 2.1 1.9 3.9
	Greens	5.6 8.2 8.3 8.4 4.8 7.3 10.1
Netherlands	CD + CP	0.1 2.5 0.5 0.8 2.5 1.0
	GL	5.6 0.9 4.1 3.5 3.7
	DG	1.3 0.2 7.0 0.4 – 0.4
Portugal	PDC	0.4 4.5 0.7 0.6 3.2
Norway	FRPn	0.7 13.0 6.3
	Stop Imm.	3.7 0.3 0.1
	Greens	0.4 –
Spain	FN + Falange	0.5 0.5 – 0.6 0.4 –
	Greens	0.2 3.0? 1.4
Sweden	NyD	1.6 5.8 5.5 6.7 5.0
	Greens	3.4 1.2
Switzerland	NA/SD	3.5 1.5 2.9 3.3
	Autopartei	2.6 5.1
	Tessin	1.4
	EDU	1.0
	Poch/Gbs	3.5 3.5 1.3
	GPS	2.9 4.8 6.1

Note: See Table 17.1 for explanation of acronyms for party names.

1995, p. 233). However, the mean mirrors just part of reality. In fact, only four countries showed a decrease in volatility in the 1980s (Denmark, the Netherlands, Norway and the UK) while *seven* experienced an increase. The four countries displaying a decrease in volatility experienced an increase in party system fragmentation in the 1970s which led to system stabilisation (and a decrease in volatility) in the 1980s. In the other countries, the 1980s' increase in volatility seems to have been linked to the formation and spread of both green and extreme-right parties, in addition to some national-specific, anti-establishment parties. Moreover, if we push the analysis forward to the early 1990s, a new wave of instability seems to be occurring. The elections recently held in France, the Netherlands, Germany, Belgium, Austria, Spain, Sweden, and, above all, Italy, show a considerable level of volatility; only the UK remains low on the volatility scale (Gallagher *et al.*, 1995, p. 235; Luther, 1995, p. 134). Voters swing more and more: but mainly because political supply (the number of parties) has increased.

To be more precise, supply is greater, but it is concentrated on the two new 'political families' – the greens and extreme-right parties. In six countries (Austria, Belgium, Germany, the Netherlands, Sweden and France), 'supply' on the far right was almost non-existent prior to 1984. Since then, it has either increased (Austria, Belgium, Germany, France) or declined (Sweden and the Netherlands). In the remaining countries which already had a sizeable extreme right party (Italy, Denmark, Norway, Switzerland) the trend has been growing everywhere. However, marginal extreme-right parties have in fact disappeared in Portugal, Greece and Spain, while in the Republic of Ireland and Finland no extreme-right party is even identifiable. Green parties were also quite weak until the mid-1980s, with two exceptions: Belgium and Switzerland. After the 1983 success of the German Grünen, and the 1984 European election which fostered the green movement, Green parties spread across most countries of Europe, with the exception of Spain, Greece, Portugal, Denmark and Norway.

Hypotheses on the Origin and Development of New Parties

How can we explain this phenomenon of new parties and new challenges to conventional party systems? The problem is twofold: on the one hand we need to examine the conditions of party system change and the likelihood of formation of new parties in general terms;

while on the other, we need to investigate the conditions that favoured Green and extreme-right parties in particular.

Socioeconomic Transformation and New Social Alignments

Conflict over economic resources has lost much of its salience since the mid-1980s as the different party programmes and government policies have become less distinctive. The allocation of resources is a much less critical issue than in the past. In this sense, the political landscape has changed radically since the 1920s when the conflicts which shaped the party systems of Europe were centred on the allocation of economic resources. The ideologies of socialism and communism mobilised large masses of people; and the same was true, to a lesser extent, for the fascist ideology which attracted millions of members and voters in the interwar years all over Europe *before* its proponents seized power. If we follow Stein Rokkan's paradigm of cleavages we could argue that in the 1920s conflict over the economy was fuelled and exacerbated by its linkage with an ideological 'friend–foe' type of opposition. Where economy and culture clashed, anti-democratic systems emerged. The (military) victory over fascism revived the conflicts of the previous generation over the allocation of resources, but with one crucial difference: one actor – fascism – had been (physically) eliminated from the political arena.

Although the most salient conflict of postwar Europe has centred on economic resource allocation, bargaining has prevailed over confrontation: even if the presence of communist parties in Catholic countries (plus Finland) exacerbated this conflict, the absence of a radical competitor on the far right prevented a repeat of the events of the 1920s and 1930s. Moreover, democracy means compromise, and in this setting the disruptive potential of the communists' own 'integrative order' was domesticated. But, as class conflict decreased, a different type of conflict over resource allocation emerged, one which no longer concerned the ownership of the means of production or state intervention in the economy. Postindustrial society is not primarily a society based on class conflict: it is a society of values conflict. This does not mean that economic issues have not retained their high relevance, and it would be naïve to disregard the importance of such themes as unemployment, inflation and welfare provision: surveys show that these are still highly salient for the bulk of the population. But it would be even more naïve to assume that these issues remain the principal axis of social conflict.

Postindustrial society signifies the decline of the interaction between human and machine. The crucial interaction is now between human beings. The implication of this epochal change is not yet clear for the political sphere. But what is clear is that the economy has lost its centrality in defining political allegiances. Again, this is not because work is less important, but because people now work in a different manner. The decline of the machine (or perhaps its substitution by a universally standardised machine, the computer) means that the *object* of conflict – the exploitation of humankind by the machine – has been displaced in favour of other *objects* of domination that are no longer in the sphere of production but in the sphere of interpersonal relations. Economic-based conflict has not been replaced by old 'integrative orders' (such as Marxism or religion), for these have collapsed too. Rather, a bric-à-brac style of value formation has emerged. Some would label this new trend 'postmodernism', emphasising the decline of 'modernity' (see Chapter 14). Others (for example, Inglehart, 1985) would challenge such ideological bricolage, arguing that new conflict dimensions are shaping Western societies – between new left and old left, or between materialist and postmaterialist politics. At any rate, class conflict over the economy has receded sufficiently to leave room for *value* conflict.

This change is not traumatic: it has been evolving slowly since the 1970s. It is a process, not a sudden revolutionary overthrow. And it has not (yet?) produced new social alignments. On the contrary, one could argue that, coherent with postmodern cultural patterns, future social alignments will be indistinct, unstable and volatile. The absence of clear and solid social configurations along the postmaterial cleavage line has limited the growth of new parties: in fact, they have failed to gain a pivotal role (legitimised by mass consent) in the various party systems. In short, the postindustrial and postmodern societies are characterised by changes in the relevance of the poles of conflict; but such changes have not yet been translated into an 'alternative set of political packages'.

A Crisis of Legitimacy?

Another way explaining the decline of established parties refers to the wider issue of the crisis of the democratic system. This problem has been variously interpreted in terms of fiscal crisis, legitimacy crisis, overload and ungovernability – described by Crozier *et al.* (1975, p. 159) as a widespread 'dissatisfaction with and lack of confidence in the functioning of the democratic system'. However, the difficulties of assessing levels of 'confidence', 'trust' and 'support' notwithstanding, this diagnosis seems to have been over-pessimistic.

In terms of the *functioning* of democracy (or 'regime efficacy' as Morlino and Montero (1995, p. 235) define it), the data provided by the Eurobarometer surveys from 1976 to 1991 indicate that 'satisfaction with democracy' was over 50 per cent in all the EU countries and that there has been no decline over time (Fuchs *et al.*, 1995). Regarding democracy *per se*, – that is, democracy as an ideal form of government – more than 90 per cent of citizens surveyed in twelve EC countries in 1991 (Eurobarometer 1991) consider it positively. The same survey shows that around 80 per cent of citizens consider democracy to be a comparatively better form of government than 'dictatorship', which Morlino and Montero (1995, p. 233) define as a high level of 'diffuse legitimacy'. However, even this response – a rather unsophisticated form of evidence in any case – does not justify the assumption that democracy faces a crisis of legitimacy. Even if the functioning or efficacy of democracy had a dramatic decline in the early 1990s – because of the sudden decline in the level of confidence in democracy in Italy (Eurobarometer) – the level of satisfaction (with the exceptions of the South European countries – Italy, Portugal, Spain and Greece – and the UK) remains very high indeed: too high to explain the development of new parties as alternatives to and antagonists of the democratic system.

We therefore conclude that the new parties are not the by-product of a generalised and acute decline of confidence in democracy. What we shall argue, however, is that distrust is unevenly distributed: it is overwhelmingly concentrated in the fringe electorates of the right and the left, and especially on the right.

This conclusion is far from new. A long tradition of analysis has demonstrated that alienated people – those who either do not have the means to interpret and master the political world, or feel excluded from society and experience a mismatch between aspirations and realisations – tend to withdraw from politics or to choose extreme positions. This approach fits better with the right of the political spectrum because of the more radical anti-system character of the far right. The Green parties also provide opportunities for 'protest', but in a rather different manner and with radically divergent aims. First, the greens tend to attract culturally sophisticated, higher-educated, relatively well-off people who want to express their opposition to the system and predominant value system by involving themselves in politics in an articulate fashion and by resorting to various forms of action. Second, the greens do not aim to overthrow the democratic system: on the contrary, their emphasis on participatory democracy and their internal organisation points to a strong adhesion to the basic principles of democratic regimes. While extreme-right parties are anti-system parties, greens are 'reformists' or 'challenging' parties: they do not seek to undermine the fundamentals of the system. Only some minor Marxist-alternative remnants, painted with a pale shade of green, radically oppose the system (the Swiss Poch, part of the Dutch Groene Link, and some Grünen *fundis*). On the whole, however, their conception of humankind is totally different: while the greens follow Rousseau and want to 'free' humans, the far-right parties 'escape from freedom' and seek control. In short, while for the former there is not enough democracy, for the latter there is too much.

Data on satisfaction with democracy by location on the right–left continuum confirm that those on the extreme right are less supportive than those in the centre or even on the extreme left. This trend is particularly evident in Spain, Italy, Greece and Portugal which show a clear correlation between left–right positioning and support for democracy: moving from left to right, the number pro-system declines while those who are anti-system increases (Morlino and Montero, 1995, pp. 246–7). This can be explained by the passage from right-wing authoritarian regimes to democracies in these countries: while the left strongly identifies with the new democratic regimes, the right is nostalgic and therefore more critical. Also, in Norway, Sweden and the USA, 'those who locate themselves on the ideological extremes tend to be most strongly alienated' and 'those on the left are more trusting than citizens on the right' (Miller and Listhaug 1993: 185).

As for extreme-right party supporters, those of the Italian MSI, the German Republikaner and French Front National display a much higher level of dissatisfaction with democracy than the mean population *and* the greens. In France, voters who are 'alienated' vote overwhelmingly for the Front National: 45 per cent support FN, while only 9 per cent would vote for the French Green Party. In Germany, 24 per cent of dissatisfied citizens would vote for the Republikaner and 9 per cent for the Grünen; in Italy, 19 per cent would vote for the MSI and 10 per cent for the Green party. The percentage of alienated voters, in the case of the greens, reflects, *grosso modo*, their share of the votes; while in the case of the extreme-right parties that percentage is more than double for the MSI, three times for the Republikaner and four times the number of FN voters. A similar pattern is discernible for the Austrian FPÖ voters, 47 per cent of whom rated the political system negatively (as against 28 per cent of the Austrian population), and 17 per cent of whom actually preferred dictatorship to democracy (compared with 5 per cent of the country as a whole) (Betz, 1994, p. 51). The

Norwegian and Danish Progress Parties follow a different pattern: the balance is slightly in favour of satisfaction (more for the Danish FRP than for the Norwegian one) – although below the national mean – but distrust towards politicians is much higher than among other parties.

In sum, the rise of new parties cannot be attributed to a crisis of democracy. On the other hand, it is true that those who feel alienated from the democratic system are concentrated on the far right and among extreme-right party voters in particular. Elements of alienation in Western democracies do exist: but the scapegoat is less democracy than its agents – political parties and politicians.

Value Change

Having dismissed either changes in cleavage structures or a deficit of democratic legitimacy as explanations for the new parties, we now turn to a third set of explanations, based on changes in value systems. Inglehart's world famous paradigm of post-materialism versus materialism was based on a 'socialisation hypothesis' which linked socialisation in an environment of 'material saturation and security' (and new high levels of education, mass media exposure and mobility), to a different value system and set of value priorities, emphasising self-affirmation, quality of life, democratic participation, equality and informal interpersonal relationships (Inglehart, 1985, p. 103). The youth revolution of the 1960s represented the first manifestation of the new value system. The critique of that period, against 'fundamental aspects of modern life such as commercialization, industrialization, political centralization, bureaucratization and democratization, cultural rationalization and pluralization' (Brand, 1990, p. 28), set the stage for a major challenge to standard beliefs in either liberal-democracy or social-democracy. The *Zeitgeist* of the late 1960s and early 1970s also contained elements of anti-modernism such as opposition to economic growth, to consumerism and to the penetration of the state into society. The novelty of the left-libertarian and green movements which adopted the postmaterial agenda was that their opposition to traditional socialist parties was based not on Marxist orthodoxy and purity (as in the case of the conventional far left) but on the basis of a completely different agenda.

In principle, the structural transformations which led to the post-material value system could have produced a radically different outcome. Why should the post-industrial process of change have favoured left-libertarian organisations? Why should post-materialists be inclined to the left of the political spectrum? Inglehart's socialisation hypothesis implies a change in value *priority* (material versus postmaterial), not in the political orientation. Conceivably, the same structural societal changes – basically, long-term economic development – could have produced postmaterial *right-wing* attitudes.

This hypothesis is consistent with the analysis of the theoreticians of mass society: the by-product of mass society was the destruction of the bonds of family, kinship and (small) community. The loss of social and affective roots would have produced insecurity and anomie, leaving the individual isolated and alienated. However, neither outcome occurred. Abundant empirical evidence shows that in Western democracies a large number of people – some 40 per cent (Cayrol, 1995, p. 183) – have an active interest in politics, and only a third, on average, never discuss politics. Those actively interested join voluntary associations, interest groups – above all trade unions (Aarts, 1995) – and they participate actively beyond the vote much more than in the past. The demand emerging from mass society did not concern the economy so much as the value system: providing a sense of community and social integration have little in common with 'material' interests. A greater degree of anomie (in Emile Durkheim's terms) has increased demands for stricter moral standards, for a more rigorous religious commitment and more pervasive religious presence, for traditional family and sexual roles, for a more hierarchical social organisation, with a clearly defined line of command, for law and order enforcement, for symbolic references to 'national' identity in terms of national pride (easily shifting to aggressive nationalism and xenophobia), and opposition to Europe and globalisation. All these issues, which constitute the 'new right' agenda, emphasise non-material concerns: they represent the right-wing (and substantially authoritarian) version of postmaterialism.

These issues found theoretical expression in the neo-conservative intellectual trend which emerged in the late 1970s as a reaction to the Keynesian social compromise, the welfare state, internationalism and libertarianism (Eatwell, 1989). Neo-conservatism differs from conservatism because it does not support the *status quo* (Girvin, 1988). Rather, it challenges modernity on its own ground by juxtaposing the post-material 'progressive' agenda with a postmaterial 'authoritarian' one (Flanagan, 1987). The importance of the conservative reaction has been underrated because the *Zeitgeist* favoured at first a libertarian–egalitarian value change and because there was initially no manifest political mobilisation on the right. While, on the left, mobilisation took the form of the 'new social movements', with a quite large popular participation in the 1980s (Aarts, 1995, pp. 249–54), there was no equivalent on the right. Those who sought a different response to postindustrial society from that of the pacifists, civil rights militants, feminists, ecologists and so on kept silent until political entrepreneurs set out explicitly to mobilise their support. When they did mobilise, their political style was quite different: while the 'new politics' parties advocated more participation and more citizen involvement, and were quite visible in the streets, extreme right parties neither supported nor exhibited similar beliefs.

The most visible presence of the extreme right came with the violent, fascist-like actions of extreme-right youth groups or small gangs of radical-right militants in the form of the 'skinhead' or 'nazi-skin' movement, frequently responsible for aggression against immigrants all over Europe (Björgo, 1995). These acts, however, involve a very small number of people and they are not the expression of anything like a social movement. What was lacking on the right was a utopian message sufficient to mobilise a collective movement. The only highly emotional and strongly symbolic messages came from the fascist and Nazi traditions – the epitome of absolute evil in postwar democracies. But the stigma associated with this symbolic imagery inhibited the formation of a large collective movement. 'Traditional' extreme-right parties – based largely on nostalgia for the inter-war Fascist movement – have almost completely disappeared, with the exception of the Italian MSI. In contrast, the latter has reached the zenith of its electoral fortunes – but only because the Italian system collapsed and the party quickly transformed itself into a less nostalgic and more forward looking party in the form of AN (Alleanza Nazionale – National Alliance).

It could be argued, then, that a right-wing value system derived either from the fascist tradition or from the radicalisation of the neo-conservative agenda, combined with novel themes emerging from the 'new right', was developing during the same period as the postmaterialist 'new politics'. The main difference was that, for some time, it was an invisible and silent 'counter-revolution' (Ignazi, 1992). Post-industrial society has therefore produced two quite opposite reactions: more self-affirmation on one side ('new politics') but also more atomisation/alienation on the other (authoritarian neo-conservatism). While the representatives of 'new politics' seek more self-management, informality and libertarianism, their right-wing counterparts search for more order, tradition, identity and security/reassurance. The direction taken depends on which ideology or cultural mood is prevailing. After the libertarianism and egalitarianism of the late 1960s and early 1970s, a rightward turn occurred in the 1980s. This shift to the right can be discerned by the diffusion of the neo-conservative cultural tendency and by its reception in the manifestos of the 'bourgeois' parties (Klingemann *et al.*, 1994). Moreover, all political families have moved to the right compared to the 1970s; but the *conservative* parties have gone further than the rest (Klingemann, 1995, pp. 190–1).

This move favoured the rise of the far right. Where conservative parties regained power, the extreme right parties also succeeded. The relationship established by Kitschelt (1988) and Rorhschneider (1993) for the Green parties – 'where the left was in government the greens grew' – goes for the far right as well. Just as the socialist parties in power were unable to manage the 'new politics' agenda, the conservatives – in *government*, not in opposition – dropped the new right agenda (with the exception of the British Thatcher government). Therefore, the new issues, introduced onto the political agenda by the neoconservative intellectual movement through established forces such as the conservative parties and their think-thanks, remained largely dormant until the extreme right parties emerged to represent *and radicalise* that agenda.

The New Parties and Spatial Analysis

The emergence of new parties has also been explained by Downs' (1957) economic model of democracy. Spatial analysts predict the appearance of a new party when the traditional parties make unprincipled, pragmatic moves along the left–right continuum and abandon to newcomers a significant, unrepresented section of the electorate (Downs, 1957, pp. 128ff). The famous example of the success of the British Labour Party, despite the presence of a large Liberal Party, is a case in point. This interpretation brings into the analysis the problem of the left–right continuum: all parties occupy a precise location on the continuum and they keep control of a certain area of the electorate by trying to conquer some part of the bordering electorate by small programmatic shifts (Shepsle and Cohen, 1990, pp. 39–40). The party system could thus be imagined as an oligopolistic market where few actors control their share of consumers/voters. The only way to break into the market is to introduce a brand new product: in other terms, only if a party offers to the electorate a new set of issues will it gain its own place in the party system. As we know, very few succeeded in doing this until the 1980s. Most were 'flash parties', short-lived and irrelevant (Pedersen, 1982; Harmel and Robertson, 1985). Moreover, they were country-specific, which means that they arose in response to specific national problems (for example, the linguistic cleavage in Belgium in the 1970s) and/or from a split in pre-existing party organisations; between 1960 and 1980, 233 new party organisations were counted but only 20 were formed by a new political groups without any role played by existing politicians, party factions or organisations (Harmel and Robertson, 1985). In sum, they did not form a new sort of party family.

The only, rather weak, attempt by a new political family to enter the party system was made by 'new-left' groups in the early 1980s. These by-products of the 1968 movement emerged in many countries, especially in Scandinavia and the Mediterranean, because of splits in the communist or socialist movements. But they were neither long-lived nor significant. Moreover, the political product supplied by these ultra-leftist parties was not exactly original, since they presented themselves as the 'true believers' of a Marxism 'betrayed' by the traditional leftist parties. In contrast, when the Green parties appeared, their agenda was genuinely new. And the same applies to those far-right groups – the postindustrial extreme-right parties – which eschew any fascist leanings.

Downs' approach leads us to test whether, in countries where new parties emerged, the pre-existing parties had previously moved along the left–right continuum leaving 'open' (that is, unoccupied) some parts of the continuum still occupied by voters. Being unrepresented, the latter awaited a new political entrepreneur attempting to fill 'the vacuum'. In this case, the political vacuum involved a set of issues introduced into the political arena by neo-conservatism and subsequently abandoned by the established conservative parties. Only marginally concerning 'economic' or 'material' questions, these centre rather on national identity, xenophobic policies, moral traditionalism (mainly concerning sex and family roles), and law and order. In the background we can discern more general attitudes such as anti-pluralism, anti-partyism and anti-parliamentarism. While significant for a sizeable number of citizens, this set of issues – especially nationalism, immigration and physical security – was disregarded by the established parties. Survey data from France and other countries show quite clearly that many people have been concerned by these issues for some time (Ignazi, 1989; Sofres, 1993). The sudden breakthrough of the French Front National has been linked precisely to the failure of the political establishment to address them. It is important to note that these issues were not 'material' issues: this is why the far-right parties which emerged in the 1980s (and their two Scandinavian antecedents) have been defined as the 'postmaterial' extreme right.

The same goes for the left: the importance of the environmental question and its salience are a major explanation for both the rise and success of the Green parties. The data provided by Hofrichter and Reif (1990) and Dalton (1994, p. 54) point out that the environmental problem was perceived as an important issue by the population at large, and that a particular section of citizens rated this problem at the highest level. When this condition materialises, a potential constituency for a 'green' party exists. Then, other factors (reaction by the established parties, the electoral system, a lack of leadership, the emergence of more salient questions, and so on) might stimulate or arrest the development of the party/movement.

Conclusion

Peter Mair (1993) correctly stresses the limited electoral support of the new parties: they are not present in all countries and in some they do not even reach 1 per cent. But if we take the eleven European countries where Green and extreme-right parties are both present, during 1988–94 they attracted some 12.3 per cent of the votes (7.2 per cent for the far right, 5.1 per cent for the Green parties), which is double the support they received in the previous (1980–7) period. If this share of votes is divided by all European countries, the new parties' impact decreases; but if, on the other hand, we add the 'anti-establishment parties', which have been excluded from this analysis, the mean increases. But it is unnecessary to play with numbers to conclude that new parties are increasing in size and number. However, none has made a real breakthrough (with the possible exceptions of the quite distinct Italian and Austrian cases): only a handful, in fact, have attracted more than 10 per cent of national election votes: the French Front National, the Belgian Green Party, the Norwegian FRP, the Italian MSI/AN, and, above all, the Austrian FPO.

On the other hand, the extreme-right parties and the Green Parties represent two quite neat 'political families': this means that common problems and common concerns coalesced in partisan organisations at different ends of the political spectrum. This phenomenon has been interpreted as a symptom of a system in crisis. But it seems clear that this is not the case: democracy is in good health. A more plausible explanation lies in value change and the related incapacity of traditional parties to represent new issues. Political parties, more than the democratic system, are under threat because they no longer adequately fulfil their functions of channelling demands. They are still strong and powerful (Mair, 1995); but they are losing their hold over (civil) society because they are not considered to be effective channels for expressing political views. While this perception has fuelled the new social movements and protest, it has also driven disaffected but active citizens to promote and participate in new political parties in order to overcome the deficiencies of the old. If the value system and the specific issues supported by these new parties continue to be salient and inadequately addressed by traditional parties of government and opposition, the new parties which have entered the political arena may endure and grow. But their future role can only be guessed at, depending on their capacity for consolidating and enlarging their constituencies and on the level of system polarisation. A growing political distance between the extremes and the collapse of the centre parties could favour institutionalised extreme-right parties and Green parties. But the reverse might be also be true: novel, more salient, issues could emerge, and/or traditional parties might recover both their expressive function and prestige.

Guide to Further Reading

2 Economic Integration and the Nation-State

There is a wide range of literature on European economic and monetary integration. Excellent studies of the politics of the most recent phase of monetary union can be found in W. Sandholtz (1993) and K. Dyson (1994). Interesting discussions by those involved in developing EMU can be found in W. Nölling (1993), and T. Padoa Schioppa (1994) while useful introductory guides, in addition to C. Taylor (1995) include R. Minikin (1993), and M. Emerson and C. Huhne (1991). For more general analyses of economic integration, see L. Tsoukalis (1997); M. Emerson (ed.) (1992); G. F. Thompson (1993); L. Davison et al. (1995) and the various contributions to N. Nugent and R. O'Donnell (eds) (1994).

3 European Integration and the Nation-State

J. Shaw (1996) offers an insightful analysis of the law and institutions of the EU. For a survey of policy-making at European level, see S. George (1991). M. Siedentopf and J. Ziller (1988) provide a comparative analysis of the implementation of EC policies at the national level. The development of functional links among parliamentary assemblies has been the focus of much attention recently: see, for example, R. Morgan and C. Tame (1996). An overview of the impact of the integration process on state regulatory policies can be found in the work of G. Majone (1994). The *Journal of European Public Policy* and *Journal of Common Market Studies* regularly provide articles on the themes covered in this chapter.

4 The Welfare State: Internal Challenges, External Constraints

For comparative analyses of the continental and Scandinavian welfare states, see the articles in G. Esping-Andersen (1996) and on specific national welfare systems, V. George and P. Taylor-Gooby (eds) (1996). On Europe, see S. Leibfried and P. Pierson (eds) (1995), L. Hantrais (1995), and M. Gold (ed.) (1993). On recent changes in welfare states, see European Commission (1995) and OECD (1994).

Since the appearance of the magisterial study edited by P. Flora (1986), there have been surprisingly few good detailed studies in English on *national* welfare systems. Exceptions are J. S. Ambler (ed.) (1991), R. H. Cox (1993),

K. E. Miller (1991), H. Milner (1994), J. Clasen and R. Freeman (eds.) (1994) and A. Cochrane and J. Clarke (1993).

5   Executives, Bureaucracies and Decision-making

Comparative analyses of West European executives are, perhaps surprisingly, rare – but for general approaches see J. Blondel and F. Müller-Rommel (1988, 1993); G. W. Jones (1991); A. Lijphart (1992); R. Elgie (1995). For UK-focused overviews of recent developments in the literature on core executives, see D. Marsh and R. A. W. Rhodes (1992) and R. A. W. Rhodes (1995); see also P. Dunleavy (1991). The EU dimension is covered in J. Peterson and E. Bomberg (forthcoming). On central administrations see A. Claisse and M.-C. Meininger (1994); E. Page (1985); G. Peters (1995); D. C. Rowat (1988); G. Warmsley *et al.* (1990); and J. Ziller (1993). On recent reforms see K. A. Eliassen and J. Kooiman (1993); G. E. Caiden (1991); B. G. Peters and D. J. Savoie (1993); J. Pierre (1995); and IIAS (1992).

6   Illicit Governance: Corruption, Scandal and Fraud

The study of 'illicit governance' is still in its infancy. For an excellent conceptual introduction, see S. H. Alatas (1990). A good international survey of corruption can be found in Heidenheimer, Johnston and LeVine (1989), while examples from Europe and Latin America are examined in W. Little and E. Posada-Carbó (1996), D. Della Porta and Y. Mény (1995) and, from a party finance perspective, C. Malamud and E. Posada-Carbó (1997). On Southern Europe, a special issue of the French journal *Confluences Méditerranée* (1995) provides a useful and up-to-date set of analyses. On party finance, the best studies to date can be found in A. B. Gunlicks (1993) and H. E. Alexander and R. Shiratori (1994). Detailed studies of particular countries are still rare. On France, however, see Mény (1992) and on Italy, D. Della Porta (1992) *Lo Scambio occulto: Casi di corruzione politica in Italia* (Bologna: Il Mulino) and D. Della Porta and A. Vanucci (1995). For a sample of Della Porta's work in English, see D. Della Porta 'The System of Corrupt Exchange in Local Government', in S. Gundle and S. Parker (1996) *The New Italian Republic* (London: Routledge) pp. 221–33.

7   Electoral Systems and Voting Behaviour

On electoral systems, the standard research work is A. Lijphart (1994a); and R. Taagepera and M. S. Shugart (1989) is a detailed exploration of the relationship between votes and seats under various formulae, district magnitudes and thresholds. A useful historical account of the evolution of the electoral system in a wide range of European countries can be found in A. M. Carstairs (1980). A number of the themes of this chapter are discussed in greater detail in M. Gallagher *et al.* (1995), especially chs 7–11.

8 European Party Systems: Continuity and Change

For further analysis of the general issues examined in this chapter, see H. Kitschelt (1989, 1994). On cleavage structures and party systems, see S. M. Lipset and S. Rokkan (1967), O. Kirchheimer (1966), and S. Bartolini and P. Mair (1990).

9 Organised Interests and the State

A critical appraisal of the role of organised interests at the European level will be found in W. Streeck and P. C. Schmitter (1991). The burgeoning literature on 'Euro-lobbying' includes S. Mazey and J. Richardson (1993); S. S. Andersen and K. A. Eliassen (1993) especially ch. 3; J. Greenwood *et al.* (1992); and J. Greenwood (1995).

10 Capitalism versus Capitalism in Western Europe

For a basic introduction to government–business relations, see G. K. Wilson (1990) and R. Whitley (1993). Also useful are the chapters on France, Germany, Italy and the United Kingdom in D. Dyker (ed.) (1992), and, for pan-European issues, see D. Dyker (ed.) (1992). For the best comparative studies, see J. Zysman (1983) and P. Hall (1986). On innovation systems, see R. Nelson (1993).

Among the best general works on Europe's largest economies, see T. Buxton *et al.*, (1994), H. D. Kurz (ed.) (1993) and E. Owen Smith (1994), P. Lange and M. Regini (eds) (1989), C. Bianchi and C. Casarosa (eds) (1991), and, for an entertaining journalistic account of the Italian system, A. Friedman (1988).

11 Regional Economic Policy and a Europe of the Regions

There is a vast literature on the politics and economics of European regions. For an overview of the issues and studies of both 'strong' and 'weak' regions, see M. Rhodes (ed.) (1995). For further information on innovation and its social context, see C. Freeman (1987) and M. Granovetter (1985). On the Community Support Programmes, see R. Leonardi (ed.) (1993). On relations between the regions of particular member states and the EU, see, for example, S. Mazey (1994); R. Rhodes (1993) and I. Tömmel (1992) and, more generally, B. Jones and M. Keating (eds) (1995). On policy networks, see A. Windhoff-Héritier (1993).

12 Foreign, Defence and Security Policy

On the early British and French nuclear programmes, see M. Gowing (1974) and W. Kohl (1971). On the more recent period see M. Clarke (1993) and S.

Croft (1994). On defence and the EC, see A. Courades Allebeck (1993) and T. Taylor (1994).

13 Environmental Policy and Politics

While the amount of literature on environmental policy and politics has grown substantially in recent years, it can still be difficult to find up-to-date material on certain issues, particularly developments within individual states. However, the OECD's *Environmental Performance Review* series provides extensive factual material as well as analysis. Regional aspects of environmental policy, particularly in Southern and Eastern Europe, can be found in S. Baker *et al.* (1994). For an extensive comparative analysis of changing policy networks in water pollution control, see H. Bressers *et al.* (1995). In addition to analyses of national policy, a number of textbooks on the EU contain chapters on environmental policy, for example, A. Sbragia (1996). For a detailed account of the potential for new instruments in European environmental policy, see G. Huppes *et al.* (1992). On the Green parties of western Europe, see D. Richardson and C. Rootes (1995).

14 Beyond Liberal Politics? European Modernity and the Nation-State

Presentations of the rise of postmodern politics are almost a glut on the market. Among the best general discussions are the books by Z. Bauman (1992a and 1992b) and W. Connolly (1991 and 1995) discussed in the text. Other writers who have worked in a similar vein and on whose excellent work I have drawn for the composite portrait presented here include R. Walker (1992 and 1994), J. Der Derian (1992), C. Mouffe (1992), J. Baudrillard (1988) and J.-F. Lyotard (1984). The writers I (rather shamelessly) lumped together as critical modernists with a shared focus on the fate of democracy include B. Barber (1995), D. Held (1995), and A. Linklater (1996). They by no means agree either with one another or with the 'postmoderns' about all the most salient characteristics of contemporary politics, but they do share a fear as to the likely fate of democracy (see also Wendt (1994) although this is not his central concern). General discussions of what I called the 'micro' level of politics are to be found especially in the work of A. Giddens (1994) but also in the work of U. Beck (1986 and 1988), on whom many 'postmoderns' would also draw. Other interesting treatments of these questions would include those of D. Harvey (1989) and F. Jameson (1989). My own general approach to the question of 'modernity' is sketched in N. J. Rengger (1995). It is applied to liberal politics with regard to the question of world order in N. J. Rengger (1996).

15 The Media and Politics

On media and politics in specific national systems, see R. Negrine (1994) for Britain, R. Kuhn (1995) for France, P. Humphreys (1994) for Germany, and G.

Mazzoleni (1991, 1995) for Italy. Broadcasting changes across Western Europe are well covered in J. Blumler (1992), which considers the impact on the public-service tradition; and K. Siune and W. Truetzschler (1992), which examines the policy context. K. Dyson *et al.* (1988) is a more advanced work on broadcasting and new media policy. For a clear and informative account of the growing policy role of the European Union, see R. Collins (1994).

16   The Integration of Feminism into West European Politics

On feminist politics in particular European countries, see, for example, L. Caldwell (1991); E. Kolinsky (1989); C. Duchen (1986). On comparative issues, overviews can be found in J. Lovenduski (1986), P. Norris (1987), United Nations (1992), and D. Stetson and A. Mazur (1995). For more theoretical approaches, see G. Bock and S. James (1992) and V. Held (1993).

17   New Challenges: Post Materialism and the Extreme Right

For a recent comparison of Green parties, see the collection edited by D. Richardson and C. Rootes (1995). On anti-party politics, see T. Poguntke and S. Scarrow (1996).

Bibliography

Aarts, K. (1995) 'Intermediate Organizations and Interest Representation', in H.-D. Klingemann and D. Fuchs (eds), *Citizens and the State* (Oxford University Press), pp. 227–57.

Aguilar-Fernández, S. (1997) 'Subsidiarity, Shared Responsibility and Environmental Policy in Spain', in U. Collier, J. Golub and A. Kreher (eds) *Subsidiarity and Shared Responsibility: New Challenges for EU Environmental Policy* (Baden-Baden: Nomos).

Aichholzer, G. and G. Schienstock (eds) (1994) *Technology Policy: Towards an Integration of Social and Ecological Concerns* (Berlin: de Gruyter).

Alatas, S. H. (1990) *Corruption: Its Nature, Causes and Functions* (Aldershot: Avebury).

Albert, M. (1993) *Capitalism Against Capitalism* (London: Whurr Publishers).

Alexander, H. E. and R. Shiratori (eds) (1994) *Comparative Political Finance Among the Democracies* (Boulder, Co: Westview Press).

Allum, P. (1995) *State and Society in Western Europe* (Cambridge: Polity Press).

Ambler, J. S. (ed.) (1991) *The French Welfare State: Surviving Social and Ideological Change* (New York and London: New York University Press).

Amin, A. and N. Thrift (eds) (199) *Globalization, Institutions and Regional Development in Europe* (Oxford University Press).

Anderson, J. (1991) 'Skeptical Reflections on a Europe of the Regions', *Journal of Public Policy*, vol. 10, no. 4, pp. 417–47.

Anderson, S. S. and Eliassen, K. A. (1993) *Making Policy in Europe: the Europeification of National Policy-Making* (London: Sage).

Andeweg, R. B. (1991) 'The Dutch Prime Minister: Not Just Chairman, Not Yet Chief?', in G. W. Jones (ed.), *West European Prime Ministers* (London: Frank Cass).

Apeldoorn, B. van (1996) 'The Political Economy of Conflicting Capitalisms in the European Integration Process: A Transnational Perspective', *Research Institute for European Studies*, Research Paper No. 31, Athens.

Armstrong, J. A. (1973) *The European Administrative Elite* (Princeton, NJ: Princeton University Press).

Avril, P. (1994) 'Regulation of Political Finance in France', in H. E. Alexander and R. Shiratori (eds), *Comparative Political Finance Among the Democracies*, (Boulder, Col.: Westview Press) pp. 85–96.

Baier, A. (1993) *Moral Prejudices* (Cambridge, Mass.: Harvard University Press).

Baker, S. *et al.*, (1994) *Protecting the Periphery* (London: Frank Cass).

Barber, B. (1995) *Jihad vs McWorld: How the Planet is both Falling Apart and Coming Together and What This Means for Democracy* (New York: Times Books).

Bartolini, S. and P. Mair (1990) *Identity, Competition, and Electoral Availability: The Stability of European Electorates 1885–1985* (Cambridge University Press).

Baudrillard, J. (1988) *Selected Writings* (ed. M. Poster) (Cambridge: Polity Press).

Baudrillard, J. (1993) *The Transparency of Evil: Essays on Extreme Phenomena* (London: Verso).

Bauman, Z. (1992a) *Postmodern Ethics* (Oxford: Basil Blackwell).

Bauman, Z. (1992b) *Intimations of Postmodernity* (London: Routledge).

Beck, U. (1986) *Risk Society* (Cambridge: Polity Press).

Beck, U. (1988) *Gegengifte: Die Organisierte Unveranvorlichkeit* (Frankfurt: Suhrkamp).

Beck, U., A. Giddens and S. Lash (1994) *Reflexive Modernization* (Cambridge: Polity Press).

Begg, I. (1985) 'Regional Dimension of the "1992" Proposals', *Regional Studies*, pp. 386–375.

Begg, I. and D. Mayes (1993) 'Cohesion, Convergence and Economic and Monetary Union in Europe', *Regional Studies*, vol. 27, no. 2, pp. 149–65.

Bennett, G. (1991) *Air Pollution Control in the European Community: Implementation of the EC Directives in the Twelve Member States* (London: Graham & Trotman).

Bennulf, M. (1995) 'The 1994 Election in Sweden: Green or Grey', *Environmental Politics*, vol. 4, no. 1, pp. 114–19.

Betz, H.-G. (1994) *Radical Right-Wing Populism in Western Europe* (New York: St Martin's Press).

Bianchi, C. and C. Casarosa (eds) (1991) *The Recent Performance of the Italian Economy: Market Outcomes and State Policy* (Milan: Franco Angeli).

Bianco, M. and S. Trento (1995) 'Capitalismi a confronto: I modelli di controllo delle imprese', *Stato e Mercato*, 43, April, pp. 65–93.

Björgo, T. (1995) *Terror from the Extreme Right* (London: Frank Cass).

Blankenberg, E., R. Staudhammer and H. Steinert (1989) 'Political Scandals and Corruption Issues in West Germany', in A. J. Heidenheimer, M. Johnston and V. T. LeVine (eds), *Political Corruption: A Handbook* (New Brunswick, NJ: Transaction Publishers) pp. 913–32.

Blondel, J. (1992) 'Executives', in M. Hawkesworth and M. Kogan (eds), *Encyclopedia of Government and Politics* (London: Routledge).

Blondel, J. and F. Müller-Rommel (eds) (1988). *Cabinets in Western Europe* (London: Macmillan).

Blondel, J. and F. Müller-Rommel (eds) (1993) *Governing Together: The Extent and Limits of Joint Decision-Making in West European Cabinets* (London: Macmillan).

Blumler, J. G. (ed.) (1992) *Television and the Public Interest* (London: Sage).

Bock, G. and S. James (eds) (1992) *Beyond Equality and Difference: Citizenship, Feminist Politics and Female Subjectivity* (London: Routledge).

Boehmer-Christiansen, S. and J. Skea (1991) *Acid Politics* (London: Belhaven).

Bogdanor, V. (1992) *Proportional Representation: Which System?* (London: Electoral Reform Society).

Boltho, A. (ed.) (1982) *The European Economy* (Oxford University Press).

Borras Alomar, S. *et al.* (1994) 'Towards the "Europe of the Regions"? Evaluation and Reflection from a Critical Perspective', *Regional Politics and Policy*, vol. 3, no. 3, pp. 1–27.

Borras Alomar, S. (1995) 'Inter-regional Cooperation in Europe During the 1980s and 1990s', in N. A. Soerensen (ed.), *European Identities* (Odense: Odense UP).

Bowler, S. and D. M. Farrell (1993) 'Legislator Shirking and Voter Monitoring: Impacts of European Parliament Electoral Systems Upon Legislator–Voter Relationships', *Journal of Common Market Studies*, vol. 31, no. 1, pp. 45–69.

Brand, K. W. (1990) 'Cyclical Aspects of New Social Movements: Waves of Cultural Criticism and Mobilization Cycles of New Middle-class Radicalism', in R. Dalton and M. Kuechler (eds), *Challenging the Political Order* (Cambridge: Polity Press), pp. 23–42.

Brants, K. (1985) 'Broadcasting and Politics in the Netherlands: From Pillar to Post', in R. Kuhn (ed.), *Broadcasting and Politics in Western Europe* (London: Frank Cass).

Brenton, T. (1994) *The Greening of Machiavelli* (London: Earthscan).

Bressers, H. *et al.*, (1995) *Networks for Water Policy* (London: Frank Cass).

Buitendijk, G. J. and M. Van Schendelen (1995) 'Brussels Advisory Committees: A Channel for Influence?', *European Law Review*, pp. 37–56.

Burley, A.-M., and W. Mattli (1993) 'Europe before the Court: A Political Theory of Legal Integration', *International Organization*, vol. 47, no. 41–76.

Bussemaker, J. and K. van Kersbergen (1994) 'Gender and Welfare States: Some Theoretical Reflections', in D. Sainsbury, *Gendering Welfare States* (London: Sage), pp. 8–25.

Buxton, T. *et al.* (1994) *Britain's Economic Performance* (London and New York: Routledge).

Caiden, G. E. (1991) *Administrative Reform Comes of Age* (Berlin: de Gruyter).

Caldwell, L. (1991) *Italian Family Matters: Women Politics and Legal Reform* (London: Macmillan).

Carl Kester, C. (1992) 'Industrial Groups as Systems of Contractual Governance', *Oxford Review of Economic Policy*, 8, 3, pp. 24–44.

Carstairs, A. M. (1980) *A Short History of Electoral Systems* (London: George Allen & Unwin).

Cartier-Bresson, J. (1995) 'L'économie de la corruption', in D. Della Porta and Y. Mény (eds), *Corruption et démocracie en Europe* (Paris: La Découverte).

Cawson, A. (1994) 'Sectoral Governance in Consumer Electronics in Britain and France', in J. R. Hollingsworth, P. C. Schmitter and W. Streeck (eds), *Governing Capitalist Economies: Performance and Control of Economic Sectors* (New York: Oxford University Press).

Cayrol, R. (1995) 'L'univers socio-politique des électeurs européens', in P. Perrineau and C. Ysmal (eds), *Le vote des douze* (Paris: Département d'Etudes Politiques du Figaro et Presses de la FNSP) pp. 181–201.

Cerny, P. G. (1993) 'The Deregulation and Re-regulation of Financial Markets in a More Open World', in P. G. Cerny (ed.), *Finance and World Politics: Markets, Regimes and States in the Post-hegemonic Era* (Aldershot: Edward Elgar) pp. 51–85.

Cerny, P. G. (1995), 'Globalization and the Changing Logic of Collective Action', *International Organization*, vol. 49, no. 4, pp. 595–625.

Chassard, Y. and O. Quintin (1992) 'Social Protection in the European Community: Towards a Convergence of Policies', *International Social Security Review*, 45, 1–2, pp. 91–108.

Chesnais, F. (1993) 'The French National System of Innovation', in R. Nelson (ed.), *National Innovation Systems: A Comparative Analysis* (Oxford: Oxford University Press), pp. 192–229.

Christiansen, T. (1996a) 'Reconstructing Space: From Territorial Politics to European Multilevel Governance', in K. E. Joergensen (ed.), *Reflective Approaches to European Governance* (London: Macmillan).

Christiansen, T. (1996b) 'Second Thoughts on Europe's Third Level: The European Union's Committee of the Regions', *Publius Journal of Federalism*, vol. 26, no. 2.

Christy, C. A. (1994) 'Trends in Sex Differences in Political Participation', in M. Githens, P. Norris and J. Lovenduski (eds), *Different Roles, Different Voices: Women and Politics in the United States and Europe* (New York: HarperCollins).

Ciaurro, G. F. (1989) 'Public Financing of Parties in Italy', in H. E. Alexander (ed.), *Comparative Political Finance in the 1980s* (Cambridge University Press) pp. 153–71.

Claisse, A. and Meininger, M.-C. (1994) *Fonctions publiques en Europe* (Paris: Montchrestien).

Clark, S. (1989) *Civil Peace and Sacred Order* (Oxford: Clarendon Press).

Clarke, M. (1993) 'British and French Nuclear Forces after the Cold War', *Arms Control*, vol. 14, no. 1, April.

Clasen, J. and R. Freeman (eds) (1994) *Social Policy in Germany* (Hemel Hempstead: Harvester).

Cochrane, A. and J. Clarke (1993) *Comparing Welfare States: Britain in International Context* (London: Sage Publications).

Cohen, B. (1994) 'Beyond EMU: The Problem of Sustainability', in B. Eichengreen and J. Frieden (eds), *The Political Economy of European Monetary Unification* (Boulder, Col.: Westview Press).

Cohen, J. and A. Arato (1992) *Civil Society and Political Theory* (Cambridge, Mass.: MIT Press).

Cole, A. and P. Campbell (1989) *French Electoral Systems and Elections since 1789* (Aldershot: Gower).

Collier, U. (1996a) *Energy and Environment in the European Union* (Aldershot: Avebury).

Collier, U. (1996b) 'The European Union's Climate Change Policy: Limiting Emissions or Limiting Powers', *Journal of European Public Policy*, vol. 3, no. 1, pp. 122–38.

Collins, R. (1993) *Audiovisual and Broadcasting Policy in the European Community* (London: University of North London Press).

Collins, R. (1994) *Broadcasting and Audio-Visual Policy in the European Single Market* (London: John Libbey).

Commission of the European Communities (1992) *Pluralism and Media Concentration in the Internal Market – An Assessment of the Need for Community Action*, COM 92 480 final (Brussels: European Commission).

Commission of the European Communities (1994) *Follow-up to the Consultation Process Relating to the Green Paper on 'Pluralism and Media Concen-*

tration in the Internal Market – an Assessment of the Need for Community Action', COM 94 353 final (Brussels: European Commission).

Commission of the European Communities (DGV) (1995) *Social Protection in Europe 1995* (Brussels: European Commission).

Connolly, W. E. (1991) *Identity/Difference: Democratic Negotiations of Political Paradox* (Ithaca, NY: Cornell University Press).

Connolly, W. E. (1995) *The Ethos of Pluralization* (Minneapolis, Minn.: University of Minnesota Press).

Cooke, P. (1992) 'Regional Innovation Systems: Competitive Regulation in the New Europe', *Geoforum*, vol. 23, no. 3, pp. 365–82.

Cooke, P. (ed.) (1995) *The Rise of the Rustbelt* (London: UCL Press).

Cooke, P. (1996) 'The Co-operative Advantage of Regions', in T. Barnes and M. Gertler (eds), *Regions, Institutions and Technology* (London: Routledge).

Cooke, P. (1996a) 'Institutional Reflexivity and the Rise of the Region State', in G. Benko and U. Strohmeyer (eds), *Space and Social Theory* (Oxford: Basil Blackwell).

Cooke, P. (1996b) 'Policy Networks, Innovation Networks and Regional Policy', in H. Heinelt and R. Smith (eds) *Policy Networks and the European Structural Funds* (Bristol: SAUS Press).

Cooke, P. and K. Morgan (1994a) 'The Regional Innovation System of Baden-Württemberg', *International Journal of Technology Management*, vol. 9, pp. 394–429.

Cooke, P. and K. Morgan (1994b) 'Growth Regions Under Duress: Renewal Strategies in Baden-Württemberg and Emilia-Romagna', in A. Amin and N. Thrift (eds), *Globalization, Institutions and Regional Development* (Oxford University Press).

Courades Allebeck, A. (1993) 'The European Community: From the EC to the European Union' in H. Wulf (ed.), *Arms Industry Limited* (Oxford: Oxford University Press, for SIPRI).

Cowles, M. G. (1995a) 'Setting the Agenda for a New Europe: the ERT and EC 1992', *Journal of Common Market Studies*, vol. 33, no. 4, pp. 501–526.

Cowles, M. G. (1995b) 'The European Round Table of Industrialists: The Strategic Player in European Affairs', in J. Greenwood (ed.), *European Casebook on Business Alliances* (Hemel Hempstead: Prentice Hall).

Cox, R. H. (1993) *The Development of the Dutch Welfare State: From Workers' Insurance to Universal Entitlement* (Pittsburgh and London: Pittsburgh University Press).

Cram, L. (1994) 'The European Commission as a Multiorganization: Social Policy and IT Policy in the EU', *Journal of European Public Policy*, vol. 1, pp. 195–217.

Crewe, I. (1985) 'MPs and Their Constituents in Britain: How Strong Are the Links?', in V. Bogdanor (ed.), *Representatives of the People? Parliamentarians and Constituents in Western Democracies* (Aldershot: Gower) pp. 44–65.

Croft, S. (1994) 'Continuity and Change in British Thinking about Nuclear Weapons, *Political Studies*, vol. 42, no. 2.

Crouch, C. (1993) *Industrial Relations and European State Traditions* (Oxford University Press).

Crozier, M., S. P. Huntington and J. Watanuki (1975) *The Crisis of Democracy* (New York: New York University Press).

d'Auria, G. (1987) 'L'administration italienne et l'intégration européenne', in C. Debbasch (ed.), *Administrations nationales et intégration européenne* (Paris: Editions du CNRS), pp. 70–84.

Dahlerup, D. (1986) *The New Women's Movement: Feminism and Political Power in Europe and the USA* (London: Sage).

Dahlerup, D. (1988) 'From a Small to a Large Minority: Women in Scandinavian Politics', *Scandinavian Political Studies*, vol. 11, no. 4.

Dalton, R. J. (1994) *The Green Rainbow* (New Haven, Conn. and London: Yale University Press).

Davernhas, O. (1986) *Droits des hommes, pouvoir des femmes* (Paris: Le Seuil).

Davison, L., E. Fitzpatrick and D. Johnson (eds) (1995) *The European Competitive Environment* (Oxford: Butterworth-Heinemann).

De Grauwe, P. (1994) 'Towards European Monetary Union without the EMS', *Economic Policy*, vol. 18, April.

De Jong, H. W. (1995) 'European Capitalism: Between Freedom and Social Justice', *Review of Industrial Organization*, 10, pp. 399–419,

Dehousse, R. (1989) '1992 and Beyond: The Institutional Dimension of the Internal Market Programme', *Legal Issues of European Integration*, vol. 1, pp. 109–36.

Dehousse, R. (1992) 'Integration v. Regulation? On the Dynamics of Regulation in the European Community', *Journal of Common Market Studies*, vol. 30, pp. 383–402.

Dehousse, R. (1994) *La Cour de Justice des Communautés européennes* (Paris: Montchrestien).

Dehousse, R. (1995) 'Constitutional Reform in the European Community: Are There Alternatives to the Majority Avenue?', *West European Politics*, vol. 18, no. 3, pp. 118–36.

Dehousse, R. and G. Majone (1994) 'The Institutional Dynamics of European Integration: From the Single Act to the Maastricht Treaty', in S. Martin (ed.), *The Construction of Europe – Essays in Honour of Emile Noel* (Dordrecht/Boston/London: Kluwer) pp. 91–112.

Dehousse, R., C. Joerges, G. Majone, F. Snyder, with M. Everson (1992) *Europe after 1992: New Regulatory Strategies*, No. 92/31 (Florence: European University Institute). Working Paper LAW.

del Castillo, P. (1994) 'Problems in Spanish Party Financing', in H. E. Alexander and R. Shiratori (eds), *Comparative Political Finance Among the Democracies* (Boulder, Col.: Westview Press) pp. 97–104.

Della Porta, D. (1992) *Lo Scambio occulto: Casi di corruzione politica in Italia* (Bologna: Il Mulino).

Della Porta, D. (1996) 'The System of Corrupt Exchange in Local Government', in S. Gundle and S. Parker, *The New Italian Republic* (London: Routledge), pp. 221–33.

Della Porta, D. and Y. Mény (eds) (1995) *Corruption et démocracie en Europe* (Paris: la Découverte).

Della Porta, D. and A. Vanucci (1995) *Corruzione politica e amministrazione pubblica: Risorse, meccanismi, attori* (Bologna: Il Mulino).

Delors, J. (1992) *Our Europe* (London: Verso).

den Boer, M. and N. Walker (1993) 'European Policing after 1992', *Journal of Common Market Studies*, vol. 31, no. 1, pp. 3–28.

Department of National Heritage (1995) *Media Ownership: The Government's Proposals*, Cm 2872 (London: HMSO).

Der Derian, J. (1992) *Anti-Diplomacy* (Oxford: Basil Blackwell).

Dimitras, P. E. (1994) 'Electoral Systems in Greece', in S. Nagel and V. Rukavishnikov (eds), *Eastern Europe Development and Public Policy* (London: Macmillan) pp. 143–75.

Doig, A. (1996) 'Politics and Public Sector Ethics: The Impact of Change in the United Kingdom', in W. Little and E. Posada-Carbó, *Political Corruption in Europe and Latin America* (London: Macmillan) pp. 173–92.

Dosi, G. (1992) 'Technological Paradigms and Technological Trajectories', *Research Policy*, vol. 11, pp. 147–62.

Dowding, K. (1995) 'Model or Metaphor? A Critical Review of the Policy Network Approach', *Political Studies*, vol. 43, no. 1.

Downs, A. (1957) *An Economic Theory of Democracy* (New York: Harper & Row).

Drysch, T. (1993) 'The New French System of Political Finance', in A. B. Gunlicks (ed.), *Campaign and Party Finance in North America and Western Europe* (Boulder, Co.: Westview Press) pp. 155–77.

Dubrulle, M. (ed.) (1994) *Future European Environmental Policy and Subsidiarity* (Brussels: European Interuniversity Press).

Duchen, C. (1986) *Feminism in France: from May '68 to Mitterrand* (London: Routledge & Kegan Paul).

Due, J. *et al.* (1994) *The Survival of the Danish Model* (Copenhagen: Jõ Forlag).

Dunleavy, P. (1991) *Democracy, Bureaucracy and Public Choice* (London: Harvester Wheatsheaf).

Dunleavy, P. and B. O'Leary (1987) *Theories of the State: The Politics of Liberal Democracy* (London: Macmillan).

Dunn, J. (1992) *Interpreting Political Responsibility* (Cambridge University Press).

Dyker, D. (ed.) (1992) *The European Economy* (London and New York: Longman).

Dyker, D. (ed.) (1992) *The National Economies of Europe* (London and New York: Longman).

Dyson, K. (1990) 'Luxembourg: Changing Anatomy of an International Broadcasting Power', in K. Dyson and P. Humphries (eds), *The Political Economy of Communications* (London: Routledge).

Dyson, K. (1994) *Elusive Union: The Process of Economic and Monetary Union in Europe*, (London: Routledge).

Dyson, K. and P. Humphreys with R. Negrine and J.-P. Simon (1988) *Broadcasting and New Media Policies in Western Europe* (London: Routledge).

Dyson, K., K. Featherstone and G. Michalopoulos (1995) 'Strapped to the Mast: EC Central Bankers between Global Financial Markets and Regional Integration', *Journal of European Public Policy*, vol. 2, no. 3, 465–87.

Eatwell, R. (1989) 'Right or Rights? The Rise of the "New Right"', in R. Eatwell and N. O'Sullivan (eds), *The Nature of the Right* (London: Pinter) pp. 3–15.

Eichener, V. (1992) *Social Dumping or Innovative Regulation?* Working Paper SPS No. 92/28. (Florence: European University Institute).

Elgie, R. (1995) *Political Leadership in Liberal Democracies* (London: Macmillan).

Eliassen, K. A. and Kooiman, J. (eds) (1993) *Managing Public Organizations: Lessons from Contemporary European Experience* (London: Sage).

Emerson, M. (ed.) (1992) *One Market, One Money: An Evaluation of the Potential Benefits and Costs of Forming an Economic and Monetary Union* (Oxford University Press).

Emerson, M. and C. Huhne (1991) *The ECU Report* (London: Pan).

Esping-Andersen, G. (1990) *The Three Worlds of Welfare Capitalism* (Princeton, NJ: Princeton University Press).

Esping-Andersen, G. (1996a) 'After the Golden Age? Welfare State Dilemmas in a Global Economy', in G. Esping-Andersen (ed.), *Welfare States in Transition: National Adaptations in Global Economies* (London: Sage), pp. 1–31.

Esping-Andersen, G. (1996b), 'Welfare States without Work: the Impasse of Labour Shedding and Familialism in Continental European Social Policy' in G. Esping-Andersen (ed.), *Welfare States in Transition: National Adaptations in Global Economies*, (London: Sage), pp. 66–87.

European Commission (1992) 'Recherche sur l'exercice du droit d'initiative de la Commission', SEC (92) 1879, 8 October.

European Commission (1993) *Community Structural Funds 1994–99* (Luxembourg: European Commission).

European Commission (1994a) *Guide to Community Initiatives 1994–1999* (Brussels: European Commission).

European Commission (1994b) *Interregional and Cross-border Cooperation in Europe* (Brussels: European Commission).

European Commission (1995).

Fallon, M. and F. Maniet (1990) *Product Safety and Control Processes in the European Community* (Brussels: Story-Scientia).

Ferrera, M. (1994) 'European Social Policy: Towards Convergence?', *Il Politico*, 59, 3, pp. 525–537.

Ferrera, M. (1996) 'The 'Southern Model' of Welfare in Social Europe', *Journal of European Social Policy*, 6, 1, pp. 17–37.

Ferrera, M. (1997), 'The Four Social Europes: Between Universalism and Selectivity', in Y. Mény and M. Rhodes (eds), *A New Social Contract? Charting the Future of European Welfare* (London: Macmillan, forthcoming).

Finer, S. E. (1975), 'Adversary Politics and Electoral Reform', in S. E. Finer (ed.), *Adversary Politics and Electoral Reform* (London: Anthony Wigram) pp. 3–32.

Flanagan, S. C. (1987) 'Value Change in Industrial Society', *American Political Science Review*, vol. 81, pp. 1303–19.

Flickinger, R. S. and D. T. Studlar (1992) 'The Disappearing Voters? Declining Turnout in Western European Elections', *West European Politics*, vol. 15, no. 2, pp. 1–16.

Flora, P. (1986) *Growth to Limits: the Western European Welfare States since World War II* (Berlin: de Gruyter).

Frears, J. (1988) 'Not Sex, the Abuse of Power: Political Scandal in France', *Corruption and Reform*, vol. 3, pp. 307–22.

Freedman, L. (1980) *Britain and Nuclear Weapons* (London: Macmillan).

Freeman, C. (1987) *Technology Policy and Economic Performance – Lessons from Japan* (London: Pinter).

Freeman, C. and L. Soete (1995) *Work for All or Mass Unemployment: Computerised Technical Change in the 21st Century* (London: Pinter).

Frieden, J. A. (1991) 'Invested Interests: the Politics of National Economic Policies in a World of Global Finance', *International Organization*, vol. 45, no. 4, pp. 539–564.

Friedman, A. (1988) *Agnelli and the Network of Italian Power* (London: Harrap).

Frognier, A.- P. (1986) 'Corruption and Consociational Democracy', *Corruption and Reform*, vol. 1, pp. 143–8.

Fromont, M. and H. Siedentopf (1987), 'L'administration de la République fédérale d'Allemagne et l'intégration européenne', in Charles Debbasch (ed.), *Administrations nationales et intégration européenne* (Paris: Editions du CNRS), pp. 15–28.

Fuchs, D., G. Guidrossi and P. Svensson (1995) 'Support for the Democratic System', in H.- D. Klingemann and D. Fuchs (eds) *Citizens and the State* (Oxford University Press) pp. 323–53.

Fukuyama, F. (1992) *The End of History and The Last Man* (London: Hamish Hamilton).

Fukuyama, F. (1995) *Trust: The Social Virtues and the Creation of Prosperity* (London: Hamish Hamilton).

Gallagher, M. (1991) 'Proportionality, Disproportionality and Electoral Systems', *Electoral Studies*, vol. 10, no. 1, pp. 33–51.

Gallagher, M., M. Laver and P. Mair (1995) *Representative Government in Modern Europe* (New York and London: McGraw-Hill).

Garcia, A. (1991) *Sexual Violence Against Women: Contribution to a Strategy for Countering the Various Forms of Such Violence in the Council of Europe Member States* (Strasbourg: Council of Europe).

Garitaonandia, C. (1993) 'Regional Television in Europe', in *European Journal of Communication*, vol. 8, no. 3, pp. 277–94.

Garrett, G. (1992) 'International Cooperation and Institutional Choice: The European Community's Internal Market', *International Organization*, vol. 41, pp. 533–560.

George, S. (1991) *Politics and Policy in the European Community* (Oxford: Clarendon Press).

George, V. and P. Taylor-Gooby (eds) (1996) *European Welfare Policy: Squaring the Circle* (London: Macmillan).

Giddens, A. (1991) *Modernity and Self Identity* (Cambridge: Polity Press).

Giddens, A. (1994) *Beyond Left and Right* (Cambridge: Polity Press).

Gilbert, N. (1992) 'From Entitlements to Incentives: The Changing Philosophy of Social Protection', *International Social Security Review*, vol. 45, no. 3, pp. 5–17.

Gillespie, R. (1993) ' "Programa 2000": The Appearance and Reality of Socialist Renewal in Spain', *West European Politics*, vol. 16, no. 1, pp. 78–96.

Girvin, B. (ed.) (1988) *The Transformation of Contemporary Conservatism* (Beverly Hills: Sage).

Glees, A. (1988) 'Political Scandals in West Germany', *Corruption and Reform*, vol. 3, pp. 261–76.

Gold, M. (ed.) (1993) *The Social Dimension: Employment Policy in the European Community* (London: Macmillan).

Golub, J. (1996a) 'British Sovereignty and the Development of EC Environmental Policy', *Environmental Politics*, vol. 6, no. 4.

Golub, J. (1996b) 'State Power and Institutional Influence: Lessons from the Packaging Waste Directive', *Journal of Common Market Studies*, vol. 34, no. 3.

Golub, J. (1996c) 'Sovereignty and Subsidiarity in EU Environmental Policy', *Political Studies*, vol. 44, no. 4.

Gonzalez Sanchez, E. (1992), 'La négociation des décisions communautaires par les fonctionnaires nationaux: les groupes du travail du Conseil', *Revue française d'administration publique*, vol. 63, pp. 391–9.

Goodhart, C. (1995) 'EMU: A Future that Works?', *Prospect*, December, pp. 70–4.

Gottschalk, P. and M. Joyce (1995) 'The Impact of Technological Change, Deindustrialization and Internationalization of Trade on Earnings Inequality: An International Perspective', in K. McFate, R. Lawson and W. J. Wilson (eds), *Poverty, Inequality and the Future of Social Policy: Western States in the New World Order* (New York: Russell Sage Foundation) pp. 197–228.

Gough, I. (1979) *The Political Economy of the Welfare State* (London: Macmillan).

Gough, I. (1996) 'Social Assistance In Southern Europe', *South European Society and Politics*, vol. 1, no. 1, pp. 1–23.

Gowing, M. (1974) *Independence and Deterrence: Britain and Atomic Energy, 1945–52* (London: Macmillan).

Grabher, G. (ed.) (1993) *The Embedded Firm: On the Socio-Economics of Industrial Networks*, (London: Routledge).

Grahl, J. and P. Teague (1990) *1992 – The Big Market: The Future of the European Community* (London: Lawrence & Wishart).

Granovetter, M. (1985) 'Economic Action and Social Structure: the Problem of Embeddedness', *American Journal of Sociology*, vol. 91, pp. 481–510.

Grant, W., W. Paterson and C. Whitson (1988). *Government and the Chemical Industry* (Oxford: Clarendon Press).

Greenwood, J., J. Grote and K. Ronit (1992) *Organized Interests and the European Community* (London: Sage).

Greenwood, J. and K. Ronit (1994) 'Interest Groups in the European Community: Newly Emerging Dynamics and Forms', *West European Politics*, vol. 17, no. 1, pp. 31–52.

Guadagnini, M. (1995) 'The Latecomers: Italy's Equal Status and Equal Opportunity Agencies', in D. McBride Stetson and A. Mazur (eds), *Comparative State Feminism* (London: Sage).

Gunlicks, A. B. (ed.) (1993) *Campaign and Party Finance in North America and Western Europe* (Boulder, Co.: Westview Press).

Haas, P., R. Keohane and M. Levy (eds) (1994) *Institutions for the Earth* (Cambridge: MIT Press).

Haigh, N. (1992) *Manual of Environmental Policy: The EC and Britain* (London: Longman).

Haigh, N. *et al.* (1986) *Comparative Report: Water and Waste in Four Countries* (London: Graham & Trotman).

Hall, P. (1986) *Governing the Economy: The Politics of State Intervention in Britain and France* (Cambridge: Polity Press).

Hall, P. A. (1994) 'The Comparative Political Economy of Europe in an Era of Interdependence', Paper presented at conference on 'The Politics and Political Economy of Contemporary Capitalism', University of North Carolina, Chapel Hill, NC, 9–11 September.

Hansen, A. (1993) 'Greenpeace and Press Coverage of Environmental Issues', in A. Hansen (ed.), *The Mass Media and Environmental Issues* (Leicester: Leicester University Press).

Hantrais, L. (1995) *Social Policy in the European Union* (London: Macmillan).

Harmel, R. and J. D. Robertson (1985) 'Formation and Success of New Parties: A Cross-National Analysis', *International Political Science Review*, vol. 6, no. 4, pp. 501–23.

Harmel, R. H. and Gibson, R. K. (1995) 'Right-Libertarian Parties and "New Values": A Re-examination', *Scandinavian Political Studies* , vol. 18, pp. 97–118.

Harmel, R. H. and J. D. Robertson (1985) 'Formation and Success of New Parties: A Cross-Analysis Survey', *International Political Science Review*, vol. 6, pp. 101–24.

Harvey, D. (1989) *The Condition of Postmodernity* (Oxford: Basil Blackwell).

Hayward, J. (1995) 'Organized Interests and Public Policies', in J. Hayward and E. C. Page (eds) *Governing the New Europe* (Oxford: Polity Press).

Heidenheimer, A. J. (1989) 'Perspectives on the Perception of Corruption', in A. J. Heidenheimer, M. Johnston and V. T. LeVine (eds), *Political Corruption: A Handbook* (New Brunswick, NJ: Transaction Publishers) pp. 149–64.

Heidenheimer, A. J. (1996) 'The Topography of European Scandals and Corruption', *International Social Science Journal*, vol. 149, September.

Heidenheimer, A. J., M. Johnston and V. T. LeVine (eds) (1989) *Political Corruption: A Handbook* (New Brunswick, NJ: Transaction Purblishers).

Heijden, H. *et al.* (1992) 'The West European Environmental Movement', *Research in Social Movements, Conflicts and Change* Supplement 2, pp. 1–40.

Held, D. (1991) 'Democracy, the Nation-State and the Global System', *Economy and Society*, vol. 20, no. 2, pp. 138–72.

Held, D. (1995) *Democracy and the Global Order* (Cambridge: Polity Press).

Held, D. and D. Archibugi (eds) (1994) *Cosmopolitan Democracy* (Cambridge: Polity Press).

Held, V. (1993) *Feminist Morality: Transforming Culture, Society and Politics* (Chicago: University of Chicago Press).

Heywood, P. (1993) 'Rethinking Socialism in Spain: *Programa 2000* and the social state', *Coexistence*, 30, pp. 167–85.

Heywood, P. (1995) *The Government and Politics of Spain* (London: Macmillan).

Heywood, P. (1996) 'Continuity and Change: Analysing Political Corruption in Modern Spain', in W. Little and E. Posada-Carbó, *Political Corruption in Europe and Latin America* (London: Macmillan) pp. 115–36.

Hildebrand, P. (1993) 'The European Community's Environmental Policy, 1957 to 1991: From Incidental Measures to an International Regime?', in D. Judge (ed.), *A Green Dimension for the European Community: Political Issues and Processes* (London: Frank Cass).

Hine, D. (1996) 'Political Corruption in Italy', in W. Little and E. Posada-Carbó, *Political Corruption in Europe and Latin America* (London: Macmillan) pp. 137–58.

Hine, D. and R. Finocchi (1991) 'The Italian Prime Minister', in G. W. Jones (ed.), *West European Prime Ministers* (London: Frank Cass).

Hine, D., H. Kassim and A. Menon (1996) *Beyond the Market? The Impact of the European Union on National Social, Environmental and Consumer Protection Policies* (London: Routledge).

Hirst, P. (1994) *Associative Democracy: New Forms of Economic and Social Governance* (Amherst, Mass.: University of Massachusetts Press).

Hirst, P. and G. Thompson (1995) 'Globalization and the Future of the Nation State', *Economy and Society*, vol. 24, no. 3, pp. 408–42.

Hodges, M. and S. Woolcock (1993) 'Atlantic Capitalism versus Rhine Capitalism in the European Community', *West European Politics*, vol. 16, no. 3, pp. 329–344.

Hoetjes, B. J. S. (1986) 'Administrative Corruption in the Netherlands: Recent Cases and Recent Developments', *Corruption and Reform*, vol. 1, pp. 133–41.

Hoffmann, S. (1966) 'Obstinate or Obsolete: The Fate of the Nation State and the Case of Western Europe', *Daedalus*, vol. 5, pp. 892–908.

Hofrichter, J. and K. Reif (1990) 'Evolution of Environmental Attitudes in the European Community', *Scandinavian Political Studies*, vol. 13, pp. 119–46.

Holman, O. (1992) 'Transnational Class Strategy and the New Europe', *International Journal of Political Economy*, 22, 1, pp. 3–22.

Holtz-Bacha, C. (1991) 'From Public Monopoly to a Dual Broadcasting System in Germany', *European Journal of Communication*, vol. 6, no. 2, pp. 223–33.

Humphreys, P. (1994) *Media and Media Policy in Germany* (Oxford: Berg).

Huntington, S. (1993) 'The Clash of Civilisations', *Foreign Affairs*, Summer.

Huppes, G. et al., (1992) *New Market-Oriented Instruments for Environmental Policies* (London: Graham & Trotman).

Hussey, G. (1995) *Ireland Today* (Harmondsworth: Penguin).

Hutton, W. (1995) *The State We're In* (London: Jonathan Cape).

Ignazi, P. (1989) 'Un nouvel acteur politique', in N. Mayer and P. Perrineau (eds), *Le Front National à Découvert* (Paris: Presses de la Fondation Nationale des Sciences Politiques) pp. 63–81.

Ignazi, P. (1992) 'The Silent Counter-Revolution. Hypotheses on the Emergence of Extreme Right-Wing Parties', *European Journal of Political Research*, vol. 22, pp. 3–34.

Ignazi, P. (1994) *L'estrema destra in Europa* (Bologna: Il Mulino).

Inglehart, R. (1977) *The Silent Revolution* (Princeton, NJ: Princeton University Press).

Inglehart, R. (1985) 'New Perspectives on Value Change', *Comparative Political Studies*, vol. 17, pp. 485–532.

International Institute of Administrative Sciences (1992) *Public Administration in the Nineties: Trends and Innovations* (Brussels: IIAS).

International Institute of Communications (1996) *Media Ownership and Control in the Age of Convergence* (London: International Institute of Communications).

International Institute for Strategic Studies (1995) *Military Balance 1995–96* (London: IISS).

Irwin, G. (1995) 'Second-Order or Third-Rate? Issues in The Campaign for the Elections for the European Parliament 1994', *Electoral Studies* vol. 14, no. 2, pp. 183–99.

Jameson, F. (1989) *Postmodernism, or the Cultural Logic of Late Capitalism* (London: Verso).

Johnson, B. (1992) 'Institutional Learning', in B. Lundvall (ed.), *National Systems of Innovation: Towards a Theory of Innovaion and Interactive Learning* (London: Pinter).

Johnson, C. and S. Collignon (eds) (1994) *The Monetary Economics of Europe* (London: Pinter).

Johnston, R. J. and C. J. Pattie (1993) 'Great Britain: Twentieth Century Parties Operating under Nineteenth Century Regulations', in A. B. Gunlicks (ed.), *Campaign and Party Finance in North America and Western Europe* (Boulder, Col.: Westview Press) pp. 123–54.

Jones, B. and M. Keating (eds) (1995) The *European Union and the Regions* (Oxford: Clarendon Press).

Jones, C. (1996) 'Aerospace', in H. Kassim and A. Menon (eds), *The European Union and National Industrial Policy* (London: Routledge).

Jones, G. W. (1991) 'West European Prime Ministers in Perspective', in G. W. Jones (ed.), *West European Prime Ministers* (London: Frank Cass).

Jones, N. (1995) *Soundbites & Spin Doctors* (London: Cassell).

Judge, D. (1993) 'Predestined to Save the Earth: The Environment Committee of the European Parliament', in D. Judge (ed.), *A Green Dimension for the European Community: Political Issues and Processes* (London: Frank Cass).

Kaplan, G. (1992) *Contemporary Western European Feminism* (London: UCL Press).

Kapstein, E. B. (1994) *Governing the Global Economy: International Finance and the State* (Cambridge, Mass.: Harvard University Press).

Kassim, H. (1994) 'Policy Networks and European Union Policy Making: A Sceptical View', *West European Politics*, vol. 17, no. 4, pp. 15–27.

Katrougalos, G. S. (1996) 'The South European Welfare Model: The Greek Welfare State in Search of an Identity', *Journal of European Social Policy*, pp. 39–60.

Katz, R. S. (1990) 'Party as Linkage: a Vestigial Function?', *European Journal of Political Research*, vol. 18, no. 1, pp. 143–61.

Katz, R. S. (1996) 'Electoral Reform and the Transformation of Party Politics in Italy', *Party Politics*, 2, 1, pp. 31–53.

Katz, R. S. and P. Mair (1992) 'The Membership of Political Parties in European Democracies, 1960–1990', *European Journal of Political Research*, vol. 22, no. 3, pp. 329–45.

Keating, M. (1993) *The Politics of Modern Europe* (Aldershot: Elgar).

Keck, O. (1993) 'The National System for Technical Innovation in Germany', in R. Nelson (ed.), *National Innovation Systems: A Comparative Analysis* (Oxford: Oxford University Press), pp. 115–157.

Keeler, J. T. S. (1987) *The Politics of Neo-Corporatism in France: Farmers, the State, and Agriculture* (Oxford University Press).

Keohane, R. and J. Nye (1971), 'Transnational Relations and World Politics: A Conclusion', *International Organization*, vol. 25, pp. 721–48.

King, A. (1991) 'The British Prime Ministership in the Age of the Career Politician', in G.W. Jones (ed.), *West European Prime Ministers* (London: Frank Cass).

King, A. (1994) 'Chief Executives in Western Europe', in I. Budge and D. McKay (eds), *Developing Democracy* (London: Sage).

Kirchheimer, O. (1966) 'The Transformation of the Western European Party Systems', in J. LaPalombara and M. Weiner (eds), *Political Parties and Political Development* (Princeton, NJ: Princeton University Press) pp. 177–200.

Kitschelt, H. (1986) 'Political Opportunity Structures and Political Protest', *British Journal of Political Science*, vol. 16, pp. 57–85.

Kitschelt, H. (1988) 'Left-Libertarian Parties: Explaining Innovation in Competitive Party Systems', *World Politics*, vol. 40, no. 2, pp. 194–234.

Kitschelt, H. (1989) *The Logics of Party Formation* (Ithaca, NY: Cornell University Press).

Kitschelt, H. (1994) *The Transformation of European Social Democracy* (Cambridge University Press).

Kitschelt, H. (1995a) 'The Formation of Party Cleavages in Post-Communist Democracies: Theoretical Propositions', *Party Politics*, vol. 1, no. 4, pp. 447–72.

Kitschelt, H. (1995b) *The Radical Right in Western Europe. A Comparative Analysis* (Ann Arbor: University of Michigan Press).

Klee, G. (1993) 'Financing Parties and Elections in Small European Democracies: Austria and Sweden', in A. B. Gunlicks (ed.), *Campaign and Party Finance in North America and Western Europe* (Boulder, Col.: Westview Press) pp. 155–77.

Klein, R. and M. O'Higgins (eds) (1985) *The Future of Welfare* (Oxford: Basil Blackwell).

Klingemann, H.-D. (1995) 'Party Positions and Voter Orientations', in H.-D. Klingemann and D. Fuchs (eds), *Citizens and the State* (Oxford University Press) pp. 183–205.

Klingemann, H.-D., R.I. Hofferbert and I. Budge (1994) *Parties, Policies and Democracy* (Boulder, Col.: Westview Press).

Kohl, W. (1971) *French Nuclear Diplomacy* (Princeton, NJ: Princeton University Press).

Kolinsky, E. (1989) *Women in West Germany: Life, Work and Politics* (Oxford: Berg).

Koole, R. (1994) 'Dutch Political Parties: Money and the Message', in H.E. Alexander and R. Shiratori (eds), *Comparative Political Finance Among the Democracies* (Boulder, Col.: Westview Press) pp. 115–32.

Koutsoukis, K.S. (1989) 'Patterns of Corruption and Political Change in Modern Greece, 1946–1987', *Corruption and Reform*, vol. 4, pp. 1–13.

Krugman, P. (1994) 'Competitiveness: A Dangerous Obsession', *Foreign Affairs*, vol. 73, no. 2, pp. 28–44.

Kuhn, R. (1995) *The Media in France* (London: Routledge).

Kurz, H.D. (ed.) (1993) *United Germany and the New Europe* (Aldershot: Edward Elgar).

La Spina, A. and G. Sciortino (1993) 'Common Agenda, Southern Rules: European Integration and Environmental Change in the Mediterranean

States', in D. Liefferink *et al.* (eds) *European Integration and Environmental Policy* (London: Belhaven).

Lakeman, E. (1974) *How Democracies Vote*, 4th edn (London: Faber & Faber).

Lamo de Espinosa, E. (1997) 'Political Corruption and Economic Ethics', in C. Malamud and E. Posado-Carbó (eds), *Financing Party Politics in Europe and Latin America* (London: Macmillan).

Landabaso, M. (1993) 'The European Community's Regional Development and Innovation: Promoting "Innovative Milieux" in Practice', *European Planning Studies*, vol. 1, pp. 383–95.

Lange, P. and L. K. Davidson-Schmich (1995) 'European Elections or Elections in Europe? The European Electoral Consequences of European Economic Integration', *Il Politico*, vol. 60, no. 1, pp. 55–91.

Lange, P. and M. Regini (eds) (1989) *State, Market and Social Regulation: New Perspectives on Italy* (Cambridge: Cambridge University Press).

Lash, S. and J. Urry (1994) *Economies of Signs and Space* (London: Sage).

Latniak, E. and G. Simonis (1994) 'Socially-Oriented Technology Policy in Germany: Experiences of a North Rhine–Westphalian Programme', in G. Aichholzer and G. Schienstock (eds), *Technology Policy: Towards an Integration of Social and Ecological Concerns* (Berlin: de Gruyter).

Lee Kaid, L. and C. Holtz-Bacha (1995) *Political Advertising in Western Democracies* (London: Sage).

Lehmbruch, G. (1991) 'The Organization of Society, Administrative Strategies and Policy Networks: Elements of a Theory of Interest Systems', in R. M. Czada and A. Windhoff-Heritier (eds), *Political Choice: Institutions, Rules and the Limits of Rationality* (Frankfurt: Campus Verlag).

Leibfried, S. (1992) 'Towards a European Welfare State? On Integrating Poverty Regimes into the European Community', in Z. Ferge and J. E. Kolberg (eds), *Social Policies in a Changing Europe* (Frankfurt: Campus Verlag and Boulder, Co.: Westview Press).

Leibfried, S. and P. Pierson (eds) (1995) *European Social Policy: Between Fragmentation and Integration* (Washington, DC: The Brookings Institution).

Leibfried, S. and P. Pierson (1995) 'Semi-sovereign Welfare States: Social Policy in a Multitiered Europe', in S. Leibfried and P. Pierson (eds), *European Social Policy: Between Fragmentation and Integration* (Washington, DC: The Brookings Institution), pp. 43–77.

Leigh, L. H. and A. T. H. Smith (1991) 'Some Observations on European Fraud Laws and their Reform with Reference to the EEC', *Corruption and Reform*, 6, pp. 267–84.

Leonardi, R. (ed.) (1993) *The Regions and the European Community* (London: Cass).

Lequesne, C. (1993) *Paris–Bruxelles: Comment se fait la politique européenne de la France,* (Paris: Presses de la Fondation Nationale des Sciences Politiques).

Lewis, J. (1992) 'Gender and the Development of Welfare Regimes', *Journal of European Social Policy*, vol. 2, no. 3, pp. 159–173.

Lewis, J. (1993) *Women and Social Policies in Europe* (Aldershot: Edward Elgar).

Lijphart, A. (1977) *The Politics of Accommodation* (Berkeley, Cal.: University of California Press).

Lijphart, A. (1984) *Democracies* (New Haven, Conn.: Yale University Press).

Lijphart, A. (1994a) *Electoral Systems and Party Systems: A Study of Twenty-Seven Democracies, 1945–1990* (Oxford and New York: Oxford University Press).

Lijphart, A. (1994b) 'Democracies: Forms, Performance, and Constitutional Engineering', *European Journal of Political Research*, vol. 25, no. 1, pp. 1–17.

Lijphart, A. (ed.) (1992) *Parliamentary versus Presidential Government* (Oxford: Clarendon Press).

Linklater, S. (1996) 'Sovereignty and Citizenship in the Post-Westphalian State', *European Journal of International Relations*, vol. 2, no. 2.

Lipset, S. M. and S. Rokkan (1967) 'Cleavage Structures, Party Systems, and Voter Alignments: An Introduction', in S. M. Lipset and S. Rokkan (eds), *Party Systems and Voter Alignments: Cross-National Perspectives* (New York: Free Press) pp. 1–64.

Little, W. and E. Posada-Carbó (eds) (1996) *Political Corruption in Europe and Latin America* (London: Macmillan).

Long, T. (1995) 'Shaping Public Policy in the European Union: A Case Study of the Structural Funds', *Journal of European Public Policy*, vol. 2, no. 4.

López-Escobar, E. (1992) 'Vulnerable Values in Spanish Multichannel Television', in J. G. Blumler (ed.), *Television and the Public Interest* (London: Sage).

Lovenduski, J. (1986) *Women and European Politics: Contemporary Feminism and Public Policy* (Brighton: Wheatsheaf).

Lovenduski, J. (1986) *Women in European Politics* (Brighton: Wheatsheaf).

Lundvall, B. (ed.) (1992) *National Systems of Innovation: Towards a Theory of Innovation and Interactive Learning* (London: Pinter).

Luther, K. R. (1995) 'Austria in Light of the 1994 Elections', *German Politics*, vol. 4, pp. 122–40.

Lyotard, J.-F. (1984) *The Postmodern Condition: A Report on Knowledge*, trans. G. Bennington (Manchester: Manchester University Press).

MacIntyre, A. (1987) *After Virtue*, 2nd edn (London: Duckworth).

Mackie, T. T. and R. Rose (1991) *The International Almanac of Electoral History*, 3rd edn (London: Macmillan).

Mair, P. (1993) 'Myths of Electoral Change and the Survival of Traditional Parties', *European Journal of Political Research*, vol. 24, no. 2, pp. 121–33.

Mair, P. (1994) 'Party Organization: From Civil Society to the State,' in R. S. Katz and P. Mair (eds), *How Parties Organize. Change and Adaptation in Party Organizations in Western Democracies* (London: Sage) pp. 1–22.

Mair, P. (1995) 'Political Parties, Popular Legitimacy and Public Privilege', *West European Politics*, vol. 18, pp. 40–57.

Majone, G. (1989) 'Regulating Europe: Problems and Prospects', in T. Ellwein *et al.*, *Jahrbuch zur Staats- und Verwaltungswissenschaft* (Baden-Baden: Nomos) pp. 159–77.

Majone, G. (1990) *De-regulation or Re-regulation? Regulatory Reform in Europe and in the United States* (London: Pinter).

Majone, G. (1994) 'Regulating Europe', in *Collected Courses of the Academy of European Law*, vol. 5 (The Hague: M. Nijhoff).

Malamud, C. and E. Posada-Carbó (eds) (1997) *Financing Party Politics in Europe and Latin America* (London: Macmillan).

Marengo, F. D. (1988) 'The Linkage Between Political Corruption and Political Scandal', *Corruption and Reform*, vol. 3, pp. 65–79.

Marks, G. (1992) 'Structural Policy in the European Community', in A. Sbragia *Euro-Politics* (Washington, DC: The Brookings Institution) pp. 191–224.

Marks, G. (1993) 'Structural Policy and Multilevel Governance in the EC', in A. W. Cafruny and G. G. Rosenthal (eds), *The State of the European Community* (Boulder, Col.: Lynne Rienner).

Marks, G., L. Hooghe and K. Blank (1995) *European Integration and the State*, Working Paper No. RSC 95/7 (Florence, European University Institute).

Marsh, D. and R. A. W. Rhodes (eds) (1992) *Policy Networks in British Government* (Oxford University Press).

Mazey, S. (1994) 'French Regions and the European Union', *Regional Politics and Policy*, vol. 4, no. 3, pp. 132–57.

Mazey, S. and J. Mitchell (1993) 'Europe of the Regions: Territorial Interests and European Integration: The Scottish Experience', in S. Mazey and J. Richardson (eds), *Lobbying in the European Community* (Oxford University Press).

Mazey, S. and J. Richardson (1993) 'Environmental Groups and the EC: Challenges and Opportunities', in D. Judge (ed.), *A Green Dimension for the European Community: Political Issues and Processes* (London: Frank Cass).

Mazey, S. and J. Richardson (1993) 'Introduction: Transference of Power, Decision Rules and Rules of the Game', in S. Mazey and J. Richardson (eds), *Lobbying in the European Community* (Oxford University Press).

Mazey, S. and J. Richardson (eds) (1993) *Lobbying in the European Community* (Oxford University Press).

Mazzoleni, G. (1991) 'Media Moguls in Italy', in J. Tunstall and M. Palmer, *Media Moguls* (London: Routledge).

Mazzoleni, G. (1995) 'Towards a "Videocracy"? Italian Political Communication at a Turning Point', *European Journal of Communication*, vol. 10, no. 3, pp. 291–319.

McAleavey, P. (1993) 'The Politics of European Regional Development Policy: Additionality in the Scottish Coalfields', *Regional Politics and Policy*, vol. 3, no. 2, pp. 88–107.

McGee, A. and S. Weatherhill (1990) 'The Evolution of the Single Market: Harmonisation or Liberalisation?', *Modern Law Review*, vol. 53, pp. 575–96.

McQuail, D. (1995) 'Western European Media: The Mixed Model Under Threat', in J. Downing, A. Mohammadi and A. Sreberny-Mohammadi (eds), *Questioning the Media* (London: Sage).

Menon, A. (1995) 'Explaining Defence Policy: the Mitterrand Years', *Review of International Studies*, vol. 21, no. 3, pp. 279–99.

Menon, A. and J. Hayward (1996) 'States, Industrial Policies, and the European Union', in H. Kassim and A. Menon (eds), *The European Union and National Industrial Policy* (London: Routledge).

Mény, Y. (1992) *La corruption de la République* (Paris: Fayard).

Mény, Y. (1996) 'Corruption French Style', in W. Little and E. Posada-Carbó, *Political Corruption in Europe and Latin America* (London: Macmillan) pp. 159–72.

Metcalfe, L. (1994) 'International Policy Co-ordination and Public Management Reform', *International Review of Administrative Science*, vol. 60, pp. 271–90.

Miller, H. A. and O. Listhaug (1993) 'Ideology and Political Alienation', *Scandinavian Political Studies*, vol. 16, pp. 167–92.

Miller, K. E. (1991) *Denmark: A Troubled Welfare State* (Boulder, Co: Westview Press).

Milner, H. (1994) *Social Democracy and Rational Choice: The Scandinavian Experience and Beyond* (London: Routledge).

Milward, A. (1992) *The European Rescue of the Nation-State* (London: Routledge).

Minikin, R. (1993) *The ERM Explained: A Straightforward Guide to the Exchange Rate Mechanism and the European Currency Debate* (London: Kogan Page).

Moerland, P. W. (1995a) 'Alternative Disciplinary Mechanisms in Different Corporate Systems', *Journal of Economic Behavior and Organization*, 26, pp. 17–34.

Moerland, P. W. (1995b) 'Corporate Ownership and Control Structures: An International Comparison', *Review of Industrial Organization*, 10, pp. 443–464.

Moravcsik, A. (1991) 'Negotiating the Single Act: National Interests and Conventional Statecraft in the European Community', *International Organization*, vol. 45, no. 1, pp. 19–56.

Moravcsik, A. (1993) 'Preferences and Power in the European Community: A Liberal Intergovernmentalist Approach', *Journal of Common Market Studies*, vol. 31, no. 4, pp. 473–524.

Moravcsik, A. (1994) *Why the European Community Strengthens the State: Domestic Politics and International Cooperation*, Working Paper No. 52. (Harvard University, Center for European Studies).

Morgan, R. and C. Tame (eds) (1996) *Parliaments and Parties – The European Parliament in the Political Life of Europe* (Macmillan).

Morlino, L. and R. Montero (1995) 'Legitimacy and Democracy in Southern Europe', in R. Gunther, N. P. Diamandouros and H.-J. Puhle (eds), *The Politics of Democratic Consolidation: Southern Europe in Comparative Perspective* (Baltimore, Md. and London: Johns Hopkins University Press).

Moses, J. (1995) 'The Social Democratic Predicament in the Emerging European Union: A Capital Dilemma', *Journal of European Public Policy*, vol. 2, no. 3, pp. 407–426.

Mouffe, C. (1992) *Rethinking the Political* (London; Verso).

Müller, W. C. and V. Wright (1994) 'Reshaping the State in Western Europe: The Limits to Retreat', *West European Politics*, vol. 17, no. 3, pp. 1–11.

Müller-Rommel, F. (1982) 'Ecology Parties in Western Europe', *West European Politics*, vol. 5, no. 1, pp. 68–75.

Müller-Rommel, F. (1989) (ed.) *New Politics in Western Europe. The Rise and Success of Green Parties and Alternative Lists* (Boulder, Col.: Westview Press).

Müller-Rommel, F. (1993) *Grüne Parteien in Westeuropa* (Opladen: Westdeutscher Verlag).

Nassmacher, K-H. (1993) 'Comparing Party Finance in Western Democracies', in A. B. Gunlicks (ed.), *Campaign and Party Finance in North America and Western Europe* (Boulder, Col.: Westview Press) pp. 233–67.

Nauwelaers, C. (1995) 'Regional Innovation Systems: Does the Concept Permeate Regional Policies?', Paper presented at STEP Group Workshop on 'Regional Innovation Systems, Regional Networks and Regional Policy', Oslo, 27–29 October.

Neckel, S. (1989) 'Power and Legitimacy in Political Scandal: Comments on a Theoretical Framework for the Study of Political Scandals', *Corruption and Reform*, vol. 4, pp. 147–58.

Negrine, R. (1994) *Politics and the Mass Media in Britain* (London: Routledge).

Negrine, R. (ed.) (1985) *Cable Television and the Future of Broadcasting* (London: Croom Helm).

Negrine, R. (ed.) (1988) *Satellite Broadcasting: The Politics and Implications of the New Media* (London: Routledge).

Negrine, R. and S. Papathanassopoulos (1990) *The Internationalisation of Television* (London: Pinter).

Nelson, R. (ed.) (1993) *National Innovation Systems: A Comparative Analysis* (Oxford: Oxford University Press).

Nölling, W. (1993) *Monetary Policy in Europe after Maastricht* (London: Macmillan).

Norris, P. (1987) *Politics and Sexual Equality: The Comparative Position of Women in Western Democracies* (Brighton: Wheatsheaf).

Norton, P. (1992) 'Does Britain Need Proportional Representation?', in R. Blackburn (ed.), *Constitutional Studies: Contemporary Issues and Controversies* (London: Mansell) pp. 136–47.

Nugent, N. and R. O'Donnell (eds) (1994) *The European Business Environment* (London: Macmillan).

O'Connor, J. (1973) *The Fiscal Crisis of the State* (New York: St James Press).

O'Doherty, D. (ed.) (1994) *Globalisation, Networking and Small Firm Innovation* (London: Graham & Trotman).

OECD (1981) *The Welfare State in Crisis* (Paris: OECD).

OECD (1994) *Environmental Indicators* (Paris: OECD).

OECD (1994) *New Orientations for Social Policy* (Paris: OECD).

OECD (ongoing) *Environmental Performance Reviews* (Paris: OECD).

Offe, C. (1983) 'Competitive Party Democracy and the Keynesian Welfare State', in C. Offe, *Contradictions of the Welfare State* (Cambridge, Mass.: MIT Press) pp. 179–206.

Ohmae, K. (1985) *Triad Power: The Coming Shape of Global Competition* (New York: Free Press).

Ohmae, K. (1995) *The End of the Nation State: The Rise of Regional Economies* (New York: Free Press).

Olson, M. (1982) *The Rise and Decline of Nations: Economic Growth, Stagflation and Social Rigidities* (New Haven, Conn.: Yale University Press).

Owen Smith, E. (1994) *The German Economy* (London and New York: Routledge).

Oxley, H. and M. Macfarlan (1995) 'Health Care Reform: Controlling Spending and Increasing Efficiency', *OECD Economic Studies*, vol. 24, no. 1, pp. 7–55.

Padoa Schioppa, T. (1994) *The Road to Monetary Union: The Emperor, the Kings and the Genies* (Oxford: Clarendon Press).

Page, E. C. (1985) *Political Authority and Bureaucratic Power: A Comparative Analysis* (Brighton: Harvester).

Passas, N. and D. Nelken (1991) 'The Fight Against Fraud in the European Community: Cacophony rather than Harmony', *Corruption and Reform*, vol. 6, pp. 237–66.

Passas, N. and D. Nelken (1993) 'The Thin Line between Legitimate and Criminal Enterprise: Subsidy Frauds in the European Community', *Crime, Law and Social Change*, vol. 19, pp. 223–43.

Peacock Committee (1986) *Report of the Committee on Financing the BBC*, Cmnd. 9824 (London: HMSO).

Péan, P. (1988) *Affaires Africaines* (Paris: Fayard).

Pedersen, M. (1982) 'Towards a New Typology of Party Life-Spans and Minor Parties', *Scandinavian Political Studies*, vol. 5, pp. 1–16.

Perez, C. (1987) 'Microelectronics, Long Waves and World Structural Change', *World Development*, vol. 13, pp. 441–63.

Peters, B.G. and D.J. Savoie (eds) *Governance in a Changing Environment* (London: McGill–Queen's University Press).

Peterson, J. (1992) 'The European Technology Community: Policy Networks in a Supranational Setting', in D. Marsh and R.A.W. Rhodes (eds), *Policy Networks in British Government* (Oxford University Press).

Peterson, J. (1995) 'Policy Networks and European Union Policy Making: A Reply to Kassim', *West European Politics*, 18, 2.

Peterson, J. and E. Bomberg (forthcoming) *Decision-Making in the European Union* (London: Macmillan).

Pierre, J. (1995) *Bureaucracy in the Modern State* (Aldershot: Elgar).

Pierson, P. (1996) 'The New Politics of the Welfare State', *World Politics*, vol. 48, no. 2, pp. 143–179.

Piore, M.J. and C.F. Sabel (1984) *The Second International Divide* (New York: Basic Books).

Plaug, N. (1995) 'The Welfare State in Liquidation?', *International Social Security Review*, vol. 48, no. 2, pp. 61–71.

Poguntke, T. (1989) 'The "New Politics Dimension" in European Green Parties', in F. Müller-Rommel (ed.), *New Politics in Western Europe. The Rise and Success of Green Parties and Alternative Lists* (Boulder, Co.: Westview Press) pp. 175–93.

Poguntke, T. (1993a) *Alternative Politics* (Edinburgh University Press).

Poguntke, T. (1993b) 'Goodbye to Movement Politics? Organisational Adaptation of the German Green Party', *Environmental Politics*, vol. 2, pp. 379–404.

Poguntke, T. and S. Scarrow (eds) (1996) 'The Politics of Anti-Party Sentiment', *Party Politics*, vol. 2, no. 2 (special issue).

Porter, M. (1990) *The Competitive Advantage of Nations* (New York: Free Press).

Porter, V. and S. Hasselbach (1991) *Pluralism, Politics and the Marketplace: The Regulation of German Broadcasting* (London: Routledge).

Purcell, J. (1995) 'Ideology and the end of Institutional Industrial Relations: Evidence from the UK', in C. Crouch and F. Traxler (eds), *Organized Industrial Relations in Europe: What Future?* (Aldershot: Avebury).

Putnam, R.D. (1993) *Making Democracy Work: Civic Traditions in Modern Italy* (Princeton, NJ: Princeton University Press).

Pyke, F. and Sengenberger, W. (eds) (1992) *Industrial Districts and Local Economic Regeneration* (Geneva: International Institute for Labour Studies).

Quermonne, J.- L. (1994) *Le système politique européen* (Paris: Montchrestien).

Rae, D. and M. Taylor (1970) *The Analysis of Political Cleavages* (New Haven, Conn.: Yale University Press).

Randall, V. (1987) *Women and Politics: An International Perspective*, 2nd edn. (London: Macmillan).

Regini, M. (1995) 'La varietà italiana di capitalismo: Istituzioni sociali e struttura produttiva negli anni Ottanta', *Stato e Mercato*, 43, April, 3–26.

Reif, K. and H. Schmitt (1980) 'Nine National Second-Order Elections: A Systematic Framework for Analysis of European Election Results', *European Journal of Political Research*, vol. 8, no. 1, pp. 3–44.

Reif, K. and H. Schmitt (1980) 'Nine Second-Order National Elections: A Conceptual Framework for the Analysis of European Parliament Election Results', *European Journal of Political Research*, vol. 8, no. 1, pp. 3–44.

Rengger, N. J. (1995) *Political Theory, Modernity and Postmodernity: Beyond Enlightenment and Critique* (Oxford: Basil Blackwell).

Rengger, N. J. (1996) *Duties Beyond Orders: World Order and the Dilemmas of Liberal Politics* (London: Routledge).

Rhodes, M. (1992) 'The Future of the Social Dimension: Labour Market Regulation in post-1992 Europe', *Journal of Common Market Studies*, vol. 30, no. 1, pp. 23–51.

Rhodes, M. (1993) 'The Social Dimension after Maastricht: Setting a New Agenda for the Labour Market', *International Journal of Comparative Labour Law and Industrial Relations*, vol. 9, pp. 297–325.

Rhodes, M. (ed.) (1995) *The Regions and the New Europe: Studies in Core and Periphery Development* (Manchester University Press).

Rhodes, M. (1995a) ' "Subversive Liberalism": Market Integration, Globalization and the European Welfare State', *Journal of European Public Policy*, 2, 3, pp. 384–406.

Rhodes, M. (1995b) 'A Regulatory Conundrum: Industrial Relations and the Social Dimension', in S. Leibfried and P. Pierson (eds), *European Social Policy: Between Fragmentation and Integration* (Washington, DC: The Brookings Institution), pp. 78–122.

Rhodes, M. (1996a) 'Globalisation and West European Welfare States: A Critical Review of Recent Debates', *Journal of European Social Policy*, vol. 6 no. 4.

Rhodes, M. (1996b) 'Globalization, the State and the Restructuring of Regional Economies', in P. Gummett (ed.), *Globalization and Public Policy* (Cheltenham: Edward Elgar), pp. 161–180.

Rhodes, M. (1997) 'Financing Party Politics in Italy: A Case of Systemic Corruption', in C. Malamud and E. Posado-Carbó (eds), *Financing Party Politics in Europe and Latin America* (London: Macmillan).

Rhodes, R. A. W (1993) 'The Europeanisation of Subcentral Government – The Case of the UK', *Staatswissenschaften und Staatspraxis*, vol. 3, no. 2, pp. 272–86.

Rhodes, R. A. W. (1994) 'The Hollowing Out of the State', *The Political Quarterly*, vol. 15, no. 2, pp. 138–51.

Rhodes, R. A. W. (1995) 'From Prime Ministerial Power to Core Executive', in R. A. W Rhodes and P. Dunleavy (eds), *Prime Minister, Cabinet and Core Executive* (London: Macmillan).

Rhodes, R. A. W. and D. Marsh (1992) 'Policy Networks in British Politics: A Critique of Existing Approaches', in D. Marsh and R. A. W. Rhodes (eds), *Policy Networks in British Government* (Oxford University Press).

Richardson, D. and C. Rootes (1995) *The Green Challenge: The Development of Green Parties in Europe* (London: Routledge).

Richardson, J. (1996) 'Water', in H. Kassim and A. Menon (eds), *The European Union and National Industrial Policy* (London: Routledge).

Richardson, J. (ed.) (1982) *Policy Styles in Western Europe* (London: George Allen & Unwin).

Richardson, J. and A. Jordan (1979) *Governing Under Pressure: The policy process in a post-parliamentary democracy* (Oxford: Martin Robertson).

Rihoux, B. (1995) 'Belgium: Greens in a Divided Society', in D. Richardson and C. Rootes (eds), *The Green Challenge* (London: Routledge).

Robins, K. and J. Cornford (1994) 'Local and Regional Broadcasting in the New Media Order', in A. Amin and N. Thrift (eds) *Globalization, Institutions, and Regional Development in Europe* (Oxford University Press).

Rodríguez-Pose, A. (1994) 'Socioeconomic Restructuring and Regional Change: Rethinking Growth in the European Community', *Economic Geography*, vol. 70, no. 4, pp. 325–43.

Rohrschneider, R. (1993) 'Environmental Belief Systems in Western Europe', *Comparative Political Studies*, vol. 26, pp. 3–29.

Rose, R. (1992) *What Are the Economic Consequences of PR?* (London: Electoral Reform Society).

Rosenau, J. (1967) 'Foreign Policy as an Issue-Area', in J. Rosenau (ed.), *Domestic Sources of Foreign Policy* (New York: Free Press).

Ross, G. (1993) 'Sliding into Industrial Policy: Inside the European Commission', *French Politics and Society*, vol. 11, no. 1, 20–44.

Rowat, D. C. (ed.) (1988) *Public Administration in Developed Democracies, A Comparative Study* (New York: Marcel Dekker).

Ruggie, J. G. (1984) 'International Regimes, Transactions and Change: Embedded Liberalism in the Post-war Economic Order', *International Organization*, vol. 36, no. 2, pp. 379–415.

Ruggie, J. G. (ed.) (1993) *Multilateralism Matters* (New York: Columbia University Press).

Rutten, C. (1992) 'Au coeur du processus de décision européen: le comité des représentants permanents (COREPER)', *Revue française d'administration publique*, vol. 63, pp. 383–90.

Sainsbury, D. (1993) 'The Politics of Increased Women's Representation: The Swedish Case', in J. Lovenduski and P. Norris (eds), *Gender and Party Politics* (London: Sage).

Sainsbury, D. (1994) 'Women's and Men's Social Rights: Gendering Dimensions of Welfare States', in D. Sainsbury, *Gendering Welfare States* (London: Sage), pp. 150–69.

Sandholtz J. and J. Zysman (1989) '1992: Recasting the European Bargain', *World Politics*, vol. 42, 95–128.

Sandholtz, W. (1993) 'Choosing Union: Monetary Politics and Maastricht', *International Organization*, vol. 47, no. 1, pp. 1–39.

Sandholtz, W. and J. Zysman (1989) '1992: Recasting the European Bargain', *World Politics*, vol. 42, pp. 95–128.

Sapelli, G. (1995) *Southern Europe Since 1945: Tradition and Modernity in Portugal, Spain, Italy, Greece and Turkey* (London: Longman).

Sartori, G. (1968) 'The Sociology of Parties: A Critical Review', reprinted in P. Mair (ed.) (1990), *The West European Party System* (Oxford University Press) pp. 150–82.

Sartori, G. (1976) *Parties and Party Systems* (Cambridge University Press).

Sartori, G. (1994) *Comparative Constitutional Engineering: An Inquiry Into Structures, Incentives and Outcomes* (London: Macmillan).

Sassoon, D. (1985) 'Political and Market Forces in Italian Broadcasting', in R. Kuhn (ed.), *Broadcasting and Politics in Western Europe* (London: Frank Cass).

Sbragia, A. (1996) 'The Push-Pull of Environmental Policy-Making' in H. Wallace and W. Wallace (eds), *Policy-Making in the European Union* (Chichester: John Wiley).

Scammell, M. (1995) *Designer Politics: How Elections are Won* (London: Macmillan).

Scharpf, F. W. (1991) *Crisis and Choice in European Social Democracy* (Ithaca, NY: Cornell University Press).

Scharpf, F. W. (1996) 'Negative and Positive Integration in the Political Economy of European Welfare States', in Y. Mény and M. Rhodes (eds), *A New Social Contract? Charting the Future of European Welfare* (London: Macmillan).

Scharpf, F. W. (1996) 'Negative and Positive Integration in the Political Economy of European Welfare States', in Y. Mény and M. Rhodes (eds), *A New Social Contract? Charting the Future of European Welfare* (London: Macmillan).

Scharpf, F. W. (1997) 'European Welfare States: Negative and Positive Integration', in Y. Mény and M. Rhodes (eds), *A New Social Contract?: Charting The Future of European Welfare*, (London: Macmillan, forthcoming).

Schedler, A. (1996) 'Anti-Political-Establishment Parties', *Party Politics*, vol. 2, no. 3, pp. 281–312.

Schneider-Lenné, E. R. (1994) 'The Role of the German Capital Markets and the Universal Banks, Supervisory Boards and Interlocking Directorships', in N. Dimsdale and M. Prevezer (eds), *Capital Markets and Corporate Governance* (Oxford: Clarendon Press) pp. 284–305.

SDE (1993) *Statement on the Defence Estimates 1993* Cm 2270 (London: HMSO).

SDE (1994) *Statement on the Defence Estimates 1994* Cm 2550 (London: HMSO).

Seligman, A. (1992) *A Theory of Civil Society* (Princeton, NJ: Princeton University Press).

Shaw, J. (1996) *The Law of the European Union* (London: Macmillan).

Shelley, M. and M. Winck (eds) (1995) *Aspects of European Cultural Diversity* (London: Routledge).

Shepsle, K. A. and R. N. Cohen (1990) 'Multiparty Competition, Entry and Entry Deterrence in Spatial Models of Elections', in J. M. Enelow and M. J. Hinich (eds), *Advances in the Spatial Theory of Voting* (Cambridge University Press) pp. 12–45.

Siedentopf, M. and J. Ziller (1988) *Making European Policies Work* (London: Sage).

Sigg, R., I. Zeitzer, X. Scheil-Adlung, C. Kuptsch and M. Tracy (1996) 'Developments and Trends in Social Security 1993–1995', *International Social Security Review*, vol. 49, 2, pp. 5–126.

Silberman, B. S. (1993) *Cages of Reason* (Chicago and London: University of Chicago Press).

Singh, A. (1995) 'Institutional Requirements for Full Employment in Advanced Economies', *International Labour Review*, vol. 134, no. 4–5, pp. 471–496.

Sinnott, R. (1993) 'The Electoral System' in J. Coakley and M. Gallagher (eds), *Politics in the Republic of Ireland*, 2nd edn (Dublin: Folens/Limerick: PSAI Press) pp. 67–85.

Siune, K. and W. Truetzschler (eds) (1992) *Dynamics of Media Politics* (London: Sage).

Sjöblom, G. (1983) 'Political Change and Political Accountability: A Propositional Inventory of Causes and Effects', in H. Daalder and P. Mair (eds), *Western Europe Party Systems* (London: Sage) pp. 369–403.

Sofres (1993) *L'Etat de l'opinion* (Paris: Seuil).

Standing, G. (1995) 'Labor Insecurity Through Market Regulation: Legacy of the 1980s, Challenge for the 1990s', in K. McFate, R. Lawson and W. J. Wilson (eds), *Poverty, Inequality and the Future of Social Policy: Western States in the New World Order* (New York: Russell Sage Foundation), pp. 153–196.

Stephens, J. D. (1996) 'The Scandinavian Welfare States: Achievements, Crisis and Prospects', in G. Esping-Andersen (ed.), *Welfare States in Transition: National Adaptations in Global Economies* (London: Sage) pp. 32–65.

Stetson, D. and A. Mazur (1995) *Comparative State Feminism* (London: Sage).

Streeck, W. (1995a) 'German Capitalism: Does it Exist, Can it Survive?', Cologne: Max Planck Institut für Gesellschaftsforschung, *Discussion Paper*, 95/5.

Streeck, W. (1995b) 'Neo-Voluntarism: A New European Social Policy Regime?', *European Law Journal*, vol. 1, no. 1, pp. 31–59.

Streeck, W. and P. C. Schmitter (1991) 'From National Corporatism to Transnational Pluralism: Organised Interests in the Single European Market', *Politics and Society*, vol. 19, no. 1, pp. 133–64.

Taagepera, R. and M. S. Shugart (1989) *Seats and Votes: The Effects and Determinants of Electoral Systems* (New Haven, Conn. and London, Yale University Press).

Taylor, C. (1995) *Emu 2000? Prospects for European Monetary Union* (London: Pinter, for Royal Institute of International Affairs).

Taylor, T. (1984) *European Defence Cooperation* (London: Routledge & Kegan Paul for Royal Institute of International Affairs).

Taylor, T. (1994) 'West European Security and Defence Cooperation: Maastricht and Beyond', *International Affairs*, vol. 70, January.

Thompson, G. F. (1993) *The Economic Emergence of Europe? The Political Economy of Cooperation and Competition in the 1990s* (Aldershot: Elgar).

Togeby, L. (1992) 'The Nature of Declining Party Membership in Denmark: Causes and Consequences', *Scandinavian Political Studies*, vol. 15, no. 1, pp. 1–19.

Tömmel, I. (1992) 'Decentralisation of Regional Development Policies in The Netherlands – A New Type of State Intervention?', *West European Politics*,- vol. 15, no. 2, pp. 107–125.

Torstendahl, R. (1991) *Bureaucratisation in Northwestern Europe, 1980–1995* (London: Routledge).

Traquina, N. (1995) 'Portuguese Television: the Politics of Savage Deregulation', *Media, Culture & Society* vol. 17, no. 2, pp. 223–38.

Traxler F. and P. Schmitter (1995) 'The Emerging Euro-Polity and Organised Interests', *European Journal of International Relations*, vol. 1, no. 2, pp. 191–218.

Tsaliki, L. (1995) 'Greek TV since Deregulation: A Case Study of "Homogenised Proliferation"', *Intermedia*, vol. 23, no. 5, pp. 37–41.

Tsoukalis, L. (1977) *The Politics and Economics of European Monetary Integration* (London: George Allen & Unwin).

Tsoukalis, L. (1997) *The New European Economy Revisited: The Politics and Economics of Integration* (Oxford University Press).

Tunstall, J. and M. Palmer (1991) *Media Moguls* (London: Routledge).

United Nations (Centre for Social Development and Humanitarian Affairs) (1992) *Women in Politics and Decision Making in the Late Twentieth Century* (Dordrecht: Nijhoff).

Van Outrive, L. (1993) 'The Administration as an Amplifier of Corruption', *Corruption and Reform*, vol. 7, pp. 125–35.

Van Schendelen, M. P. C. M. and R. H. Pedlar (1994) Lobbying the European Union: companies, trade associations and issue groups (Aldershot: Dartmouth).

Van Straaten, J. and J. Ugelow (1994) 'Environmental Policy in the Netherlands: Change and Effectiveness', in M. Wintle (ed.), *Rhetoric and Reality in Environmental Policy* (Aldershot: Avebury).

Verwey, W. (1994) 'HDTV and Philips: Stepping Stone or Snake Pit?', in R. H. Pedlar and M. Van Schendelen (eds), *Lobbying the European Union: Companies, Trade Associations and Interest Groups* (Aldershot: Dartmouth).

Vipond, P. A. (1993) 'The European Financial Area in the 1990s: Europe and the Transnationalization of Finance', in P. G. Cerny (ed.), *Finance and World Politics: Markets, Regimes and States in the Post-hegemonic Era* (Aldershot: Edward Elgar) pp. 186–106.

Virilio (1990) *L'Intertie Polaire* (Paris: Christian Bourgeois).

Volcansek, M. L. (ed.) (1992) *Judicial Politics and Policy-Making in Western Europe* (London: Frank Cass).

Walker, R. B. J. (1992) *Inside/Outside: International Relations as Political Theory* (Cambridge University Press).

Walker, R. B. J. (1994) 'The Concept of the Political', in K. Booth and S. Smith (eds), *International Relations Theory Today* (Cambridge: Polity Press).

Walker, W. (1993) 'National Innovation Systems: Britain', in R. Nelson (ed.), *National Innovation Systems: A Comparative Analysis* (Oxford: Oxford University Press), pp. 158–191.

Warmsley, G. *et al.* (1990) *Refounding Public Administration* (London: Sage).

Waters, M. (1995), *Globalization* (London and New York: Routledge).

Weale, A. (1992) 'Vorsprung durch Technik? The Politics of German Environmental Regulation', in K. Dyson (ed.), *The Politics of German Regulation* (Aldershot: Dartmouth).

Weber, M. (1968) *Economy and Society* (edited by Guenther Roth and Claus Wittich) (Berkeley and Los Angeles: University of California Press).

Weidner, E. W. (1955) 'Decision-making in a Federal System', in A. W. Macmahon (ed.), *Federalism – Mature and Emergent* (Garden City, NY: Doubleday) pp. 363–83.

Weiler, J. H. H. (1981) 'The Community System: the Dual Character of Supranationalism', *Yearbook of European Law*, vol. 1, p. 267.

Weiler, J. H. H. (1985) *Il Sistema Comunitario europeo* (Bologna: Il Mulino).

Weiler, J. H. H. (1991) 'The Transformation of Europe', *Yale Law Journal*, vol. 100, pp. 2403–83.

Weiler, J. H. H. (1994) 'A Quiet Revolution – The European Court of Justice and its Interlocuters', Comparative Political Studies, vol. 26, pp. 510–34.

Wendt, A. (1994) 'Collective Identity Formation and the International State', *American Political Science Review*, vol. 88, no. 2, pp. 384–96.

Wessels, W, (1990) 'Administrative Interaction', in William Wallace (ed.), *The Dynamics of European Integration* (London: Pinter) pp. 229–41.

Westlake, M. (1995) 'The European Parliament, the National Parliaments and the 1996 Intergovernmental Conference', *Political Quarterly*, vol. 66, pp. 59–73.

Whitley, R. (ed.) (1993) *European Business Systems: Firms and Markets in their National Contexts* (London: Sage).

Wilcox, C. (1991) 'The Causes and Consequences of Feminist Consciousness Among Western European Women', *Comparative Political Studies*, vol. 23, no. 4.

Wilensky, H. (1981), 'Democratic Corporatism, Consensus and Social Policy: Reflections on Changing Values and the Crisis of the Welfare State', in *OECD, The Welfare State in Crisis* (Paris: OECD), pp. 185–95.

Wilks, S. and M. W. (eds) (1987) *Comparative Government–Industry Relations: Western Europe, the United States and Japan* (Oxford: Clarendon Press).

Wilson, G. K. (1990) *Business and Politics* (London: Macmillan).

Wise, M. and Croxford, G. (1988) 'The European Regional Development Fund: Community Ideals and National Realities', *Political Geography Quarterly*, vol. 7, no. 2, pp. 161–82.

Windhoff-Héritier, A. (1993) 'Policy Network Analysis: A Tool for Comparative Political Research' in H. Keman (ed.), *Comparative Politics: New Directions in Theory and Method* (Amsterdam: VUP).

Wyatt-Walker, A. (1995) 'Globalization, Corporate Identity and European Technology Policy', *Journal of European Public Policy*, vol. 2, no. 3, pp. 427–46.

Ziller, J. (1993) *Administrations Comparées* (Paris: Montchrestien).

Zysman, J. (1983) *Governments, Markets and Growth: Financial Systems and the Politics of Industrial Change* (Ithaca and London: Cornell University Press).

Zysman, J. (1994) 'How Institutions Create Historically Rooted Trajectories of Growth', *Industrial and Corporate Change*, vol. 3, no. 1, pp. 243–83.

Zysman, J. (1995) 'National Roots of a "Global" Economy', *Revue d'Iconomie Industrielle*, 71, 1, pp. 107–121.

Index